"Unapologetically materialist and with meticul[...] explains that socialism is far more than a moral appeal for a better world, [it is] an absolute necessity for the continued survival of our species. A sobering analysis of our current crisis seamlessly linked with a revolutionary communist optimism – a must read for all those terrified of the future but willing to change it."

★★★★★ – Seán Ó'Maoltuile,
National Education Officer, Connolly Youth Movement

"Reese recovers a Marxist analysis of automation and makes original contributions to the environmental question. The refreshing focus on production, as opposed to consumption, makes it clear that Marxists need not abandon the promise of a world of plenty."

★★★★★ – Laure Kwame Richardson

"A sprawling and diverse work. While there is an enormous amount of Marxist work available as regards history, we are sorely lacking any real attempts at analysing the current situation. This is a noble attempt at doing just that."

★★★★ – Kali Koba, *Desperate Times*

"Either the world's last history book or a roadmap to its salvation."

★★★★★ – Andrew George

"Engaging, not too hard to follow, and truly the best write-up I've seen on the current accumulation crisis. Bleak, but without being fatalistic. I think you'll walk out with a solid understanding of the mechanisms of capitalism, why the usual arguments for it utterly fail, and some hope that there's a bright future on the other side."

★★★★★ – Alejandro Salvador, Goodreads

"Who can argue that we face a choice between socialism or barbarism? No one if they have read this book."

★★★★★ – David Ellis, Goodreads

"Reese has done something that no other Marxist theorist had yet achieved, bringing together all of the major strands of our historical moment, from the climate emergency to the long running crisis in the global economy. He walks the reader through the current macro trends, where all roads lead to deepening malaise and breakdown. This would have been enough to make this a significant theoretical work, but then he does something far more ambitious – he illuminates the solution."
★★★★★ – Donal Costello, Goodreads

"I would challenge the most vociferous proponent of capitalism to refute the well-researched, scientifically-backed statements that Reese makes throughout the course of *Socialism or Extinction*."
★★★★★ – Aidan Wallace, *Philosophical Malady*

"Reese lays out the dangers of late-stage capitalism and the possibilities of socialist revolution with a rare clarity and thoroughness."
★★★★★ – Emma Norman

"A sobering analysis of the reality of current efforts to stop the climate crisis, but a book that still provides hope for a better future."
★★★★★ – Luci Brăn, Communist Party of Britain (personal capacity)

"An excellent, insightful book with a clear grasp of history, politics and the economic reality that capitalism is undercutting itself."
★★★★★ – Hugh Mann, Amazon review

"As surreal as some things may appear, this is undoubtedly the reality of our world. This book should be a household read."
★★★★★ – Shay Thomas, Amazon review

SOCIALISM
OR
EXTINCTION

Text copyright © Ted Reese, January 2021
First published November 2019 (e-book); updated January 2021
ISBN: 9798554968730
Cover art: James Bell

SOCIALISM
OR
EXTINCTION

CLIMATE, AUTOMATION AND WAR
IN THE FINAL CAPITALIST BREAKDOWN

TED REESE

Contents

Acknowledgements	xii
Introduction	1
1. The greatest ever overaccumulation of capital, the greatest ever capitalist crisis	16
2. Breakdown theory is crisis theory	24
3. Defining automation: the fourth industrial revolution?	52
4. 'Technological unemployment' and fearful rulers	60
5. Workerless factories, globalisation in retreat and the crisis of imperialism	65
6. The final contradiction?	83
7. Factory fragmentation	87
8. Rescuing Marx's 'The Fragment on Machines'	91
9. The fantasy of fully automated capitalism	99
10. The final breakdown: destined to strike much earlier than a zero rate of profit	107
11. Keynesian fantasies	134
12. Proletarianisation and the historical demands of the productive forces	161
13. Man vs machine: Postcapitalist techno-utopia or dictatorship of AI?	174
14. Capitalism wants the most destructive world war yet – but even that can't save it	181
15. Humanity's emancipation: Higher communism and the single automated society	196
16. Against extinction: For a green (hemp-based) industrial revolution that is actually green	208
Conclusion: Socialism or extinction	258
Afterword	265
Update: The covid-19 crash	277
Notes	288

Acknowledgements

This is an independent piece of work without any institutional backing and the views stated are mine alone. I would, though, like to thank the Revolutionary Communist Group for helping my development as a Marxist over the past few years, especially members of the editorial board of *Fight Racism! Fight Imperialism!*

For all of their help, enthusiasm, incisive and constructive criticism and comradeship, I would also like to thank Luke Beesley, Laurie Kwame Richardson and especially James Bell, the latter also for his eloquent artwork and several contributions to the text, particularly the sections on modern warfare and the united front.

"Find a factory anywhere in the world built in the
past five years – not many people work there."
– James Manyika, McKinsey Global Institute director, June 2017

"As soon as labour in the direct form has ceased to be the great
wellspring of wealth, labour time ceases and must cease
to be its measure.... Capital thus works towards its own dissolution
as the form dominating production."
– Karl Marx, "The Fragment on Machines", *Grundrisse*, 1858

"The fundamental difference between the [automation] revolution in capitalist countries and its counterpart in the socialist states consists in its leading to the breakdown, instead of the consolidation, of the existing relations ... of production.... *Its consummation is incompatible with capitalism.*"
– Genrikh Volkov, *Era of Man or Robot?
The Sociological Problems of the Technical Revolution*, 1967

"The law of breakdown is the fundamental law that governs
and supports the entire structure of Marx's thought....
Despite the periodic interruptions that repeatedly defuse the tendency towards breakdown, the mechanism as a whole tends relentlessly towards its final end with the general process of accumulation. As the accumulation of capital grows absolutely, the valorisation of this expanded capital becomes progressively more difficult. Once the counter-tendencies are themselves defused or simply cease to operate, the breakdown tendency gains the upper hand and asserts itself in the absolute form as the final crisis.... There is an absolute limit to the accumulation of capital and this limit comes into force much earlier than a zero rate of profit."
– Henryk Grossman, *The Law of Accumulation
and Breakdown of the Capitalist System*, 1929

"The decrease in the interest rate is ... a symptom of the growing domination of capital in the process of perfecting itself – of the estrangement which is growing and therefore hastening to its annulment."
– Marx and Friedrich Engels, *Economic and Philosophic Manuscripts*, 1844

"It is unthinkable to obtain the new types of energy
without automation."
– Volkov

"Hemp will be the future of all mankind, or there won't be a future."
– Jack Herer

Introduction

"Let us not, however, flatter ourselves overmuch on account of our human victories over nature. For each such victory nature takes its revenge on us."[1]

Friedrich Engels, *The Dialectics of Nature*, 1883

On 8 October 2018, the world's leading climate scientists warned in a report for the United Nations' (UN) Intergovernmental Panel on Climate Change (IPCC) that there were only 12 years for carbon emissions to be cut sufficiently if global warming is to be kept to a maximum of 1.5° Celsius (C), the target limit agreed at the 2015 Paris Climate Conference. Beyond this point, even half a degree will "substantially" worsen the risks of droughts, floods, extreme heat and destitution for hundreds of millions of people, creating what the UN's special rapporteur on extreme poverty Philip Alston termed "climate apartheid", where "the rich escape overheating, hunger, and conflict... while the rest of the world is left to suffer".

Previously, it had been thought that a 2°C rise would be safe. That point is going to be reached, on the current trajectory of rising emissions, by 2050, or when the pre-industrial atmospheric CO_2 concentration of 280 parts per million (ppm) has doubled, ie since fossil fuel burning began.

The figure in 2018 stood at 411ppm – up from 400 just two years earlier – the highest it has been in three million years.[2] It then hit 415 in May 2019, when steep increases in ppm were recorded for the seventh consecutive year. In the 1990s, the average annual growth rate was about 1.5ppm, but in the past decade that has accelerated to 2.2ppm.

Preventing a rise higher than 2°C would have required an annual cut in carbon emissions of 20% by 2030 and then to zero by 2075. To keep to 1.5°C, however, the reduction must increase to 45% by 2030 and then to zero by 2050. Achieving this, the IPCC said, requires "rapid, far-reaching and unprecedented changes in all aspects of society".

While the report's warning was stark, it obscured just how bad the situation really is. Among other more pessimistic readings, climate scientist Ian Mauro from the University of Winnipeg has said that emissions need to peak in 2020.[3]

Climate data is incredibly complex to analyse with certainty, so scientists tend to understate the possible outcomes. This is undoubtedly compounded by political interference. Scientists complained that a 2014 IPCC report was significantly "diluted" under pressure from some of the world's biggest greenhouse gas (GHG) emitters, including Saudi Arabia, China, Brazil and the United States (US).[4] A report in March 2019 revealed that the largest five stock market listed oil and gas companies – Chevron, BP, ExxonMobil, Shell and Total – spend nearly $200m (£153m) a year lobbying to delay, control or block policies aimed at tackling climate change.[5]

The Grantham Research Institute on Climate Change said the IPCC's final 2018 report was "incredibly conservative" because it did not mention the danger of "points of no return" that could trigger runaway extreme warming; or the likely rise in climate-driven refugees. The UN puts the figure at 200 million – but with a high-end estimate of one billion – by mid-century,[6] when parts of the Middle East and North Africa may become uninhabitable.[7] Making similar points, a report published in Australia warns of "outright chaos" on the way to the end of human civilisation by 2050.[8]

The planet's average surface temperature has risen by more than 1°C since 1850, peaking in 2016 at 1.38°C. The *rate* of warming though has "really moved into exceptional territory" in the past 30 years, according to Gavin Schmidt, Director of the National Aeronautics and Space Administration's (NASA) Goddard Institute for Space Studies. He said in August 2016:

> "It's unprecedented in 1,000 years. There's no period that has the trend seen in the 20th century in terms of the inclination [of temperatures]. Maintaining temperatures below the 1.5°C guardrail requires significant and very rapid cuts in CO_2 emissions or co-ordinated geo-engineering. That is very unlikely. We are not even yet making emissions cuts commensurate with keeping warming below 2°C."[9]

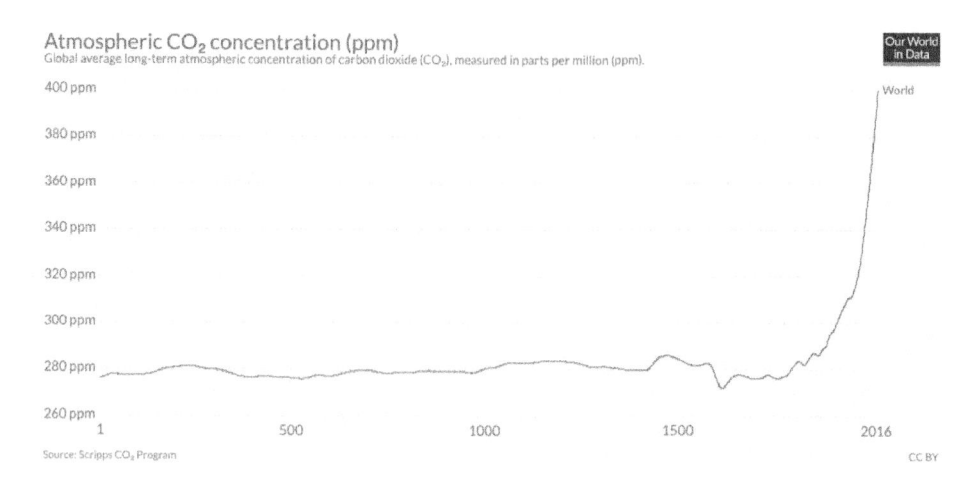

Atmospheric CO_2 concentration (ppm)
Global average long-term atmospheric concentration of carbon dioxide (CO_2), measured in parts per million (ppm).

Source: Scripps CO_2 Program

The rate of warming will continue to accelerate, especially as the numerous effects of climate change compound each other, such as melting Arctic ice reflecting increasingly less sunlight back into space while also releasing trapped gas. An aggregate of 369 billion tonnes of snow and ice is disappearing every year, at a rate 18% higher than had been thought in 2013.[10]

The East Antarctic Ice Sheet, previously thought to be relatively unaffected by climate change, is now showing signs of melting. In June 2019 a study found that permafrost had begun thawing in the Canadian Arctic *70 years* earlier than expected, at a rate six times the long-term average.[11]

In the same month fires in the Arctic emitted 50 megatonnes of carbon dioxide – four weeks before what used to be the start of the typical fire season – a figure equivalent to Sweden's annual emissions and more than the amount released by June fires in the Arctic between 2010 and 2018 combined.

At the beginning of the "The Uninhabitable Earth", an article in *New York Magazine* that previewed the book of the same title, David Wallace-Wells writes:

> "Arctic permafrost contains 1.8 trillion tonnes of carbon, more than twice as much as is currently suspended in Earth's atmosphere. When it thaws and is released, that carbon may evaporate as methane, which is 34 times as powerful a GHG warming blanket as carbon dioxide when judged on the timescale of a century; when judged on the timescale of two decades, it is 86 times as powerful. In other words, we have, trapped in Arctic permafrost, twice as much carbon as is currently wrecking the atmosphere of the planet, all of it scheduled to be released at a date that keeps getting moved up, partially in the form of a gas that multiplies its warming power 86 times over."[12]

At 2°C "the ice sheets begin their collapse".[13] Wallace-Wells says that while "most people talk as if Miami and Bangladesh still have a chance of surviving ... most of the scientists I spoke with assume we'll lose them [to rising sea levels] within the century, even if we stop burning fossil fuel in the next decade". More than 600 million people live within 30 feet of sea level. At just 3°C sea levels would rise by 50 metres.[14] London, Brussels, New York, Buenos Aires and Mumbai, to name a few, would be permanently under water.

The climate crisis is an extremely serious existential threat. Before the IPCC's 2018 report, it could feel as if the topic barely registered with politicians, the media or the general public, either in collective denial or complacent about its supposedly distant effects. But now a collective eco-consciousness is taking hold – the effects are already being felt and can no longer be ignored.

Since 2005, the number of floods has increased by a factor of 15, extreme temperature events by a factor of 20, and wildfires sevenfold; the 20 warmest years since records began have been in the past 22 years.[15] Since 1980, the planet has seen a 50-fold increase in the number of places experiencing dangerous or extreme heat.[16] The number of heatwaves affecting the planet's oceans tripled in the past couple of years, having already jumped by more than 50% in the three decades to 2016, killing swathes of sea-life "like wildfires that take out huge areas of forest", according to the Marine Biological Association.[17] This is adding to ocean acidification, whereby the CO_2 in the oceans rises at the expense of oxygen, suffocating the coral reefs that support as much as a quarter of all marine life.

Meanwhile, 95% of the world's population is breathing dangerously polluted air, killing at least nine million people a year, damaging our cognitive ability and respiratory systems and even our DNA. Pollution "endangers the stability of the Earth's support systems and threatens the continuing survival of human societies", according to the Commission on Pollution and Health.[18]

Inextricably linked to the climate emergency is a broader environmental crisis. A third of Earth's land is now acutely degraded, with fertile soil being lost at a rate of 24 billion tonnes a year through intensive farming.[19] The UN said in 2014 that if current rates of degradation continue, all of the world's topsoil (the 5-10 inches where most of Earth's biological activity takes place) could be gone within 60 years.[20] 95% of our food presently comes from the soil. Unless better approaches are adopted, arable and productive land per person in 2050 will equate to only a quarter of the level in 1960. The equivalent of 30 football pitches of soil are being lost every minute.

Heavy tilling, overharvesting and the use of petroleum-based agrochemicals have increased yields at the expense of long-term sustainability.

Temperature anomaly from 1961-1990 average, Global
Global average land-sea temperature anomaly relative to the 1961-1990 average temperature in degrees celcius (°C). The red line represents the median average temperature change, and grey lines represent the upper and lower 95% confidence intervals.

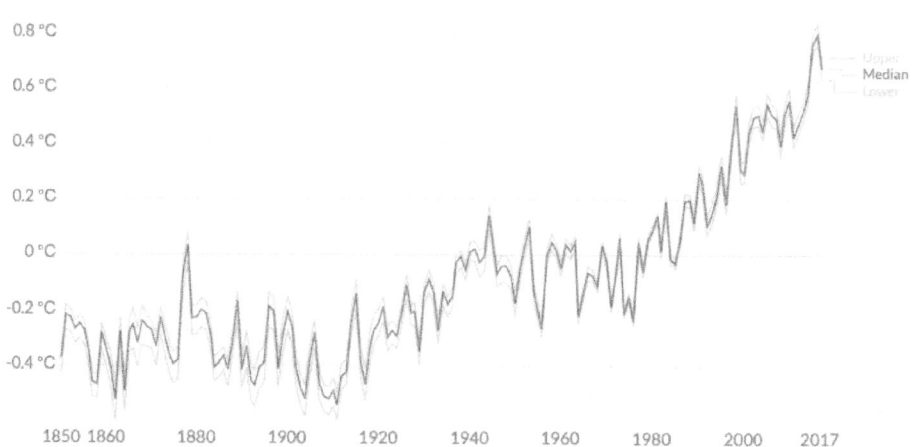

Our World in Data

Source: Hadley Centre (HadCRUT4)   CC BY

Monoculture (the practice of keeping animals or crops of the same species and with nearly identical genomes) has economised production but destroyed biodiversity. Three quarters of the world's food is generated from just 12 plants and five animal species. The expansion of intensive agriculture is the number one reason for deforestation. In the past 20 years, agricultural production has increased threefold and the amount of irrigated land has doubled, often leading to land abandonment and desertification. Decreasing productivity has been observed, due to diminished fertility, on 20% of the world's cropland, 16% of forest land, 19% of grassland, and 27% of rangeland.

Furthermore, tropical forests have become a source rather than a sink of carbon.[21] Forest areas in South America, Africa and Asia – which have until recently played a crucial role in absorbing GHGs – are now releasing 425 teragrams of carbon annually, more than all the traffic in the US. This is due to the thinning of tree density and culling of biodiversity, reducing biomass by up to 75%. Scientists combining 12 years of satellite data with field studies found a net carbon loss on every continent. Latin America – home to the world's biggest forest, the Amazon, which is responsible for 20% of Earth's oxygen – accounted for nearly 60% of the emissions, while 24% came from Africa and 16% from Asia. Every year about 18 million hectares of forest – an area the size of England and Wales – is felled. In just 40 years, possibly one billion hectares, the equivalent of Europe, has been torn down. Half the world's rainforests have been razed in a century and they will vanish altogether at current rates within another.

Earth's "sixth mass extinction"[22] is well underway: up to 50% of all individual animals have been lost in recent decades and almost half of land mammals have lost 80% of their range in the last century. Vertebrate populations have fallen by an average of 60% since the 1970s, and in some countries there has been an even faster decline of insects – vital, of course, for aerating the soil, pollinating blossoms, and controlling insect and plant pests.

It would be beyond foolish to think that, without urgent radical change, the human race is not going to be next. The difference between now and the last ice age was 4.5°C. While the IPCC says the current rate of emissions puts us on course for a 4°C rise by the end of the century,[23] other studies have put the figure at 8°C,[24] at which point humans at the equator and in the tropics would not be able to move around outside without dying; while sea levels would swell 200 feet higher, leaving hardly any arable land on the face of the planet.[25] Another projection anticipates the disappearance of clouds and a 12°C rise.[26] Even more frighteningly, a 3.5°C rise is considered by some to be "the extinction point", because

> "the food chain collapses, oceanic plankton dies off, and terrestrial vegetation is severely limited. The grasslands we use for agriculture are threatened the most. The extinction of species will create chaos. For

example, the disappearance of bees will create enormous problems with pollination. The acidification of the oceans depletes the oxygen in the waters. Temperatures higher than the extinction point are being predicted, not by crackpots, ideologues or sci-fi writers, but by serious scientists."[27]

In the grand scheme of things, very little is being done to tackle this bleak reality. The Paris Climate Accord in 2015 was nothing more than an international ruling class trade deal committing to crimes against humanity.[28] In principle, it agreed to *aim* to limit warming to 1.5°C, but none of the commitments were legally binding and the IPCC said that the actual commitments made still amounted to 3.2°C by 2100. Even if they were honoured, annual carbon emissions would rise from 50 billion tonnes to 55-60 billion tonnes by 2030 when they need to be cut by at least 36 billion tonnes just for a 50/50 chance of avoiding the 2°C tipping point. Even the expense of these minimal commitments proved too much for the US, which pulled out of the Accord in 2017, having never ratified the Kyoto Protocol that it signed up to in 1998, either.

In July 2019 it was revealed that only 20 of 160 of the biggest emitting companies had been meeting the targets agreed in Paris.[29] Around the world, 302 new oil and gas pipelines are at some stage of development, about 51% of them in North America, adding another 559 million tonnes of CO_2 each year by 2040.[30] Between 2015 and 2018, 33 global banks invested a combined $1.9 trillion in fossil fuel companies. The oil and gas industry is set to spend $4.9 trillion on exploration and extraction of new fossil fuel fields over the next decade.

Elsewhere, the majority of European firms have no CO_2 reduction targets.[31] While about a third of the GHG reductions needed by 2030 can be provided by the restoration of natural habitats, such a solution has attracted just 2.5% of the funding for tackling emissions.[32] The list goes on.

In 2017, around four billion metric tonnes of CO_2 emissions were added to the annual total compared to the year before, a 2% rise to 41 billion. Emissions had increased by 0.25% in the three years from 2014, when economic growth had been weaker. In 2018, US emissions rose by 3.4%. Meanwhile, as Richard Seymour writes, in the Arctic:

"World powers view this disaster as a commercial and military opportunity to be deliriously pursued. NATO (North Atlantic Treaty Organization) conducts grandstanding exercises in the region, the US and Canada invest in new fleets of ice-cutters, Denmark successfully trials its first commercial voyage in the transpolar sea route, and Russia reopens military bases. The British government anticipates $100bn worth of investment in the new, blue Arctic, while the US looks forward to mining vital oil and gas reserves hidden under the thinning ice."[33]

Converging crises
The above summary barely covers the true extent of the crisis. As Wallace-Wells says at the very start of his book, "It is worse, much worse than you think." And yet this overwhelming existential threat is hardly the only crisis humanity is faced with. Since the global financial crash and 'Great Recession' of 2008-09, the debt-fuelled recovery has been the weakest in the so-called post-war era (since the end of World War II (WWII)). Whereas total outstanding credit in the US after the Wall Street Crash grew from 160% to 260% of GDP between 1929 and 1932, the figure ballooned from 365% in 2008 to 540% in 2010. That does not include the increasingly unregulated derivatives market, whose nominal outstanding value is at least four times GDP. This hedge-betting on the future prices of underlying assets – which aims to guarantee profits, boost earnings or hide debt liabilities (money owed on accounts, loans, expenses, bonds, deferred taxes, etc) – has been the source of three back-to-back 'once-in-a-century' financial bubbles since 1990.[34]

The 2008-09 crash has been followed by a decade of austerity (significant cuts to wages, welfare and public services) and a rising right-wing populism, including the stunning ascendency of property tycoon and celebrity demagogue Donald Trump as the President of the US in 2016.[35] The British public's vote in June 2016 to leave the European Union (EU) delivered another shock of global significance. A chronic drift towards trade wars and protectionism is accelerating and in January 2018, US Defence Secretary Jim Mattis said that "great power competition, not terrorism, is now the primary focus of US national security", putting Russia, China and – yes – Europe in the crosshairs of the world's long-time dominant economic and military power.

Adding to this age of anxiety is the accelerating automation revolution. What should be an emancipatory and utopian development only generates insecurity at the prospect of unprecedented mass unemployment.

It can be no coincidence that all these crises are converging at exactly the same time. They cannot be explained away by cynical and shallow generalisations about 'human nature'. In the course of this investigation we will see that in fact all of these crises have a common root cause: the decaying *nature* of capitalism and its *tendency towards breakdown*. Indeed, average Gross Domestic Product (GDP) growth rates in the world's richest countries have fallen in every decade but one since the 1960s and are clearly closing in on zero. Recent technological leaps, especially in computing power, have seen manufacturing and consumer prices accelerate towards zero. In the longer-term, over centuries, rates of profit (both nationally and globally) and real interest rates (which tend to track economic growth) have also trended downwards, ever-closer to zero.

Drawing on Polish Jewish communist Henryk Grossman's vital clarification of Karl Marx's methodology in economic theory, we shall see that capitalism is heading inexorably towards a final, insurmountable breakdown that is destined to strike much earlier than a zero rate of profit. Indeed, we shall also see that *worldwide hyper*inflation is likely to strike sooner rather than later – and that the intensifying competition the economic crisis is spurring between nation-states threatens the most destructive world war to date.

Humanity therefore stands at a world-historic juncture. Far from facing an entirely hopeless situation, our investigation will show that if we change course, and choose the right one, we can prevent the Apocalypse promised by capitalism, liberate humanity from the dictatorship of capital and – while stabilising the climate – build a world of abundance for all that is clean, green and sustainable.

Precisely because these crises share one common cause, they share one common solution: socialism (the lower stage of communism), capitalism's historically necessary successor. That there remains so much confusion as to what exactly this entails comes down to mistaken understandings of how capitalism works and the poor application of Marx's methodological approach to economic theory – just as it did a century ago. It is therefore necessary to 'go back to basics'. By applying Marx's methodology to an economic analysis of capitalism we will see that the law of (exchange) value governs not only all production under the present system, but also its rise and fall.

Just as Marx's methodological method provides an objective analysis of capitalist development, the materialist concept of history developed by Marx and Friedrich Engels provides an objective analysis of how to establish the lower and then higher stages of communism. By tracing the historical (as in necessary) development of the productive forces, we shall see that the

'High income' countries' average GDP growth rates.
Horizontal line represents decade average.
Source: World Bank

'Leninist' road – of revolution, proletarian dictatorship and centrally planned 'state' socialism – remains *necessary*. By drawing on the work of the Soviet Russian philosopher Genrikh Volkov, we shall see that the Leninist road opens up the path to a Single Automated Society – fully automated production in a *de facto* one-state world, the final stage of the socialist transition to global, stateless communism. We shall establish precisely why this road is the solution that must be pursued if humanity is to combat the climate crisis and survive to realise its full potential in what Marx called "the beginning of human history".

The political debate around the climate crisis remains glaringly absent of any serious Marxist argument. But communists too have yet to sufficiently address the question. The vague contention that the economy must be decarbonised via the replacement of fossil fuels by renewable energy is inadequate when the new infrastructure continues to rely on the fuel-intensive and environmentally-damaging extraction of metals (which are also a finite resource). Resource extraction is responsible for 50% of global emissions, with minerals and metal mining responsible for 20% of emissions even before the manufacturing stage.[36] The 'green' industrial revolution proposed by social democrats may end up with a carbon neutral system of production by the time it is finished, but in the meantime it would be anything but.

That mankind and nature have been so profoundly alienated from each other under capitalism requires that they be reunited if the planet is to remain habitable.[37] One of the ways that this alienation has been most concretely institutionalised has been through the international prohibition and under-utilisation of the hemp and cannabis plants, the most prolific and versatile crops on Earth that were used for thousands of years before capitalism for food, fuel, medicine, clothing and construction. As we shall see, hemp (along with other fibrous plants) remains capable of providing for most of humanity's needs; and is *the key* not only to reversing desertification and stabilising the climate, but also furthering technological and industrial progress. A green industrial revolution must be precisely that – green.

We therefore argue that saving Earth's habitability is bound up with ending this alienation – so that man can once again rely on nature for survival instead of having to sell his ability to work – and completing the historical economic transition from anarchic, labour-intensive, extraction-based, for-profit commodity-production; to planned, hemp-based, fully-automated, break-even utility-production. Indeed, the Latin *cannabis sativa*, the scientific name given to cultivated hemp – because it is one of the few plant species that provides food, medicine and fibre – means 'useful'.[38]

Raising consciousness
With all this in mind, we argue that the agitational work of socialists in the coming crucial period should – in the clearest possible terms – primarily focus

on raising consciousness not just of class but of capital *per se* if we are to *sufficiently* raise consciousness and break the ideological stranglehold of social democracy, liberalism and fascism. We argue that the following points should be put at the forefront of communist agitation and serve as an introduction to Marxist education:

1) Capitalism is heading into its greatest ever crisis – one so deep that it may amount, in strictly economic terms, to the final breakdown of the entire system, whereby *all* fiat currencies collapse against precious metals, leading to widespread – perhaps near-universal – immiseration across the world.

Aggregate global debt keeps hitting new records, expressing the fact that the overaccumulation of capital – surplus capital that is unprofitable to (re)invest – is at an all-time high. Official global debt in 2017 was $184 trillion, 225% of global GDP. This equates to $86,000 for every person in the world, 2.5 times the average per capita annual income. According to some estimates, though, official figures are understated by a factor of 2.5, making actual global debt $460 trillion, 560% of GDP and $215,000 per person. The debt is also increasingly greater than the money supply, clearly making it unsustainable.

Capital itself is a generally *ever-increasing* fetter on investment and productivity growth, which are experiencing record periods of stagnation. As well as money hoarding, surplus capital can take the form of speculation and under-utilised and unused factories/land.

The overaccumulation crisis has necessitated the savage austerity of the past decade, since the growth of capital is increasingly dependent on public subsidies. Record levels of inequality have followed, since sustaining the accumulation process also requires the sufficient centralisation and concentration of capital.

2) The general rate of profit tends to fall, not just in cycles of years or decades, but *historically towards zero*. The world rate of profit fell in an overall trend from an estimated 43% in the 1870s to 17% in the 2000s, a trajectory taking it to zero by 2055. Similarly, real interest rates have been trending downwards towards zero – where they have been stuck since 2010 – for 700 years.

These trends are reflected in the rapid fall towards zero of manufacturing costs and consumer prices – the more abundantly things are made, the cheaper they become – driven by the tendency for computing power to double every two years, in turn accelerating the speed of production. Whereas the price of the world's fastest supercomputer in 1975 was $5m ($32m in 2013's money), the price of an iPhone 4 released in 2010 with the equivalent performance was $400. Aerospace companies producing engines in 2010 for $24m in 24 months are now 3-D printing their engines for $2,000 in two weeks; while human genome sequencing (preventative health care) that cost billions of dollars only 30 years ago will soon cost next to nothing.

3) The historical tendency towards fully automated production – a necessary development due to capital accumulation's ever-rising demand for higher productivity – is the final expression of capital's self-abolishing tendency, as the source of surplus value, exchange-value and profit – the exploitation of commodity-producing human labour – is becoming obsolete. Hence the historical fall towards a zero rate of profit. *All profit is essentially unpaid labour*. Machines cannot sell labour-power and therefore cannot be exploited/produce surplus value. The overaccumulation of capital is at the same time an underproduction of surplus value.

4) The decaying *nature* of capitalism is also illustrated by GDP growth rates, which are already closing in on zero. Average GDP growth rates have been falling for 50 years in what the World Bank defines as 'high-income countries', from: 5.59% in the 1960s; to 4.15% in the 1970s; 2.93% in the 1980s; 2.35% in the 1990s; and 1.78% in the 2000s. The figure rose slightly to 2.1% in 2010-2018 – but with the largest ever global recession on the horizon: the respective technology and housing bubbles of the 1990s and 2000s have been eclipsed by a bond (debt) market bubble encompassing *every* asset class in the financial system – an unprecedented 'everything bubble'.

Before the end of August 2019, a remarkable $17 trillion of government bonds, 30% of the worldwide market, were trading at *negative* yields (meaning bondholders were getting less back than they invested) – something unheard of before 2013 – having shot up from $15 trillion at the start of the month. Because investment in production is increasingly unprofitable, the demand for government bonds as a store-holder of value – considered the 'safest' bonds, since the state can print money – has exploded. Rising demand pushes their prices up but their yields (interest rates) down, making government debt cheaper to repay. Ending a recession, however, typically requires an interest rate cut of 5-6% – and rates across the world are already close to zero (they had *never* gone as low as zero in the US or Britain before 2010). Deepening negative rates would increasingly disincentivise investment in government bonds, eventually pushing yields back up, making sky-rocketing government debt more expensive to pay off and collapsing the tax base. Even if investors tolerate deepening negative rates, there is a definite limit to the amount of cash that can be converted into bonds and stocks, which would be bought increasingly via money printing – rapidly devaluing the money supply and risking the highest levels of hyperinflation ever seen.

Since demand for currency rises in a crisis, a match in supply via printing is required to limit deflation. If, however, demand falls or collapses due to bankruptcies and high or mass unemployment, and the supply remains high in an effort to raise prices or boost consumption, then inflation becomes abnormally high (above 2%). This is now the risk, since bonds held by central banks would normally be sold back on the private market before inflation becomes a problem – but the private sector is also increasingly dependent on central banks as the purchaser of corporate bonds. The record amount of money that has been printed since 2008 could therefore become worthless.

Wealthy investors are being advised to take their money out of the banks and buy gold in the expectation that the purchasing power of *all* fiat currencies will collapse against precious metals. Inflation is also used as a weapon to burn debt, taxes and wages.

All this fits with the historical devaluation of fiat (unbacked paper) currency. British pound sterling and the US dollar have now lost nearly 100% of their purchasing power during their lifetimes – almost all of that since 1970 (93.5% for sterling; 85% for the dollar).

5) Eventually the system must come up against an *absolute* overaccumulation of capital, ie an *absolute historical maximum to accumulation* and, therefore, a *final capitalist breakdown*, which is destined to strike *much earlier than a zero rate of profit*. This is because the size of the exploitable working class and the amount of time it works cannot be expanded indefinitely. The global workforce has now been all but totally deindustrialised – ie, shifted predominantly to services, from manufacturing – hence the fall in profit rates and manufacturing costs. *For the first time*, therefore, socialism is becoming an economic *necessity* – the fight for which is the *historical mission* of the *international* working class.

6) Each economic crisis requires the sufficient devaluation of capital and labour-power in order to restore accumulation (ie, to restore the value of total surplus value to over and above the value of total capital). In the 20th century, massive overaccumulation *necessitated* the destruction of capital via two world wars and fascism before sufficient devaluation was achieved, resulting in the post-war productivity boom amid a new, *early stage* of capital accumulation.

Now, a *late stage* of accumulation is again intensifying competition between nation-states over profit, trade and (neocolonial and domestic) assets, thereby *forcing* the ruling classes of the advanced global powers – the US, Britain, Germany, France, Japan, China and Russia – into direct confrontation, *inevitably* manifesting at first in protectionist nationalism and trade wars.

A world war now, however, *surely cannot save capitalism*. While it would accelerate the final devaluation to zero prices – via an arms race involving further automation – the record level of overaccumulation means that such a war would also have to be the most destructive to date: a probable nuclear conflagration that would annihilate human civilisation and the habitability of the planet. *Only world socialism can end this apocalyptic threat for good.*

7) Socialism is capitalism's historically necessary successor, just as capitalism necessarily succeeded feudalism. This can be explained through Marx's

materialist conception of history, ie by tracing the historical development of the productive forces:

a) the historical tendency of capital to monopolise production shows that the productive forces and accumulation itself demand a 'final merger' into an absolute monopoly. Once all production has come under the ownership of the state (society), this monopoly has been achieved by definition;

b) the increasing necessity for long-term central planning *within* private corporations shows a historical tendency towards central planning of the economy as a whole;

c) the private sector's ever-increasing dependence on state subsidies is trending towards 100% of income and, therefore, nationalisation.

These developments provide an incredible opportunity for the international working class to take over industrial capacities that it did not have at the start of previous socialist construction, when primitive peasant economies had to be industrialised.

The need to plan the economy as a whole necessitates the foundation of a new Communist International, which will guide the final merger and construction of a Single Automated System, ie a *de facto* one-state world, the final stage before (global, stateless) communism.

8) Just as the dictatorship of capital (an all-capitalist state) *is* the capitalist mode of production, the dictatorship of the proletariat (an all-socialist state) *is* the socialist mode of production (the lower stage of communism), which will replace the shallowness of representative democracy with participative/direct democracy, fully enfranchising the working class, starting with a democratically agreed new constitution in every country. Once every nation has become socialist and as the productive forces become fully automated and relatively localised – made much more possible than in the past thanks to 3-D printing, personal computers, open source coding, etc – bringing about abundant (ie extremely plentiful) material wealth *for all*, the state will become increasingly obsolete and wither away into (the higher phase of) communism.

9) Capitalism *per se* is responsible for the existential climate crisis: the labour-intensity (profitability) involved in extracting fossil fuels and metals and converting them into commodities makes plundering nature *increasingly* necessary. The ever-rising demands of capital accumulation require an ever-greater intensity and expansion of extraction and an ever-greater mass of commodities. The Green New Deal proposed by social democrats may aim to replace fossil fuels with renewable energy, but because it remains a capitalist solution, the materials being used to build wind turbines, solar panels and batteries rely on an ever-greater (fuel-intensive) extraction of metals, and will therefore only continue to increase greenhouse gas emissions exponentially and jeopardise the habitability of the planet. The real solutions include:

i) capitalism's replacement by socialism, a higher and more efficient mode of production, whereby the decommodification of labour will mean that value-creation becomes dependent on utility-production instead of exploitation – ending the absolute need to plunder the environment, since all labour will become productive. (Under capitalism, only commodity production is productive.)

ii) the nationalisation and then internationalisation of all natural resources, controlled by an independent global trust, making them the common patrimony of humanity;

iii) an incentivised transition towards communal ways of living in order to achieve large efficiency gains, reduce urban concentration and resolve urban-rural contradictions;

iv) extensive, ongoing investment in: nuclear power (which is now safe but unprofitable); building rational, eco-friendly infrastructure; cleaning up the environment; recycling (especially metals); rewilding; reforestation; permaculture farming; urban agriculture; and lab-grown food and jewellery.

v) a green industrial revolution that is actually green – ie hemp-based. Hemp is Earth's most prolific and versatile crop and can be converted into 50,000+ applications, including bioplastics up to ten times stronger than steel yet lighter than carbon fibre. Before capitalism, hemp was used for at least 10,000 years for food, fuel, clothing, medicine and construction. Hemp grows quickly, heals even the most damaged soil and rapidly draws down carbon dioxide from the atmosphere. Whereas a standard average sized house emits 48 tonnes of carbon, an equivalent hemp-based house sequesters 5.5 tonnes. Hemp is key not only to stabilising the climate and reversing desertification, but the next technological and industrial advancements. As a battery and conductor it outperforms lithium and graphene both in terms of ability and longevity – at 1,000th of the cost, *because its production is not labour-intensive*. If humanity is to have any chance of surviving and thriving, civilisation's infrastructure must be largely rebuilt from hemp and other fibrous plants (banana peel can be made into sodium-ion batteries, for example) (and mycelium, a type of fungus that can be rapidly grown and manipulated into numerous useable structures) both to stop and reverse the environmental and climate crises and to address the finite nature of fossil fuels and metals.

10) Communists must keep faith in the *masses* and appeal to their *immediate needs*. The Bolsheviks had only 8,000 members just four months before the 1917 Revolution. While we must endeavour to lead the masses, we cannot run too far ahead of them in rhetoric or deed. We must appeal to the widest possible strata of society in order to turn as quickly as possible to the *urgent* priority of saving the habitability of the planet. Widespread immiseration and the threat of extinction, which personally concerns the whole of humanity, will necessarily produce a reaction from the whole of humanity. This

necessitates the use of the united front as a tactic – appealing to the leaders of reformist parties for joint action, even if only for reforms at first, in order to address and win over the reformist rank and file. The Canutes who oppose the fight for socialism can only do so in the name of barbarism and extinction; the promise of amnesty should be at the forefront of agitation to encourage defectors who come to their senses.

11) Socialism will nationalise the land. To weaken support for counter-revolution, communist parties should vow to cancel *all* outstanding mortgages and personal debt, and entitle *all* households, *regardless of class*, to remain in (and own) the property in which they presently live, with the land leased from the state according to differential convenience or amenity of land. (Compensation for expropriations in general will be offered where possible.) As the process of building socialism progresses, those who are required to leave their homes, due to the need to revive the environment or build new infrastructure, will be compensated with the new, eco-friendly, high-quality housing, in a location as close as possible, that the state will embark upon building for everyone. Unused properties will be given to the homeless and those presently living in inadequate accommodation; with some transformed into care homes and mental health retreats, run by patient-led councils.

12) Fiat currency (which is anyway dying 'a natural death') will be replaced by digital voucher credits pegged to labour time (the real measure of value). In combination with the social ownership of production and full employment, this will end exploitation and underpin equal rights, since each worker will accrue all the value created by their labour time, rather than having part (most) of it appropriated by capitalists; minus only direct taxes to control inflation and fund universal public services, such as health care, social care and education, which will be free at the point of use. The voucher system will include a grading system, set according to type of work/productivity to incentivise work where it is needed. Consumer goods will be priced according to the labour time it took to produce them, adjusted according to supply and demand to ensure stability (ie break-evenness), thereby abolishing inherent economic recession. Free time will increasingly become the measure of social wealth, revitalising individual craftsmanship. Full employment (including earn-as-you-learn apprenticeships), a lower retirement age (with guaranteed public pensions) and a reduced working week (differing according to circumstances and development in each country) should be implemented as quickly as possible. State debt will be cancelled, including that 'owed' from 'developing' to 'developed' nations.

The rest of this book will substantiate this summary of our arguments in theoretical detail.

1. The greatest ever overaccumulation of capital, the greatest ever capitalist crisis

"As the accumulation of capital grows absolutely, the valorisation of this expanded capital becomes progressively more difficult."[39]

Grossman

In a scene towards the end of the US TV series *Breaking Bad* (2008-13), Skyler White tells her husband Walter – a genius chemistry teacher who pays for his cancer treatment by becoming a meth kingpin – that they have accrued more money "than we could spend in 10 life-times". Capitalism shares a similar problem: overaccumulated capital.

We will show why capital overaccumulates in theoretical detail in the next chapter, but we should start by grasping this concept as an inherent defect of the system that results in periodic capitalist crisis. On average, recessions (two consecutive quarter-year periods of negative growth) strike roughly every ten years. Put simply, overaccumulated capital is surplus capital – it *cannot* be (re)invested in production because it cannot yield profit. Capital itself then is a barrier to investment, productivity growth and the development of the productive forces (humans and technology). Since the demands of accumulation tend to increase, this barrier is generally ever-growing both relatively and absolutely (it recedes partly and temporarily when capital is cheapened).

In an example of how capitalists fail to understand the nature of their own system, Larry Fink, the head of BlackRock, the largest asset manager in the world, with a $4.65 trillion portfolio, wrote in April 2015 to the chief executives of the 500 biggest firms listed on the US stock market to accuse them of "underinvesting in innovation, skilled workforces or essential capital expenditures necessary to sustain long-term growth".[40] Why would they invest in things that are not profitable?

Europe's most well-known 'democratic socialist'[41] and self-proclaimed Marxist, Yanis Varoufakis, Greece's former Minister of Finance, fared little better in his analysis when he said in January 2016 that investors were simply "too terrified" to reinvest because of "low demand" from increasingly poor populations.[42] But why are they "terrified"? To suggest such a thing implies that the solution is simply to restore the confidence of investors. All governments have to do therefore is put money in the pockets of the public so that demand again rises. Varoufakis does not give a Marxist explanation of the crisis but a mystifying theory of 'underconsumption'. He cannot explain exactly why demand is low; nor the cause of the "twin peaks", as he calls them, the mountains of debt and idle capital which sit alongside one another.

Put simply: debt rises *to 'plug the gap' created by the lack of profit which surplus capital cannot yield.*

Debt and currency devaluation

According to the International Monetary Fund (IMF), private debt has trebled since 1950, "making it the driving force behind global debt". It put global debt in 2017 at a record high of $184 trillion, 225% of global GDP, 11 percentage points up on 2009. This worked out at $86,000 for every person in the world, 2.5 times annual per capita income. According to financial analyst Ron Surz, once 'off the books' costs such as social security are included, the figure is understated by a factor of 2.5, making actual global debt $460 trillion, 560% of GDP and $215,000 per person.[43] If that is the case, then the true number is even higher. The IMF figure only includes households, governments and non-financial corporates, whereas analysis by the Institute of International Finance (IIF) also includes the outstanding debt of financial institutions (and is more frequently updated). The IIF put global debt in the third quarter of 2017 at $233 million, 327% of GDP.

Because of the lack of profitable opportunities in production, investors have increasingly bought short-term government debt, which at the same time has enabled the government to prop up the tax base. As the demand for this debt has increased, however, prices have risen and yields have therefore fallen – all the way to zero, something that had *never* happened before 2010 in the US or Britain. This debt then is becoming increasingly unattractive, since investors are only getting back what they lent, during which time inflation may have eroded its value. Long-term government debt, however, is less attractive (hence their higher yields) than short-term debt, since there is simply longer for something to go wrong and returns are needed in the short-term to pay for short-term bills and expenses. Central banks have therefore needed to purchase long-term debt at high-prices, a method of 'front running' that incentivises investors to buy long-term debt and then sell it on to central banks at a profit.

This unconventional monetary policy – ie, influencing the money supply, as opposed to a government's fiscal (tax and spend) policies – is known as 'quantative easing' (QE). The central bank increases its reserves by 'printing' electronic money (thereby devaluing the existing supply) and then 'expands its balance sheet' by using it to buy longer-term debt. The US's monetary base exploded from $842bn in August 2008 to $2.9 trillion in January 2013.[44]

Central banks set a target 'base' rate with the aim of maintaining economic growth and employment levels without letting inflation run out of control. The base rate therefore tends to stay close to the rate of GDP growth. Because government debt is so high though (higher rates increase debt-to-GDP) the Fed kept rates at zero (down from 6.4% before the housing crash) for an extraordinary seven years after 2009, even as growth edged upwards, albeit sluggishly (they were held at 1%, down from 6.4%, for 12 months after the 2001 recession). Lower rates (achieved by issuing more debt) cheapen loan capital[45] – now made all but free (the borrower returns what they borrowed without paying much, if any, interest) – so that banks don't stop lending, sustaining cashflows; to increase subsidies to the private sector; and to make government debt cheaper to repay (service/finance).

Surplus capital in all its forms tends to rise. In 2008, the 963 non-financial companies in the S&P Global 1200 index sat on cash piles totalling $1.95 trillion. By 2012, total reserves had surged by 62% to $3.16 trillion.[46] Citing figures from asset management firm GMO, in July 2013 Robin Harding reported in the *Financial Times* (*FT*) that

> "profits and overall net investment in the US tracked each other closely until the late 1980s, with both about 9% of GDP. Then the relationship began to break down. After the recession, from 2009, it went haywire. Pre-tax corporate profits are now at record highs – more than 12% of GDP – while net investment is barely 4% of output."[47]

In November 2013, Credit Suisse published similar conclusions, saying that "US net business investment has rebounded – but, at around 1.5% of GDP, still only stands at the trough levels seen during the past two recessions".[48] It showed that since the early 1980s, the peaks reached by net business investment as a share of GDP have been declining in each economic recovery. As John Smith writes in *Imperialism In The Twenty-First Century*:

> "A notable effect of the investment strike is that the age of the capital stock in the US has been on a long-term rising trend since 1980 and started climbing rapidly after the turn of the millennium, reaching record levels several years before the [2008-09] crisis."[49]

Smith points out that in the UK the biggest counterpart to the government's fiscal deficit (the difference between annual total revenue and total expenditure) of 8.8% of GDP in 2011 was "a corporate surplus of 5.5% of GDP, unspent cash that sucked huge demand out of the UK economy".[50]

The problem is even worse in Japan, where huge corporate surpluses and low rates of investment have been the norm since the early 1990s. According to Martin Wolf in the *FT*, "the sum of depreciation and retained earnings of corporate Japan was a staggering 29.5% of GDP in 2011, against just [sic] 16% in the US, which is itself struggling with a corporate financial surplus".[51]

In 2012, the United Nations Conference on Trade and Development (UNCTAD) reported that "despite the gradual advance of international production by transnationals (TNCs), their record levels of cash have so far not translated into sustained growth in investment levels. UNCTAD estimates that these cash levels have reached more than $5 trillion, including earnings retained overseas."[52] In 2014, investment-to-GDP ratios in the 'developed world' were close to their lowest levels in 60 years.[53]

As David Yaffe noted in the British communist newspaper *Fight Racism! Fight Imperialism! (FRFI)*, in July 2016 the ratings agency Fitch "calculated that there is now a remarkable $11.7 trillion worth of sovereign debt in the global market that carries *negative* interest rates", meaning investors (mainly pension and hedge fund managers) receive less money back than the amount loaned.

> "This increased by $1.3 trillion in June alone and includes $2.6 trillion long-term debt (more than seven years maturity). The amount of bonds with a yield that used to be considered normal, that is above 2%, is barely worth $2 trillion. Most of this negative debt is in Japan and the eurozone, but rate expectations in the UK are falling as well. Recently Royal Bank of Scotland and its subsidiary NatWest warned businesses they may have to charge them to accept deposits due to low interest rates. This move would make them the first UK banks to introduce negative interest rates."[54]

Capital is dirt cheap and yet it isn't cheap enough. From the perspective of buyers of government debt (bondholders), they are willing to lend the state $100 now in return for $99 later in the hope that $99 later will be worth relatively more than $100 is now. It's risky, but not as risky right now as investing that same capital in production.

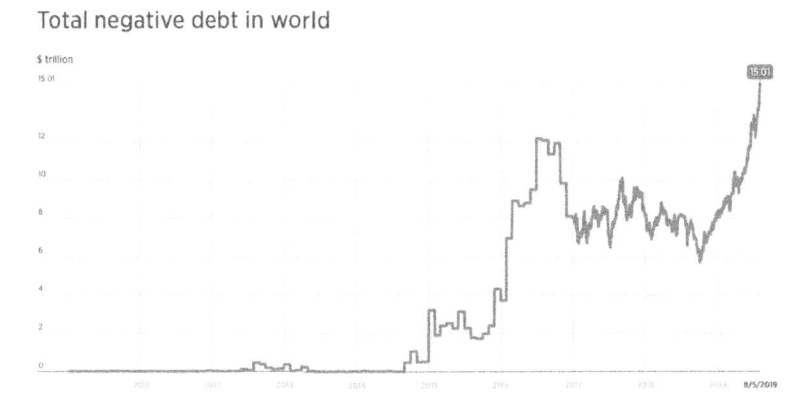

Total negative debt in world

Source: Deutsche Bank

The quantity of negative-yielding debt – which barely existed before 2014 – hit $14 trillion in the first half of 2019, $15 trillion at the start of August and $16.7 trillion before the end of the month. In the middle two weeks of August the proliferation of negative-yielding bonds erupted – 30% of global, tradeable bonds were being sold at a guaranteed loss.

The necessity of austerity
As well as sitting idle in corporate bank accounts, surplus capital can be channelled into speculation on stock markets (where ownership shares of businesses are bought and sold) or hoarded in offshore tax havens, waiting for profitable conditions to return.

At the same time, the 'private sector' becomes increasingly dependent on government (ie public) subsidies, including bail-outs and tax cuts. The US corporate tax rate has been cut gradually from 48% in 1951 to 13% in 2017.[55] Britain's was 52% in 1973, and will be cut from 19% to 17% in 2020.[56] Tory contestants vying to replace Theresa May as Prime Minister spoke about making the rate as low as 12.5% in order to "turbocharge the economy".[57]

As a result, tax revenues and state budgets shrink, at least in relative terms per capita. National (public) debt inevitably grows in order to at least partially cover the shortfall, having already risen from subsidising the private sector. It grew enormously, of course, after the bailout of the banks in the wake of the financial crash. The British government did so to the tune of £456bn: £124bn in loan or share purchases, requiring an actual cash injection to the banks and costing taxpayers up to £5bn a year just to service the loan; and £332.4bn in guarantees and liabilities. The money is supposed to be paid back after 20 years but the government has admitted that at least £27bn will never be recouped. All this is without taking into account losses from the recession. Britain's national debt-to-GDP rose from 35% in 2008 to 80% in 2014. In the US the bailouts reportedly reached $14.4 trillion in 2010.[58]

In 2019, the US's official national debt stood at $22 trillion, 106% of its GDP; up from 62% in 2007 and by 2% since Trump took office two years earlier. It increased under his predecessor Barack Obama (2009-17) by 74% ($8.6 trillion), following a 101% rise ($6.1 trillion) under George W Bush (2001-09), putting the two in the top five highest borrowing US presidents.[59] With the next recession certain to be even – considerably – worse than the last one, US national debt is set to rise above the 118% record of 1946, after WWII, indicating a record level of overaccumulation. That the figure was 39% in 1937, having risen from 16% at the onset of the Great Depression in 1929, *before a world war*, and having risen back up to over 100% from 31% in 1974, without a world war, tells us just how deep this crisis is compared to a century ago.

National debt is owed to the government's creditors: bondholders, ie people, companies and foreign governments; international organisations such as the World Bank; private financial institutions; and central banks. During

2010-19, the US government spent $2.5 trillion on net interest payments, compared to $1.5 trillion on veterans benefits and $1.1 trillion on education.[60]

So state spending goes towards both the public and the private 'sectors', but is paid for by taxes on profits and wages. Private investors and companies are therefore continually lobbying the government, especially when profit rates are falling, to lower taxes or spend less on welfare and public services so that more can be spent on private subsidies. They will claim that government spending is 'crowding out' private investment but this is merely their invented justification for plundering the working class.

Rising public debt just happens to coincide with stagnant investment in production. One study suggests that 77% of debt-to-GDP is the point at which "national debt levels begin to have an adverse effect on growth", with each additional percentage point of debt costing 0.017 percentage points of annual real growth. In 'developing' countries the figures are 64% and 0.02%.[61]

Money printing alone does not add to public debt, but state spending without repayment would risk too much demand compared to supply and, therefore, above normal general inflation. Inflation targets are usually 2%; high enough to incentivise lending and inspire spending confidence (because deflation indicates a recession) but low enough for businesses to plan their expenditure. Bond financing therefore curbs the inflationary potential of the money printing it is backed by, since debt obligations keep demand in check.

Quantitive easing, however, has now been going on for far longer than originally planned, since attempts to 'turn off the taps' have pushed the economy towards recession. Government bonds are explicitly intended to be parked at the central bank only temporarily, to be sold back into the private sector when monetary policy needs to be tightened, ie when interest rates, which cannot go down forever, need to be raised to reign in demand and lower general inflation. But if debt is not or cannot be repaid it becomes increasingly difficult to attract creditors, and so more bond financing is required. The central bank could cancel public debt, but that would reduce the general tax burden and therefore increase demand and inflation.

Austerity, based on the socialisation of private debt, has been, therefore, an economic *necessity* – not only an unfair and immoral 'political choice', as is claimed by left-wing reformists.

That public spending as a share of national income in Britain in 2017 (39.6%) stood at the same level as in 2007 (39.6%), after seven years of debt servicing via savage cuts to state welfare and public services, suggests national income must have fallen per capita. Indeed, official forecasts suggest that GDP per adult in 2022 will be 18% lower than it would have been had GDP grown by 2% a year since 2008 (it has averaged 1.1%), broadly the expected rate of growth at that time. As of July 2017, public spending per capita had fallen by 3.9%.[62] This figure, though, obscures the fact that the government is allocating proportionally less of its budget to welfare and public services. Per person, day-to-day spending on public services has been cut to about four-fifths of what it was in 2010.[63]

The government slashed public sector employment by 15.5% between September 2009 and April 2017, a reduction of nearly one million jobs, primarily affecting women, who make up around two-thirds of the public sector workforce. Overall, £22bn of the £26bn in 'savings' since June 2010 have been shouldered by women.[64] Lone mothers (92% of lone parents) have experienced an average fall in living standards of 18% (£8,790). Black and Asian households in the lowest fifth of incomes are the most affected, with an average of 19.2% and 20.1% – £8,407 and £11,678 – respectively.[65] The Office of Budget Responsibility (OBR) has said that the cumulative scale of cuts to welfare are "unprecedented", with real per capita welfare cap spending in 2021-22 projected to be around 10% lower than its 2015-16 level.[66]

The Conservative-Liberal Democrat coalition government initially aimed to eliminate the deficit by 2015 but weaker-than-expected growth pushed the date back to 2025. The government tried to spin this as a generous easing of austerity, but it was merely giving itself more time to take on the deficit. In December 2017 the OBR said that GDP per person would be 3.5% smaller in 2021 than was forecast in March 2016. Contradicting the government, the OBR said the deficit would not be eliminated until 2031. The Institute for Fiscal Studies (IFS) added that national debt – then standing at £1.94 trillion, with an annual servicing cost of £48bn – may not return to pre-crisis levels until the 2060s. Pressure on the public finances, primarily from health and social care, is only going to increase. In all of the OBR's scenarios, spending grows faster than the economy. With health costs running ahead of inflation, the National Health Service (NHS) – already suffering from a £4.3bn annual shortfall – requires a 4% minimum annual increase in funding to maintain expenditure per capita amid a growing and ageing population.

The attacks on the working class have been focused on what for capital is its most 'unproductive' sections. In Britain, a study by the *British Medical Journal* accused the Tory government of "economic murder" after finding that cuts to health and social care had led to 120,000 excess (more than expected) deaths in England alone between 2010 and 2017.[67] In August 2015 the government was forced to reveal statistics showing that 90 people were dying every month after being declared "fit to work", which denied them their right to benefits. A UN inquiry reported that welfare reforms in Britain had disproportionately affected disabled people and led to "grave and systematic violations" of disabled people's rights. In May 2019, Philip Alston, UN rapporteur on extreme poverty, compared Conservative welfare policies to the creation of 19th century workhouses and said that Britain's poorest people face lives that are "solitary, poor, nasty, brutish, and short".

Attacks on the working class in Britain have faced some active opposition from those most affected, such as Disabled People Against Cuts; low-paid service workers striking for pay rises; and the Focus E15 mothers in East London, who defeated the Labour council trying to evict them from their social housing. While most opposition has remained limited to vocal condemnation, much of the initial support the government did secure for austerity measures has started to ebb. Now that austerity is starting to affect the middle classes, it has 'gone too far'.

Following an outcry in 2015 from the House of Lords and among his own Members of Parliament (MPs), then Chancellor of the Exchequer George Osborne cancelled planned cuts to tax credits that would have cost families £1,000 a year. But if the government decides to halt cuts to welfare it either has to raise taxes, take on more debt or make further cuts to public services (or a combination of all three). As the blog *Flip Chart Fairy Tales* points out:

> "Public service providers have already cut all the easy stuff, or the things that people can't see, like regulatory and support services. The next round of cuts is likely to fall on far more visible areas, like roads, parks and rubbish collection."[68]

This then would be as unpopular as further welfare cuts. As with tax credits, it is no longer just 'the Left' which is complaining. In 2017 the Conservative chairman of the Local Government Association warned that councils would be unable to deliver core services by the end of the decade. But the Resolution Foundation calculates that stopping the cuts to public services and welfare spending would cost the state over £30bn. The government is stuck between a rock and a hard place.

The dictatorship of capital
Economics, by definition, is about managing scarce resources. The rich must continually take from the lower classes to sustain their own wealth amid a relative contraction (per capita) of exchange-value. Far from being simply a political choice, for capital austerity has been an economic necessity. In terms of reducing the deficit and the national debt, the cuts to public spending have in fact been nowhere near deep enough, despite having been very significant.

Governments have had to pursue austerity in order to sustain the profitability of the economy as a whole. It is clear then that the capitalist mode of production *is* the *dictatorship* of capital. This reality is expressed politically by a dictatorship of the bourgeoisie (capitalists) – a plutocratic oligarchy – but bourgeois governments are compelled to make most of their decisions in response to overaccumulation. The needs of capital are paramount and determine the development of the system as a whole. The working class is made to pay the price, with more and more debt heaped onto its back.

2. Breakdown theory is crisis theory

> "The breakdown tendency, as the fundamental tendency of capitalism, splits up into a series of apparently independent cycles which are only the form of its constant, periodic reassertion. Marx's theory of breakdown is thus the necessary basis and presupposition of his theory of crisis, because ... crises are only the form in which the breakdown tendency is temporarily interrupted and restrained from realising itself completely."[69]
>
> Grossman

That capitalism requires indefinite accumulation is obvious. A profit-based system implies growth – investors are disincentivised from investing if returns are not higher than the amount invested. What is and has been in dispute for nearly two centuries is whether or not accumulation *can* go on indefinitely.

Those within left-wing trends who believe capital accumulates harmoniously, interrupted only by external forces and economic mismanagement (underspending, deregulation, insufficient redistribution) are known as harmonists; while those who uphold Marx point to capitalism's inherent contradictions that result in its tendency towards breakdown. Few, in truth, have accurately upheld the latter position.

Before we go into breakdown theory, though, we must show that (i) the exploitation of commodity-producing human labour is the sole source of surplus value (represented in our formulas as s), exchange-value, and profit; and (ii) that due to the needs of capital accumulation, constant capital (c, the outlay on machinery and other material inputs) tends to grow relative to variable capital (v, the outlay on labour). For if variable capital alone returns new value but shrinks relative to constant capital, then it is clear that the proportion of the value-creating component in the organic composition of capital (constant capital plus variable capital, $c+v$) tends to shrink historically towards zero.

That constant capital grows relative to variable capital is indisputable – that the means of production (M) grows relative to living labour (L) is historical, and therefore true of every mode of production. What needs to be shown is that under capitalism the process is governed by the law of value, ie the labour theory of value.

Human labour power (the ability to work) is a *unique* commodity in that it produces *surplus value* – the amount of value that goes to the capitalist after the worker has been 'paid' for the part of the day that equates to the amount they and their family need to live on.

The working day is split into two parts: necessary labour time and surplus labour time. Necessary labour time is the time it takes the worker (on average) to produce enough value to buy the commodities they need to reproduce themselves, ie to stay what is socially considered healthy enough to continue working. Surplus labour time is the time the worker works beyond necessary labour time. Since the going rate for labour power is necessary labour time, surplus labour time is surplus value that goes to the capitalist, *realised* through the sale of the commodities workers produce.

For example: a worker in a toy factory is paid £10 a day to work 10 hours; she produces 10 toys a day, and each toy is worth £10 each. The capitalist is only paying the worker for her ability to work one hour each day to produce enough value to reproduce herself (one toy = one hour's labour = £10). Her necessary labour time is one hour, and her surplus labour time that goes to the capitalist is nine hours. If the worker needs £10 a day to reproduce herself, then that £10 is the value of her labour power. If the capitalist cuts the daily wage below £10, he has pushed the wage below the value of labour power. (Indeed, struggles for better wages are usually struggles to push them back up to the proper value.)

The price of labour power is determined like the price of any other commodity – on average, the cost of its production, ie necessary labour time. But if commodities are sold for the cost of their production then how does the capitalist make any profit?

The capitalist purchases the worker's human labour power but, *uniquely*, *always* ends up with more than the amount it cost to purchase the commodity. The wage *obscures* the fact that the capitalist has only paid for necessary labour time. (Marx calls the social relations that are concealed by economic relations 'commodity fetishism'.) *Profit then is essentially unpaid labour.* Wage labour is – especially for the poorest workers whose daily subsistence depends exclusively on the sale of their labour-power – *wage-slavery*.

Marx's investigations led him to realise that his analysis of capitalism must start with the commodity, since capitalism "presents itself as an immense accumulation of commodities".[70] What all commodities have in common is that they are all exchangeable – they all possess *exchange-value*. And as they are all products of labour, what they all have in common which gives them this exchange-value is *general human labour in the abstract*. Therefore, the total value of all commodities is determined by *total socially necessary labour time* – how long they took to produce. (The socially necessary labour time of each finished product includes that of each component, or primary commodity.) Therefore, when labour-saving technology reduces total socially necessary labour time (per commodity – for an increase in the number of commodities made may increase socially necessary labour time in absolute terms), there tends to be a relative fall in the surplus value contained in the total value of commodities, ie less surplus value per commodity, despite the fact that the rate of exploitation has increased, ie that each worker is now giving the capitalist more surplus labour time and therefore producing more surplus value relative to their necessary labour. As Grossman says:

> "Technological progress means that since commodities are created with a smaller expenditure of labour their value falls. This is not only true of the newly produced commodities. The fall in value reacts back on the commodities that are still on the market but which were produced under the older methods, involving a greater expenditure of labour time. These commodities are devalued."[71]

The possibility of crisis *originates in the dual character of the commodity*. It is at once an object of use, a *use-value*, and something that can be exchanged for another thing, an *exchange-value*. In a dialectical (bidirectional/interactional) unity of opposites, the more abundant a use-value becomes, relative to demand, the less exchange-value it contains. The capitalist produces goods in greater abundance, *yet is compelled to expand absolute production yet further to make up for his falling profit rate*.

Since different commodities contain different magnitudes of value and therefore cannot be directly exchanged, the creation of money (gold being the historical money-commodity) proceeds logically from this contradiction. It is not the exchange of commodities which regulates the magnitude of their value, but the magnitude of their value which controls their exchange-value. Exchange-value is the only form in which the value of commodities can be expressed. Someone will buy a use-value because they need or want it, but only if they can exchange it for something else, ie money. If they do not have enough money, they cannot buy it, and profit goes unrealised.

But to focus on this final 'surface level' aspect is what produces the mistaken underconsumptionist theory, for it forgets or ignores where it arose from – the dual character of the commodity. This is why a proper Marxist analysis always has to come back to the point or mode of production. And the point of production is accumulation. Grossman writes:

> "The specific nature of capitalist commodity production shows itself in the fact that it is not simply a labour process in which products are created by the elements of production M and L. Rather the capitalistic form of commodity production is constructed dualistically – it is simultaneously a labour process for the creation of products and a valorisation process. The elements of production M and L figure not only in their natural form, but

at the same time as values c and v respectively. They are used for the production of a sum of values, w, and indeed only on condition that over and above the used up value magnitudes c and v there is a surplus s (that is, $s = w - c + v$). The capitalist expansion of production, or accumulation of capital, is defined by the fact that the expansion of M relative to L occurs on the basis of the law of value; it takes the specific form of a constantly expanding capital c relative to the sum of wages v, such that both components of capital are necessarily valorised. It follows that the reproduction process can only be continued and expanded further if the advanced, constantly growing capital $c + v$ can secure a profit, s. The problem can then be defined as follows – is a process of this sort possible in the long run?"[72]

It is then simplest to think of the problem as follows: the purpose of commodity production is to convert the surplus value extracted from living labour into capital. But accumulation – the reproduction *and* expansion of capital – does not happen unless a *sufficient* magnitude of surplus value is produced. If the surplus value generated is insufficient then it only reproduces the *part* of capital that it is equal in value to – the rest becomes surplus capital. Capital is only fully "valorised" if it is reproduced and expanded. Grossman therefore says overaccumulation is produced by "imperfect valorisation". This abstraction can be applied to 'individual capital', the capital owned by each individual capitalist, and total capital.

Imperfect valorisation therefore explains cyclical crises. The total investment in production tends to grow faster relative to the growth of profits returned, because constant capital has to grow relative to variable capital. The mass of capital has continued to rise but at a declining rate. This is expressed as a falling rate of profit. There is a lack of surplus value relative to total capital – an underproduction of surplus value is at once an overaccumulation of capital.

The declining rate of profit

To shore up our understanding of the declining rate of profit it is helpful to represent capital production with the formula $c + v + s$.

The value of c is not increased in production but merely preserved by it, whereas v is the only part of capital that enables the capitalist to increase the value of their capital. s is the portion of the newly created value appropriated by the capitalist. The rate of surplus value is therefore s/v and the rate of profit is the ratio between surplus value and total capital, that is $s/(c+v)$. The organic composition of capital, $c+v$, measures the difference between the rate of surplus value, s/v, and the rate of profit – ie, in general, the higher the organic composition of capital, the more *capital*-intensive the industry, and the lower the rate of profit; the more *labour*-intensive, the higher the rate of profit.[73]

Because the demands of capital accumulation, as well as the need to stay ahead of or keep up with competitors, *compels* capitalists to innovate in order to raise productivity, the *fundamental* tendency of the capitalist system is to increase the ratio of constant capital to variable capital. But when the organic composition of capital, $c+v$, increases, other things being equal, the profit rate, $s/(c+v)$, declines.

Restoring the accumulation process

Imperfect valorisation *compels* the capitalist class to restructure their businesses and the system as a whole. "This involves groping attempts at a complete rationalisation of all spheres of economic life."[74] It includes:

1) increasing the production of surplus value by raising the rate of exploitation; by

a) increasing the production of *absolute surplus value*; that is, increasing the number of exploited workers, the length of the working day, intensification of effort (limited by the number of hours in the day, the physical health and ability of workers; the effectiveness of workers' resistance);

(b) increasing the production of *relative surplus value*; that is, reducing the value of labour power by cheapening production through innovation; ie, increasing surplus labour time and reducing necessary labour time (limited by the development of technology and the effectiveness of workers' resistance);

(c) driving down the costs of labour below the value of labour power (super-exploitation) through wage cuts (relative and absolute); redundancies and sackings; attacks on workers' rights and conditions, etc (limited by the effectiveness of workers' resistance).

2) dedicating more surplus value to the expansion of capital by *redirecting* portions of it from public spending (welfare, public services) to the 'private sector' (state subsidies, tax cuts), including the privatisation of state assets and public services.

3) the *sufficient* devaluation of currency and centralisation and concentration of capital (both in terms of money and privately owned production).

But the contradiction remains and the cycle repeats itself: the capital investment needed to raise productivity through innovation means constant capital grows relative to variable capital and also, therefore, the surplus value produced by variable capital. *Surplus value is converted into capital faster than it is produced* and so capital once again over-accumulates. And because the overall mass of capital is now even greater than before, an even greater magnitude of surplus value is required alongside an even greater devaluation and concentration of capital in order to reproduce and expand it yet further.

Crisis is therefore inherent to the system, as increasing magnitudes of capital become dormant while waiting for profitable conditions to return, and cannot be put down merely to 'greed', hoarding or the 'bad' or 'erroneous choices' of capitalists, politicians, economists and civil servants. Private and public debt rises not because of arbitrary overspending but in order to *make up for the insufficient production of surplus value*. Imperfect valorisation expresses an inherent defect in the accumulation process; and because, with each crisis, overaccumulation arises from an ever-greater base of accumulation, with living labour shrinking relative to constant capital, the problem tends to become more severe both relatively and absolutely. As Marx says:

> "The *real barrier* of capitalist production is *capital itself*. It is that capital and its self-expansion appear as the starting and the closing point, the motive and the purpose of production.... Capitalist production constantly strives to overcome these immanent barriers, but it overcomes them only by means that set up the barriers afresh and on a more powerful scale."[75]

Marx's *Capital* showed that this would eventually result in an *absolute* limit to accumulation (see chapter 10). In the meantime, however, modifying counter-tendencies devalue capital and labour power sufficiently to temporarily restore the 'equilibrium' between total capital and surplus value, along with, therefore, the process of accumulation on an expanded level, keeping the breakdown to a partial one, ie a temporary – to one extent or another – economic crisis.

Harmonist crisis theory
The harmonists rejected breakdown theory and came up with other explanations for crises, either correcting Marx's 'errors' or claiming he did not propose a theory of breakdown at all. This was because they made the mistake – deliberately or not – of taking "only secondary surface appearances that stem from the essence of capital accumulation as their primary basis",[76] said Grossman, who put the record straight:

> "To be sure, Marx himself referred only to the breakdown and not to the theory of breakdown, just as he did not write about a theory of value or a theory of wages, but only developed the laws of value and of wages. So if we are entitled to speak of a Marxist theory of value or theory of wages, we have as much right to speak of Marx's theory of breakdown."[77]

Grossman lamented "a whole generation"[78] of Marxists for producing "unsatisfactory literature" on Marx's scientific method and for an immaturity that had seen them write "extensively on the political revolution [while neglecting] to deal theoretically with the economic aspect of the question and [failing] to appreciate the true content of Marx's theory of breakdown".[79] Because they went "straight for results... without bothering to ask by what methodological means were those results established and what significance they contain within the total structure of the system", they ended up taking surface level phenomena as the starting point of their analysis, instead of the point of production and the accumulation process. Theoretical errors led to practical errors.

In 1899, Eduard Bernstein, a 'Marxist' in the German Social Democratic Party[80] (SPD), dismissed breakdown theory as "purely speculative"[81] on the basis that the living standards of the working class had risen, meaning that socialism was no longer an economic necessity – a notion that of course seems to be more popular today than ever (see chapter 12).

Taking a slightly different angle, Vladimir Simkhovitch – who called Marxism the "crudest and most unfinished doctrine of social philosophy" – said Marx's theory may have seemed sound at the time it was written but that it could no longer be taken seriously because of "an unprecedented improvement of the working class in the industrial countries".[82] On the same evidence, Werner Sombart could say that Marx was wrong because the revolutionary basis of his message was a theory of immiseration,[83] while Arthur Spiethoff said it had been based on a theory of underconsumption that had also been proven wrong.[84] But Marx never denied that the living standards of the working class could rise. In fact *he* pointed out that the factor exerting an upward pressure on real wages was the growing intensity of labour demanded by capital accumulation. His argument was that wages and living standards would re-deteriorate, not because of a theory of immiseration or underconsumption, but because of the breakdown tendency.

Karl Kautsky, a long-time leading Marxist thinker who ended up rejecting the revolutionary road, claimed "a special theory of breakdown was never proposed by Marx and Engels".[85] Instead, unlike earlier socialist thinkers, they had foreseen in the working class an "increase in its training and organisation, its maturity and power".[86] Only this, and not economic crisis, would lead to socialism.

In 1927 Kautsky said that it was "no longer possible to maintain that the capitalist mode of production prepares its own downfall".[87] He declared – just two years before the Wall Street Crash – that "capitalism stands today, from a purely economic point of view, stronger than ever".[88] He even claimed that Marx himself proved that capitalism could go on *ad infinitum* in the second volume of *Capital*.[89]

But if capitalism could go on forever, and the living standards of the working class therefore continued to rise, why would the working class risk a conflict with the bourgeoisie in order to get rid of capitalism, or even just to improve it? Only on the "hopes we have that the proletariat attains sufficient strength", said Kautsky, "that the productive forces grow sufficiently to provide abundant means for the welfare of the masses... finally, that the necessary economic knowledge and consciousness develop to ensure a fruitful application of these productive forces".[90]

Grossman thought it "quite sad to watch a thinker of such exceptional merit, towards the closing stages of his active life, rejecting his entire life's work at a single stroke", adding:

"The conclusions Kautsky draws constitute an abandonment of scientific socialism. If there is no economic reason why capitalism must necessarily fail, then socialism can replace capitalism on purely extra-economic – political or psychological or moral – grounds."[91]

Mikhail Tugan-Baranovsky sang from the same hymn sheet as Kautsky, saying that capitalism "could never collapse from purely economic causes, whereas it is doomed for moral reasons".[92] Otto Bauer of the Social Democratic Workers' Party of Austria, Rudolf Hilferding and Kautsky, both of the German SPD, took on this idea, that the working class would seek socialism in search of moral or social justice, ignoring Marx's labour theory of value. Such a romantic assessment of the working class views it as morally homogenous and treats the slogan that class struggle is the motive power of history with a basic and fetishistic literalism – while, in practice, holding back the working class by promoting misguided theory and an illusory route to socialism through bourgeois democracy.

For Bauer, crises could be explained by temporary adjustments of accumulation to the growth of population.[93] Hilferding claimed crises only emerged because production was not properly regulated. With a proportional distribution of capital in the individual branches of industry, "production can be expanded indefinitely without leading to the overproduction of commodities", he claimed, which Kautsky agreed with.[94] Hilferding saw finance capital as "a socialising function" because once it had "brought the most important branches of production under its control", centralised banking set the stage for capitalism's straightforward replacement by socialism, justifying the SPD's opportunism and anti-communism.[95]

Hilferding, because he underrated the importance of production, had it the wrong way round. Although the contradiction between industry and banking worked itself out through a fusion of the two into finance capital, within that relationship the increasing tendency is for industry – which continues to work towards integrating everything under one sphere – to dominate the banks, not vice-versa. "Industry becomes increasingly more independent of credit flow because it shifts to self-financing through depreciation and reserves," Grossman points out.[96] "There is a tendency for the share of equity funds to increase at the expense of borrowed funds, or for the company to acquire its own assets in the banks.... this is one of the reasons why banks have been turning to the stock exchange by way of investments."[97]

Hence why the banks proved to be the weakest link in capital's chain in the 2008 crash. They were compelled to speculate. It is only in the early stage of capitalist development that the banks dominate, when industry relies on an outside supply of credit to build itself up. "The historical tendency of capital is not the creation of a central bank which dominates the whole economy through a general cartel, but industrial concentration and growing accumulation of capital leading to the final breakdown due to overaccumulation," says Grossman.[98]

Distortions of breakdown theory

The few Marxists who upheld a breakdown theory failed to grasp the root cause of breakdown. The Polish Jewish communist Rosa Luxemburg contended that overaccumulation resulted from the capitalist countries increasingly running out of 'non-capitalist' markets with regards to exporting commodities. If this were the case, capitalism would suffer from an overproduction of surplus value that could therefore not be realised. Capitalism has an insatiable thirst for surplus value; it is the underproduction of surplus value which creates crisis. Luxemburg did not base her analysis in the immanent laws of accumulation, shifting "the crucial problem of capitalism from the sphere of production to that of circulation".[99]

Nikolai Bukharin, a Bolshevik, failed to provide "a serious account ... and simply ends up with nebulous phrasemongering about [expanding] 'contradictions'".[100] Bukharin put the revolution in Russia down to the misery brought about by war, but could not explain what had brought the war about in the first place. Louis Boudin, a Russian-born US Marxist, "correctly says that breakdown can be understood and explained with the help of Marx's theory of value" but "offers no proof" and therefore "it is not surprising that he falls back"[101] on Luxemburg's theory. Elsewhere, Grossman says that Bukharin

> "only speaks generally about the 'limit given to *a certain degree by the tension of capitalist contradictions*' that 'will inevitably lead to the collapse of capitalist rule', without providing the theoretical explanation of why these contradictions must culminate in the final impossibility of balance. Just as little does this interpretation provide concrete indicators by which the 'degree' of critical tension in the contradictions that make breakdown 'unavoidable' can be identified in advance. This can only be determined

after the fact, after the advent of the breakdown. Then, however, the theory of breakdown is superfluous as an instrument of scientific knowledge."[102]

It fell to Grossman then, on the eve of the Wall Street Crash, to clarify Marx's breakdown theory and to prove its validity.

The three stages of Marx's method

Marx's method, the method of *successive approximation*, consists of three stages: an abstract reproduction scheme, generating a mathematical pattern, as a tool of theoretical analysis; hypothetical, simplifying assumptions which form its basis; and subsequent corrections to the scheme whereby the assumptions are lifted, one by one, in order to move back from abstraction to empirical reality, as a process of verification. Grossman explains that:

> "The question I shall examine is whether fully developed capitalism, regarded as an exclusively prevalent and universally widespread economic system relying only on its own resources, contains the capacity to develop the process of reproduction indefinitely and on a continually expanding basis, or whether this process of expansion runs into limits of one sort or another which it cannot overcome."[103]

Any scientific investigation of the real world of concrete, empirically-given appearances has to start with simplifying assumptions. If the essence of something could be known from its appearance, there would be no need for science. Marx therefore started with a fictional reproduction scheme of the accumulation process and made various simplifying assumptions to gain an understanding of the inner structure of the object under investigation. The assumptions made are that:

1) the capitalist economy exists in isolation – that there is no foreign trade;
2) there are only two classes – capitalists and workers;
3) there are no landowners, hence no ground rent;
4) commodities exchange at value and without the mediation of merchants;
5) the value of labour power is constant;
6) the rate of surplus value is constant and corresponds to the magnitude of the wage, ie a rate of surplus value of 100% (so that surplus labour time matches necessary labour time);
7) there are only two spheres of production, producing means of production and means of consumption;
8) the rate of growth of population (the accumulation of variable capital) is a constant magnitude
9) in all branches of production capital turns over once a year.

The conclusions established from these assumptions have a purely provisional character and therefore have to be followed up by a concluding stage, a process of correction that takes account of the factors that were disregarded.[104] "In this way, stage by stage, the investigation as a whole draws nearer to the complicated appearances of the concrete world and becomes consistent with it," says Grossman.[105] It was the failure or inability of so many economists, Marxist or otherwise, to grasp this basic methodological principle that caused them to misunderstand and misrepresent Marx's findings. "They failed to notice the purely provisional nature of the initial stages and ignored the fact that in the methodological construction of the system each of the several fictitious, simplifying assumptions is subsequently modified. Provisional conclusions were taken for final results."[106]

Grossman starts by taking a reproduction scheme produced by Bauer that had been cited by the harmonists as proof of their theory. The scheme: takes account of technological advances which produce an ever-increasing organic composition of capital; sets a simplifying rule that constant capital grows twice as fast as variable capital, the former by 10% per annum, the latter by 5%; although capitalist consumption (k) increases absolutely, increases in productivity and the mass of surplus value allow a progressively greater portion of the surplus value to be earmarked for accumulation; both departments I (production of the means of production) and II (production of means of consumption) annually devote the same percentage of surplus value to accumulation; and the rate of profit behaves according to the Marxist law of its tendential fall.[107] Constant capital starts from 200,000 and variable capital 100,000; 120,000 of the constant capital is apportioned to Department I and 80,000 to Department II.

The second stage of Marx's method

Proceeding from these assumptions, Bauer believed his scheme showed that capital could accumulate indefinitely. The portion of surplus value reserved for the individual consumption of the capitalists represents a continuously declining percentage but grows absolutely, thereby providing the motive that drives capitalists to expand production.[108]

"We might imagine that Bauer's harmonist conclusions are confirmed," says Grossman. "The percentage fall in the rate of profit is of no concern because the absolute mass of profit can and does grow as long as the total capital expands more rapidly than the rate of profit falls.... Is the falling rate of profit a real threat to capitalism? Bauer's scheme appears to show the opposite. By the end of year four both the fund for accumulation and the fund for capitalist consumption have grown absolutely." And yet, precisely with Bauer's scheme, Grossman shows that Bauer's harmonist conclusions represent a "banal delusion".[109]

The source of Bauer's mistakes came down simply to intellectual laziness, in that he limited his scheme to four years. "If Bauer had followed through the development of his system over a sufficiently long timespan he would have found, soon enough, that his system necessarily breaks down."[110]

Following Bauer's system to year 36, the portion of surplus value reserved for capitalist consumption, which amounts to 86,213 in the fifth year and grows over the following years, "can only expand up to a definite high-point. After this it must necessarily decline because it is swallowed up by the portion of surplus value required for capitalisation."[111]

On this point, Grossman explains that for accumulation to occur, surplus value must be deployable in a threefold direction and divided into three corresponding fractions: additional constant capital (a_c); additional variable capital (a_v) or additional means of subsistence for workers; and a consumption fund for the capitalists (k). "If the available surplus value could cover only the first two, accumulation would be impossible. For the question necessarily arises – why do capitalists accumulate? To provide additional employment to workers? From the point of view of capitalists that would make no sense once they themselves get nothing out of employing more workers."

Despite the falling rate of profit, accumulation accelerates because the scope of accumulation expands not in proportion to the level of profitability, but in proportion to the base of the already accumulated capital. As Marx says: "Beyond certain limits a large capital with a small rate of profit accumulates faster than a small capital with a large rate of profit."[112]

Grossman concludes:

"We can see that after ten years the original capital expands from a value of 300,000 to 681,243, or by 227%, despite a continuous fall in the rate of profit. In the second decade the rate of expansion of capital amounts to 236%, although the rate of profit falls even further from 24.7% to 16.4%. Finally in the third decade the accumulation of capital proceeds still faster, with a decennial increase of 243%, when the rate of profit is even lower. So Bauer's scheme is a case of a declining rate of profit coupled with accelerated accumulation. The constant capital grows rapidly, it rises from 50% of the total product in the first year to 82.9% of the annual product by year 35. Capitalist consumption (k) reaches a peak in year 20 and from the following year on declines both relatively and absolutely. In year 34 it reaches its lowest level only to disappear completely in year 35.

"It follows that the system must break down. The capitalist class has nothing left for its own personal consumption because all existing means of subsistence have to be devoted to accumulation. In spite of this there is still a deficit of 11,509 on the accumulated variable capital (a_v) required to reproduce the system for a further year. In year 35 Department II produces consumer goods to a total value of 540,075 [the 525,319 advanced as variable capital at the beginning of the year plus 14,756 accumulated variable capital] whereas, on Bauer's assumption of a 5% increase in population, 551,584 of variable capital is required.

"Bauer's assumptions cannot be sustained any further, the system breaks down. From year 35 on any further accumulation of capital under the conditions postulated would be quite meaningless. The capitalist would be wasting effort over the management of a productive system whose fruits are entirely absorbed by the share of workers.

"If this state persisted it would mean the destruction of the capitalist mechanism, its economic end. For the class of entrepreneurs, accumulation would not only be meaningless, it would be objectively impossible because the over-accumulated capital would lie idle, would not be able to function, would fail to yield any profits: 'there would be a steep and sudden fall in the general rate of profit'."[113]

Profitability depends on the relationship between the rate in the increase of profit and the magnitude of capital. Overaccumulation is, at a specific stage of accumulation, "inevitable":[114]

"A falling rate of profit is a permanent symptom of the progress of accumulation through all its stages, but at the initial stages of accumulation it goes together with an expanding mass of profits and expanded capitalist consumption. Beyond certain limits, however, the falling rate of profit is accompanied by a fall in the surplus value earmarked for capitalist consumption (in our scheme this appears in year 21) and soon afterwards of the portions of surplus value destined for accumulation. 'The fall in the rate of profit would then be accompanied by an absolute decrease in the mass of profit.... And the reduced mass of profit would have to be calculated on an increased total capital.'"[115]

The other side of the accumulation process

Grossman then stresses the importance of looking at the other side of the accumulation process – since this could only be assessed by extending Bauer's four-year scheme – that alongside unemployed capital grows unemployed labour:

"Imperfect valorisation due to overaccumulation means that capital grows faster than the surplus value extortable from the given population, or that the working population is too small in relation to the swollen capital.... Towards the closing stages of the business cycle the mass of profits (s), and therefore also its accumulated constant (a_c) and variable (a_v) portions, contract so sharply that the additional capital is no longer sufficient to keep accumulation going on the previous basis. It is therefore no longer sufficient to enable the process of accumulation to absorb the annual increase in population. Thus in year 35 the rate of accumulation requires a level of 510,563 a_c + 26,265 a_v = 536,828. But the available mass of surplus value totals only 525,319. The rate of accumulation required to sustain the scheme is 104.6% of the available surplus value; a logical contradiction and impossible in reality.

"From this point onwards valorisation no longer suffices to enable accumulation to proceed in step with the growth of population.... The extension of Bauer's scheme shows that in year 35 there are 11,509 unemployed workers who form a reserve army.

"In addition, because only a part of the working population now enters the process of production, only a part of the additional constant capital (510,563 a_c) is required for buying means of production. The active population of 540,075 requires a total constant capital of 5,499,015; the result is that 117,185 represents a surplus capital with no investment possibilities."[116]

There was no theory of immiseration – immiseration is explained by the theory of breakdown. With the consumption fund for the capitalists falling, they are bound to try to reverse this tendency. They must either cut their expenditure on wages

"or cease to observe the conditions postulated for accumulation, that is, the condition that constant capital must expand by 10% annually to absorb the annual increase in the working population at the given technological level.

	c	v	s	accumulation	k
Commencement	200	100	100	20+ 5= 25	75
After 20 years	1222	253	253	122+13=135	118
After 30 years	3170	412	412	317+21=338	74
After 34 years	4641	500	500	464+25=489	11
After 35 years	5106	525	525	510+26=536	-11

Bauer's reproduction scheme taken to year 35.
In this variation, Grossman merges the departments (the separated version is not in the abridged book) to make Bauer's schema more realistic, since without competition the rate of profit would vary from sphere to sphere. Competition has the affect of equalising rates of profit across departments, which in turn cause production prices to deviate (increasingly) from values (labour time).

This would mean that from now on accumulation would proceed at a slower rate, say 9.5% or 8%. The tempo of accumulation would have to be slowed down, and that, too, permanently and to an increasing degree. In that case accumulation would fail to keep step with the growth of the population."[117]

The installation of new machinery slows down and a growing reserve army forms, even if wages are assumed to remain constant. At any rate, the outcome would not be due to an increase in wages.[118]

The third stage of Marx's method

Marx's proof procedure is deductive. Having seen that capitalism in its purest form, with an ideal trajectory of accumulation, has a tendency to break down, we now have to see if this remains the case when the factors that were omitted from the scheme for the purpose of simplification are reintroduced. Do they help or hinder valorisation? Can any of them suppress the breakdown tendency altogether?

There is a logical shortcut to answering this question. For any counter-tendencies *spring from the breakdown tendency*. The breakdown tendency and the counter-tendencies are *part of the same piece of elastic*. If capitalism breaks down in ideal conditions then it logically breaks down in imperfect conditions, too.

The crisis *compels* the capitalist to act in a certain way in order to save his business interests. He has to rationalise and, if he can – many enterprises are of course wiped out – expand production.

Exporting capital to countries with a lower organic composition of capital, thereby finding a source of labour that can be exploited at a higher rate; a sharp devaluation of constant capital, bringing its value in line with the magnitude of surplus value; wage cuts which raise the magnitude of surplus value – all of these are made *necessary* in order to counter the breakdown tendency. If this were not the case, there would be no economic explanation, and we would no longer be studying economics.

The counter-tendencies convert the breakdown into a temporary crisis, after which accumulation picks up again on an expanded basis. But "restored accumulation will again generate the very same phenomena of overaccumulation and imperfect valorisation".[119]

We will run through some of the main counter-tendencies to prove the point and show how capitalism has developed the way it has out of necessity. We therefore need to see what happens to the breakdown tendency when we reincorporate foreign trade, landowners who live off ground rent, merchants and the middle classes, and allow the rate of surplus value or the level of wages to vary.

Several theories, however, have already been disproven: firstly, that crisis is caused by an underproduction of capital; secondly, given the assumed state of equilibrium, any disproportionality theory – justifying the claim that crisis can be avoided if capitalism it is properly regulated or 'planned',[120] with wealth redistributed according to population growth; and, thirdly, given that the breakdown tendency set in despite assumed full employment and a constant value of wages, underconsumption theory.

Devaluation
Since we have already established that technological improvements demanded by accumulation devalue labour power, commodities and capital, it is obvious that the assumption of constant values cannot be maintained.

Before, the value of the constant capital used up in the process of production was transferred intact to the product; the values created in each cycle of production were accumulated in the next cycle without undergoing any quantitative changes. (Some values are of course destroyed in consumption.) But "devaluation necessarily flows out of the mechanism of capital even in its ideal or normal course":[121]

> "Devaluation of capital goes hand in hand with the fall in the rate of profit and is crucial for explaining the concentration and centralisation of capital that accompanies this fall...
>
> "The result of the devaluation of capital is reflected in the fact that a given mass of means of production represents a smaller value. The result is analogous to that which arises from growing productivity – cheapening of the elements of production and a faster growth of the mass of use-values as compared with the mass of value. However in the case of rising productivity the elements of production actually start off cheaper whereas here we are dealing with a case where the elements of production produced at a given value are only subsequently devalued.
>
> "With devaluation the technological composition of capital remains the same while its value composition declines. Both before and after devaluation the same quantity of labour is required to set in motion the same mass of means of production and to produce the same quantity of surplus value.
>
> "But because the value of the constant capital has declined, this quantity of surplus value is calculated on a reduced capital value. The rate of valorisation is thereby increased and so the breakdown is postponed for some time. In terms of Bauer's scheme, periodic devaluation of capital would mean that the accumulated capital represents a smaller value magnitude than shown by the figures there and would, for example, only reach the level of year 20 as late as year 36.

"In other words, however much devaluation of capital may devastate the individual capitalist in periods of crisis, they are a safety valve for the capitalist class as a whole. For the system devaluation of capital is a means of prolonging its life span, of defusing the dangers that threaten to explode the entire mechanism. The individual is thus sacrificed in the interest of the species."

Since the share of the value-creating variable capital has shrunk, however, the same tendency that has staved off breakdown goes on to reproduce breakdown. "A capital that fails to fulfil its function of valorisation ceases to be capital; hence its devaluation."[122]

Fixed capital
Fixed capital is the fixed component of constant capital (the non-fixed part comprising circulating capital, ie wages, raw materials, rents etc); it is machinery. In the assumed scheme, the life cycle of fixed capital equals one period of reproduction. It is more realistic to suppose that the fixed component of constant capital operates over several cycles of production and does not need to be renewed annually. "In this case even if the value of the fixed capital is transferred to the product in a smaller annual rate of depreciation, it nevertheless helps in creating a growing mass of value, and therefore of surplus value, in proportion to its actual durability."[123] The valorisation of the given capital is furthered. That technological improvements progressively consolidate the physical durability of fixed capital strengthens this factor.

However, technological improvements, which become increasingly rapid – because, like capital accumulation, they always arise from a higher base – also increase the rate of moral depreciation. That is, fixed capital, despite its improved durability, is replaced more frequently by new and improved fixed capital, which can do the job even more efficiently, and so, through disuse, it loses its use-value and its value in less and less time, long before expiring physically. This reduces the total mass of value and surplus value which it forms. "Hence, the greater the scale on which fixed capital develops... the more does the continuity of the production process or the constant flow of reproduction become an externally compelling condition for the mode of production founded on capital," says Marx.[124]

Prices, competition and centralisation
Since we have established that value is created only by human labour, we know that price rises have no impact on the mass of profit because the existing value is unaffected. They play a role in centralising existing value, and only really when the value of money falls. Neither is it the extension of credit that produces an upturn in prices – credit extends to cover the lag in the realisation

of profit, ie the underproduction of surplus value. What capital needs to do is create new value.

The most important renovations and expansions in the productive apparatus are made *in periods of depression when commodity prices are low*, paving the way for an upturn as expansion, even without updating technical methods, allows a reabsorption of the unemployed back into work, thereby restoring the base for both surplus value production and the realisation of profit (not simply because supply creates demand but because paid work revives purchasing power). In the everyday world, production is not immediately regulated by the law of value but by the prices of production, which (increasingly) diverge from their abstract values, as surplus value is divided up by various surface level demands (particularly the need to centralise capital). If prices do not fall then production only continues on the existing scale and expansion cannot take place, and vice-versa. Prices are bound to fall.[125] Grossman says:

> "At first only further expansion of production becomes unprofitable; reproduction on the existing scale is not affected. But with each cycle of production this changes. The portion of the surplus value earmarked for accumulation each year goes unsold. As inventories build up the capitalist is forced to sell at any price to obtain the resources to keep the enterprise going on its existing scale. He is compelled to reduce prices and cut back on his scale of production. The scale of operations is reduced or they shut down completely. Many firms declare bankruptcy and are devalued. Huge amounts of capital are written off as losses."[126]

Commodities have become unsaleable not simply because purchasing power has diminished but because surplus capital *cannot be put to use* – and so competition intensifies as each individual capital attempts to expand itself by taking capital from other individual capitals. Until now, we have treated the capitalist class as a single entity, but now we have to reckon with the competition between many capitals.

"A capitalist working with improved but not as yet generally adopted methods of production sells below the market price, but above his individual price of production; his rate of profit rises until competition levels it out,"[127] says Marx. He goes on to explain that when crisis strikes, the fight for the division of profit becomes a fight to minimise losses, to pass them on to a rival. "For the class as a whole, the loss is unavoidable. But how much each individual member has to bear, now becomes a question of strength and cunning, and competition then becomes a struggle of hostile brothers."[128]

Intensifying competition itself necessitates mergers. Two individual capitals can only outcompete a third and fourth rival if they combine forces. The new enterprise resulting from the merger has a higher organic composition, resulting in an increase in the productivity of labour, which cheapens commodities, including the commodities that go into workers' consumption. The elements of variable capital are thereby cheapened, the value of labour power declines and surplus value and the rate of surplus value increase. Surviving rivals are forced to follow suit in order to keep up, raising total surplus value still further. Those who cannot go bust, and the surviving corporations have the option of buying up their depreciated capital, further centralising capital overall. But this does not stop the cycle from repeating itself in the long run, since the value-creating part of capital has again shrunk.

The rise of ever-greater monopolies is therefore inevitable. The smaller capitalists fail or refuse to grasp this. In their 2018 book *The Myth of Capitalism: Monopolies and the Death of Competition*, Jonathan Tepper and Denise Hearn complain that US Americans live under a "fake" version of capitalism.[129] They show that four corporations control 90% of American beer; four airlines dominate airline traffic, often enjoying complete local monopolies regionally; the top two insurance companies have 80-90% market share between them in many states; four companies control the entire US beef market and have "divided up the country"; three companies control both 70% of the global pesticide market and 80% of the US corn-seed market; 75% of US households can only access one provider for high-speed internet; Google's share of internet search traffic is 90%; and so on.

The 'Big Five' institutional investors – Blackrock, Vanguard, State Street, Fidelity, and JP Morgan – "now own 80% of all stock" in the Standard & Poor's (S&P) 500 (measuring the performance of the 500 largest US publicly traded companies). This is mirrored internationally.[130] Another study shows that BlackRock, Vanguard and State Street Global Advisors manage more than $14 trillion of assets and account for over a quarter of the votes cast by the directors of the US's 500 biggest companies. The study says that over the next 20 years their control is on course to extend to 41% of voting rights. BlackRock is the world's largest investor in coal plant development and owns more oil, gas and thermal coal reserves than any other investor.[131] A 2011 study found that, of 43,000 international corporations based in 116 countries, 40% of them were owned or controlled by just 0.5% of the world's biggest companies.[132]

The tendency towards monopolisation accelerates during economic crises. The 20 years before the 2008 crash saw the greatest frenzy of mergers and acquisitions since the first decade of the 20th century. Brian Becker of the Party for Socialism and Liberation in the US writes in his book *Imperialism in the 21st Century* that "nowhere is this more apparent than in the financial sector itself…. In 1995, the six largest banks in the US owned assets worth 17% of the size of the entire US economy. This had risen to 55% … by 2006. Bank concentration accelerated from 2006 to the third quarter of 2010, when the top six banks increased their assets to 64% of GDP."[133] Bear Stearns, for example,

Wall Street's fifth largest bank and worth $20bn in 2007, was absorbed by JP Morgan for just £240m, with the taxpayer footing a £30bn subsidy.

As smaller competitors have been swallowed up by monopolies, over half of all firms have disappeared over the past 20 years: "On this trend, by 2070 we will only have one company per industry," say Tepper and Hearn.[134] "The scale of mergers is so extreme, you would almost think American capitalists were trying to prove Karl Marx right."[135]

The reserve army of labour
Once Bauer's scheme is extended, the development of a reserve army of labour is shown to become inevitable. Marx says:

> "The greater the social wealth, the functioning capital, the extent and energy of its growth, and, therefore, also the absolute mass of the proletariat and the productiveness of its labour, the greater is the industrial reserve army. The same causes which develop the expansive power of capital, develop also the labour power at its disposal. The relative mass of the industrial reserve army increases therefore with the potential energy of wealth. But the greater this reserve army in proportion to the active labour army... the greater is official pauperism. *This is the absolute general law of capitalist accumulation.*"

The reserve army means labour is abundant and cheap. The mass of the unemployed exert a downward pressure on the level of wages so that they fall below the value of labour power (because the threat of unemployment compels those who are employed to accept lower wages). This partially transforms "the labourer's necessary consumption fund into a fund for the accumulation of capital".[136] Far from underconsumption producing the crisis, depressing the cost of labour power helps to solve it, exposing "the complete superficiality of those theoreticians in the trade unions who argue for wage increases as a means of surmounting the crisis", says Grossman.[137] Communists support progressive reforms, including wage rises – especially as such struggles develop the organisational and fighting capacities of the working class – but clearly wage rises eat into the surplus value available to capital, and therefore deepen the crisis, or bring its onset forward.

At the same time as depressing wages, capital has created a problem for itself by reducing the valorisation base. Capital ideally desires full employment in the productive sectors.

Circulation and use-values
Clearly the scheme's reproduction periods of one year apiece are unrealistic, for in the real world the speed of production is continually increasing, while turnover time also varies from one branch to another. Better productivity in

turn produces better means of production and therefore a quicker circulation of capital through improved transportation and communications. A £10m investment returning £11m is a 10% rate of return, but becomes 20% if the return can be achieved in six months instead of 12. A greater amount of surplus value is available sooner, and the portion of capital that has to remain in circulation is also reduced, meaning more can be dedicated to productive capital. Improvements to transportation allow the capitalist to reduce storage costs. Therefore, the time during which capital takes to transform itself from the commodity form to the money form tends to become progressively shorter.[138] The rate of profit rises.

These same counter-tendencies produce pressures in the opposite direction. More surplus value is produced in less time, but the total value of commodities is determined by socially necessary labour time – there is an average fall in value in relative terms per commodity the quicker they are made. The law of value giveth and taketh away.

The same can be said for the fact that every time reproduction is renewed on an expanded or higher basis, the multiplicity and mass of use-values expands,[139] reabsorbing part of the surplus population and expanding the valorisation base. But the use-values are made more efficiently and against an expanded constant capital, and the counter-tendency snaps back in the opposite direction.

The renewal of capital

There is an opposing, albeit weaker tendency to the increasing concentration of capital to be taken into account, which explains why small enterprises do not disappear altogether:

> "... the centralisation of capitals already existing in a few hands and the decapitalisation of many ... would entail the rapid breakdown of capitalist production, if counteracting tendencies were not constantly at work alongside this centripetal force, in the direction of decentralisation."[140]

Marx shows that there is a continual penetration by capital into new spheres in which

> "portions of the original capitals disengage themselves and function as new and independent capitals. Besides other causes, the division of property, within capitalist families, plays a great part in this. With the accumulation of capital, therefore, the number of capitalists grows to a greater or lesser extent."[141]

Because the minimum amount of capital required to sustain larger enterprises, with their higher organic composition, is very high and continually growing, smaller capitals "crowd into spheres of production which modern industry has only sporadically or incompletely got hold of".[142] The result is a lower organic composition, creating room for experimentation and invention (and therefore an expansion of use-values), a relatively larger mass of workers, a rise in the rate of profit and the creation of new investment opportunities. "Superfluous capital is reabsorbed," says Grossman, but "gradually there is a new accumulation of capital which is destined to become superfluous."[143] The organic composition eventually rises or/and the business merges with another to stay afloat.

This counter-tendency partly explains why the petty bourgeoisie in Britain is so disproportionately large compared to perhaps all other countries, and with it the particular conservatism of British politics. Grossman comments:

"British capitalism is deeply symptomatic of these processes. While the traditional industrial centres of the North, of Scotland and Wales have been in a chronic crisis, a whole series of new industries have begun to spring up in the South, in the Midlands and in the areas surrounding London.... these industries have a much lower organic composition of capital.... Even if the development of such industries does relieve the general impact of the economic depression it cannot compensate for the catastrophic consequences of the decline of the older branches which formed the basis of Britain's domination."[144]

This sounds strikingly familiar to the process of 'deindustrialisation' that took place in Britain after the economic crisis of the 1970s (see chapter 11).

Rents and levies
So far we have looked at the reintroduced factors that, at least initially, counteract the breakdown tendency. Some just assist it. Landlords, for instance, eat into the profits of industrial capitalists by charging them ground rent, a clear source of division within the ruling class.

Commercial rent has the same impact as ground rent (as do other levies and interest). It takes a share of profit away from capital without participating in production. This inspires a struggle against intermediary trade in order to reduce the costs of sales and import transactions. The ability to eliminate the trader is one reason which makes merged enterprises superior. They economise by integrating trade and export into their own organisations. Commercial agents cannot be done away with though because they fulfil necessary roles in the process of circulating industrial capital. We know that the role of commerce has in fact expanded hugely. Marx anticipated this:

"The extent to which products enter trade and go through the hands of merchants depends on the mode of production, reaching a maximum with the full development of capitalist production, where the product is produced simply as a commodity and not at all as a direct means of subsistence."[145]

A new middle stratum of commercial wage-workers emerges, increasing the outlay of the industrial capitalist without directly raising surplus value, since it is an outlay for labour employed "solely in realising value already created".[146] It also reduces the fund available for the employment of productive workers. The increasing role of commerce therefore, in spite of the efforts made to streamline it, works against the counter-tendencies.

'Third persons' and consumers

Other 'third persons', such as bureaucrats, the professional strata, rent receivers and so on, have the same effect. They do not create surplus value and are therefore *unproductive*. "They do not enlarge the mass of actual products but, on the contrary, reduce it by their consumption," Grossman points out,[147] "even if they perform various valuable and necessary services by way of repayment." Their *revenues* are materially derived from the wages of the productive workers. There is overlap here with consumers as a whole. Grossman explains:

> "Of course these groups perform various services in return, but the non-material character of such services makes it impossible for them to be used for the accumulation of capital. The physical nature of the commodity is a necessary precondition of its accumulation. Values enter the circulation of commodities, and thereby represent an accumulation of capital, only insofar as they acquire a materialised form.
>
> "Because the services of third persons are of a non-material character, they contribute nothing to the accumulation of capital. However, their consumption reduces the accumulation fund. The larger this class, the greater the deduction from the fund for accumulation."

Grossman noted that in Britain, "where there is a large number of such persons, the tempo of accumulation will have to be slower". Nearly a century on, the services sector (ie, non-goods-producing) now accounts for around 80% of economic activity in Britain.[148] (The figure was the same in the US in 2012.) Although services workers produce value if they are employed by capital (as opposed to by a customer) they tend to add relatively little value compared to manufacturing workers, as they tend to handle finished or near-finished products (the delivery of a commodity to the consumer is part of the production process), if they do so at all.

Britain's wealth, of course, is largely a legacy of its Empire. But how has it sustained this if the bulk of its workers are relatively unproductive? The rate of surplus value production tends to be higher in imperialist nations due to their advanced technology. There is another factor, however. This brings us to another, very important, counter-tendency.

Capital exports
Towards the end of the 19th century, capitalism passed into its highest stage – imperialism, or monopoly/finance capitalism, effectively a fusion of banking and industrial capital. The industrialised countries had long exported capital in periods of crisis but their dependency on doing so now became constant and grew enormously. This was not simply a conscious decision, a wrong turn or an accident, but a necessary development in order to sustain accumulation and the system as a whole.

The colonial powers became capitalist through the direct plunder and enslavement of their colonies. This 'primitive accumulation' enabled them to embark on domestic industrialisation, which further accelerated technological advancements and the efficiencies of mass production, creating dominant large-scale enterprises, specialisation in production and a skilled workforce that made Britain the 'workshop of the world' and its leading superpower. But Britain would soon come up against the limits of its population, ie the valorisation base.

Capitalism had to expand. British capital was increasingly compelled to export its surplus capital to widen its valorisation base, by colonising and industrialising the interior of colonised continents (colonisation having previously been generally limited to coastal enclaves).[149]

At some point, around the 1870s, it started to become more profitable to export capital (means of production and interest-bearing loan capital) than it did to export consumer goods. By taking advantage of a lower organic composition of capital and a higher rate of exploitation, goods could be imported at a cheaper price than producing them domestically.

Capital exports were increasingly needed to push back the breakdown tendency. This parasitism necessarily offsets British capitalism's decaying nature. Today, Britain is the most parasitic imperialist power, exporting capital equatable to 560% of its GDP in 2015.[150] In bulk, Britain's capital outflows come second only to that of the US, which became the dominant world power after WWII, partly because the fighting had not taken place on its turf. Its enormous and integrated industrial base gave it huge advantages over Europe anyway; but Britain had to hand the US large parts of its empire in return for support in defeating Germany. The US further advanced its power by exporting capital to rebuild Europe. In response, France and Germany have taken steps to form a European imperialist bloc – through the formation of the EU – that can compete with the US, while Japan is the weakest of the imperialist nations (something that could potentially change after Britain leaves the EU).[151]

Foreign trade in general pushes back the limits of surplus value. It expands the base of productive workers and the multiplicity of use-values, reduces costs and relatively increases the speed of the circulation of capital. But imperialism also reintroduces competition in foreign exchange, and commodities no longer exchange at value. Grossman explains:

"If we look at the sphere of production it follows that the economically backward countries have a higher rate of profit, due to their lower organic composition of capital, than the advanced countries. This is despite the fact that the rate of surplus value is much higher in the advanced countries and increases even more with the general development of capitalism and the productivity of labour. Marx gives an example where the rate of surplus value is 100% in Europe and 25% in Asia, while the composition of the respective national capitals is 84c +16v for Europe and 16c + 84v for Asia. We get the following results for the value of the product:
Asia: 16c + 84v + 21s = 121. Rate of profit 21/100 = 21%
Europe: 84c + 16v + 16s = 116. Rate of profit 16/100 = 16%

"International trade is not based on an exchange of equivalents because, as on the national market, there is a tendency for rates of profit to be equalised. The commodities of the advanced capitalist country with the higher organic composition will therefore be sold at prices of production higher than value; those of the backward country at prices of production lower than value. This would mean the formation of an average rate of profit of 18.5% so that European commodities will sell for a price of 118.5 instead of 116. In this way circulation on the world market involves transfers of surplus value from the less developed to the more developed capitalist countries because the distribution of surplus value is determined not by the number of workers employed in each country but by the size of the functioning capital."

This relationship continues today. According to one study, between 1980 and 2012 the net outflows of capital from 'developing and emerging' countries being funnelled into 'developed' ie imperialist nations totalled $16.3 trillion.[152]

This was backed up by a study published by UNCTAD in 2013, which found that 67% of the total 'value added' (the difference between the sale price and the production cost) generated in 'global value chains' (world trade) is captured by multi- and transnationals which are based in rich nations.[153]

Britain may have lost most of its Empire but it retains 143 permanent military bases in 42 countries (only the US has more). Its economy still depends on what could be called neocolonialism – it is inherently parasitic. According to a 2016 War on Want report, for example, 101 companies listed on the London Stock Exchange controlled more than $1 trillion of mining and energy resources in 37 Sub-Saharan African countries.[154] Much of the wealth created by the workers they employ is funnelled back into the City of London, Britain's parasitic financial centre.

The profit from each commodity produced goes towards the GDP of the country in which it is sold, rather than where it is made. As described in John Smith's 2012 "The GDP Illusion" article in *Monthly Review*:[155] a garment worker in Bangladesh is 'paid' €1 for making 18 t-shirts in a 10-hour shift. Each t-shirt is sold in Germany for €4.95 by the Swedish retailer Hennes & Mauritz (H&M); H&M pays the Bangladeshi manufacturing firm €1.35 for each T-shirt, 28% of the final sale price; H&M keeps 60 cents in profit per t-shirt; the German state captures 79 cents through Value Added Tax (VAT) at 19%; the net profit goes towards Germany's, not Bangladesh's GDP. Another example: the workers who cultivate and harvest coffee which is exported to imperialist nations receive less than 2% of its final retail price. In 2009, according to the International Coffee Organization, the roasting, marketing, and sale of coffee added $31bn to the GDP of the nine biggest coffee-*importing* countries, more than twice the total export earnings that year of all coffee-producing nations.

This neocolonial relationship tends to strengthen the rate of profit in the imperialist countries, while under-developing, ie slowing the development, of the oppressed nations,[156] many of which lurch from one bankruptcy to the next.

The World Bank's World Development Indicators (WDIs) add further clarity to this relationship, providing data on Manufacturing Value Added (MVA) growth (for 1990 and 2002) and on growth in export of manufactures (for 1990 and 2004) for 55 'low- and middle-income' nations and 16 'high-income' nations.[157] Manufactured exports from the 55 low-wage nations increased by 329% between 1990 and 2004 (434% if China is included), yet their combined MVA grew by only 46.3%.[158] Between 1996 and 2005, high-income nations' share in global MVA declined only moderately from 80% to 74%, with the share of low- and middle-income nations rising from 20% to 26%. The MVA of the 55 low- and middle- income nations fell from 1.8 times the value of its exports of manufactures in 1990 to 0.6 in 2002.[159]

"Such transfers become a matter of life and death for capitalism," says Grossman, because at advanced stages of accumulation "it becomes more and more difficult to valorise the enormously accumulated capital".[160] This explains the aggression of imperialist 'foreign policy' – the destruction of Afghanistan, Iraq, Libya, Syria and so on, just recently – for

> "accumulation of capital at a late stage entails intensified competition of all capitalist countries on the world market. The drive to neutralise the breakdown tendency through increased valorisation takes place at the cost of other capitalist states. The accumulation of capital produces an ever more destructive struggle among capitalist states, a continuous

revolutionisation of technology, rationalisation, Taylorisation or Fordisation of the economy – all of which is intended to create the kind of technology and organisation that can preserve competitive superiority on the world market."[161]

It is important to stress that imperialism developed in order to counter the breakdown tendency. Even Vladimir Lenin's *Imperialism: The Highest Stage of Capitalism* comes in for stick from Grossman for not doing this.

"Lenin linked [the tendency of stagnation and decay] to the growth of monopolies. That there is such a connection is indisputable, but a mere statement is not enough. After all, one is not dealing simply with the phenomena of stagnation.... Imperialism is characterised by both stagnation and aggressiveness. These tendencies have to be explained in their unity; if monopolisation causes stagnation, then how can we explain the aggressive character of imperialism. In fact both phenomena are ultimately rooted in the tendency towards breakdown, in imperfect valorisation due to overaccumulation. The growth of monopolisation is a means of enhancing profitability by raising prices and, in this sense, is only a surface appearance whose inner structure is insufficient valorisation linked to capital accumulation."[162]

Grossman's point remains evident: the export of surplus capital accelerates during a crisis (after initially receding), showing the vitality of his breakdown theory, that it is able to explain new or intensifying manifestations of the capitalist system as it ages.

Kautsky saw imperialism simply as a ruling class "policy" to conquer the non-capitalist agrarian parts of the world, reducing its essence to the level of psychology and greed.[163]

Eugen Varga, an economic advisor to Joseph Stalin, denied that there could be a saturation of capital in any single country, simply saying that higher rates of profit were the attraction for capital exports.[164] In a devastating critique, given Varga's position, Grossman said that this flatly contradicted the law of value because

"to suppose that capital can expand without limits is to suppose that surplus value can likewise expand without limits, and thus independently of the size of the working population. This [would mean] that surplus value does not depend on labour."[165]

While imperialism is necessary to stave off breakdown, it also has the opposite effect, at least in those capitalist countries which are exploited by it and frozen out of the monopolies on raw materials. And since imperialism leeches off of those countries, the repercussions are felt 'at home':

> "With the progress of accumulation the number of countries grows in which accumulation approaches absolute limits. In proportion to the growth in the number of countries which export capital, competition and the struggle for profitable outlets is bound to intensify. The repercussions of this will necessarily sharpen the crisis at home. If the early crises of capitalism could already lead to wild outbreaks, we can imagine what crises will be like under the growing weight of accumulation when the capital exporting countries are compelled to wage the sharpest struggles for investment outlets on the world market."[166]

A growing number of developing countries are now emerging as increasingly independent, with significant international influence and the confidence to stand up to the bullying of the US and Britain, which by contrast are in relative decline. From 1980 to 2008, foreign direct investment from the imperialist to the developing nations grew from $503bn to 13.6 trillion, leading to the latter's share of economic growth rising from 30% to 75%.[167]

Capitalism's decaying nature led to imperialism – and further breakdown leads to intensifying imperialist rivalry. We will look at the role of war later as we consider the ever-growing prospect of a Third World War, but suffice to say that the destruction war entails is the ultimate method of devaluing capital and labour power. War is therefore caused by and a temporary solution to the breakdown tendency. Eventually imperialism must either destroy civilisation or be replaced by a higher system of production:

> "Despite the periodic interruptions that repeatedly defuse the tendency towards breakdown, the mechanism as a whole tends relentlessly towards its final end with the general process of accumulation. As the accumulation of capital grows absolutely, the valorisation of this expanded capital becomes progressively more difficult. Once these counter-tendencies are themselves defused or simply cease to operate, the breakdown tendency gains the upper hand and asserts itself in the absolute form as the final crisis."[168]

3. Defining automation: The fourth industrial revolution?

"If each of the instruments were able to perform its functions on command or by anticipation ... so that the shuttles would weave themselves and picks play the lyre, master craftsmen would no longer have a need for subordinates, or masters for slaves."[169]

Aristotle

Humans have longed to be free of toil. The Greek poet Antipater, a contemporary of the Roman statesman Cicero, welcomed the invention of the water mill, which worked "without labour or effort", as the foundation of a "Golden Age" and the liberator of slaves.

After a long and painful evolutionary road, and now living in the epoch of late-stage capitalism, the possibility of a post-work world – with the ongoing development of robotic machinery, artificial intelligence (AI) and other forms of increasingly sophisticated automation – seems like a tangible reality. The bourgeois narrative trumpets this as the 'fourth' industrial revolution. Is this accurate?

The evolution of production is a process of developing man's mastery over nature, of harnessing nature to serve our needs. New technologies give rise to new needs. For centuries – comprising the primitive communal, slave-owning and feudal systems – manual labour determined the technological basis of society. As the continual improvements and specialisations of the implements of labour reached their limits and slavery and feudalism became fetters (restraints) on the further development of the productive forces as a whole, mechanisation (machine-aided production) necessarily replaced manual labour. Man was no longer the source of power which wielded the implements of labour.

Consolidating capitalist relations of production, this was the first industrial revolution – it marked a radical change in the *technological* mode of production, ie *the mode of combining man and technology*. Where man had controlled and wielded the inanimate elements of work, machines now dictated the inputs of man and relieved him as, in Marx's words, "chief actor";[170] but, in creating a division of labour, did not free him. "The hand tool makes the worker independent – posits him as proprietor. Machinery – as fixed capital – posits him as dependent, posits him as appropriated."[171]

Dominant versions of history tell the story that – since it was the most obvious contrast between machine production and the handicrafts and ordinary manufacture of small 'cottage industry' workshops – the upgrade of the steam engine made by Scottish engineer James Watt around 1775 was the fundamental catalyst of the first industrial revolution. By extension, it was the primary factor behind the rise of British capitalism and the ensuing industrial and economic dominance of its Empire. All thanks to the individual genius of Watt – or was it his 'Britishness'?

This is an example of idealism, the theory that man's ideas or ever-improving rationality determine the course of history. Marx's method of dialectical materialism – that political and historical events are driven by conflict or interaction between social forces – enables the understanding of history *per se*, rather than individual versions of it. (Indeed, it also explains man's ever-improving rationality.) That it was Watt who made this innovation is merely a 'historical accident' – if he had never been born someone else would have realised this inevitable evolutionary development.[172]

Behind this 'accident' lay the driving necessity to develop machinery and liberate industry from the confines imposed by nature in terms of a power source. The development of steam power removed the reliance on water power and therefore enabled industry to be moved to other locations more freely. With steam power, the primary factor became access to coal, the source of the energy needed to generate steam, which in turn enabled greater access to coal. With the development of electrical power, industry was further liberated, and has therefore invariably moved to wherever the cheapest labour can be found.

The origins of the steam engine can actually be traced back to the ancient Greek mathematician Hero of Alexandria. Within a system of slavery, though, it could not be utilised. Marx therefore argues:

"The steam-engine itself, such as it was at its invention during the manufacturing period at the close of the 17th century, and such as it continued to be down to 1780, did not give rise to any industrial revolution. It was, on the contrary, the invention of machines that made a revolution in the form of steam engines necessary. As soon as man, instead of working on the object of labour with a tool, becomes merely the motive power of a machine, it is purely accidental that the motive power happens to be clothed in the form of human muscles; wind, water or steam could just as well take man's place."[173]

In his 1967 book *Era of Man or Robot? The Sociological Problems of the Technical Revolution*, Russian Soviet philosopher Genrikh Volkov writes that what made an industrial revolution for Marx

> "pivoted on finding the correct methodological approach. His examination focused on changes in the joint working mechanism and the combination of the inanimate and human elements of the process of production. Whether the machine is driven by an animal, a man or steam, Marx showed, is immaterial. The source of power, being part of the machine, only serves the system of working machines."[174]

What is defined as the second industrial revolution by bourgeois scholars was therefore merely the ongoing development of the first. Taking place in the decades before WWI, it saw the growth of existing industries and establishment of new ones, with electric power enabling ever-greater mass production. Major technological advances included the telephone, light bulb, phonograph and the internal combustion engine.

The ongoing digital revolution – with the emergence of digital record-keeping, the personal computer, the internet, and other forms of information and communications technology – is considered to be the third industrial revolution. This is, perhaps, more arguable. The instruments described certainly amplify man's mental capacity. But the digital revolution is a technological revolution and actually *part* of the automation revolution; not an industrial revolution by itself:

> "Mechanisation begins with the transference to technology of basic *physical* working functions, while automation begins when the basic *'mental'* functions in a technological process actually materialise into machines. This becomes possible with the appearance in production of supervising, controlling or programming cybernetical installations."[175]

The productivity of machines is slowed down by the physiological limits of human bodies, and so automation becomes necessary; man is increasingly excluded from direct production and now works *alongside* fully mechanised machines, calling forth a radical change in the man-technology relationship. As Marx said of automation:

"Labour no longer appears so much to be included within the production process; rather, the human being comes to relate more as watchman and regulator to the production process itself."[176]

The point of automation therefore, says Volkov,

"should be to remove the contradiction between the inanimate and human elements, between man and machine, to break the shackle that made man and machine a single working mechanism, to act as Hercules setting Prometheus free to perform his great deeds. Potentially, automation can enable man to become Man with a capital letter, and the machine to become Machine in the full sense of the word. Freedom for man's development is, at the same time, freedom for technological progress."[177]

In *Automation and Social Progress* (1956), English socialist Sam Lilley defined automation provisionally as "the introduction or use of highly automatic machinery or processes which largely eliminate human labour *and detailed human control*".[178]

The term is of course applied to a very broad field ranging from semi-automatic machinery to automatic factories. These are qualitatively different notions and so must be understood carefully. Volkov writes:

"Semi-automatic technology (semi-automatic machine-tools and lines, so-called cyclic automatons) represents a transitional form from ordinary to automatic machines. In this form, 'automation' is usually affected by mechanical means without, as a rule, recourse to cybernetical devices. The worker is still directly included in the process, which he supplements with his nervous system, intellect and, partly, muscular energy (loading and unloading of machines). At this stage, the new technology does not yet constitute automation proper and lacks its most characteristic features. As a matter of fact, semi-automatic technology stretches to the limit the adverse aspects of mechanisation by simplifying things still more, robbing working operations of all their creative content and contributing to their further fragmentation."[179]

Automation proper can therefore be subdivided into three stages:

1. *Initial or partial automation* (separate machine-tools fitted with programme control, separate cybernetically controlled automatic lines). Here, the worker has relative freedom of action. They are included in the process only in so far as their duties include the overall supervision of operations, maintenance and adjustment of the machines.

2. *Developed automation*, eg, automatic factories equipped with overall electronic control of all production processes, regulation of equipment, loading and unloading, transportation of materials, semi-finished and finished products. In this stage of automation the worker takes no direct part in the production process.

3. *Full automation*, which ensures automatic operation of all sections of production, from planning to delivery of finished products, including choice of optimum conditions, conversion to a new type of product, and auto-planning in accordance with a set programme. The planning of production as a whole and the overall control of its operation are also to a considerable extent transferred to automatic installations. "Automation of this kind is equivalent to automatic production on the scale of the entire society," says Volkov. "Here, not only the labour of workers, but that of technicians and, to a considerable extent, of engineers as well, is excluded from the direct technological process. This does not mean, of course, that such work disappears altogether. It is only shifted to another sphere, becomes more creative and closer related to scientific work."[180]

Under capitalism in the first part of the 21st century, we are still a fair way from achieving full automation. But that does not mean we are not witnessing an industrial revolution. The first industrial revolution began before and necessitated the rise of capitalism, just as the second begins before and necessitates the rise of socialism.

An industrial revolution has far-reaching consequences that go beyond the framework of technology and even beyond that of material production. The first affected the character of labour (manual to mechanised); social structure (artisan and peasant turning into worker);[181] the correlation of economic branches (agriculture being supplanted by industry); and, finally, the political and economic field (capitalist relations superseding feudal relations). Volkov spells out the most characteristic features of the second industrial revolution.

1) The production of material wealth has a tendency to turn into fully automated production "on a society-wide scale". The second industrial revolution therefore "marks the *completion* of the establishment of industry". At first, large-scale machine industry had a relatively limited area of diffusion, having taken the place of handicrafts and ordinary manufacture. But with the second industrial revolution, "industrialisation tends to spread also to the whole of agriculture, beginning with mechanisation, followed by comprehensive mechanisation and, eventually, by automation. Industrialisation is spreading to house-building, distribution, the community services (eg public catering) and even intellectual, scientific work. In this way, industry becomes the *universal form* of producing material wealth."

2) While the first industrial revolution was *local* in character, being limited to a few developed European countries, the second industrial revolution "tends to involve all the countries of the world" as newly industrialising countries begin by installing the most up-to-date industrial equipment involving comprehensive mechanisation and automation. "This presents features of the first and second industrial revolutions at one and the same time. Consequently, the second industrial revolution is *global* in character, *laying the groundwork for a subsequent economic and social integration of nations.*"[182] [Our emphasis – see chapter 15.]

3) The modern industrial revolution leads to substantial structural changes in the various spheres of social activity. Because of the ever-decreasing need for manpower for material production, scientific production increases both quantitatively and qualitatively and tends to assume priority over the direct production of material wealth. "Hence, science is the *helmsman of the modern industrial revolution.*"

4) The dominant feature of the automation revolution concerns its social implications. As we know, the first industrial revolution led to the consolidation of capitalist exploitation. Large-scale industry spelt wholesale ruin for artisans and peasants, longer working hours, intensification of labour and narrow specialisation. In contrast, the modern industrial revolution that was underway in the socialist nations "leads to a shortening of working hours, an easing of labour, a modification of its nature (work becoming more creative and free), and to the elimination of the essential distinctions between town and countryside, and between mental and manual labour. While yielding the industrial basis for an abundance of material wealth and to

distribution according to need, it also opens up possibilities for unlimited spiritual improvement of man's personality."

Volkov adds:

"The second industrial revolution resolves the contradiction between the machines and those who operate them, ie the contradiction within the joint working mechanism. By completing the automation of production, it paves the way for the implementation of the principles of *socialist humanism* in society. Hence, the very logic of the second industrial revolution *strengthens man's personality and humanism*.

"In capitalist countries, however, this logic and the above-mentioned features of the second industrial revolution contradict the very essence of the relations of exploitation. All the same, mechanised labour gives way to automation, the antithesis between mental and physical labour tends to disappear. And the cultural and technical standard of the workers tends to rise. Substantial changes also occur in the social structure and in the relation between the various economic branches. In other words, many of the essential elements of an industrial revolution are distinctly on hand.

"The fundamental difference between the revolution in capitalist countries and its counterpart in the socialist states consists in its leading to the *breakdown*, [our emphasis] instead of the consolidation, of the existing relations under the conditions of the private ownership of the means of production. The modern industrial revolution has strained to the utmost all the contradictions of capitalism.... It does not reform capitalism. Instead, it creates the material preconditions for a social revolution and paves the way for the eventual replacement of capitalist relations of production by communist relations."[183]

The technological determinists who see automation as the fourth industrial revolution do not put the development of technology in its proper socio-historical context, but instead in isolation from the human component of the productive forces. They fail to see "the genuine dialectics of the forces and relations of production, [and] deny the inverse influence of the relations of production on the productive forces and the development of science and technology".[184]

To summarise: over many centuries, manual labour determined the technological basis of society. The technological mode of production, the mode of combining inanimate and human elements, was *subjective*.

The next stage, paved by the specialisation of implements in manufacture, began when the main working function – control of partial implements – of the 'living mechanism', the worker, transferred to the mechanical mechanism, the machine. From human-inanimate, the working mechanism became inanimate-human. The technological mode of production became *objective* and labour became mechanised. This is then the first industrial revolution.

Finally, the third historical stage in technological development is ushered in by automation. The working mechanism becomes fully *technical* and the mode of combining man and technology becomes *free* and labour itself is automated. This then is the second industrial revolution.

We therefore reject the bourgeois definition that posits the automation revolution as the fourth industrial revolution.

4. 'Technological unemployment' and fearful rulers

"The shadow of Frankenstein's monster hangs over the entire capitalist world."[185]

Volkov

In the past, industrial and technological progress has, says *The Economist*,[186] voice of the industrialist ruling class, "always created as many jobs as the number displaced", or at least enough in time to contain the resulting social and political instability from this "technological unemployment" to what the influential British economist John Maynard Keynes called a "temporary phase of maladjustment",[187] preventing a level of unrest that could have sparked revolution.

But, the magazine acknowledges, the "pace of change this time is unrivalled" – and, it warns, "no government is prepared". With the severe rationing of state welfare in imperialist nations already well underway, the result is a growing level of uncertainty in both imperialist and 'developing' nations about where a 'lost generation' is going to find work or subsistence.

Some have considered the revolutionary implications. "Marx and Engels may again become relevant," Bank of England (BoE) Governor Mark Carney warned business leaders at the Canada Growth Summit in April 2018. There is then genuine concern within the bourgeoisie that underconsumptionist theories of capitalism's downfall have some validity: that unemployment will become so high in the age of automation that the working class will not be able to afford the commodities made by the machines that have replaced them, and so realising profit will become increasingly impossible.

Manufacturing labour as a share of the US workforce fell from 40% during WWII to 8.7% in 2015. According to a study by the National Bureau of Economic Research (NBER), around 670,000 jobs in the US were "lost to robots" between 1990 and 2007.[188] Each industrial robot introduced coincided with the elimination of 6.2 jobs within the commutable area. Wages also saw a slight drop of between 0.25% and 0.5% per 1,000 employees when one or more robots was added to the workforce. Another study in 2019 found that 1.7 million manufacturing jobs across 29 advanced economies had been lost to robots since 2000, with a further 20 million to come by 2030. It also found that robots in poorer regions trigger the loss of almost twice as many jobs as in wealthier ones.[189]

Any claims that as many skilled jobs will be created as displaced by automation so far seem highly dubious. Dr Carl Frey at the Oxford Martin School found that only 0.5% of the US workforce has found employment in the high-tech industries that have emerged since the turn of the century.[190] Start-ups, for example, may be bought up for tens or hundreds of millions of pounds by tech monopolies, but the algorithms and technology they use employ few people. Instagram employed just 13 when it was sold to Facebook in 2012 for $1bn. In 2018 Goldman Sachs said that a trading desk occupied by 500 people 15-20 years ago was now staffed by three.[191]

Frey has led three studies on automation since 2013. One estimates that up to 47% of all jobs in the US are at high risk of being automated by 2033, with a further 19% facing medium risk.[192] Another says the figure rises to 80% for jobs in transport, warehousing and logistics.[193] We are already familiar with self-serving kiosks in supermarkets, fast-food chains and cinemas. In February 2018, Amazon launched the world's first "cashierless store" and the British Retail Consortium expects almost a third of three million retail jobs to disappear by 2025. Increasingly susceptible are workers who operate machinery, prepare fast food, collect and process data, originate mortgages and do paralegal and accounting work.

Even jobs that require dexterity are starting to be replaced. In October 2018, the US's "first robot farm" featuring "incredibly intelligent" machines opened in California.[194] Cows on industrial farms are milked by machines. In May 2019, the world's first raspberry-picking robot went on trial in Britain, where farms have faced increasing labour shortages since the Brexit vote. Each robot will be able to pick more than 25,000 raspberries a day, 10,000 more than a human worker.[195] Fieldwork Robotics, a spinout from the University of Plymouth, intends to lease them to farmers for less than the £1-2 per kilogram of raspberries paid to workers.[196]

Andy Haldane, the BoE's chief economist, warned in 2015 that a "robot revolution" threatens up to 15 million jobs in Britain. Haldane said the transformation of the global economy over the next 20 years would cut the costs of doing business but exacerbate social inequality.

According to the Office for National Statistics, 8.7 million people aged 16 to 64 in February 2018 were already 'economically inactive', ie, not working and not seeking work. While this includes students and pensioners, it also includes many who have been forced to give up looking for work, some due to the dehumanising effects of being "interviewed by algorithm".[197] Those who are economically inactive are discounted from unemployment figures, one of the technicalities that has enabled the Conservative government to say that unemployment is at an all-time low. Of course, in-work poverty and underemployment are at record highs.[198] The restructuring of the labour market has seen a boom in casualised labour and zero hours contracts; ie, the emergence of 'the gig economy',[199] whereby workers can be paid per task – robbing them of the standard employee entitlements of regular 37.5-hour weekly income, holiday and sick pay, etc. Gig economy workers more than doubled in size to 4.7 million in Britain between 2016 and 2019.[200]

It can be easy to overstate the impact technology has on employment. In the past 60 years automation has only eliminated one occupation: elevator operators.[201] But Professor Richard Susskind, author of *The Future of the Professions and Tomorrow's Lawyers*, stresses that we should also be wary of downplaying just how much super-computers might change the working world. While being in a creative or people-focused industry may keep your job safe for the next 10 years or so, he says, the same cannot be said for the next 20. "What you're going to see for a lot of jobs is a churn of different tasks," he says. "So a lawyer today doesn't develop systems that offer advice, but the lawyer of 2025 will.[202] They'll still be called lawyers but they'll be doing different things." He believes the 2020s are going to be a decade not of unemployment, but of redeployment. Beyond that, however, the picture is far less clear: "I don't think anyone can do long-term career planning with any confidence."

In the short term, technology will mainly continue to supplement – albeit a relatively smaller number of productively employed – human workers. Productivity in office-based sectors' increased in the UK by 84% in the 33 years from 1970 thanks to the huge advances in Information Computer Technology.[203] An office worker in 2013 could do in one hour what an office worker in 1970 took five hours to do.[204]

How can that productivity possibly be raised still further? The answer is artificial intelligence (AI). AI means computers are increasingly able to 'think' and 'learn', performing analytical tasks that until now required human judgement. This already includes composing original music and beating professional players at complex board games.

Many well-paying middle class professions are threatened as much as low-paid working class jobs. As Stanford University academic Jerry Kaplan writes in *Humans Need Not Apply*, automation is now "blind to the colour of your collar".[205] McKinsey Global Institute, known as the world's number one private sector think tank, says that up to $9 trillion in global wage costs could be saved as computers take over 'knowledge-intensive' tasks.[206] The 'cognitive' services work that replaced manufacturing jobs is now being replaced as well.

The processing power in a typical smartphone is already far superior to that used by NASA to take man to the moon in 1968. The world's fastest supercomputer in 1975 was worth $5m ($32m in 2013's money), while an iPhone 4 released in 2010 with the equivalent performance was $400.[207] According to Moore's Law, named after Intel co-founder Gordon Moore, processing power tends to double roughly every 18 months.[208] In theory this means that

> "in just under half a century (48 years, 32x18 months) processing power will increase 4.3 billion times. But if it keeps on increasing at the same rate, over the next 48 years it will increase another 4.3 billion times from a massively higher base. Even if absolute physical limits begin to slow the pace of progress, we will be able within 50 years to deploy unimaginably massive quantities of computing power, and as that computing power becomes available, multiple work activities which till now have resisted automation will become automatable."[209]

This quote is from former UK Financial Services Authority chairman Adair Turner and his theoretical paper *Capitalism In The Age of Robots*. He writes that at some point the advent of machine learning means that "we [will] not have to write code specifying how to lay a brick, or sew a shirt, but can simply move robot arms through the process, with the machine coding itself to achieve perfect future repetition".[210] This will lead to a 'singularity' whereby robots can build and programme new, ever-better robots *without any* human input. McKinsey and Co expects "the near-complete automation of existing job activities" somewhere between 2060 and 2100, with the "most technologically optimistic" scenario putting the date at 2045.[211]

The myth of 'technological unemployment'
Keynes popularised the term 'technological unemployment', "unemployment due to our discovery of means of economising the use of labour outrunning the pace at which we can find new uses for labour".[212] Much of the Left continues to parrot this mystification. 'Technological unemployment' is

merely an appearance obscuring *economic unemployment*. Workers only go unemployed because capital cannot afford to employ them. The 'setting free' of workers through machinery is something quite different. It is, says Grossman

> "a technical fact produced by the growth of M relative to L and as such is not a specifically capitalist phenomenon. All technological advance rests on the fact that labour becomes more productive, that it is economised – or set free – in relation to a given product…. This process of the setting free of workers will occur in any mode of production, including the planned economy of socialism."[213]

Marx could not possibly have deduced the breakdown of capitalism from this technical fact. The most important factor is not the change in the technical composition of capital, $M:L$, but in the *organic* composition of capital, $c:v$, in the course of the process of accumulation. Grossman said "the existing literature has totally ignored" the fact that the growth of the reserve army

> "is not rooted in the technical fact of the introduction of machinery, but in the imperfect valorisation of capital specific to advanced stages of accumulation. It is a cause that flows strictly from the specifically capitalist form of production. Workers are made redundant not because they are displaced by machinery, but because, at a specific level of the accumulation of capital, profits become too small…"[214]

Franz Oppenheimer accused Marx of basing the finding that the reserve army inevitably grew on a purely empirical 'impression' that Marx gained from a study of British capitalism. He added a third kind of setting free, arguing that more labour is displaced in the countryside than in industry, and concluded that "the process of setting free can have nothing to do with changes in the organic composition of capital".[215] Grossman set him straight:

> "Oppenheimer overlooks something quite elementary… Marx is concerned with the condition of workers who already function as wage labourers. In the countryside the setting free is a setting free of small producers; it is their proletarianisation and conversion to wage labour."[216]

★

5. Workerless factories, globalisation in retreat and the crisis of imperialism

"The aggressive character of imperialism ... necessarily flows from a crisis of valorisation. Imperialism is striving to restore the valorisation of capital at any cost, to weaken or eliminate the breakdown tendency. This explains its aggressive policies at home (an intensified attack on the working class) and abroad (a drive to transform foreign nations into tributaries). This is the hidden basis of the bourgeois rentier state, of the parasitic character of capitalism at an advanced stage of accumulation. Because the valorisation of capital fails in countries at a given, higher stage of accumulation, the tribute that flows in from abroad assumes ever-increasing importance."[217]

Grossman

From water mills to clocks, the long and fascinating history of self-governing systems predates capitalism by millennia. We are concerned, however, with a specific type of production under capitalism, that of automatic machinery. Factory production has, of course, become increasingly semi-automated over the past two centuries. But, writes Lilley, "it is only in the post-war period – and largely as a result of technical advances initiated during the war – that it has become possible to apply automation to technical processes in general".[218]

A Soviet piston factory which started work in 1950 was "the most complete example of automation in the world", says Lilley in an eye-witness account, with a ball-bearing factory there not far behind. The Soviet Union had only taken "investigatory steps". Rather than the piecemeal approach taken by the US and Britain, where automated parts of the production process have been introduced gradually, the USSR, precisely because of its socialist character, was able to concentrate its efforts on building a handful of near-fully automated factories in order to pave the way for future generalisation.

In the US, the first industrial robot, called Unimate, arrived on the General Motors assembly line in 1962. Automation has since played an increasingly large role in everyday life, from automatic teller machines in the 1970s to the autonomous Roomba vacuum cleaner in 2002 and beyond. The exponential improvement in computing power and its combination with ever-improving machinery has consistently taken the quality, ability and efficiency[219] of technology and productivity to higher levels. A 2015 report from investment bank Bank of America Merrill Lynch says that:

> "The pace of disruptive technological innovation has gone from linear to parabolic in recent years. Penetration of robots and AI has hit every industry sector and become an integral part of our daily lives. One major risk ... is the potential for increasing labour polarisation, particularly for low-paying jobs such as service occupations, and a hollowing-out of middle income manual labour jobs."[220]

The authors calculate that the total global market for robots and AI is expected to reach $152.7bn (£99bn) by 2020, boosting productivity in some industries by an estimated 30%. Among Japan's carmakers, robots are able to work unsupervised 24/7 for up to 30 days, so lights and air conditioning do not need to be turned on.[221] While 'offshoring' manufacturing jobs – ie, exporting capital – to the 'low-income economies' is said to save up to 65% on labour costs, replacing human workers with robots saves up to 90%.[222] Unlike workers, robots do not need breaks, sick days, holidays or pensions.

In 1970, the number of industrial robots employed worldwide was 1,000. In 2016 the figure reached 1.8 million, and should hit three million in 2020.[223] In 2016, worldwide robot sales increased by 16% to 294,312 units, a new peak for the fourth year in a row. Since 2010, the demand for industrial robots has "accelerated considerably due to continued technical improvements".[224] In 2016, there were on average 74 robots per 10,000 workers worldwide, up from 66 the year before. In the car manufacturing sector the number in 2016 was 2,145 in South Korea, 1,261 in the US, 1,150 in France, 1,131 in Germany, 1,131 in Spain and 505 in China.[225]

In some factories robotic arms work so quickly that they are put behind shatter-proof glass screens to ensure the safety of the few staff that remain. German sportswear giant Adidas has opened its first 'Speedfactory' in Bavaria, where the time it takes to make a trainer from the design stage to finished product has been slashed from 18 months to five hours.[226] It employs only 120 workers, compared to roughly 1,000 in each of its Asian factories.

While this remains a very small part of Adidas's operations, and for limited-edition sportswear, it hints at the direction mass production is potentially heading: if the rest of the company's production were to become equally automated, the roughly one million workers employed in its supply chain across the world would fall by over 90%.[227]

In the Association of Southeast Asian Nations (Asean) economic area – including Cambodia, Indonesia, Thailand and Malaysia – 90% of garment and footwear workers are at risk from automated assembly lines dubbed 'sewbots'. The International Labour Organisation (ILO) says that nine million people, mostly young women, are susceptible to losing their jobs to the new robot workforce.[228] Sewbot factories will be relocated to Europe and the US to save on transit costs, but will create few jobs.

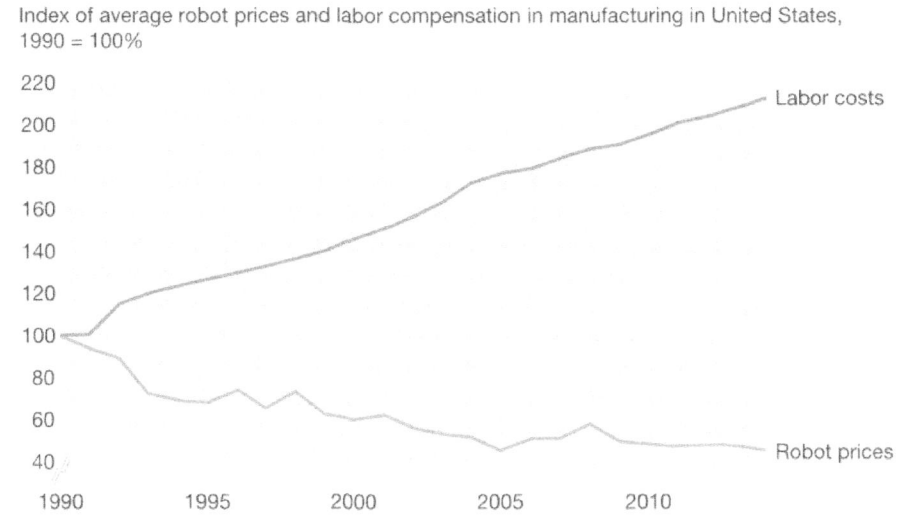

Index of average robot prices and labor compensation in manufacturing in United States, 1990 = 100%

Source: Economist Intelligence Unit; IMB; Institut für Arbeitsmarkt- und Berufsforschung; International Robot Federation; US Social Security data; McKinsey analysis

Costs of automation: labour vs robots

Chinese garment manufacturer Tianyuan Garments Company has announced a new automated clothing factory in the US. Tianyuan is partnering with a US company, SoftWear Automation, to supply high-tech sewbots for the factory. The sewbot technology was developed at Georgia Tech's Advanced Technology Development Center, with part of its funding coming from the US Department of Defense. The robots operating in the planned Tianyuan factory will be able to produce 1.2 million t-shirts a year across 21 automated production lines. The price to produce each shirt will be approximately $0.33, "significantly cheaper than what is currently possible with even the cheapest labour in the developing world".[229]

"Factories today chase cheap labour around the world and we have ended up with an unsustainable supply chain. SoftWear Automation's Sewbots can move that manufacturing closer to the customer or the raw materials," says SoftWear's CEO Palaniswamy Rajan.

In China,[230] the early 21st century's 'workshop of the world', wages for striking factory workers have been rising. The necessary reaction, as far as factory owners have been concerned, has been to replace ever-more costly human workers with robots. In one factory visited by the *FT*, nine robots manufacturing sinks now do the job of 140 full-time workers.[231] Even the final quality check is carried out by a computer-linked camera. "These machines are cheaper, more precise and more reliable than people," the factory owner told the newspaper. "I've never had a whole batch ruined by robots. I look forward to replacing more humans in future."

Thousands of factories in China have been turning to automation, subsidised by the government. AI superiority by 2030 is China's strategic goal, and around two thirds of global investment in AI now takes place in China. The Communist Party of China's (CCP) 2013 economic reform plan proposed changing China from a low-wage, labour-intensive manufacturing power based on exports, to a high-waged economy based on technology-driven productivity growth and an expanding services sector. China launched its Made in China 2025 policy in 2015, focusing on ten sectors, including robotics and renewable energy, semiconductors, scientific and medical research and AI.

At one factory owned by Foxconn – the notorious Apple supplier known for high rates of suicide among its staff – the introduction of robots reduced the number of employees from 110,000 to 50,000 in one fell swoop.[232] The company is dealing with regular uprisings by replacing workers with 'Foxbots' that it claims will eventually build enough robots to replace all its workers. Japanese company Mujin, meanwhile, claims to be close to commercialising the world's first "humanless warehouse", and already has operations up and running in China.[233]

Three-dimensional printing
Supply chain jobs are also coming under threat from new technology, with some car manufacturers, for example, experimenting with three-dimensional (3-D) printing to produce lighter and cheaper parts and spares, reducing the costs associated with shipping and distribution. Private space company Rocket Lab's Rutherford engine is the first oxygen-hydrocarbon engine to use

3-D printing for all primary components, reducing costs and build time from months to days, and also enabling rapid scalability. With six printers the engine can be manufactured in 24 hours. Another space company, Relativity Space, aims to build an entire rocket structure from 3-D printing – measuring 90 feet tall, seven feet wide and capable of carrying 2,000 pounds into orbit – by the mid-2020s. It will take a month to build and all but eliminate the human labour that still accounts for 90% of the production costs.[234] Furthermore, rather than having globalised supply chains, the company foresees the entire rocket being built in the US.[235] Prices are nosediving. In 2017 Bob Richards of Moon Express said that, "Our first quote from an unnamed aerospace company from our propulsion system in 2010 was $24m in 24 months; we're now printing our engines for $2,000 in two weeks."

3-D printing is a form of additive manufacturing, which is far more flexible than traditional manufacturing since products are built by layering component materials from the bottom up. While commercial prices of 3-D printers fell from $100,000 in 1988 to $1,400 in 2015, open source designs can be assembled for as little as $300. The first printers have only been able to print in plastic or steel, but the development of continuous composite printing means printers will be able to work with multiple complementary materials simultaneously. Scientists have even developed the ability to print living human kidneys and artificial skin. Edible products like structures made of chocolate or sugar can also be printed and decent sized housing structures can already be printed for as little as $5,000. In the future it is likely that printers will be capable of producing goods at the molecular level, ie capable of printing anything comprised of the molecules used. Ben Reynolds in *The Coming Revolution* (2018) describes additive production – which "fulfils the promise of the personal computer as a means of production" – as a paradigm shift from industrial production to distributive production.

> "It is conceivable that the logical fulfilment of distributed production – nearly instant production of anything, at will, anywhere in the world – will arrive within the lifetime of children born at the time of this writing…
>
> "Distributed production fundamentally erodes the basic pillars of capitalism…. Any industry that finds itself competing with a form of distributed production will no longer have the option of adaptation through monopolisation. Instead, that industry will flail wildly as prices fall back toward their values and as its entire business model disintegrates in slow motion."[236]

Deindustrialising the developing world

The march of the machines around the world has accelerated as a result of sharp falls in the price of industrial robots and a steady increase in their capabilities. The effect on developing nations is profound, as the *FT* says: "Developing countries, from India to Indonesia and Egypt to Ethiopia, have long hoped to follow the example of China's rapid economic growth, but new automation now means that industrialisation is likely to generate significantly fewer jobs."[237] Surplus labour is expected to be particularly high in Africa, where the population is projected to increase by over four times by 2100. Turner writes that:

> "Between 1800 and 1950 a huge gap opened up between the standard of living of the rich countries – in particular in North America and western Europe – and most of the rest of humanity. Over the past 70 years, a small number of countries have achieved a remarkable catching up, growing per capita income far faster than rich countries operating at the frontier of technology, and at least partially closing the gap thanks to a development model of export oriented labour-intensive manufacture."[238]

This opportunity for "catching up" is "being destroyed"[239] because "endlessly advancing automation possibilities mean that the rich world does not need cheap emerging economy labour to provide low-priced footwear, apparel, or other goods".[240] All this includes new automation in developing nations themselves. Citing the example of India, which despite its recent rapid growth is still a 'low income' nation, Turner writes:

> "Given demographic trends, India needs to create 10 to 12 million new jobs per annum to keep unemployment and underemployment stable, but despite GDP growth now running at 6-7% per annum, recent job creation falls far short of that level. Indeed there are signs that formal employment in leading sectors such as export oriented manufacture, IT, back-office processing, and generic pharmaceuticals may already be declining as Indian companies apply state-of-the-art technology to automate their activities even though labour is available at extremely low cost."[241]

Even Latin America and Sub-Saharan Africa have been deindustrialising – shifting from predominantly manufacturing to services-based workforces – in the past decade, from a much lower starting point than Asia.[242] Whereas industrialisation peaked in western European countries at income levels of around $14,000, India and many Sub-Saharan African countries appear to have reached their peak manufacturing employment at income levels of $700 (both at 1990 levels).[243]

The inevitable intensification of trade wars

The trend towards automation both within and without the imperialist nations can help explain the protectionist turn and 'right-wing populism' in the US and Europe, expressed most prominently by the rise of US President Donald Trump and his intensified trade war policies. With his 'America First' sloganeering he set out in the direction of economic nationalism in response to a deteriorating domestic industrial base and an unsustainable trade deficit that is no longer being financed to the extent that it had been a decade ago by China.

In 2011, the US generated 23.7% less demand for the rest of the world's net exports than it would have done had the 2008-09 crash never happened. Foreign net capital flows ending up as loans to US corporations fell drastically from $500bn in 2006 to -$50bn in 2011; and US assets attracted 57% less capital than they were projected to before the crash.[244]

When, as is starting to happen, the organic composition of capital rises to a level in developing nations that generates insufficient profits, capital exports may provide less and less of a cushion for the breakdown tendency (especially when the option exists to make commodities at home without having to shell out on a workforce and transit costs, although this may be limited by things like the cost of land).

Protecting the domestic economy therefore increasingly becomes more of a priority, especially for those capitalists who rely on domestic markets more than international trade – such as land owners like Trump. While the messy business of politics still plays an important role, the base for economic nationalism has been apparent and growing since the early 1990s, as a larger part of the bourgeoisie has become increasingly dependent on forms of rent. The likes of Trump therefore tend to be more socially regressive and parochial than liberals and rely on more hardline and overt nationalist and bigoted rhetoric to stoke divisions in the working class, appealing especially to those workers who see their own fortunes as tied to the success of the nation or their private sector employer, usually a privileged layer which has risen to the position of home-ownership and, therefore, in reality, the lower middle classes. When this petty bourgeois layer is threatened with proletarianisation or re-proletarianisation, a significant proportion cling to their nationalist ideologies and, having been manipulated by the media (as much by censorship by omission as anything else), continue to scapegoat migrants, benefits "scroungers"[245] and anything else that contributes to higher taxes, potentially creating a mass base for fascism.

Trump promised to re-industrialise the Midwest and 'bring back jobs' that have been 'outsourced' overseas. This hasn't happened. When Toyota announced plans to invest a further $750m in the US in March 2019 it said this would create just 600 jobs. The value-creating part in the composition of capital is disappearing. Toyota then said that tariffs placed on foreign cars may stop the investment in its tracks. Some of the – mainly white – workers who voted for Trump have started to lose faith in him and his promises.

It has been predicted that between 2.5 million and 7.5 million US jobs, mainly in manufacturing, will be lost during 2019-21 because of the overvalued dollar – making imports cheaper but US exports more expensive – and an increasing current account deficit. The US goods trade deficit is expected to increase to between $1.2 trillion and $2 trillion in 2020, an increase of $400bn to $1.2 trillion above the $807bn US goods trade deficit in 2017. When General Motors (GM) announced that it would be closing plants and laying off around 15,000 staff by the end of 2019, it was treated as a canary in the coal mine in that GM was clearly moving to protect itself from an expected downturn. The Economic Policy Institute (EPI) commented:

> "The collapse in output, especially in the capital-intensive manufacturing sector, will decimate investment – and taken together, both will result in large additional job losses as income and spending collapse, resulting in a steep recession if nothing is done to reduce the overvalued dollar. The dollar must fall by at least 25-30% (on a real, trade-weighted basis) to rebalance US trade and avert the coming trade tsunami that's baked into the economy as a result of the rising trade deficit."

But – such are the contradictions of capitalism in decay – a devaluation of the dollar will weaken the US's control of the international market. The dollar's role as the reserve currency for foreign exchange has until now enabled the US to strong-arm most countries into complying with its demands. The EPI said Trump's economic policies had reinforced the dollar's inflation, because his corporate tax cut – from 35% to 21%, the biggest US corporate tax cut ever – had naturally increased the federal budget deficit, which is projected to exceed $1 trillion by 2020. This is "driving up short- and long-term interest rates, attracting even more foreign capital – and further strengthening the dollar". But Trump had to cut corporation rates because of low corporate profitability and he needs to attract foreign capital for the same reason, to finance the deficit.

The US wants China to be dependent on US industry rather than vice-versa. Trump has repeatedly framed China as a "trade cheat" and vowed to address the US's goods trade deficit with China. He tried to do this by protecting US industry with tariffs of 10-25% on $250bn of Chinese imports, about half of the total US imports from China. This forced China to devalue its currency by about 10% against the dollar. As a result, the US trade deficit with China increased faster (11.6%) than the US deficit with the world as a whole (10.4%), reaching a new record of $419.2bn in 2018, up from $375.6bn in 2017. China also retaliated by placing tariffs on US agricultural goods, damaging the Midwest Trump had promised to rejuvenate.

US tech firms are affected, too: Qualcomm sells 65% of its products to China, Microsoft 50%, Broadcom 50% and Intel 23%. China produces 60% of the world's rare earth minerals, which are used in electronic devices. US tariffs on China raise, for example, Apple's prices in the US because the company uses components made in China.[246] Trump though doubled down, placing tariffs of 10% on the remaining $300bn of Chinese imports. The US Chamber of Commerce, which represents more than three million US companies, said these tariffs would "only inflict greater pain on American businesses, farmers, workers and consumers". China – which appreciated its currency in 2010 after intense US lobbying – responded by allowing its renminbi to weaken by 1.4%, past the key seven-per-dollar level for the first time in more than a decade, "due to the effects of unilateralist and trade-protectionist measures and the expectations for tariffs against China". Trump then designated China a "currency manipulator" in a significant escalation that caused international stock markets to fall as investors fled to the traditional havens of gold and the Swiss franc. China accused the US of "deliberately destroying the international order" and holding its own citizens hostage.

Whatever Trump or any other US President tries will necessarily fail to rejuvenate US industry. Jobs can only be 'brought back' by making US labour power cheaper than the machinery or overseas labour that capitalists would otherwise employ – and that would mean another savage attack on wages and workers' rights in the US (which protectionists on the Left, if we're being generous, don't understand). Even then, reverting to former technological methods which employed more workers would have to be pursued – an impractical and expensive nonstarter that would weaken productivity.

Senile imperialism

What we are seeing then is this: *the highest stage of capitalism has gone past its own high point and is elapsing as a historical epoch* – automation is undoing the economic relations that underpin the system. The productive forces now demand a higher mode of production altogether. Monopoly capitalism could survive despite the turmoil it wrought 100 years ago because it was still in its infancy and full automation was a distant reality. Today imperialism is old and senile with nowhere left to go but 'home', and highly developed automation has brought the expiration of the law of value into view.

This is being expressed, even as the world economy becomes increasingly integrated technologically, through the weakening of 'globalisation', which, contrary to neoliberal propaganda, was in retreat before the emergence of Britain's 'Brexit' from the EU and the election of Trump. In 2015-16, the G20 economies introduced a record number of trade-restrictive measures, at 21 per month.[247] More precisely, the rising organic composition of capital in developing countries is undermining imperialist economic relations. Over-accumulations of capital are now so great that it is becoming more and more unprofitable to invest at home *or* overseas. *Capital's ability to expand its valorisation base is increasingly exhausted.*

Imperialism in the post-war era has been a kind of neocolonialism, where instead of direct occupation (although, of course, the US military has around 800 overseas military bases) collaborating bourgeoisies are given privilege and power, backed up with 'aid' – especially of the military variety – to defend imperialist interests. Those nations, including capitalist ones, which attempt to operate independently by keeping control of their own resources, face suffocating isolation as the imperialists impose economic sanctions that block imports and threaten or indeed carry out military invasions (including by proxy, ie by arming far right terrorists and insurrectionists).[248] Since losing the protection of the Soviet Union, Yugoslavia, Iraq, Afghanistan, Libya and Syria have all been destroyed, while others have capitulated and accepted onerous International Monetary Fund (IMF) loans and privatisation programmes in order to spare themselves a similar fate. Iran, Cuba, the Democratic People's Republic of Korea, Bolivia and Venezuela remain in the imperialist crosshairs today for retaining or reasserting their independence, along with Russia and China for emerging as direct competitors.

Since 2008, the crisis of imperialism has deepened significantly – precisely because, as David Yaffe of the Revolutionary Communist Group (RCG) has consistently pointed out, in the case of Britain, for example, its "unbalanced economy – its critical dependence on the earnings from its vast overseas assets and particularly those of its parasitic banking and financial services sector – makes it extremely vulnerable to any external economic or political shocks".[249]

Yaffe calls Britain a "weak link in the imperialist chain", a phrase Lenin used to describe Russia.[250] For around 40 years, Yaffe has kept track of the nature and size of Britain's external assets and their impact on the character of British capitalism, pointing in particular to "the increasingly dominant role of banking and commercial capital in sustaining and advancing British imperialism's interests throughout the world".[251] He exposes just how dependent Britain's economy is on wealth created by workers in the neo-colonies. His update at the end of 2015 explained:

"In 1962, UK external assets were around half Britain's Gross National Product (GNP), with UK banking and commercial assets 18% of the total. By 1977, UK external assets had expanded to 107% of GNP, and banking and commercial claims had become the dominant component of these assets, 70% of the total and equivalent in size to 75% of GNP.

"These developments have now reached unprecedented levels. In 1997 UK external assets were 244% of GDP, in 2005 they reached 395% of GDP, and as the financial crisis of 2008-09 broke out they had grown to five times Britain's GDP. A few years later, when the financial derivatives of UK banks were added to UK external assets by the Office of National Statistics (ONS), and they were reconfigured to take this into account, those external assets at the end of 2008 were £10.98 trillion, nearly 7.5 times Britain's GDP....

"These dramatic changes were in the main ignored by economic commentators until very recently, when a serious deterioration in the balance of payments current account [the difference in value between imports and exports of goods and services] needed to be confronted and explained. That deterioration in the current account was due to negative earnings on the UK investment account – the difference between what the UK earns on its overseas assets and what the rest of the world earns on its assets in the UK. The investment account had contributed on average a positive 1.4% of GDP a year to the current account throughout the pre-financial crisis 2000s. After 2011 those net earnings on the UK investment account fell rapidly, and in 2012 were barely positive. In 2013 and 2014 they turned increasingly negative, registering a deficit of 1.96% of GDP in the second quarter of 2015.

"Britain's overseas assets ... are rising again, reaching £10.17 trillion at the end of 2014 – equivalent to nearly six times Britain's GDP. Of these assets, loans and deposits abroad by UK banks (called 'other investments') were £3.54 trillion, that is 1.95 times GDP, and financial derivatives were £2.83 trillion, that is 1.6 times GDP – together they make up 62.6% of total overseas assets – a gigantic usury [high interest] capital. 12.1% of these overseas assets, £1.23 trillion, were direct investments (an investment in an enterprise abroad with 10% or more shares or voting stock), and 24.7%, £2.51 trillion, were portfolio investments (investment in shares, bonds and money market instruments).

"These foreign assets were matched by even greater foreign liabilities of £10.63 trillion, leaving a net external debt of -£454.1bn, or 25% of GDP. This is 86.1% higher than the net external debt of the previous year. In 2014 Britain's net earnings on its investment account were negative, at -£32.0bn, following negative net earnings of -£16.0bn in 2013, and barely positive net earnings of £0.9bn in 2012. This should be compared with net earnings of £20.0bn on the investment account in 2011 and significant net earnings in previous years. This is a serious development for the balance of payments current account, which had a record deficit of £92.9bn in 2014, equivalent to 5.1% of GDP. This threatens a run on the pound, forcing its devaluation, and is a serious threat to the standard of living of people in Britain."[252]

In 2015, the exposures (the maximum potential loss of lenders) of UK banks to the 'emerging market' economies totalled $820bn or 150% of their core capital, with that to China alone at $540bn. Of the top five British banks, HSBC and Standard Chartered are especially vulnerable to any economic shocks in Asia. In addition, the exposures of UK banks stood at $655bn in the US and $960bn in the euro-area.[253]

In October 2017, the Office for National Statistics revealed that Britain was "£490bn poorer than thought" and no longer had a net reserve of foreign assets.[254] The half a trillion pounds that "went missing" equated to 25% of GDP. Britain's stock of wealth dropped from a surplus of £469bn to a net deficit of £22bn.

It is only in the context of the British economy's decaying and parasitic nature that the Brexit crisis can be properly understood.[255] Britain's relative decline means it can no longer withstand competition from the US and EU as an independent imperialist power. Sooner or later it was going to have to make a shift towards allying more decisively with one or the other. Either way the importance and independence of the City of London as a world financial centre was bound to be undermined.

The ruling class is split between those whose economic interests are mainly tied to Europe, the 'Remainers', and those whose are mainly tied to the US, the 'Brexiters'. The latter also want to cut taxes and devalue the pound to make it more competitive.[256] Nationalists who depend mostly on the domestic market also see Britain's contributions to the EU as a drain on British capital. Much like the humiliated Mussolini, these nationalists think they can rebuild an empire (with direct colonialism working like the extension of the domestic market) in the face of ascendent opposition and without an industrial base.

Whereas much analysis in Britain has simply blamed the crisis on former Tory Prime Minister David Cameron for deciding to call a referendum, seeing it as a capitulation to the far right, the RCG has been arguing since 2006 that the ruling class would be forced sooner or later to choose between the US and Europe.[257] It has been one of very few left-wing organisations in Britain which did not opportunistically take a side with a faction of the imperialist bourgeoisie.[258]

Some, such as the Socialist Party, Momentum and Left Unity, have sided with Remain under the fantastical notion that 'a socialist EU is possible'.[259] As Lenin wrote: "A United States of Europe is possible as an agreement between the European capitalists… but to what end? Only for the purpose of jointly suppressing socialism in Europe, of jointly protecting colonial booty against Japan and America…"[260]

Others, such as the Socialist Workers Party, Communist Party of Britain and Communist Party of Great Britain (Marxist-Leninist) (CPGB-ML), along with the trade unions Unite and the National Union of Rail, Maritime and Transport Workers (RMT), have backed leave under a so-called 'Lexit' slogan, a 'left-wing' or even 'socialist' Brexit, as if Britain would not remain capitalist and imperialist either way. This has been partly motivated by the idea that EU law forbids Britain from nationalising its utilities and industries, so leaving the EU is seen as the best way to protect and expand state jobs. But if and when Britain leaves, it will import all EU law into British law, and the British ruling class will resist nationalisations at least as much as the European ruling class. By backing Brexit these organisations have lined up alongside the far right to support the wholly regressive step of ending the free movement of workers between Britain and Europe. The contortions made by the CPGB-ML to justify its opportunism culminated predictably in outright reaction when it called for a vote for Nigel Farage's hard-right Brexit Party in the May 2019 European elections. All the while, hate crimes against minorities have been rising.

The long run stalemate in Parliament only served to reinforce the RCG's analysis. The only position communists and anti-imperialists could take was to boycott the referendum while highlighting the reactionary and idealistic intentions of both sides. To choose either side would not only have been unprincipled and reactionary, it would have amounted to lying to the working class with the fantasy that their conditions could improve either way. Capitalist crisis and austerity will continue to deepen regardless of the outcome.[261]

Deindustrialisation in the imperialist nations
The neoliberal era in the imperialist nations (precipitated by the economic crisis of 1973) has been characterised by deindustrialisation,[262] ie the marked decline in manufacturing jobs, not of industrialisation *per se* – absolute output is greater than ever – in Britain for example from a peak of 8.9 million in the 1960s to 2.9 million in 2016.[263] We are often told by the Left that production was relocated to poorer countries as "one of the solutions the bourgeoisie adopted to counter rising worker militancy in Europe and North America in the 1960s", to quote one example.[264] But this has it the wrong way round – worker militancy rose because the imperialist bourgeoisie was relocating production, ie because overaccumulation and falling profit rates compelled capitalists to export capital.

That the low-productivity services sector now accounts for around 80% of economic activity in Britain underscores both the country's dependence on parasitism and the tendency of automation to create 'non-direct' labour. The US labour market has followed the same trend.[265]

As the oldest imperialist nation, it makes perfect sense that Britain is the most deindustrialised – it is naturally the most decayed. It has the lowest rate of profit (see chapter 10), probably in the world, because of its high organic composition of capital. An Office for National Statistics report in November 2017 stated that the UK had the lowest gross fixed capital formation – spending on non-financial assets such as land, buildings, machinery, tools and software – of 34 Organisation for Co-operation and Development (OECD) countries. From the first quarter of 2008 to the second quarter of 2009, this form of investment fell by 18% in the UK; the largest proportionate fall of any OECD country. Between 1997 and June 2017 the UK spent, on average per year, just 16.7% of its GDP on gross fixed capital formation; the lowest of all the OECD countries.

Britain was the 'workshop of the world' into the 1870s but, as Grossman wrote, "the technological stagnation of Britain and her loss of industrial leadership were rooted in the faltering of her rate of accumulation due to the already huge accumulation of capital".[266] This was already true by 1856 when,

> "the Englishman Bessemer reported the discovery of a new process that was destined to revolutionise the metal working industries and to replace the dominance of iron by steel. But for 20 years Britain ignored the discovery of the Bessemer process and stuck to the puddling process until the competition of Germany, France and Belgium forced her to take it over and refine it. This was repeated again when in 1879 Thomas discovered the basic process named after him. Britain received the finding with pure indifference and let foreigners buy it until, in three years, it revolutionised all the plants on the continent. The British monopoly was a thing of the past as the leadership in iron and steel production gradually passed into other hands."[267]

Lenin made the same point – that even though the richest countries accumulate the most capital in absolute terms, they are the most decayed in relative terms: "On the whole, capitalism is growing far more rapidly than before; but this growth is not only becoming more and more uneven in general, its unevenness also manifests itself, in particular, in the decay of the countries which are richest in capital (England)."[268] That Britain was unable to hold on to its empire proved his point.

Thanks to the massive devaluation of capital that resulted from the two world wars, the process of capital accumulation was revived and investment in British manufacturing, aided by the Keynesian state,[269] enjoyed a new lease of life. This was only possible during this *early stage* of accumulation, when production was unencumbered by the fetter of surplus capital. But a new overaccumulation built up and growth of 6.5% in 1973 suddenly plummeted to -2.5% in 1974. What academics refer to as 'neoliberalism' and 'globalisation' – ie the political action that was *required* to achieve the sufficient rationalisation of capital and labour power – became necessary in order to restore the accumulation process.

Crises within the imperialist countries take surplus capital to higher levels, forcing capitalists to send more of it overseas. This was happening in the half-decade before the financial crash as interest rates in the imperialist countries were already unusually low, forcing investors to look abroad for higher rates of return. Smith writes that between 2003 and 2007,

> "the so-called emerging markets (EMs) in Africa, Asia, and Latin America

grew at a faster rate than at any time since the Second World War, more than twice as fast as imperialist countries. Their average rate of growth during these years exceeded 7% (5.9% if China is excluded), compared to 2.6% in rich countries. Even in the most crisis-affected year, 2009, they grew by 2.9% (0.9% excluding China), compared to a 3.7% decline in imperialist countries, and in 2010 growth rates in EMs shot back up to 7.7% (6.9% excluding China). Even though EM growth rates declined in each of the next four years, in 2014 they still grew on average by 4.3% (3.1% excluding China), compared to 1.7% GDP growth in the imperialist countries."[270]

It is clear that global growth has been sustained mostly by the developing nations in the past 10 years, especially given that the GDP growth of imperialist countries *per se* depends significantly on wealth created elsewhere anyway.

The crisis in the 'developing world'
The start of the millennium saw the beginning of the 'commodities supercycle' with rising world prices of the metals, oil and other primary commodities upon which many developing nations depend for the bulk of their export earnings, particularly in Africa and Latin America. This supercycle was driven by China's massive upswing in demand for raw materials as its continued 'post-Mao' economic 'opening up', combined with its huge labour base and the infrastructure that socialism had enabled it to build, made it the ideal location for the 'outsourcing' surge. *The Economist* noted that a credit boom in the EMs "was in large part a response to the credit bust in the rich world. Fearing a depression in its richest export markets, the authorities in China brought about a massive increase in credit in 2009. Meanwhile a flood of capital escaping the paltry yields on offer in developed economies pushed interest rates lower in developing ones."[271]

High rates of growth in EMs were therefore a reflection of deteriorating economic conditions in the imperialist countries. But, as Smith says, before the crisis

> "it was possible to pretend that buoyant economic growth in emerging nations was a sure sign of their progress toward convergence with imperialist nations; since then it has become abundantly clear that their fate is hostage to the actions of imperialist investors and of central banks beholden to them."[272]

Post-crash, a net total of $2.2 trillion in capital flooded into the fifteen largest EMs, between July 2009 and June 2014, when the flow "abruptly reversed and began gushing out, reflecting a dramatic loss of confidence by imperialist investors in the prospects for developing countries".[273] Total net outflows from the fifteen largest EMs rose to $600.1bn over three quarters to the end of March 2015, higher than the $545.2bn in outflows seen during the crisis-ridden three quarters to April 2009.[274] As the *FT* said in April 2015,

> "one big and insidious trend is working to forge a common destiny for almost all EMs. The gush of global capital that flowed into their economies in the six years since the 2008-09 financial crisis is in most countries now either slowing to a trickle or reversing course to find a safer home back in developed economies."[275]

This shows that imperialists cannot avoid overaccumulation forever simply by exporting capital. But "a safer home back in developed economies" only means turning to speculation, taking advantage of corporate tax cuts and wages that have been lowered; and production methods that have been cheapened, which will, as we have seen, therefore produce lower rates of surplus value in the long run, especially in the case of workerless factories.

It is clear that the mutual dependence of the imperialist countries and the developing nations they colonise with capital is being weakened by the inherently contradictory relations that govern that dependence – stagnant or declining demand in the imperialist countries poses an obvious threat to the export-oriented industrialisation strategies pursued by developing nations, but an economic crisis in the developing world, particularly in China, would be acutely felt in the US and Europe, and the world as a whole.

That is what is going to happen, though. Citing China's economic slowdown, sudden currency devaluations and dramatic falls in its stock market, Andrew Haldane, BoE chief economist, described in September 2015 what he called

> "the latest leg of what might be called a three-part crisis trilogy. Part one of that trilogy was the 'Anglo-Saxon' crisis of 2008-09. Part two was the 'euro-area' crisis of 2011-12. And we may now be entering the early stages of part three of the trilogy, the 'emerging market' crisis of 2015 onwards."

China's GDP growth dropped from 6.8% in 2017 to 6.6% in 2018,[276] having averaged 9.55% between 1989 and 2018, peaking at 15.4% in the first quarter of 1993.[277] Growth of 6.2% in the second quarter of 2019 was China's slowest quarterly growth rate since 1992, while its industrial output in July also hit a 17-year low.

The speed of the build up in debt in the emerging economies has been described as "staggering" by Hung Tran, the executive managing director of the Institute of International Finance (IIF).[278] According to the IMF, the total corporate debt of indigenous non-financial firms in major emerging markets snowballed from $4 trillion in 2004 to $18 trillion in 2014, 73% of GDP.[279] Almost all of this growth was recorded after the beginning of the financial crash.

By autumn 2015, total EM corporate debt had reached $23.7 trillion, 90% of total EM GDP.[280] In 2015 Chinese non-financial companies alone accounted for more than half of total EM corporate debt, with their $12.5 trillion debt to banks and bondholders costing them an estimated $812bn in annual interest payments.[281] According to the *FT*, this is "significantly more than China's projected total industrial profits this year", and amounts in real terms to $1.35 trillion[282] once account is made of factory gate prices, which had fallen in 42 consecutive months to September 2015 and were by then declining by around 6% a year.[283] Deflation in producer prices saw real interest rates in China rise sharply, reaching 10.8% in March 2015.[284]

Chinese firms are far from alone in suffering from falling product prices: by 2015, nine of the top ten emerging markets were experiencing falling producer prices, with only Indonesia bucking the trend.[285] As Smith says:

"Rising debts and falling product prices are a fatal combination that threaten a wave of corporate bankruptcies, with the potential to torpedo the banking systems in the affected countries. The IMF warns that 'shocks to the corporate sector could quickly spill over to the financial sector and generate a vicious cycle', especially in those EMs where loans to corporations form a high proportion of bank assets. Indicating the global extent of the phenomenon, the most-exposed banking systems, excluding China, are to be found in Turkey, the Philippines, Chile, and Bulgaria."

The extent of this rising debt and the emerging crisis it promises underpins the crisis of imperialism and enables us to appreciate the likelihood that the next global crash will be even – considerably – worse than the one that rocked the world in 2008.

6. The final contradiction?

> "The worker becomes an ever cheaper commodity the more commodities he creates. With the increasing value of the world of things proceeds in direct proportion the devaluation of the world of men."[286]
>
> Marx

A report by a Canadian investment bank, Macquarie, goes so far as to say that, unlike what it calls the first three industrial revolutions, which "aimed to supplement" human workers, the fourth "aims to replace humans completely", making it "intrinsically far more disruptive".[287] In a seemingly Marxist explanation, the report puts the global economic crisis down to "declining returns on humans", warning investors of "deglobalisation", intensifying trade wars and a booming "lumpenproletariat".[288]

If it is possible and true that the automation revolution aims to "replace human workers completely", then it inadvertently aims to cut off the key social relation in the process of capital accumulation, ie the exploited human labour that goes into commodity production. Machinery cannot produce surplus value because, unlike workers, it cannot sell labour power – it cannot be exploited. "Declining returns on humans" is therefore an apt diagnosis, and once again shows, to the chagrin of all its would-be grave-diggers both on the Left as well as the Right, that the labour theory of value remains correct and, indeed, more relevant than ever.

As we have seen, when labour-saving technology reduces total socially necessary labour time, there is a relative fall in the value contained in the total value of commodities, ie less value per commodity, despite the fact that the rate of exploitation has increased; ie, that each worker is now giving the capitalist more surplus labour time and therefore producing more surplus value relative to their necessary labour.

The total automation of productive labour would therefore make commodities free of exchange-value. In the meantime, the commodities that are no longer produced by human labour will still command a share of the overall mass of surplus value, but at an ever-decreasing rate.

The more abundantly something is made, the less profit it contains. In recent decades, we have witnessed an accelerating historical trend of the price of manufacturing prices and technological goods towards zero – despite the inflation that erodes the purchasing power of currency. Sony's Playstation 4 (PS4), a home games console released in 2013, was twice as powerful as the PS3 (launched in 2006) but, at $400, cost $200 less. That was 1/100,000th of the cost of the world's leading supercomputer in 1996, the ASCI Red ($55m) which the PS3 matched for processing power.[289] Another recent example: the price of photovoltaic (PV) cells, the main technology for generating solar power, has fallen by 20% every time capacity has doubled over the past 60 years. When the technology was deployed for the first time aboard NASA's Vanguard 1 satellite in 1958, each panel was able to generate a maximum half a watt of energy at a cost of many thousands of dollars each. By the mid-1970s, that figure had fallen to $100 per watt, and in 2016, to 50 cents. This tallies with the Henderson Curve, the principle calculated by banking consultant Bruce Henderson that the cost of manufacturing tends to fall by around 20% every time capacity doubles.[290]

As Grossman says:

"As a consequence of this fundamentally dual structure [of the commodity], capitalist production is characterised by insoluble conflicts. Irremediable systemic convulsions necessarily arise from this dual character, from the immanent contradiction between value and use-value, between profitability and productivity, between limited possibilities for valorisation and the unlimited development of the productive forces. This necessarily leads to overaccumulation and insufficient valorisation, therefore to breakdown, to a final catastrophe for the entire system."[291]

It is worth quoting a passage at length from Ernest Mandel's *Late Capitalism*[292] here to drive home the point:

"The following numerical examples show how serious are the consequences of this tendency for the quantity of value-creating labour to diminish as a result of automation. As will be seen, it profoundly affects the ability of late capitalism to halt the fall in the rate of profit by raising the rate of surplus value and its ability to prevent the intensification of social tensions by increasing real wages. Let four successive cyclical peak years be called A, B, C, and D, and the distance between them approximately 10 years. In the starting year of our comparison let the total number of man-hours worked by the productive labourers in both Departments together be 10 billion (approximately 5 million productive workers working 2,000 hours annually, or 6 million working 1,666 hours annually). Let the rate of surplus-value be 100%, ie 5 billion hours are devoted to the production of surplus-value. As a result of increased employment despite growing automation, in the year B 12 billion instead of 10 billion hours of productive labour are expended. We assume that the rate of surplus value now rises from 100% to 150% (instead of using half of their labour time for the production of the equivalent of their real wages, the productive workers now use only two-fifths for this purpose). The mass of surplus value rises from the product of 5 billion to the product of 7.2 billion working hours, ie it rises by 44%. Since the productive workers henceforth produce the equivalent of their wages in 4.8 instead of 5 billion working hours, a total increase of 30% in real wages of all workers (a modest annual growth rate of 2.6%) would necessitate a 35% increase in the productivity of labour in Department II [commodity production]. This remains in the framework of the possible; it indeed accords with the development of the last 25 years.

"In year C of our comparison, automation has already halted the rise in the mass of employment or of the man-hours worked. It remains constant at 12 billion. For example, in order to make up for the increase in the organic composition of capital (which has risen by 50% between A and B and between B and C) the rate of surplus value would have to rise once more from 150% to 233.33%, ie instead of disposing of 4 working hours in 10 to produce the equivalent of his real wages, the productive worker now has a mere 3 out of 10 at his disposal for this purpose. The total mass of surplus value has now risen to a product of 8.4 billion hours, ie by a whole 16.6%. If the workers, however, are to be able to achieve a further 30% increase in real consumption (in the mass of products or use-values) in the 3.6 billion working hours still available to them for the production of the equivalent of their consumer goods, as compared to the 4.8 billion working hours of ten years previously, the productivity of labour in Department II would have to be increased by 70%, ie an annual growth rate of 5.4%. This is still just on the edge of the possible.

"Let us now consider the fourth year, D. In order to neutralise the rise in the organic composition of capital (approximately 70% since the year C), the rate of surplus value would now have to go up from 233.33% to 400%, ie the productive worker would now be left with only 1 working hour in 5 to produce the equivalent of his wage. Let us say, however, that automation has reduced the total number of man-hours worked from 12 billion to 10 billion. The absolute mass of surplus value is now equivalent to 8 billion working hours, or in other words, *despite a massive increase in the rate of surplus-value*, from 233% to 400%, *the mass has declined*. For the mass of surplus-value to remain at least the same, the rate of surplus value would have to be 525% instead of 400%, so that a mere 1.6 billion working hours would remain for the production of the equivalent of real wages. But even if the rate of surplus value 'only' rose to 400%, a further 30% increase in real wages over ten years would necessitate that the mass of products made in the 2 billion working hours in the year D increase by 30% over the mass of products produced in 3.6 billion working hours in the year C, ie an increase of 140% in the productivity of labour in Department II: the realisation of an average growth rate of 9.1% needed to achieve this goal would seem to be impossible. This would still be much less than the annual average necessary to guarantee a 30% increase in real wages by the year D with only 1.6 billion available man-hours, ie where the mass of surplus value remains constant. In this case, the productivity of labour would have to rise, in the course of the decade, by as much as 192.5%, ie an absolute unattainable growth of 11.4%.

"The conclusion is obvious: with increasing automation, increasing organic composition of capital and the onset of a fall in the total man-hours worked by productive labourers, it is impossible in the long run seriously to continue to increase real wages and at the same time maintain a constant mass of surplus value. One of the two quantities will diminish. Since under normal conditions, ie without fascism or war, a significant decline in real wages can be excluded, there emerges *an historical crisis of the valorisation of capital* and an inevitable decline, first in the mass of surplus value, and hence there follows an abrupt fall in the average rate of profit. In our numerical example, even if real wages were to stagnate in the year D while the mass of surplus value fell from 8.4 billion to 8 billion working hours, this would still mean that the productivity of labour would have increased by 80% (an annual rate of increase of 6%). If the mass of surplus value remained constant as well as real wages, labour productivity would have increased by 125%, ie an unobtainable growth rate of 8.4% annually."[293]

7. Factory fragmentation

"In the manufacture stage, the worker was still required to possess skill and a knowledge of the tricks of the trade. The machine simplified even these functions. The machine warps man in a way, adapting him to the performance of monotonous mechanical work and making him a slave. In all logic, it should be the other way round."[294]

Volkov

In *Capital*, Marx quotes Scottish Professor Andrew Ure, calling his work "the classical expression of the spirit of the factory". Ure attained infamy for an experiment in which he sent electric bolts through the body of an executed criminal, Matthew Clydesdale – a skilled weaver. At the time of this experiment, 1818, the General Association of Operative Weavers had been declared illegal.

In 1820 the organisation led a revolt which was crushed and its leaders were publicly executed and ritually dismembered. Ure became obsessed with a desire to create an obedient workforce and allay his fear of militant trade unionism. He was unable to turn Clydesdale into an enslaved zombie, but "the fingers moved nimbly like those of a violin performer".[295]

As Jeff Sparrow writes in an article for *Counterpunch*,

"the professor thus made a dead weaver bend to his will in a fashion that the Scottish industrialists were manifestly unable to achieve with Clydesdale's living comrades. Galvanisation itself might have proved a failure, but the possibility that science might transform recalcitrant workers into obedient automatons remained alluring."[296]

Ure required a new method. In 1985 he published *The Philosophy of Manufactures*. Ure argued that technology provides industrialists with a crucial weapon against their employees, since "when capital enlists science into her service, the refractory hand of labour will always be taught docility".

Machines sped up productivity, but also broke down the artisanal skills that gave workers independence. "On the handicraft plan," Ure explained,

> "labour more or less skilled, was usually the most expensive element of production – *materiam superabat optis*;[297] but on the automatic plan, skilled labour gets progressively superseded, and will, eventually, be replaced by mere overlookers of machines. The principle of the factory system then is to substitute mechanical science for hand skill, and the partition of a process into its essential constituents, for the division or graduation of labour among artisans."[298]

The machine itself is a metonym for the factory, which, Ure says, should be understood as a "vast automaton, composed of various mechanical and intellectual organs, acting in an uninterrupted concert for the production of a common object, all of them being subordinated to a self-regulating moving force". As Sparrow says: "It's an image of the entire workforce recast as Clydesdale's corpse, labouring as directed by the galvanic power of the owner."

Ure hailed the mill owners who employed a spinning contraption, the 'Iron Man', "a creation destined to restore order". In his book, Ure writes: "The news of this Herculean prodigy spread dismay through the union, and even long before it left its cradle, so to speak, it strangled the Hydra of misrule."

But, Sparrow points out, the consequences were double-edged:

> "The transformation of skilled weavers into automatons broke down the barriers of sectionalism, laying the basis for workers everywhere to recognise each other as equivalents rather than seeing only isolated practitioners of particular skills. As representatives of a distinctive craft, the weavers were destroyed. But as members of a global working class, they arose in an infinitely more powerful incarnation."

Taylorisation and Fordism

The process of deskilling continued apace during the 19th century with the emergence of Taylorisation, which is defined as "a set of principles governing the design of jobs which entail the separation of mental from manual labour, subdivision of tasks, deskilling, close managerial control of work effort and incentive wage payments". This meant breaking down work into its constituent parts as various "physical motions" which could be precisely timed. Frederick Winslow Taylor's "scientific management" of work was intended to make trade unions obsolete as co-operation in the workplace would be ensured through the application of scientific principles and "each worker pursuing their individual self-interest". Mind-numbing assembly-line work – reducing workers to appendages of machines; automatons performing one repetitive task – developed and patented by Ransom E Olds, was the natural successor at the beginning of the 20th century, later turned into the *moving* assembly line by Henry Ford.

The postmodernists of neoliberalism would have it that the rise of white collar work – the managerial apparatus of administration, supervision and planning that in reality has been increasingly required by capital – ushered in an era of skilled and satisfying mental work. But a survey in 2013 found that, across the world, only 13% of people consider their jobs to be satisfying.[299] What is now recognised as a "mental health epidemic" – with *The Lancet* medical journal declaring in October 2018 that *every* country in the world was experiencing a crisis of "monumental suffering" – only serves to show that, on the whole, the opposite is true, that the monotony and alienation of Taylorist authority persists, and has, if anything, intensified.

The 21st century Ures are still motivated to subjugate the workforce. The neo-Luddite David Noble's work on numerically controlled machine tools – technology central to the vision of workerless factories – argues that the drive to automate machining cannot be explained solely by the requirements of a purely technical efficiency but is marked by the managerial imperative to gain control over the shop floor, and in particular to break the power of skilled unionised machinists. Noble shows that this has been demonstrated by the suppression of technological options that would allow workers some control over newly automated processes. As Nick Dyer-Witherford explains in his book *Cyber Marx*:

> "Even when this participation might have improved the operations of the system – by allowing for revision of programmed instructions according to circumstances – the managerial decision to eliminate the human element prevailed. The whole thrust of capitalism's use of information technology in the workplace is, according to Noble, fundamentally anti-human, predicated on a model of 'progress without people'."[300]

A famous example took place recently. Asked about taxi monopoly Uber's long-term viability when so many of its employees were expressing dissatisfaction about the job and the company, its chief product officer responded: "Well, we are just going to replace them with robots."

It is a mistake, however, to say that worker militancy is the primary motive force behind innovation. While there is a dialectical relationship, the initial impetus comes from the demands of capital accumulation, which compel the capitalist to cut their outlay on wages in the first place, and in turn the workers to fight back. Marx says that capitalism continually strives to push wages down towards zero:

"The zero of [the labourers'] cost is therefore a limit in a mathematical sense, always beyond reach, although we can always approximate more and more nearly to it. The constant tendency of capital is to force the cost of labour back towards this zero."[301]

As Grossman says:

"In reality the constant devaluation of labour power accomplished by continual cuts in wages runs up against insuperable barriers. Every major cut in its conditions of life would inevitably drive the working class to rebellion. In this way, and through the very mechanism that is internal to it, the capitalist system moves incessantly towards its final end, dominated by the 'law of entropy of capitalist accumulation'."[302]

8. Rescuing Marx's 'The Fragment on Machines'

"It is clear how absurd Lauderdale is when he wants to make fixed capital into an independent source of value, independent of labour time."[303]

Marx

In a remarkable passage known as "The Fragment on Machines", written in *Grundrisse* 160 years ago, Marx – having witnessed the development of semi-automatic factory machines – appears to anticipate the eventual rise of full automation and the accompanying tendency towards the abolition of profit, speaking of the "value-creating power of the individual labour capacity [becoming] an infinitesimal, vanishing magnitude".[304] He writes that,

"... once adopted into the production process of capital, the means of labour passes through different metamorphoses, whose culmination is the *machine*, or rather, an *automatic system of machinery* (system of machinery: the *automatic* one is merely its most complete, adequate form, and alone transforms machinery into a system) set in motion by an automaton, a moving power that moves itself; this automaton consisting of numerous mechanical and intellectual organs, so that the workers themselves are cast merely as its conscious linkages."[305]

He could almost be writing about AI when he says

"... it is the machine which possesses skill and strength in place of the worker, is itself the virtuoso, with a soul of its own in the mechanical laws acting through it; and it consumes coal, oil etc ... just as the worker consumes food, to keep up its perpetual motion...."[306] The accumulation of knowledge and of skill, of the general productive forces of the social brain, is thus absorbed into capital, as opposed to labour, and hence appears as an attribute of capital."[307]

Anticipating the ultimate contradiction of capital accumulation, he says:

"To the degree that labour time – the mere quantity of labour – is posited by capital as the sole determinant element, to that degree does direct labour and its quantity disappear as the determinant principle of production – of the creation of use-values – and is reduced both quantitatively, to a smaller proportion, and qualitatively, as an, of course, indispensable but subordinate moment, compared to general scientific labour, technological application of natural sciences, on one side, and to the general productive force arising from social combination in total production on the other side – a combination which appears as a natural fruit of social labour (although it is a historic product). Capital thus works towards its own dissolution as the form dominating production."[308]

And:

"As soon as labour in the direct form[309] has ceased to be the great wellspring of wealth, labour time ceases and must cease to be its measure. Capital itself is the moving contradiction, [in] that it presses to reduce labour time to a minimum, while it posits labour time, on the other side, as *sole measure* [our emphasis] and source of wealth. Hence it diminishes labour time in the necessary form so as to increase it in the superfluous form; hence posits the superfluous in growing measure as a condition – question of life or death – for the necessary. On the one side, then, it calls to life all the powers of science and of nature, as of social combination and of social intercourse, in order to make the creation of wealth independent (relatively) of the labour time employed on it. On the other side, it wants to use labour time as the measuring rod for the giant social forces thereby created, and to confine them within the limits required to maintain the already created value as value. Forces of production and social relations – two different sides of the development of the social individual – appear to capital as mere means, and are merely means for it to produce on its limited foundation. In fact, however, they are the material conditions to blow this foundation sky-high."[310]

It would be at best imprecise and at worst a fatal theoretical blunder to conclude that automation *per se* is abolishing profit. As we have established, employment and technological progress are determined by the needs of capital at a given stage of accumulation. To say that capital is tending towards abolishing itself, via the abolition of exchange-value, is therefore more accurate, and this is merely expressed through the second industrial revolution and its tendency towards its logical endpoint, ie the complete automation of productive labour. But, as we shall see, Marx does not say or suggest that this means capitalism automatically dissolves into socialism.

Misreadings and distortions

"The Fragment" has been – wilfully or not – invariably misinterpreted by various left-wing theorists. Italian Antonio Negri speciously described it as "Marx beyond Marx" while his fellow autonomist Paolo Virno claimed that its ideas "are not present in any of his other writings and in fact seem alternative to the habitual formula".[311]

In his 2015 book *Postcapitalism: A Guide To Our Future*, British social democrat Paul Mason follows this train of thought. "In the 20th century, the Left had seen state planning as the route out of capitalism," he says, but in "The Fragment", which was not published in Germany until 1939 or translated into English until 1973, "we are confronted with a different model of transition: a knowledge-based route out of capitalism… [which] collapses because it cannot exist alongside shared knowledge [which is reducing the costs of production inputs towards zero].[312] The class struggle becomes the struggle to become human and educated during one's free time."[313]

What this nebulous "knowledge-based route out of capitalism" concretely entails is not explained at all clearly. Mason speaks of a "conflict that results in the abolition of the market system and its replacement by postcapitalism"[314] but does not specify if this conflict is between people, classes or mechanisms. We're told that "postcapitalism could take many different forms" and that "we'll know if it's happened if a large number of goods become cheap or free, but people go on producing them irrespective of market forces".[315] Socialism will emerge without anyone even realising – just like that!

Not only does Marx give up the class struggle, he supposedly replaces the proletariat with 'the general intellect', a term Mason interchanges with 'the networked individual'. Because technology is blurring the distinction between work and leisure, we are required to create value across our whole lives, says Mason, not just in the workplace. True enough. "This gives us multiple economic personalities, which is the economic base on which a new kind of person, with multiple selves, has emerged. It is this new kind of person, the networked individual, who is the bearer of the postcapitalist society that could now emerge."[316] Mason recognises that people are having to work harder and longer but fails to see this as their increasing proletarianisation.

Marx says machines are

> "organs of the human brain, created by the human hand; the power of knowledge, objectified. The development of fixed capital indicates to what degree general social knowledge has become a direct force of production, and to what degree, hence, the conditions of the process of social life itself have come under the control of the general intellect and been transformed in accordance with it."[317]

Mason thinks general social knowledge has come under the control of 'the general intellect', but they are one and the same thing. The general intellect has not replaced the proletariat.

Mason wonders why Marx "did not pursue this idea more widely? Why does the general intellect disappear as a concept except on this one unpublished page? Why does this model of the market mechanism being dissolved by social knowledge get lost in the writing of *Capital*?"[318] The "obvious" answer, he claims, is because "capitalism itself at the time did not bear out the proposition". And so Marx "retreated"[319] from the ideas set out in "The Fragment", and the 20th century revolutionaries who followed his teachings in *Capital* – "a doctrine of state socialism and crisis-driven transition"[320] – were therefore misled by Marx himself, explaining, for Mason's money, their failures and defeats, and justifying his fantasy of a parliamentary road out of capitalism.

"As a theory of crisis, Marxism is flawed,"[321] claims Mason, who decries Bolshevism as the "forced-march abolition of the market" – God forbid! Marx apparently underestimated capitalism's ability to "mutate".[322] This mutation is "the exhaustion of an entire structure – of business models, skill-sets, markets, currencies, technologies – and its rapid replacement by a new one". But what is this surface level phenomena caused by? The answer, of course, is the need to rationalise, to sufficiently devalue capital and labour power. The idea that Marx's model "could not accommodate structural adaptation" is a laughably arrogant attempt by Mason at claiming to have corrected Marx's theory. Grossman, who was at pains to show the Marxists of his day that their supposed improvements on Marx were also wrong, states that crises "are only surmounted through … a structural reorganisation of the economy",[323] with capitalists being forced to cut production costs, find new, cheaper sources of raw materials, and so on. Grossman says that "Marx repeatedly draws attention to the elastic power of capital".[324]

Mason's confusion becomes self-parodic when he says: "The doom premonitions of the Marxist Left in the 1890s were proved false. They would first have to live through a massive upswing of capitalism, then through chaos and collapse in the years 1914-21."[325] Presumably the chaos and collapse of a horrific world war – that indeed resulted in the consummation of Russian capitalism's breakdown in the form of the first consolidated proletarian revolution – do not fit Mason's definition of doom!

Capital, lest we forget, is an exposition of capitalism's historical transience. In it, as we have seen, Marx speaks of the "ever-decreasing" role of variable capital.[326] Does this not imply a fall towards zero? In volume III[327] Marx anticipates developments that "put the majority of the population out of [work]" and therefore "cause a revolution".[328]

But perhaps Marx is incorrect because he declares "the majority of the population" to be the decisive revolutionary force, rather than free information! Marx's apparent retreat has been imagined. At no point does Marx suggest in "The Fragment" that automation or social knowledge provide a "different" transition out of capitalism. Mason should read the text again more carefully. Marx explicitly states that "the workers" – not the general intellect or the networked individual! – must seize the means of production in order to realise the new social relations that the productive forces demand:

"[Capital's] tendency [is] always, on the one side, *to create disposable time, on the other, to convert it into surplus labour*. If it succeeds too well at the first, then it suffers from surplus production, and then necessary labour is interrupted, because *no surplus labour can be realised by capital*. The more this contradiction develops, the more does it become evident that the growth of the forces of production can no longer be bound up with the appropriation of alien labour, but that *the mass of workers must themselves appropriate their own surplus labour.*"[329] [Our emphasis.]

Nothing in "The Fragment" goes against Marx's theory of breakdown and revolution. Marx explicitly writes that as value produced from surplus labour time diminishes "production based on exchange-value *breaks down*". [Our emphasis.] Mason's claim that 20th century revolutionaries were somehow incorrectly led away from reformism is nonsense. He is not, as he imagines, backed up by Marx.

In *Fully Automated Luxury Communism*, Aaron Bastani falls into the same sort of idealism. Bastani does a good job of showing that manufacturing costs are falling not only faster than bourgeois economists have been able to anticipate but rapidly towards zero. We have already seen how this is happening in particular with regards to 3-D printing.

Perhaps the best example is in Human Genome Sequencing, which, in line with socialist principles, is set to revolutionise healthcare by making it preventative. "It took 13 years and billions of dollars to sequence the first human genome. By 2007 the cost of performing the same process for a single individual had fallen to around $1m, a far steeper performance in the price curve than any other information technology," says Bastani. "By January 2015, sequencing a genome had fallen to $1,000 and two years later the biotech company Illumina unveiled a machine expected to do the job for under $100." While it took 13 years to map the first human genome, Ilumina's machine performs the same task in under an hour. The cost of sequencing a genome has fallen by a factor of between five and 10 times a year. It could cost as little as $30 by the late 2020s, although according to Raymond McCauley, who worked at Illumina, it will cost "as little as flushing a toilet" by 2022. The cost of food grown in labs is also plummeting towards zero (see chapter 16). Because technological capacity tends to double from an already doubled base, technological prices are falling evermore rapidly, and are on course to close in on zero around mid-century. Nobody reading Bastani's book, therefore, can honestly disagree with his conclusion that capitalism is "passing away".

A good description of technological development and the effect on prices does not explain accurate economic theory, however, and Bastani's is some way off. Firstly, he contends that competition is the imperative behind innovation. While it plays an important role, we have shown that the primary driving force is the need to valorise capital, and that intensified competition stems from the same factor.

He then asserts that "information is the basis of value under modern capitalism" and that because information is becoming free, capitalism's ability to reproduce itself is disappearing.[330] Such an extraordinary claim deserves a rigorous theoretical explanation, but none is forthcoming. Bastani just quotes Peter Drucker, a theorist of management, who said in 1993, "that knowledge has become the resource, instead of a resource, is what makes our society postcapitalist";[331] and Paul Romer, former chief economist of the World Bank, who defined technological advance as "an improvement in the instructions for mixing together raw materials", meaning, says Bastani, that "value increasingly arises from the instructions for materials rather than from the materials themselves".[332] When did *exchange*-value ever arise from materials? It arises from the exploitation of labour. Other than that, like Mason, Bastani just points out that digital software can be copied for nothing, that Wikipedia has made physical encyclopaedias all but redundant, and so on.

As we have seen, Marx did say that the more developed fixed capital becomes the more "general social knowledge has become a direct force of production", and Bastani does quote "The Fragment", where Marx says that, "the creation of real wealth comes less to depend on labour time and on the labour employed than on the power of the agencies set in motion during labour time, whose 'powerful effectiveness' … depends rather on the general state of science and on the progress of technology, or the application of this science to production". Certainly then, information has become "a direct force of production", but exchange-value is still only produced "during labour time". Under capitalism, higher quality information contributes to increasing the rate of exploitation.

Bastani does not once mention the labour theory of value and does not therefore explain why information, or at least copying it, has become free, ie that, thanks to the digital revolution – a feature of the second industrial revolution – it no longer requires any necessary labour time.

Because Bastani does not base his analysis on the labour theory of value, he goes on to give a confused, vague explanation of capitalism's end: a transitional combination of voting through the capitalist state, "municipal protectionism", Universal Basic Services, "socialised finance" and "worker-owned businesses". At some point the state suddenly becomes a "postcapitalist state" but conveniently he does not outline how.

He cites Wlodzimierz Brus and Kazimierz Laski, followers of the "Marxist-Keynesian" Michael Kalecki, Soviet 'reformers' who claimed that under 'market socialism', "publicly-owned firms would have to be autonomous". Such thinking led not to communism but the return of capitalism, plunging living standards and millions of excess deaths. Like them, Bastani is advocating a fantastical capitalist road to communism, without socialism.

Although Bastani recognises that the system is beset by crisis roughly every ten years, his vision of capitalism's incremental end can only be based on the theory of harmonious capital accumulation. We just have to wait for falling prices to reach zero and then we have communism. That capitalism will break down before then (see chapter 10) has not occurred to him.

Furthermore, his capitalist road is an imperialist one, dependent on the accelerated plunder of the 'Global South' he purports to care so much about.[333] Extraction in the neo-colonies involves the forcible displacement of local communities and, invariably, proxy wars over the control of resources – the expanded extraction of which will accelerate rising emissions (see chapter 16).

Although we have no problem with the rhetorical description of communism as fully automated luxury for all[334] – communism has always been destined to be as such; and the need to debunk the myth that it means 'poverty for all' is obvious – his use of the slogan is empty. It may as well be 'accelerated imperialism and extinction for all'.

Yes, imperialism is the final stage of capitalism before socialism, but that does not mean we support it. Socialists in an imperialist country such as Britain should be demanding the cancellation of all debts 'owed' to us by the neo-colonies and the withdrawal of British-based multinationals so that the land and productive forces are returned and countries can realise real self-determination.

9. The fantasy of fully automated capitalism

"Capitalism is incompatible with automation in the whole of industry and agriculture, because this no longer allows the creation of surplus value or valorisation of capital. It is hence impossible for automation to spread to the entire realm of production in the age of late capitalism."[335]

Mandel

Automation is not wiping out the source of profit overnight, of course. Like all technological advancements it is having some temporary counteracting effects on the breakdown tendency. Human labour still goes into making robots and computers, including and especially the human labour needed to extract the raw materials for their construction in countries where child soldiers multiply faster than androids. Some jobs are harder to automate than others. Many will be unaffected in the short to medium term, and robots replacing unproductive labour will save costs for capitalists without affecting the production of surplus value.

Automation is obviously increasing the multiplicity of use-values tremendously – brand new commodities that have been created by the needs of the new technology or that were not possible to make under the old method of production. This creates new jobs, whether in services or production.[336]

The demand for living labour to extract and make the components that go into robotics and the new use-values they spawn counteract decay – but only for a time. Eventually new cycles of overaccumulation make automating those jobs necessary as well, at least if a cheaper alternative source of labour cannot be found, and found where capital needs it.

The question is: are we already approaching that stage? In June 2017, McKinsey Global Institute Director James Manyika said: "Find a factory *anywhere in the world* [our emphasis] built in the past five years – not many people work there."

As we have seen, instead of creating more jobs in the developing nations, there is a trend away from 'outsourcing' towards 'insourcing' – building automated factories inside the imperialist nations that create few jobs.

Capital ideally seeks the largest possible base of surplus value, which means it actually desires full employment in commodity-producing sectors. Because of the system's inherent deficiencies, though, this is only possible at an *early* stage of accumulation.

As we have seen, levels of employment are determined not by labour-saving technology but by the needs of capital at a given stage of accumulation – if it is unprofitable to invest in a company it is unprofitable to employ the labour that would run it. If a company goes bust because low profits force investors to pull their funding, workers lose their jobs regardless of whether the company planned to automate them. A boss operating in a country with weak labour rights can sack all of their workers and bring in cheaper replacements. If long-term profits are going to be higher by replacing a given number of workers with innovative machinery that will raise productivity, that is what determines the decision to do so; and so on.

We are in a *late* stage of accumulation, the greatest level of accumulation and overaccumulation ever, and therefore we are facing the greatest ever crisis of capitalism. *That* is why unemployment, underemployment and in-work poverty are going to continue to rise acutely. This given stage of accumulation requires that increasing amounts of capital lie dormant, waiting for profitable conditions to return, with surplus labour increasing alongside surplus capital.

The sort of boom in use-values required to resolve the crisis *as it currently stands* is not possible – it would only be possible at an early stage of accumulation, in a scenario like the post-1945 productivity boom, after a world war that had reset the value of capital. As the Macquarie paper says, while investors "might argue that… higher value jobs will eventually emerge… eventually could take a very long time".

Lilley in *Automation and Social Progress* wrote that the *rate* of technical progress "gathered speed" in capitalism's early days "of the later 17th century and early 18th,[337] and constantly – apart from occasional slumps – accelerated until the 1890s, far surpassing anything in previous history". But it "fell away dramatically after the 1890s", as capitalism grew into its monopolistic stage, with a revival seen "only in the extraordinary circumstances of WWII".[338]

The rate of technological progress, like that of profit, goes up and down for numerous reasons. Thanks to the breakthrough of the internet and digital, it enjoyed a big upswing in the 1990s.

As Michael Elsby has shown, however, "investment-specific technological change" has been marked by a "considerable slowdown" since 2000.[339] This is despite the decline in labour's share of compensation and ongoing advances that produce myriad new use-values in gadgetry and computing, which give most people the impression, helped by the commercial propaganda of advertising (the costs of which are passed on to consumers!), that the rate of technical progress is always rising. Like capital accumulation, technology may be advancing and accelerating in absolute terms – because its reproduction always begins again from a higher base – but the rate of advancement is slowing down. The opposite only *appears* to be true. Silicon Valley has constructed quite the shiny facade around capitalism's rotting interior.

Capitalism's survival has therefore *massively slowed down* the development of automation, exposing the idealism of bourgeois economists in the process. In 1957, German 'Marxist' Fritz Sternberg claimed that the US under capitalism would seamlessly become a fully automated, classless society by 1975![340]

In the same year, Lilley made a rough calculation – based on the rapid *rate* of improving living standards in the Soviet Union – that if Britain were socialist, the development of automation would reduce the working week there to 25 hours by 1990, 12 hours by 2000, and six hours by 2010.[341] If Britain developed even faster than the Soviet Union, as would have been likely due to its 250-year industrial head start, a Britain that became socialist in 1965 could have had a working week of six hours by 1995.

This squandered history is profoundly depressing – there can be little doubt that, had a world revolution followed Russia's, as Lenin expected, we would already be living in a fully automated communist society.

Capitalism's education problem
The problem of capitalist development is also expressed through its inability to educate and train enough highly skilled workers, a situation which has persisted and grown despite the bourgeoisie's genuine desire to solve it. As Volkov explains:

"The more far-sighted among the bourgeois economists and sociologists have long been aware that in the scientific and technological revolution which we are now witnessing, automation requires an increasingly higher level of culture among even the rank and file workers and that the production of material wealth is becoming more and more dependent on the spiritual wealth of the members of society and on the level of their intellectual development. They are beginning to realise that education of the mass of workers has become *an economic necessity*.

"The well-known American economist Leonard Silk notes that scientific and technological progress exerts its influence on people chiefly in two ways: a) it creates an enormous demand for people able to use their brains and b) leads to greater increases in production than in population, thus solving the problem of the satisfaction of man's physical needs. He stresses that the growing demand for educated people is already evident in all spheres of American life.

"But it is a demand that capitalist society is unable to satisfy on the necessary scale. Bourgeois ideologists are compelled to admit the lack of skilled workers, technicians and engineers capable of operating the latest automatic equipment. As a result, the productive forces of capitalist society run into a *deep-going contradiction between the level of technology and that of the working population*....[342]

"The ideologists of capitalism would show as little concern for the spiritual condition of the exploited masses as they did in the past century if it were not for the fact that their profits have become greatly dependent on it. Nowadays, *the productive forces have reached such a stage when all further development requires the practice of genuine humanism*. [But] to fulfill this demand, capitalist society would have to cease."[343]

How can a country be truly rich when it is compelled to forego educated specialists, the most important factor in economic and social development? The problem was recognised by the British even during capitalism's post-war 'golden years'. Lilley quotes a Professor TU Matthews, who put it bluntly at the Margate Conference of the Institution of Production Engineers in 1955:

"Scientific discovery and invention has far outstripped the assimilation capacity of most British industries for new ideas, new materials and new automatic control equipment and means of production.... Automation will not in this country come as an avalanche but by easy stages proceeding from the automobile industry and gradually extending to other mass production industries. The reason that it will be relatively slow arises from the fact that there are neither the machine-toll manufacturers to build the machines nor the specialist engineers, mechanics and technicians to man the factories."[344]

Lilley adds: "We have not got anything like enough scientists, production engineers and engineering technologists to enable us to develop automation (or industrial technique in general).... Nor is it a specifically British problem." He cites a US Congressional subcommittee naming a shortage of scientists, technicians and skilled labour. "This inability to provide enough highly trained people turns out to be another of the general failures of capitalist economies. Britain's position, as the oldest of them, is worse than most; but the trouble is universal."[345] He goes on:

"For every million of the population, Britain annually turns out 57 engineers of university degree standard. Corresponding figures for other countries are: France, 70; Switzerland, 82; West Germany, 86; USA, 136. Every important capitalist country produces more than we do. But even the US figures are far exceeded by those of the USSR, with its 280 engineering graduates each year per million people. In addition, it is now usually agreed that the four or five year courses of the USSR give higher standards than our normal three years."[346]

Volkov also contrasted the problems faced under capitalism with the Soviet Union, where

"scientific and technological progress, particularly automation, leads to a far-reaching change in the relation of the productive and unproductive spheres. The proportion of people employed in the unproductive branches of the economy went up approximately 50% between 1941 and 1962. However, despite the common tendency of the unproductive sphere to grow, the changes in the structure of the labour force in the USSR and the USA are essentially different.

"Whereas in the USA the increase of the unproductive sphere mostly occurs in the financial and state apparatus, in the USSR this growth is chiefly observed in science, the health services, art and education, ie in branches that serve man's needs directly. In 1962, the number of people employed in education was twice that of 1940, and more than 150% higher in the health services and 570% higher in science, whereas the number of people employed in the state and economic machinery went down by half a million.

"In the US the picture is quite different: between 1940 and 1958 the number of civil servants of the federal administration almost doubled, while the development of public health, social security and education fell far short of the nation's needs. Whereas the state-machinery and the advertising and financial agencies are being expanded out of all proportion, the development of branches vital to society is mainly attained through the pressure exercised by the working people and the demands exacted by technological progress."[347]

The idea that socialism is more 'bureaucratic' than capitalism, even in a country historically lagging in industrial development and therefore democratic experience, is clearly a lie.

Under-utilisation and absolute limits

Even current estimates of the ongoing development and implementation of automation are bound to be overly-optimistic. Raising the capital necessary for such a high organic composition is increasingly difficult. Nothing else can explain static productivity growth at a time of such extraordinary technological capacity.[348]

This ongoing reality foils Turner's claim that "the productivity question has been solved", or that it is being solved, by automation. Like any other technological advancement under capitalism its development is interrupted and slowed by economic crises (not to mention that overproduction and uneven distribution persist and worsen). It doesn't matter what form of technology is producing commodities, if a company goes bust, production stops.

"Competition entails an enormous squandering of the productive forces through the struggle for sales outlets, the overproduction of commodities on one side and unemployment on the other," says Grossman. "After the war underutilisation of capacity became a general phenomenon in the leading capitalist countries. This is the celebrated 'regulation' of production by the cartels and trusts – not a planned calculation and distribution of production according to needs, but restrictions on the utilisation of productive capacity in order to push up the level of prices and profits."[349] This wasteful underutilisation is unaffected by technical capability because it is determined by the capitalist relations of production.

Bob Colwell, director of DARPA (the Defense Advanced Research Projects Agency) – an arm of the US Department of Defense – has predicted the end of Moore's Law, not necessarily because of physical but economic limits:

> "[It takes] huge amounts to build the fab plants, and yet more... to pay for the design teams to design new chips.[350] Intel makes these investments,

which are in the billions [of dollars], because they expect to reap way more billions in profits in the following years.

"But if there is doubt that those profits will arrive, and possibly if they just doubt they can come up with the necessary silicon improvements, they may not want to make the investment at all. Should a major player like Intel make such a call, that would effectively end Moore's Law all by itself, because then the various companies that make the super expensive tools for chip production will themselves not make the investments needed to keep Moore's Law alive."

Monopoly capital limits technological development at the best of times, because its domination of the world market restricts competition. A company that introduces a new commodity (or a new method to produce commodities), has by definition a monopoly over it and thereby the opportunity to set its price above its value, as high as the market can bear, through the phenomenon of artificial scarcity – creating an undersupply of something that could be made available much more widely.[351] US industry operates at just over 75% of capacity and this figure has been in a long-term decline since well before 1970.[352]

These self-imposed and inescapable fetters are very bad news for capitalism. Because all other means of raising the rate of profit have been, historically, all but exhausted, there is a permanent pressure to accelerate technological innovation, as is seen in the increasingly quicker and wasteful turnover of fixed capital.

The profit rates of individual capitals in different branches of production are of course fluctuating all the time. Mandel, writing in 1975, pointed out that some automation initially lowered the organic composition of capital:[353]

"... just as in the first phase of machine-operated large industry, the large machines were themselves produced not by machine but by hand, so in the first phase of automation currently in progress the automatic machine aggregates are not constructed automatically but on the conveyor belt. In fact, the industry which produces electronic means of production has a *notably low* organic composition of capital. In the mid-1960s the share of wage and salary costs in the gross annual turnover of this branch of industry in the US and Western Europe fluctuated between 45% and 50%. This explains why the massive amount of capital which has streamed into it since the beginning of the 1950s has lowered rather than raised the average social composition of capital and, correspondingly, has raised rather than lowered the average profit rate."[354]

This is possible when the relative share of constant capital in the average commodity value increases but is accompanied by a decrease in the absolute expenditure on constant capital per commodity. As the implementation of automation becomes more and more capital-intensive, however, the same conclusion established earlier becomes inescapable:

"The automatic production of automatic machines would hence be a new qualitative turning point, equal in significance to the appearance of the machine-production of machines in the mid-19th century... For we have arrived at the absolute inner limit of the capitalist mode of production. [This] lies in the fact that the *mass of surplus value necessarily diminishes as a result of the elimination of living labour from the production process in the course of the final stage of mechanisation-automation.*"[355]

10. The final breakdown: destined to strike much earlier than a zero rate of profit

"The periodic nature of crises has not stopped the downward trend of the rate of profit in the long term. Against those claims of the inexhaustible capacity of capital to restore the rate of profit and its own vitality… it is necessary to assert its inevitable historical transience, in the light of empirical evidence."[356]

Esteban Ezequiel Maito

After the financial crash, with global economic growth turning negative for the first time since 1945 and unemployment rising by 31 million people by the end of 2010, mainstream economists and political pundits repeatedly insisted that "no one saw it coming" and were at a loss as to why. The crash was later blamed on the poorly regulated speculation of 'greedy', 'reckless' bankers, particularly with regards to the US subprime mortgage sector. Their actions, though, were encouraged – subsidised – by the state. Mortgages were approved for people who would never be able to meet repayments once interest rates rose. This debt was then sold on in search of shorter-term returns by bundling it up with other forms of debt (into 'collateral debt obligations' (CDOs)) in order to conceal its high-risk, with credit ratings agencies responsible for evaluating the risks of assets giving them the lowest possible risk rating (AAA).[357] When the bubble burst, $14 trillion of household wealth in the US alone and $40 trillion of equity globally suddenly vanished. All along, this capital had been fictitious. The returns on the debt became too small, setting off panic selling, as had been the case with internet stocks on a smaller scale in 2000.

The crash, though, was the manifestation of a deeper malaise. Marxists had been predicting a crisis of such magnitude for years. Fidel Castro, the late, great communist leader of Cuba, saw it coming very clearly in a speech given on 24 August 1998 – nearly 10 years earlier. "Nothing has been invented nor can anything be invented which can avoid it," he said, describing capitalism as a "savage, chaotic and uncontrollable beast".[358]

Marx speaks in *Capital* of the decennial business cycle, ie of 10-year average periods between each recession, or crisis. That hasn't changed much, if at all, despite all the counter-tendencies that have continually shortened the reproduction cycle, such as the enormous technological advances in telecommunications and transit which have sped up the circulation and turnover of capital. Since WWII, Britain, for example, has suffered recessions in 1956, 1961, 1974-5, 1980-1, 1990-1 and 2008-9 – roughly every nine and a half years on average between the end of one recession and the beginning of the next. The next recession is therefore 'due', and is being largely staved off only through austerity and massive debt accumulation. In the US, the 10-year period of 1991-2001 was the country's longest period of uninterrupted growth on record. The end of July 2019 saw that record surpassed.

REAL GDP GROWTH DURING EXPANSIONS

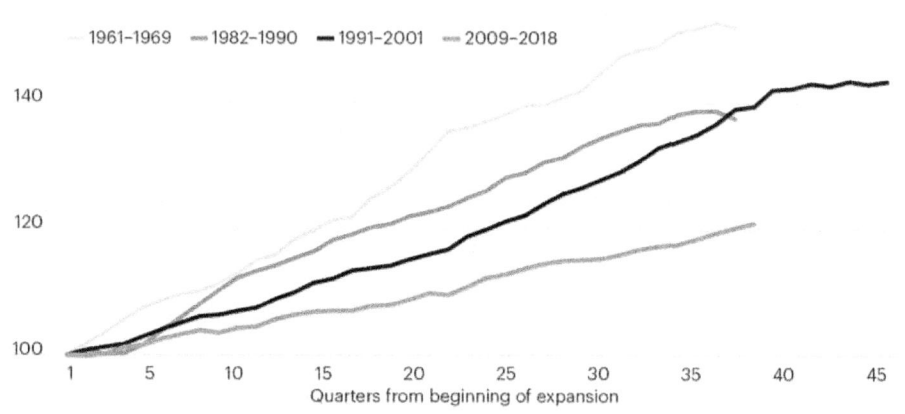

Source: Federal Reserve Bank of St. Louis, quarterly data through Q1 2018.

Despite that, the recovery from the last recession has been the weakest in the post-war era. US GDP grew by 43% over the first 39 quarters of the 1991-2001 expansion. In the first 39 quarters of the current expansion, through to March 2019, GDP grew by only 22%. At the current rate, the current expansion would have to continue for another six years to equal the aggregate growth of 1991-2001, and nine more years to match the 54% aggregate GDP growth recorded over 1961-69.[359]

Corporate profits peaked in 2015. While Trump's massive tax cut saw after-tax profits resume an upward turn, the effects are already wearing off, indicating that the last period of expansion is coming to an end. In August it was reported that the US yield curve had inverted for the first time since 2007.

A yield curve inversion means that the interest rate on 10-year government debt has fallen below the rate on the two-year equivalent. At the time, two-year Treasuries Bills (T-Bills) were trading at a yield of 1.634%, while 10-year T-Bills offered only 1.628% (having trended downwards from 14% since 1980). The longer-dated government debt normally offers a better rate of return. Inverted yield curves therefore imply that investors are more pessimistic about growth and they usually precede recessions. The news prompted investors to snap up long-term US government debt, sending the interest rate on 30-year T-Bills to record lows.

August updates also revealed that Germany's economy had contracted by 0.1% in the second quarter, while Britain's shrank by 0.2%.[360] The yield curve inversion in Germany was worse than in the US and Britain. Berlin responded by auctioning €2bn of new 30-year government bonds at a zero interest rate, meaning it would simply take money and promise to return the same amount in 2049, by which time inflation will have eroded much of its value. Pension funds, insurance firms and fund managers would therefore not be able to grow their clients' wealth this way.

The signs have been increasingly ominous. The UN's *World Investment Report 2018* said that global Foreign Direct Investment (FDI)[361] fell by 23% in 2017,[362] with 'inward' FDI flows to the developed economies falling even more, by 37%. The global average return on foreign investment fell to 6.7%, down from 8.1% in 2012.

In October 2018, the IMF warned that the world economy is "at risk" of another financial crash, citing the 60% surge in global debt over the past decade. Despite years of austerity, the gross debt across advanced economies stood at 106% of GDP in 2016, significantly higher than the 72% in 2007,[363] *before* the crash. The global economy shrank by 1.7% in 2009. That was bad enough, the worst in the post-war era, and yet all the indications are that the next one will be considerably worse.

This isn't just another crisis.

There is more than just a risk of it happening – it is going to happen, not because governments and regulators have failed to sufficiently reform the banks, as is claimed by the IMF, but because it is baked into the system.[364]

The decaying nature of capitalism is clearly illustrated by average GDP growth-rates, which have fallen in every decade for 50 years in what the World Bank defines as 'high-income countries', from 5.59% in the 1960s, to 4.15% in the 1970s, 2.93% in the 1980s, 2.35% in the 1990s, and 1.78% in the 2000s. The figure rose slightly, based on debt and austerity, to 2.15% in the years 2010-2018, but this minor reprieve will not last much longer.

The ever-decreasing portion of living labour

Although GDP is not a measure of the profit rate *per se* it is obviously indicative. Its undeniable trend is consistent with and reflects Marx's assertion that "the gradual growth of constant capital in relation to variable capital must necessarily lead to *a gradual fall of the general rate of profit*".[365] He called this "the most important law of political economy"[366] which "testifies to the merely historical, transitory character of the capitalist mode of production".[367]

It is important to stress that capitalism does not go into crisis "because the rate of profit tends to fall", as callow Marxist converts are wont to say. A falling rate is simply the *expression* of a relative decline in the mass of profit – even though it continues to rise absolutely – and, therefore, surplus value: "The fall in the rate of profit ... expresses the falling ratio of surplus value itself [to] the total capital advanced."[368] The magnitude of surplus value does not match, let alone exceed, the magnitude in the value of capital.

How the rate of surplus value expresses itself depends on the different volumes of constant capital (c) and consequently of the total capital (C), because the rate of profit (p') = s/C. If the rate of surplus value is 100% (ie surplus labour time matches necessary labour time):[369]

If $c = 50$, and $v = 100$, then $p' = 100/150 = 66⅔\%$;
$c = 100$, and $v = 100$, then $p' = 100/200 = 50\%$;
$c = 200$, and $v = 100$, then $p' = 100/300 = 33⅓\%$;
$c = 300$, and $v = 100$, then $p' = 100/400 = 25\%$;
$c = 400$, and $v = 100$, then $p' = 100/500 = 20\%$.

We see that, with the growth of constant capital, the rate of profit falls so long as the rate of surplus value, or the intensity of exploitation, remains the same. But even when the rate of exploitation rises, we know that the capital advanced grows quicker, that the organic composition of capital rises, that every individual product, "considered by itself, contains a smaller quantity of labour than it did on a lower level of production, where the capital invested in wages occupies a far greater place compared to the capital invested in means of production".[370] Therefore the hypothetical series above is "the actual tendency of capitalist production".[371] And so "the portion of living labour, unpaid and objectified in surplus value, must also stand in an *ever-decreasing* ratio to the value of total capital applied".[372]

Contemporary empirical evidence

According to Michael Roberts, the US's general rate of profit fell by more than 30% between 1947 and 2011.[373] It zigzagged up and down, of course, but that averages out at a decline of 0.49% per year. "Most of that fall was between 1965 and 1982, when it fell by over 20%. Then there was a recovery in the rate of nearly 20% from 1982 to 1997. Since then, the rate has fallen about 9%, only half the rate of the previous down-phase." He puts this last point down to a rise in the rate of exploitation. In a more recent update he says that the rate of profit fell slightly "for three consecutive years from a post-crash peak in 2014... the US rate of profit has not returned to the level of 2006, the registered peak in the neoliberal period... Indeed, in 2017 it was 17% lower than in 2006."[374]

In *The Long Depression*, Roberts writes that the general rate of profit also fell in a secular trend in Britain over a 45-year period: in 1963-75, the rate of profit fell by 28% (note: not percentage points) because the organic composition of capital rose by 20% and the rate of surplus value fell by 19%; from 1975-96, the rate of profit went back up by 50%, with the organic composition rising by 17% and the rate of surplus value going up by 66%; in 1996-2008, the rate of profit fell by 11%, with the organic composition rising by 16% compared to a rate of surplus value that flatlined. Overall during 1963-2008, the organic composition of capital rose by 63% compared to the weaker rate of growth in surplus value of 33%.[375]

Roberts has compared a number of studies of the rate of profit which use slightly different methods of calculation. While the figures vary somewhat, they all show the same trend. For example, he compared data from the UK's Office for National Statistics (ONS) and other series compiled by the BoE (a) with the work of Esteban Maito (b), who has published a study on the 'world rate of profit'. The two use slightly different source data and Maito does not include variable capital in his calculations due to the difficulty of tracking it:[376]

> "Although the rates of profit differ between (a) and (b), the trend and turns for the 150 years are much the same. This is an important confirmation of the robust nature of the results in both. And the results could not be clearer: the rate of profit on UK capital since 1855 has been in secular decline: in (a) from around 25% in the 1850s to about 10% [in the 2000s] and in (b) from about 30% to 5%. In (a) the rate of profit has fallen to 39% of its level in the 1850s and in (b) it has fallen to 26%."[377]

Maito's work shows Britain to have the lowest rate of profit of the countries studied.[378] Again, this makes sense given that it is the oldest imperialist country and therefore most likely to have the highest organic composition of capital. His figures put Britain's rate of profit consistently around 30% for the second half of the 19th century, slipping slightly in the decade after and then tumbling to 15.5% in 1920-24. After pulling itself back up in fits and starts to 28.5% in 1940-44, the figure falls again to 17.9% in 1945-49 and does not recover. By 1965-69 it falls below 10% (9.6%) and never rises back above that threshold. (1970-74: 7.6%; 75-79: 4.6%; 80-84: 3.9%; 85-89: 6.1%; 90-94: 5.3%; 95-99: 8.5%; 2000-04: 7.5%; 2005-09: 7.3%). Even Japan does not slip below 10% until 2005-09. Again, it is only in this context that the Brexit crisis can be fully understood.

Furthermore, British pound sterling lost *99.5%* of its purchasing power between 1694 (the year the currency was officially adopted) and 2011.[379] When the starting point, however, is taken from 1970, it can be seen that the vast amount – 93.5% to 2019 – has been lost since the end of the post-war boom and the gold standard (see next chapter). (The US dollar devalued by 97% between 1635 and and 2019; but the figure is 91% when the starting point is taken from 1947, when the US became the world's leading imperialist power; and 85% since 1970. That means today's dollar was worth nine cents in 1949 and 15 cents in 1970. The dollar's rate of inflation has been 3.92% per year since 1970, compared to 0.46% per year before then. Even the 2019 Chinese renminbi is worth only 22% of its 1987 equivalent.)[380]

Maito published his study in 2014. The calculations are based on 14 countries: six 'core' countries (to use his terminology);[381] the US, Britain, Germany, the Netherlands, Japan and Sweden; and eight 'peripheral' countries; Argentina, Australia, Brazil, Chile, China, Korea, Spain and Mexico.[382] The study shows that in recent decades, the rate of profit of the core countries has fallen more compared to that of the peripheral nations, especially China. The periphery experiences higher and lower rates of profit,

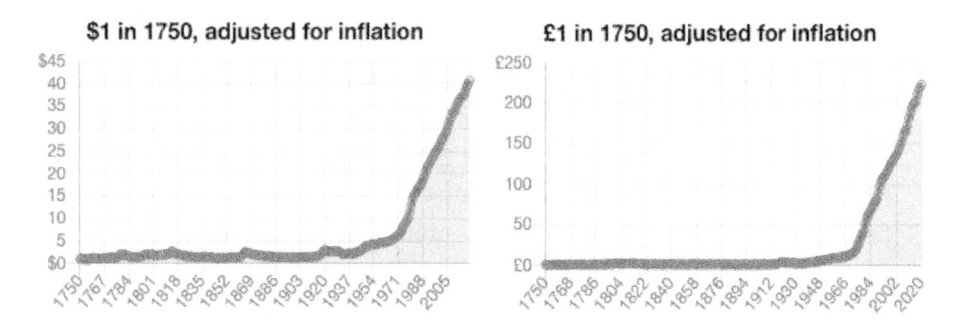

Source: Officialdata.org

while the fluctuations in the core are more stable by comparison, confirming the theory that the core benefits from unequal exchange.

Most importantly the study reveals that "the rate of profit in the long run shows a clear downward trend" in *every* country.[383] A falling secular trend is recorded from an overall average of around 43% in the 1870s to 17% in the 2000s. The profit rate averaged around 30% just before the end of the 19th century and again during the post-war boom, having shot up and down wildly during and between the two wars. It then hovered above 20% in the last quarter of the 20th century.

Although the sample is not exhaustive, it is more than enough to confirm the theory. Socialists should be explicit about this: it is not enough to say that the rate of profit tends to fall – it must be at the forefront of our agitation that it falls historically towards zero, to expose the embedded ideology that capitalism can go on forever.

Interest: tending historically towards negative rates
The history of interest rates provides further evidence of the same phenomenon. Paul Schmelzing, an economic historian from Harvard University, has produced the most comprehensive survey to date of long-term interest rates going back to the 14th century. His work shows that today's low yields follow a downwards historical trend over the past five centuries.

"The century-average safe real rate peaked in the 15th century at 9.1%, and declined to 6.1% in the 16th century, followed by 4.6% in the 17th, 3.5% in the 18th century, and 1.3% (thus far) for the 21st century... My new data showed that long-term real rates – be it in the form of private debt, non-marketable loans, or the global sovereign 'safe asset' – should always have been expected to hit 'zero bounds' around the time of the late 20th and early 21st century, if put into long-term historical context."[384]

Even negative long-term real rates "have steadily become more frequent".[385] Schmelzing says, therefore, that low rates cannot be explained merely by 'secular stagnation', ie a long-term period of low or no economic growth, as is claimed by mainstream economists.[386] Former US Treasury Secretary Larry Summers, for example, blames demographics and technology – an ageing population does not want to bet its money on risky investments; while information technology pushes down the cost of starting and running a business, so the actual supply of risky debt falls. Others, such as the Berlin-based economist Eckhard Hein, put the onus on the rise of monopoly power alongside the decline of organised labour. The 'libertarian' right blame central banks and the severing of the gold standard. The overall trend, though, has

> "persisted across a variety of monetary regimes: fiat- and non-fiat, with and without the existence of public monetary institutions... The long-term historical data suggests that, whatever the ultimate driver, or combination of drivers, the forces responsible have been indifferent to monetary or political regimes; they have kept exercising their pull on interest rate levels irrespective of the existence of central banks, (*de jure*) usury laws, or permanently higher public expenditures. They persisted in what amounted to early modern patrician plutocracies, as well as in modern democratic environments, in periods of low-level feudal Condottieri battles, and in those of professional, mechanised mass warfare."[387]

The decline in real interest rates has been a long-term trend
Nominal bond yields, GDP- and arithmetically-weighted, 1314-2018

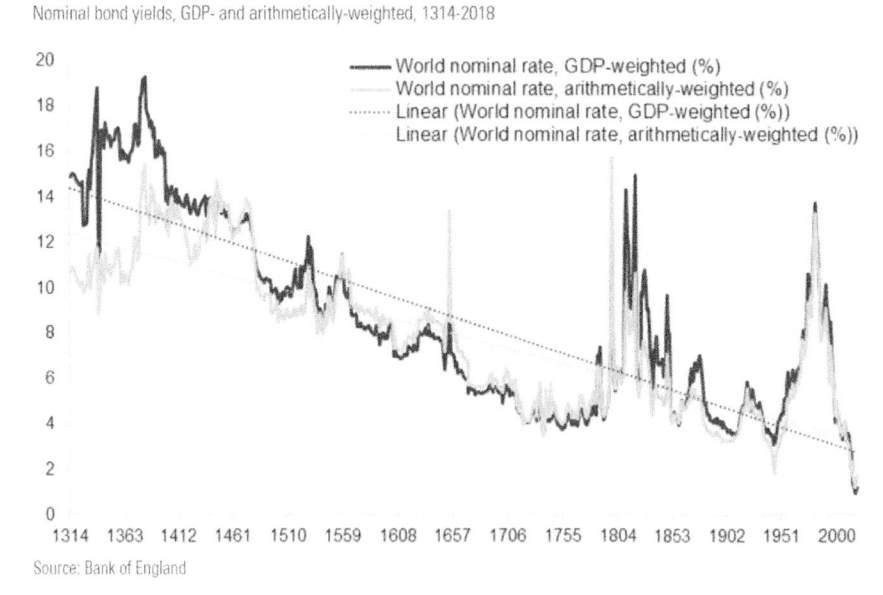

— World nominal rate, GDP-weighted (%)
World nominal rate, arithmetically-weighted (%)
······· Linear (World nominal rate, GDP-weighted (%))
Linear (World nominal rate, arithmetically-weighted (%))

Source: Bank of England

Schmelzing concludes that short-term yields on government debt will go *permanently* negative by 2030, followed by long-term yields by 2050.[388]

Negative rates have hit nations before during periods of massive crisis and high inflation, mainly during or after the world wars, notably in Germany, Italy and Japan.[389] The long-time imperialist powers Britain and the US, however, had never gone as low as zero before 2010. Indeed, Schmelzing notes that "England exhibits notably elevated real rates over the entire early modern period".[390]

Most mainstream economists believe that there is a 'natural' interest rate, determined by people's long-term expectations of growth. Schmelzing's work demolishes this idea. He himself notes that falling interest rates have coincided with greater overall capital accumulation and pent-up reserves.[391] Commenting on Schmelzing's findings, Paul Mason writes:

"There is ... one major economist who theorised the long-term fall in rates of return on capital as a product of technological development... Marx expected technology, science and human development to exert a deep, underlying downward pull on the ability of capital to extract profits from our work – and thus on the ability of financiers to extract interest from both capitalists and workers. If Schmelzing is right, his chart simply tells the story of the technological maturity of capitalism. In the long run, as I argued in *Postcapitalism*, it means there are just not going to be rates of return to sustain an economic model based on markets and private ownership."[392]

The final breakdown

If aggregate profit and interest rates fall historically to zero (and beyond), it follows that there *is* a historical maximum accumulation of capital that cannot go any higher. This makes perfect sense according to Grossman's emphasis on a progressively unvalorisable accumulation of capital. As he wrote in 1932:

"It is easy to calculate that with continuing accumulation on the basis of an ever-higher organic composition of capital, a point must come when all accumulation ceases... the immanent laws of capital accumulation themselves progressively weaken the counter-tendencies... If crisis is the tendency to breakdown that has not fully developed, the breakdown of capitalism is nothing other than a crisis that is not checked by counter-tendencies."[393]

If it were not the case that there is a historical maximum limit to accumulation, there would be no materialist justification for Marx's assertion that capitalism is a historically transient mode of production. The harmonists would be right and the struggle for socialism would be based only on extra-economical factors – moral or subjective factors that have yet to bring capitalism down, despite the system's unending crimes against humanity. Marx's critics – some of them still high on the idea that the destruction of the Soviet Union proved him wrong and signalled 'the end of history' (as if the fight to replace slavery and feudalism with capitalism never experienced setbacks) – could use Marx himself to rightly point out that capitalism can rejuvenate itself forever. But they would be wrong – that capitalism will end is an *economic and scientific certainty*. It is not only the falling rate of profit that indicates this. As we have seen, commodity prices are accelerating towards zero. How can anybody make a profit when history has made everything free?

Maito's work does show that each crisis tends to push back the trajectory of the rate of profit's fall towards zero.[394] So in 1900, the profit rate was on course to hit zero in 1989. By 1944 this had changed to 2025; and by 2010 to 2054 (roughly in line with the trajectory of technology prices falling to zero). However, the trajectory for 1970 and 2010 is almost the same, and in 1980 it was actually brought forward to 2043. This further shows that capitalism needs crises to survive, with the slowdown in accumulation extending its lifespan, although the counter-tendencies can themselves counter the delaying tendency by restoring and accelerating accumulation. Either way, the trajectory continues to fall towards zero at one speed or another.

Again, it would be imprecise to say that automation *per se* is taking the profit rate towards zero; rather it is the final manifestation of the self-abolishing tendency of capital. The declaration made by Marx and Engels in *The Communist Manifesto* that capitalism's replacement by socialism and then communism is "inevitable", in solely economic terms, remains justified.[395] It was not a prophetic claim, but a scientific fact.

Grossman also stands vindicated. He was right to assert that Marx's theory was a theory of breakdown and that capitalism would eventually come up

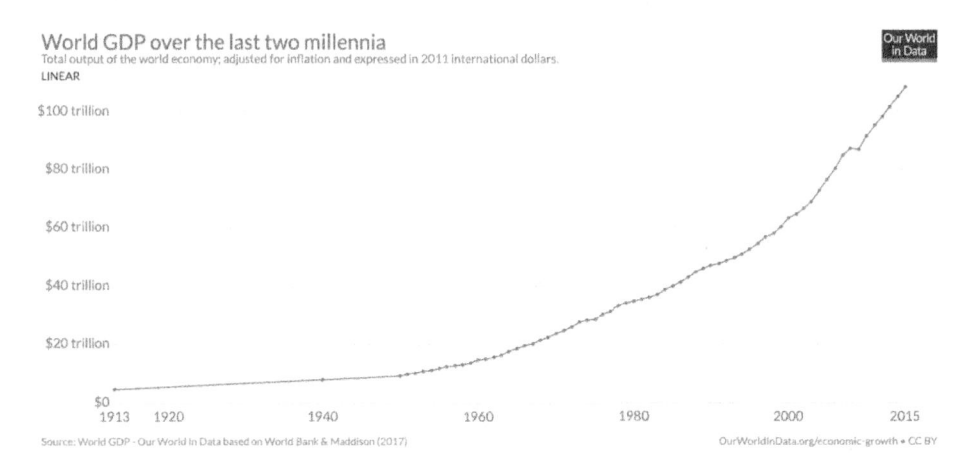

The ever-steepening trajectory of total capital accumulation indicates that it must eventually come up against an absolute limit, an absolute historical maximum.

against absolute limits of accumulation. But Grossman has one more lesson for us. Whereas Bauer and his fellow neo-harmonists thought that the rate of profit "could tend downwards indefinitely, getting closer and closer to zero without ever disappearing altogether",[396] Grossman stressed:

> "There is an absolute limit to the accumulation of capital and this limit comes into force *much earlier* [our emphasis] than a zero rate of profit."[397]

He said it was "completely false" to assert that only in the case of a zero rate of profit "can we speak of an absolute overaccumulation of capital", that "as long as capital yields a profit, however small, we cannot speak of overaccumulation in an absolute sense because the capitalist would rather be content with a small profit than have no profit at all".[398] Grossman goes on:

> "In identifying the conditions on which this limit depends mere empiricism is quite useless. For instance in the utilisation of fuel the experience of almost 100 years has shown that it was always possible to obtain a greater quantity of heat from a given quantity of coal. Thus experience, based on several decades' practice, might easily suggest that there is no limit to the quantity of heat obtainable through such increases. Only theory can answer the question whether this is really true, or whether there is not a maximum limit here beyond which any further increases are precluded. This answer is possible because theory can calculate the absolute quantity of energy in a unit of coal. Increases in the rate of

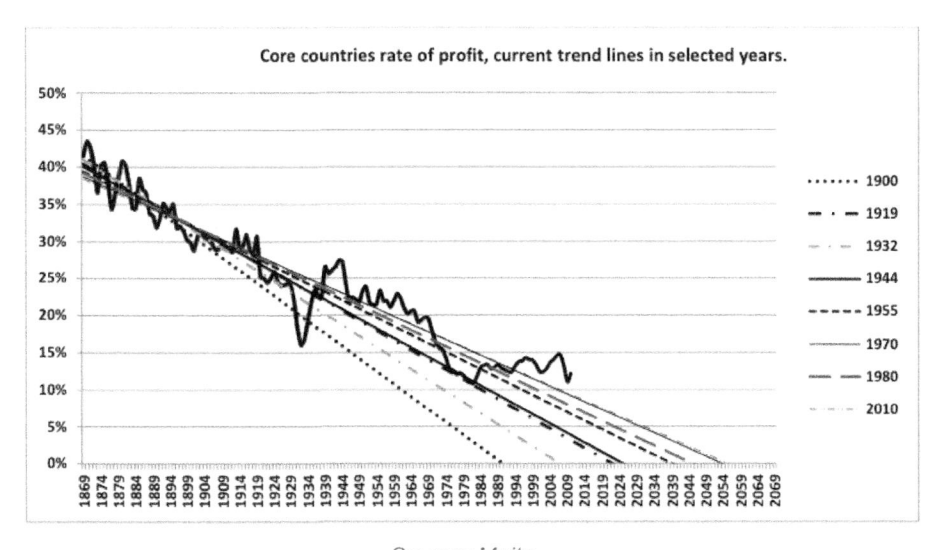

Source: Maito

utilisation cannot exceed 100% of the available quantity of energy. Whether this maximum point is reached in practice is of no concern to theory."[399]

The same logic is applicable to capital accumulation. As coal is converted into heat, living labour is converted into accumulated or 'dead' capital. In a very material sense, all of the productive human labour ever expended has paved the way to socialism.

"The limit of capitalist production is the surplus time of the labourers," says Marx.[400] But stretching the surplus labour time of the working class to 100% is not possible without returning to absolute slavery. Capital cannot even afford to exploit an ever-increasing part of labour, a surplus population that grows alongside surplus capital, while workers in the growing services sector are also relatively unproductive. "As the capitalist mode of production develops, an ever larger quantity of capital is required to employ the same, let alone an increased, amount of labour-power," says Marx.[401]

> "As soon as capital would, therefore, have grown in such a ratio to the labouring population that neither the absolute working time supplied by this population, nor the relative surplus working time, could be expanded any further (this last would not be feasible at any rate in the case where the demand for labour were so strong that there were a tendency for wages to rise); at a point, therefore when the increased capital produced just as much, or even less, surplus value than it did before its increase, there would be absolute overproduction of capital."[402]

Grossman stresses that there are absolute limits to the counter-tendencies. Stocks, wages and commercial profits must meet a definite limit. The counter-effects of capital exports are also only temporary, as competition on the world market intensifies over what remains profitable. "For this reason too, the tendency to break down must become more intense, at a definite point." The expansion in fixed capital

> "does not have a different effect. At higher levels of capital accumulation, at which fixed capital accounts for a larger component of constant capital, the contraction of production during the crisis has ever-smaller significance: a firm's burden of depreciation and interest payments for fixed capital does not decline when production is reduced."

After absolute overaccumulation can be countered no longer – since the surplus time of both domestic and overseas workers can be stretched no further – the consumption fund of both the capitalists and the workers shrinks absolutely. The capitalist's attacks on the working class must go into overdrive and production begins to grind to a halt. The working class must fight back or starve. For Marx, says Grossman,

> "class struggle and revolution are inevitable concomitants of the immanent economic necessity with which development drives towards socialism. So capitalism approaches its end as a result of its inner economic laws."[403]

The present crisis

Given all we have assessed, the question arises: are we already on the brink of the final breakdown?

In May 2019 the crisis deepened as US manufacturing suffered its worst slowdown since September 2009, prompting further calls for an interest rate cut – including from Wall Street and Trump, ahead of the 2020 election, of course – to make access to capital cheaper and delay a spiral into recession. At the end of July the Fed cut the rate from 2.25% by 0.25%. That the US yield curve inversion followed on the heels of a cut was described by Michael Pento, author of *The Coming Bond Market Collapse*, as "very remarkable".[404]

But as Ambrose Evans-Pritchard pointed out in *The Age*: "It typically takes 500 basis points of cuts [ie 5%] to lift the US economy out of recession: the Fed has barely more than 200 to play with.[405] Rates in the eurozone are stuck at -0.4%. They cannot go any lower. Europe is trapped."[406]

This isn't just another crisis. As Marx says:

> "The decrease in the interest rate is … a symptom of the annulment of capital only inasmuch as it is a symptom of the growing domination of capital in the process of perfecting itself – of the estrangement which is growing and therefore hastening to its annulment."[407]

Base interest rates before the Great Recession were riding above 5%. Central banks are more and more caught between a rock and a hard place. The Fed needs to push the base rate lower not only to make capital cheaper to borrow, preventing a 'credit crunch' whereby banks stop lending, but so that the government can afford to service its debt, since higher interest rates increase the debt-to-GDP ratio. In 2016, the US deficit stood at $500bn, funded through debt issuance. Interest payments of an overall 1.9% comprised 7% of the US federal debt. If rates were to rise again due to a panic sell-off and debt deflation, repayment rates of 6% or so on $25 trillion would become all but impossible. *Even greater debt issuance would be required.*

Issuing debt is increasingly necessary, anyway, because, in the absence of productive opportunities, investors need to store value in government bonds, considered the safest option since the state can print money. Rising demand pushes bond prices up and yields down, making government repayments cheaper. With yields now so low, though, the prospect of debt deflation becomes increasingly likely, whereby demand for bonds declines, prices fall and rates start to go back up – soaring government debt becomes more expensive and therefore riskier, creating a debt panic and massive sell-off. Investors will switch *en masse* to hard assets, especially precious metals, the prices of which will therefore (potentially hyper)inflate. Normally interest rates would be raised to bring inflation down, but if that happens the Fed will be choosing to burst the biggest financial bubble in history and collapse the tax base. If it tries to reinflate the bubble instead, it will have to print ever-greater quantities of money to purchase dumped bonds in a scramble to reverse the situation, sending the national debt even higher and accelerating the devaluation of money. Whatever central banks do, countries are at some point going to default, meaning most bondholders won't get their money back. Most major banks will go bankrupt, large corporations will default on their debt, unemployment will go through the roof and consumers will lose access to credit. Rising high inflation, and then hyperinflation, is surely coming – the only question is when.

The US's budget deficit grew by another 23.1% in the first nine months of the fiscal year 2018-19, from $607bn to £747.1bn – putting it on track for £1 trillion. Until a deal was finally reached in September, the government did not have borrowing power after March when the congressionally mandated debt ceiling kicked in. Extraordinary measures have already been taken to raise that debt ceiling on a number of occasions. CNN reported that, "As lawmakers trade fire over contempt votes and impeachment, there's been no progress toward reaching a budget agreement or extending the federal government's ability to borrow before September [when the government's credit line runs out]. That's raising the ugly prospect of more than $100bn in mandatory cuts as well as an unprecedented default on US debt – a situation that could trigger a worldwide economic catastrophe."[408]

Official US debt-to-GDP has surpassed 100%. Historically, a nation that surpasses 90% is considered to be bankrupt (meaning it is highly unlikely to ever repay its debt). We have seen smaller economies default on their debt plenty of times before, when the IMF bails them out with high-interest loans in return for privatisations and austerity. But we are talking about the collapse of the highest stage of capitalism, a system that is now global and technologically integrated. If the parasitic imperialist economies collapse, it's because the whole damn system has collapsed.

Right-wing economist Jim Rickards suggests the IMF is preparing to bail out the Fed via 'Special Drawing Rights' (SDRs), foreign exchange reserve assets, that would replace the dollar. SDRs represent a claim to currency held by the IMF. Given that the dollar is the world's reserve currency, the IMF effectively *is* the US. If the dollar fails and no other currency is strong enough to replace it, SDRs would probably have to be backed by a highly inflated gold standard. Even if it is possible for the IMF to somehow keep the Fed afloat for, say, another decade, there would be no institution left to bail out the IMF after the following crisis.

Rickards predicts that if gold became the world currency standard, its price would rise 700% to $10,000 per ounce, from $1,400 per ounce (as of August 2019, having risen from about $250 in 2000). In preparation for what is coming, central banks bought 145.5 metric tonnes of gold during the first quarter of 2019, compared to 86.7 metric tonnes in the first quarter of 2018, a 68% spike, according to the World Gold Council. The overall figure in 2018 was 651.5 metric tonnes, up by 74% from 2017 and the second highest yearly total on record.

Rickards promotes the subjective theory of value – that something is worth what someone is willing to pay for it (despite recognising that GDP growth depends on the size and productivity of labour!). He therefore mocks Marx's contention that gold has no intrinsic value – but Marx is right. Once the economy bottoms out, gold will be as worthless, at least to most people, as fiat money – and gold production too is being automated.

Is China's capital virile enough to potentially come to the rescue? While its interest rate was higher in 2019, at around 4.5%, it may be in a better position to ramp up capital exports, but with demand for Chinese goods from the US and Europe set to collapse, it is hard to see how China's economy is going to fare that much better. (What use is a trade surplus when what you are owed cannot be paid?)

There is no way of knowing how long it will be before high inflation (which could strike simply if the demand for goods outstrips collapsing supply) turns into hyperinflation – or how far rates will turn negative before they start going back up (see next section). Governments will likely delay the spiral by making huge emergency cuts. But worldwide hyperinflation is becoming increasingly likely. To prevent it, central banks will have to 'turn off the taps' and reverse QE by reducing the money supply, causing hyperdeflation and the worst depression of all time, which would follow hyperinflation anyway.

Worldwide hyperinflation is, of course, unprecedented under capitalism. The US has never meaningfully defaulted on its debt. We may be on the verge of a total economic meltdown.

If manufacturing prices are on course to fall to zero around 2050, aligning with a zero rate of profit, and all accumulation ceases "much earlier" – with the magnitude of devaluation required taking the rate of profit too close to zero – then we should not be surprised if a final breakdown strikes sooner rather than later. Remember, too, as spelt out by Volkov and Mandel, that full automation cannot be realised under capitalism.

We are already in the middle of a worldwide 'long depression', with a decade of austerity cutting public services close to the bone. The privatisation of the public sector is the plundering of the public purse. This last resort source of valorisation – bear in mind that state ownership of health care and education is the most economically efficient way of reproducing the working class – is already running dry.[409]

Capitalism is in permanent crisis mode. Average productivity growth rates in the 'high income countries' have been spluttering below 2% for the past two decades and below 1% for the last one. We have seen that the rate of surplus value in Britain flatlined in the period up to 2008, and that the value of pound sterling has almost bottomed out. The rate of surplus value in the US was 5% in 1997-2016, down from 16.4% in 1982-1997.[410] Combine all this and the weak 'recovery' fuelled by soaring and record levels of debt, and it was already clear that a crash of unprecedented scale is imminent, especially given that the crisis is reaching its 'third stage' in Asia, whose growth has been keeping the world economy afloat.

While Keynesians continue to dismiss the size of debt as unimportant – claiming that countries that print their own money can do so without limit – it is not only Marxists who can see an epic crash coming. Pento, who anticipated the housing crash, predicts that the US is approaching "the end stage of the biggest asset bubble in history". In recent interviews he has said that at the time of writing his book,

"not even I would ever have imagined that there could ever be negative yielding sovereign debt, much less to the tune of $10 trillion. That means that governments are borrowing money and paying you back no interest and less than your principal payment. That has never before happened in the history of the world. But it's not just happening in the US. It's a global bubble.... There's going to be a collapse in asset prices like we've never seen before, and that's going to bring about a recession like we've never seen before."

Pento has predicted that *all* fiat currencies will "lose their purchasing power in spades against precious metals, and then you're going to see inflation run out of control" – and compared the situation to the end of the Roman Empire. He advises investors to take "all of their money out of the banks and put it in gold".[411]

In June 2017, "legendary investor" Jim Rogers, 75, told *Business Insider* that the next crash would be "the biggest in my lifetime":

"The bubble's going to collapse, and you should be very worried.... In 2008, we had a problem because of debt. That debt is nothing compared to what's happening now. In 2008, the Chinese had a lot of money saved for a rainy day. It started raining. They started spending the money. Now even the Chinese have debt, and the debt is much higher. The Fed's balance sheet is up over five times since 2008....

"What's going to happen is, they're going to raise interest rates some more. Then when things start going really bad, people are going to call and say, 'you must save me, Western civilisation is going to collapse'. And the Fed, which is made up of bureaucrats and politicians, will say, 'well, we better do something'. And they'll try, but it won't work. It'll cause some rallies, but it won't work this time.... You're going to see governments fail. You're going to see countries fail. You're going to see parties disappear. You're going to see institutions that have been around for a long time – [investment bank] Lehman Brothers [which went bankrupt in 2008] had been around over 150 years – gone."[412]

Financial analyst Graham Summers calls it 'the everything bubble', the title of his book (2017):

"Because [Treasury] bonds serve as the bedrock (the 'risk-free' rate of return) for the US financial system, once they went into a bubble, *everything* went into a bubble... The bubble comprises numerous smaller, individual debt bubbles... in corporate debt, municipal debt, consumer debt, commercial debt, etc. As such, the entire $60 trillion in debt securities floating around the US financial system is vulnerable to debt deflation when the everything bubble bursts… The bond bubble is too large for the Fed to truly contain when it pops. The US internet tech bubble was $7 trillion in size. The US housing bubble was $14 trillion in size. The US bond bubble is $20 trillion in size. When you include junior [secondary] debt instruments, it swells to over $60 trillion. When you include derivatives associated with bond yields, it's over $124 trillion."[413]

But capitalist breakdown can only be consummated by revolution. Until then, the ruling classes will do everything they can to implement the necessary counter-tendencies, as was the case between 1914 and 1945. This time, because automation is so advanced and the environmental crisis so dire, a 1945 that breathes another century of life into the system is surely not possible. Nevertheless, the most right-wing sections will attempt to revert to fascism, absolute slavery (a probable impossibility given it ended because it was not enforceable in urban settings, where the vast majority of people are now situated), mercantilism and direct colonialism (risking world war; see chapters 14 and 17).[414] As long as the working class does not seize power or production is not socialised, a husk of the capitalist system will cling on, with ever-greater rates of poverty, hunger and misery, and through increasingly oppressive, reactionary and genocidal means. Eventually, though, capital must surely betray one too many people.

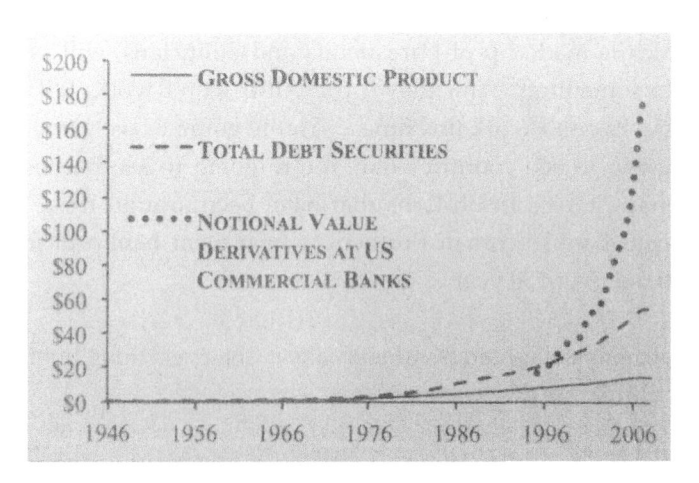

Total US debt securities, GDP, and notional value of derivatives outstanding at US commercial banks; trillions US dollars (1946-2008).
Source: Summers. Data adapted from Federal Reserve Bank of St Louis.

Negative interest rates

Since 1958, rate cuts per recession in the US have actually averaged 6.2%. The highest was 10.5% in 1981-3; the lowest 3.5% in 1957-8.[415] If the base rate is running at 2% ahead of the next recession, reinflating the bubble to a yet bigger size – following a wave of bankruptcies (since there is no way the Fed can prop up everything) and once a firm systematically important to the banking system starts to fail, threatening 'contagion' – could potentially see the rate pushed down to something like -4%. This would be incredibly politically toxic – for starters, it would mean people and companies would have to pay banks to deposit money. But since pushing down long-term rates is achieved by converting cash into stocks, things would have to go much further than that.

In *The Everything Bubble*, Summers highlights the Fed's preparations to intensify a long run 'war on cash' – in what would surely amount to the greatest centralisation of capital in history. He argues that this would involve: bans on high denominations of physical cash (similar to Roosevelt's confiscation of gold in 1933); a carry tax on smaller denominations (enforced by adding metallic strips to notes); a global wealth tax; and 'bail-ins', whereby – instead of being bailed-out by an external source – savings deposits will be seized or frozen and converted into the given bank's equity (something that has already happened in Cyprus). While all of this would attract massive cross-class resistance, Summers believes that, after the initial outrage, most people and institutions would rather lose some of their investment if the only alternative is to let the banking system fail and lose all of it (while consumers will also benefit from reduced debt repayments). Germany's three-month government bond yield already fell to -0.8% in 2016.

In the past few years, France, Italy, Spain and other EU members have banned the use of physical cash transactions over a certain amount (usually €1,000 or higher). India even removed over 86% of all physical cash from its economy by banning the 500 rupee and 1,000 rupee notes, the two most common bills in circulation. Other countries are drawing up similar legislation. In 2000, the Fed published a research paper proposing a carry tax on smaller denominations.[416] "Rather than a ploy to raise taxes, the author states clearly that this is about stopping people from sitting on cash," Summers points out. Larry Summers and Ken Rogoff, former chief economist to the IMF, are among those calling to ban $500 bills. In 2010, Congress passed Title II of the Dodd-Frank Wall Street 'reform' bill, giving the Federal Deposit Insurance Corporation (FDIC) legal authority to intervene should a systematically important firm (SIFI) start to fail. According to this legislation, the FDIC would take over the SIFI's business, 'remove' senior management, and "apportion losses to shareholders and unsecured creditors" – meaning people who own stock or unsecured debt would lose some, if not all, of their money. With the plundering of the working class all but exhausted, the ruling class must turn to accelerating the proletarianisation of the petty bourgeoisie. "Because deposits are liabilities, which the FDIC want to reduce, any capital you keep in a bank above the FDIC insured limit of $250,000 could simply be written down… meaning a percentage, if not all, of these funds would be wiped out," says Summers. The bank's stock price would, of course, collapse. During the Bank of Cyprus's bail-in in 2013, 50% of all uninsured deposits were converted into shares in the bank at a nominal value of €1 per share. Ultimately only 37.5% of these deposits were used. "What ever initial relief these depositors felt was promptly erased when shares in the bank collapsed to €0.20 on the open market – they lost 80% of their capital."[417]

While negative rates will drag down short-term yields, Summers estimates that bringing down long-term yields will require "nuclear" amounts of QE, something like $100-250bn per month, in contrast to the $25-80bn that followed the housing crash. This will involve allowing the Fed to make US debt payments itself.

> "We'd actually reach the point through which the Fed would be *actively printing money* to finance US debt payments. This would represent the end game for Fed policy: a situation in which the Fed would acquire most if not all new debt issuance from the US (usually by buying it from financial firms that would be front-running the Fed's QE programmes) and then printing new money to pay the interest on the negative yields."[418]

This is a recipe for hyperinflation – almost certainly at astronomical rates the likes of which have never been seen before.

Furthermore, there is only so much physical cash, most of which never really leaves the system. Of about $117 trillion in wealth in the US financial system, only $13.5 trillion is stored in cash and only $1.5 trillion is in the form of physical coins and bills, little over 1% of the total. The rest is in the form of electrons stored in a bank server or brokerage account. The banks don't have trillions in physical dollar bills lying around in vaults – this would be physically impossible – to meet redemptions if people start demanding their money in actual physical cash (when investors sell stocks they effectively 'buy cash'). When the US state runs out of ways to incentivise or compel the conversion of cash into stocks, the greatest round of unstoppable debt deflation in history will take off.

Japan

Keynesians and other economists who claim money can be printed without limit will point to Japan, where interest rates have been held at zero for 16 years, sending its debt-to-GDP ratio to 230% and counting, having cleared 100% in the 1990s. (Manufacturing labour as a share of the workforce in Japan fell from 27.4% in 1970 to 16.6% in 2012.) In 2016, the Bank of Japan (BoJ) became the single largest shareholder for one quarter of Japan's 225 largest publicly traded companies. It is the number one owner of Japan's debt and stock market. Because the US prints the world's reserve currency, Summers believes the US could get away with even more extreme measures.

In 2000, the BoJ's balance sheet hit 14% of GDP – rising to 90% in 2016. "I wouldn't go so far as to claim the Fed will be able to pull off a similar balance sheet expansion (for one thing, the world is a lot further down the monetary rabbit hole today than it was in 1999)," says Summers. "However, the Fed has already taken its balance sheet from 6% of US GDP in 2008 to 27% in 2016." QE of $160bn per month, $3.8 trillion in two years, would take the Fed's balance sheet to $8 trillion, 45% of US GDP. "At that level, if the Fed was its own country it would be the second or third largest country in the world."[419]

The US's situation is not that far behind Japan's, and it is catching up. Japan, of course, invests heavily in US debt. Its Government Pension Investment Fund (GPIF) is the largest public pension fund in the world, with over $1.5 trillion worth of assets. Negative yielding bonds in Japan can be turned into higher-yielding bonds bought from the US. This stopgap solution cannot last forever.

Amazon: the ultimate monopoly

The model that serves as the basis of the tech conglomerates that have taken over the world also indicates that something is very awry. According to *The Economist*, data is now more valuable than oil.[420] While data use and storage certainly create massive demand for physical commodities and fuel – and therefore labour power – the only labour base for data itself is in its initial formatting and entry. Copying it is virtually instantaneous, and vast swathes of it is created by device sensors and AI. Data then can only be worth as much as it is by bundling it up and selling it on via services, to marketing firms, etc. Hence its rapid monopolisation – its worth is rent-based.

In the US in 2016, Google and Facebook, which provide free services, accounted for almost all the revenue growth in digital advertising. Amazon, the so-called 'everything store' and the world's highest net worth company, captures around half of all dollars spent online in the US, yet it did not pay a single cent of federal tax for the second successive year in 2018, despite doubling its profits to $11.2bn. In fact, it received an income tax rebate for the previous two years totalling almost $270m. It was also offered $3bn in tax incentives to build its second headquarters in New York before the company pulled out due to an unexpectedly strong backlash from lawmakers, activists and union leaders, who rightly thought that so much government money could be better spent.

Amazon is hugely dependent on the state on the one hand and, on the other, because it does not make the vast majority of the products it sells – it simply runs services – most of the capital it does make independent of the state represents a rentier-parasitism that is *almost totally dependent on workers employed by other capitals.*

In its first few years as a public company, Amazon ran at a loss. When it first reported a quarterly profit in the fourth quarter of 2001, it came in at a lowly $5m. But, much to the displeasure of his shareholders and Wall Street, Amazon CEO Jeff Bezos always maintained that investing in future growth would be more important than hitting quarterly earnings targets. In the final quarter of 2017 – 58 quarters after its May 1997 initial public offering (IPO) – the company's net income suddenly spiked at $1.86bn, equalling all the previous profit it had accumulated in the previous 14 years. (This was bolstered significantly by Trump's corporate tax cut, which added about $790m in accounting terms.)

Bezos became the world's wealthiest man in July 2017 when his estimated net worth increased to more than $90bn, a figure that had risen to £151bn at the beginning of 2019. His is the so-called 'flywheel' philosophy, a cycle in which cutting prices "attracts customers, which increases sales and attracts more customers, which allows the company to benefit from economies of scale (bundling together logistics and other routine costs), until, ultimately, the company can cut prices again, spinning the flywheel anew".[421] This is also known as "blitzscaling". But it is nothing more than the logic of ever-intensifying capitalist competition.

Absolute monopoly is becoming a fact. Never before has one single company had such an impact on the devaluation process. The price cuts have extended to postage and packaging – next-day delivery is free for Amazon Prime members who pay an annual fee ($99 in the US).

Membership numbers exceeded 100 million in April 2018. The lower prices and free posting entices members to make frequent orders, doing all their shopping on the website for the inexpensive convenience, which of course reduces their personal travelling expenses. Such high demand empowers Amazon to command reduced payments to middle men and couriers, squeezing their profits, the losses of which are passed onto courier drivers, the number of which has exploded (although Amazon plans to replace them with drones).

The low wages, constant demand and competition for work has created a perfect storm forcing couriers to accept casualised self-employed status with no rights and long hours, further deepening their rate of exploitation.

To stomp out competition Amazon needs to retain and grow its membership base. It is not, though, responsible for the quality of the vast majority of the products it sells. Amazon has solved this problem by empowering customers to post product reviews and ratings. On one hand, this represents a democratisation of consumerism that potentially forces retailers and manufacturers to raise standards, further squeezing profit margins. On the other, Amazon has amassed a legion of unpaid non-productive (neither productive nor unproductive)[422] workers who provide free content, creating a revenue stream from commercial data mining. Once you factor in the unpaid work of customers – and, of course, *they* are actually paying Amazon – with the low wages paid to the company's workforce,[423] it is clear that Amazon's average outlay on wages is almost negligible.

Everybody works for Jeff Bezos. An increasing number of consumers, retailers and manufacturers alike are paying rent to Amazon, out of necessity. Many productive capitalist enterprises are being drawn into Amazon's orbit and, to some extent, turned into its *de facto* subsidiaries. They cannot compete with Amazon and are therefore becoming dependent on it, even as it eats into their profits. Bezos is the ultimate monopoly capitalist, in both senses of the word. Amazon is the last capitalist ship on which the rest of industry is being forced to board. It will surely sink under the weight of its own monopoly.

Other companies now following the blitzscaling model are not going to be as successful as Amazon. In April 2019 *The Economist* analysed 12 of the most prominent venture-backed 'unicorn' companies (start-ups worth more than $1bn which are moving towards IPOs, when the stock of a company is offered on a public stock exchange for the first time). It found that a "remarkably high" 84% of them "have no profits".[424] The companies are collectively £47bn in the red, a figure that more than doubled between 2016 and the end of 2018. As *The Economist* says, "this is profligate even by the standards of Amazon, which before and after its IPO was seen as a particularly profit-averse company; it had cumulative losses of $3bn between 1995 and 2002. Uber lost almost $4bn just last year, excluding exceptional items."

These 12 firms are looking at a combined valuation of £350bn, yet their "overheads are scant" and they have just $6bn of fixed assets between them "and not many staff". Despite that their operating margins are around -30%. *The Economist* adds:

> "Based on a discounted cashflow model, in aggregate the dozen firms will need to increase their sales by a compound annual rate of 49% for ten years to justify that valuation [and the average unicorn is considered to be overvalued by 60%]. That is the same as the average growth of Amazon, [Google parent] Alphabet and Facebook in the decades after their IPOs. ... But that is not enough. Justifying the valuation means not just staggering increases in sales, but also a very large improvement in margins. In aggregate these would have to increase by 34 percentage points. That would be truly unprecedented. The average for Amazon, Facebook and Google was only 19 percentage points.
>
> "Google almost quadrupled in value in the year after floating, which bought tech a lot of diffuse goodwill. No one expects Uber to do that. If today's unicorns turn out to have created most of their value for private investors before floating, the public will take note."

Like Amazon, Google and Facebook, these companies are offering (often free) services, extracting rent from consumers and other (often productive) capitals. As this parasitic online landlordism continues to make the latter two poorer, this model can only serve to undermine its own source of income. It is unsustainable.[425]

Speculation's role in the concentration of capital
The counter-acting tendencies that kicked into gear to curtail the last breakdown have not been enough to prevent the next one, or, it seems, from making it even worse.

Growth in the US picked up slightly in 2017 and 2018, mainly as a result of Trump's tax cut. But because this allowed corporations to partially reabsorb surplus labour, this also meant that, for the first time since 1997-2001, wages also picked up noticeably, between 2015 and 2017. Both those periods were marked by very low rates of unemployment (3.6% as of May 2019, the lowest since 1969). Again, we see that wages eat into profits and the profit rate falls as a result.

Capitalism cannot tolerate high employment (by its standards) for long.[426] Economists consider anything below 4% unemployment to be a sign of impending recession and had predicted that the figure would fall to a remarkably low 3.4% in 2019.

Rising absolute wages led to rising inflation and so prompted the Federal Reserve Board to raise interest rates in the last quarter of 2017 and in all four in 2018, up from a record low of close to zero. This had the desired effect as wage growth in 2019 started to slow down again. The rate was put on hold at 2.25-2.5% and a planned increase to 3% was postponed in January 2019 amid complaints that monetary policy was making borrowing too expensive. The growing expectation of lower rates therefore encouraged a rise in speculation on global equity markets – foreign investors channelled a record $9bn into Chinese equities in January 2019, reviving Chinese stocks after a slump in 2018, while bonds and stocks in the US rallied in June as productivity continued to slow down.[427]

FT Advisor reported that "Bruce Stout, who runs the £1.6bn Murray International investment trust… is not convinced that the rise in share prices since the start of 2019 is justified. He feels the market is ignoring the reason interest rates are not rising at the pace previously expected, which is that economic conditions are deteriorating, and worsening economic conditions will have a negative impact on company profits."[428]

But this is what is bound to happen. It is only once the economic situation improves that credits are displaced from the exchange into production. In 1985, financial profits accounted for about 15% of US profits, rising to 40% by 2008 (whereas services, the main source of employment, never exceeded 10% in that time). The fraction of national income appropriated by rentiers, the owners of financial assets, rose in every OECD country for which data was available from the 1970s to the 1990s. Among non-financial companies the manufacturing sector led the trend of industrialisation,[429] confirming Lenin's definition of finance capital. In 2003, for every $1 of world income, $1.80 of derivatives circulated; but by 2007, that ratio had shot up by *640%*, with every $1 of world income corresponding to almost $12 worth of derivatives.[430]

In his book, published on the eve of the Wall Street Crash, Grossman observed a similar situation, saying that there were "enough signs to suggest that America is fast approaching a state of overaccumulation":

"The basic characteristic of the economic year 1927 is that industry and commerce have watched their production fall, their sales decline and their profits contract. Reduced sales and lower production release a portion of the capital which flows into the banks in the form of deposits. The banks attract industrial profits for which there are no openings in industry and commerce. At the end of 1927 the holdings of the member banks of the US Federal Reserve System were $1.7bn more than a year earlier. This constitutes a rise of 8% against the 5% considered normal. The retrogression in industry and commerce contrasts sharply with the overabundance of cheap credit money."[431]

He also points out that:

"The relationship between the banks and speculation which is discernible in the specific phases of the business cycle is also reflected in minor fluctuations within any given year. In periods when the banks can employ their resources elsewhere the exchange is subdued; it becomes brisk only when those resources are again released. Speculation is a means of balancing the shortage of valorisation in productive activity by gains that flow from the losses made on the exchange by the mass of smaller capitalists. In this sense it is a power mechanism in the concentration of money capital."[432]

The rise in industrial capital deposited in banks is bound to depress the interest rate. When the discounts and the outflow fail to change the depressed state of industry, as in 1927, an expansion of speculation and speculative driving up of shares is bound to follow. But this too cannot last:

"The worst orgies of speculation are possible in a period when, with the transition from individual forms of property to its social form in share capital, enormous fortunes accumulated over several decades are thrown on to the market and sacrificed on the stock exchange. These are the flotation periods bound up with vast regroupments and concentration of wealth.... But once this process of concentration of share capital has already reached an advanced level, with the general progress of accumulation and through the mediation of the stock exchange, the exchange itself is left only with the residual stock capital in the hands of the public. Under these conditions speculation is badly debilitated, not of course through the conscious intervention of banks which supposedly centralise command over the economy into their own hands, but because there is not enough material for the exchange to digest. At an already advanced level of concentration of share capital, speculation on the stock exchange is bound to lose its impetus as its middle-class base of small rentiers, workers, civil servants and so on, dries up."[433]

Trump boasted about record prices on the stock market, but this is only a sign of a bubble forming before it bursts. Wall Street breathed a sigh of relief after a pronounced slump in February 2018 turned into the biggest upwards curve in a year. By the end of August, the market value of Apple and Amazon had each surpassed $1 trillion, and Alphabet flirted with $900bn. The combined market value of the 'big' five reached $3.6 trillion. But suddenly towards the end of the year, investors dumped shares in Facebook, Amazon, Apple, Netflix and Alphabet, wiping more than a $1 trillion off their combined market value from their high points. In January 2019 Apple issued poor trading figures and a further 9% was taken off its value.

One of these spontaneous bursts of panic selling is sooner or later bound to tip over into a full-scale crash – triggering a financial and economic crisis that will make the Great Recession look like an unexceptional blip.

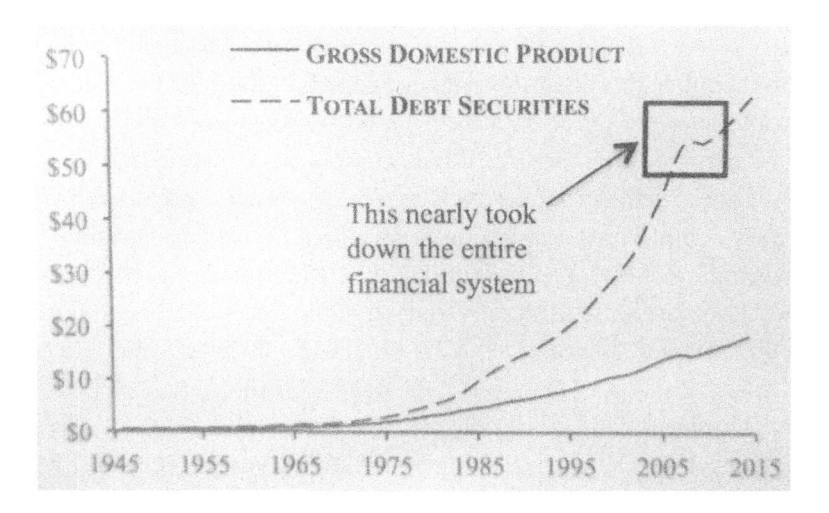

Debt deflation of the 2008 crisis in total US debt securities and its impact on US GDP; trillions US dollars (1945-2016). Source: Summers.

11. Keynesian fantasies

"We used to think you could spend your way out of a recession and increase employment by cutting taxes and boosting government spending. I tell you in all candour, that option no longer exists."

Prime Minister James Callaghan,
Labour Party Conference 1976

The Macquarie report (see chapter 6) warns investors that "there is no modern precedent to the degree of state control that we envisage in the coming years". Indeed, then Labour Shadow Chancellor John McDonnell – a Keynesian who wishes to emulate the post-war Labour government that embarked on a minimal nationalisation programme – claimed that Labour's left-wing had "won the argument" and pushed then Tory Prime Minister Theresa May towards talk of a "state interventionist" economic policy. "It's time to remember the good government can do," she told the Conservative Party conference in October 2016. "Where markets are dysfunctional, we should be prepared to intervene. Where companies are exploiting the failures of the market in which they operate, where consumer choice is inhibited by deliberately complex pricing structures, we must set the market right."

According to the Resolution Foundation, pledges made by the Tories going into the December 2019 general election would increase the proportion of annual government spending to 41.3% of GDP by 2023 and likely to beyond the 42% average recorded between 1966 and 1984 – this from a party accusing Labour (planning 43.3%) of wanting to take Britain back to the 1970s – once extra outlays on the NHS are taken into account. The average for the 20 years up to 2008 was 37.4%.

In reality, any ideological back-pedalling has been forced upon the Conservative Party – which supposedly stands more or less for limiting the state to, conveniently, the provision of law and order and national defence – by the deepest capitalist crisis in almost a century. While electoral pressure from Labour has played its part, so have the needs of profit. Capital accumulation demands productivity growth, which stalled in Britain at an average of 0.3% in the five years to the end of 2017 – the longest period of low growth since the 19th century. This was the motivation for then Chancellor Philip Hammond's £31bn investment in a National Productivity Fund, with £500m for projects such as AI and driverless cars. In his 2017 Autumn Budget, he claimed to be putting Britain "at the forefront" of the world's "imminent technological revolution".

McDonnell, a self-described democratic socialist, says stagnant productivity is caused by the government's 'political choices' of austerity and low state investment in infrastructure. But productivity growth is not low because of low investment growth, state-led or otherwise – both are low because of the fetter of overaccumulation. Falling profits inevitably mean falling tax revenues, meaning less public money is available for the state to spend. Indeed, by the time McDonnell gets to raise taxes he is likely to be doing so against a relatively smaller profit base (not to mention the likelihood of increased tax evasion and capital flight).

McDonnell wants to spend far more than Hammond, pledging in July 2016 that a Labour government would mobilise £500bn of investment and lending from the creation of a national investment bank, with £350bn coming directly from the public purse. He claims the extra borrowing would "pay for itself" and that nationalising railways and utilities would "cost nothing". Asked in November 2017 how much his plans would add to Britain's annual £48bn cost of servicing the ever-rising national debt – nearly £2 trillion and 90% of GDP as of April 2018 – McDonnell said: "We are talking about it paying for itself, a one-to-one multiplier. That's the standard analysis by the Office for Budget Responsibility and others. When you invest, you grow the economy and as a result of that you cover your costs."

But credit extended to either private or nationalised enterprises would not expand real capital, because credit is fictitious capital. Any expansion of production under nationalised enterprises would not create new exchange-value because the surplus labour time of workers would go to the state instead of private capital. Production could grow without broadening the valorisation base – until, that is, surplus value is redirected to the private sector through subsidies or any nationalised industry is re-privatised. Keynesianism's real and necessary function then is to save capitalism, to intervene and 'hold the fort' where private ownership becomes unprofitable, to lay the groundwork for re-privatisation when profitable conditions eventually return.

The only way Keynesianism expands capital is by taking the burden of production and rationalising costs away from private capital, so that the remains of private industry can buy parts etc at lower costs, thereby improving profit margins. Keynesianism therefore subsidises the private sector while increasing social debt. Indeed, a heavy dose of 'Keynesianism' was used to bail out the banks.

Like all Keynesians – who say that the size of national debt does not matter because the state can print money – McDonnell is wrong about debt, because it must be serviced and repaid from real, profitable returns on production. After all, it is owed to someone who probably owes it to someone else. Debt matters and eventually countries will default on their debt. They may be able to restructure their debt by either extending its due date or devaluing their currency; but these options cannot last forever; usually involve taking on more long-term debt to pay off short-term debt; and are often met at first by investment withdrawal.

The extension of credit can only cover a lag in the *realisation* of profits, which are underproduced at the best of times, for so long. It is no more than fictitious capital, creating bubbles that are sooner or later bound to burst. The extension of credit McDonnell plans – "quantitive easing for people instead of banks" – would raise demand relative to supply and therefore have inflationary consequences. As Reynolds points out, deficit spending on wages for state employees inflates the value of commodities relative to wages denominated in currency and therefore has a secondary effect of producing a reduction in real wages and a rise in a rate of exploitation.[434]

For the working class to benefit at the expense of capitalists, wages would have to be pegged to the cost of living. That would not survive capitalist reaction without a powerful working class movement on the streets and a strong social democratic party dominating the state apparatus, especially the military.

The New Deal myth

The Keynesian myth starts with Franklin D Roosevelt's New Deal in the US in 1933-37. It was implemented before the destruction of WWII, but it still followed massive devaluation, the deflationary process of 1929-1932, when national income plummeted by more than 50% following the Wall Street Crash. Keynesians still claim that the New Deal worked or that it failed only because it was 'not Keynesian enough'.

Keynesianism, though, is essentially little different to the economism that has always dominated the reformist wing of the socialist movement. Economism maintains that the economic struggles of the workers for the improvement of their immediate working and living conditions should be the chief preoccupation of Marxists. Lenin called this "slavish cringing before spontaneity", arguing that while Marxists should support wage rises they also had a duty to stress at all times that working class gains could only be sustained by revolution.

Paul Mattick, who upheld Grossman's understanding of capitalism, skewered the myth of the New Deal in 1977:

> "... deficit financing [ie funding the economy via government borrowing] in order to cope with extraordinary government expenditures is as old as and older than capitalism. Since it was always practiced in times of war, it was obvious that it would also be used in the 'war' against the depression. Even the idea of the 'multiplier effect' of government-induced production made its appearance long before Keynes formulated his theories. But despite the lack of a realistic theory of capital production, the bourgeoisie felt intuitively that government deficit financing may be an effective short-term expedient but could not possibly be a long-term solution. It is clear, of course, that any large-scale investment, from whatever source, will increase production, and that this increase will lead to some additional production apart from the initial investment. But behind the desire for a balanced budget lies the instinctive recognition that a continuous expansion of production by way of government deficit financing must finally destroy the capitalist system."[435]

Roosevelt was more or less attacked as a Marxist by Republicans. But he regarded his greatest achievement as having saved capitalism. The 'Keynesian turn' had in fact begun, out of necessity, under the Republican president Herbert Hoover. "Some aid was dispensed via the creation of the Reconstruction Finance Corporation in 1931, which was authorised to lend money to banks, businesses, and farms to shore up the faltering economy. Public works to help both private business and the unemployed led to large deficits, despite the desire for a balanced budget," says Mattick.

Roosevelt merely expanded this, albeit on a much larger scale than any Republican could have been seen to tolerate. To begin with he brought hope to the masses and inspired a spirit of sacrifice and compromise – of class collaboration. However,

> "he too was for a balanced budget... Aware of the fact that only inflationary methods could block a further decline of the economy, Roosevelt still searched for a type of inflation that would not unduly

enlarge the national debt. He tried, on the one hand, to reduce the costs of government and, on the other, to increase the money supply through the issuing of unsecured currency and through the devaluation of the dollar. The devaluation raised prices to some extent and provided the monetary means to finance the recovery programme."

Regulation included the Agricultural Adjustment Administration (AAA) which aimed to raise farm prices – while swathes of the country went hungry – through crop reductions. And we are supposed to believe that Keynesianism works!

"Credit was extended to [farmers] in return for their reduction of production. Foodstuffs of all descriptions were dumped and covered with poison and quicklime to prevent the hungry from using it. Wheat and cotton were plowed under, millions of pigs and cows were destroyed in the hope of raising prices, through artificial scarcities... Farmers were rewarded for not producing commodities, although this was of benefit only to the larger agricultural enterprises, not to the small farmers.... crop limitation allowed the landlords to drive their tenant farmers from the land and at the same time to pocket their share of government subsidies. 'Recovery' of this type merely increased the misery of tenants and share-croppers."

The government worried that the unemployed needed training for when employable conditions returned, so a conscious effort was made to stigmatise 'idleness'. 18- to 25-year-old men were sent to labour camps called the Civil Conservation Corps (CCC). They were more or less prepared for military life and received no more than "pocket money". They planted trees, built minor roads, tracks and dams, and fought against soil erosion.

But "the costs of work relief are far higher than those of direct relief" and so the Civil Works Administration had to be closed and more than four million people returned to regular benefits, "which cut government expenses by more than half and subjected the relief recipients once again to the humiliations of the 'means test', that is, the proof of total destitution".

A year later, however, "Roosevelt found it necessary to reinstitute public employment and to launch the Works Progress Administration (WPA), which hired about three million people out of more than twenty million relief recipients. The WPA paid somewhat more than was allotted to welfare cases, but less than the prevailing wage rates, so as not to 'encourage the rejection of opportunities for private employment'."

Meanwhile, the right-wing of the Democratic Party inevitably felt public spending was too high. "To keep the party intact and to retain its leadership, Roosevelt tried to balance the contrary interests by means of compromises, which either advanced or retarded the New Deal." The National Industrial Recovery Act (NRA), the cornerstone of the New Deal "was thus destined to fall apart without, and independently of the fact that the Supreme Court of the United States declared it in violation of the Constitution and therefore invalid, together with the AAA and some other New Deal legislation".

The NRA involved more planning designed to end the state of fierce competition that brought prices and wages down. "The cat is out of the bag," wrote Rexford Tugwell, one of Roosevelt's early advisers. "There is no invisible hand. There never was. We must now supply a real and visible guiding hand to do the task which that mythical, non-existing, invisible agency was supposed to perform but never did."

But this planning consisted, says Mattick, "exactly of those measures that had hitherto been the results of unconscious market forces, that is, the increasing concentration of capital and its acceleration in times of crisis and depression. To facilitate this process, antitrust laws had to be set aside to allow trade associations to fix their own prices and profit margins through a 'fair' distribution of market shares in all industries."

To try to keep labour on side, the NRA, through special legislation, was to guarantee the right to the independent formation of trade unions and collective bargaining. Union membership, which comprised about 12% of all employed workers in 1922, had fallen to 6% by 1932. From then on, however, the number of strikes to defend both wages and unions increased rapidly, *"which merely led to a further deterioration of the economy"*. [Our emphasis.]

The NRA had been a product of underconsumption theory. Boosting consumption would raise prices and supposedly revive the economy. "It was all so simple; it only ignored the fact that wages are costs of production, so that the higher they are, the lower will be profits," says Mattick. The NRA's objective "was to be attained through the restraint of competition, without regard for the actual profitability of capital, on which the state of the economy, and therewith the state of competition, depends. Monopolisation, being the effect of competition, was now to be reached without competition, by means of gentlemen agreements that assured everyone the required profits and the workers a living wage."

In practice, "things worked out quite differently, or rather they worked out in the only way they could within the confines of capitalism":

> "Although most industries subscribed to NRA codes, or at least paid lip service to them, the codes were written up, and the authorities therewith created were dominated by big business and its special interests to the detriment of small producers, the workers, and the public at large. The control over prices and production granted to the various trade associations reduced itself finally to mere price fixing, which broke the deflationary spiral but did not enhance the economy to any noticeable extent. It did, however, accentuate the further concentration of capital and, in that sense, was one of the preconditions for the resumption of the capital-expansion process. The unlamented demise of the NRA by verdict of the Supreme Court led to some shadowboxing on the part of Roosevelt, although it merely removed the legal sanction from the 'natural' course of events, namely, the increasing monopolisation of capital."

Union activity and militancy rose significantly because workers had the confidence that the government would not send in the army. But "rank-and-file initiative again subsided to make room for the ordinary bargaining procedures of the labour market, thus revealing the hollowness of labour's victories, which had only served to integrate the unions more thoroughly into the capitalist system".

Growing union activity also reflected a slightly improving global economic outlook. Roosevelt decided to reign in public works "in a new effort to balance the budget in response to the demands of the business world". For the neo-Keynesians this is where Roosevelt was 'not Keynesian enough'. He should have built more labour camps!

"Concerns about the budget deficit sabotaged the New Deal from ending the Depression's global economic catastrophe," writes Kimberly Amadeo.[436] But if you do not disempower and expropriate the capitalist class then sooner or later you have to reckon with its demands. She points to strong economic growth during the New Deal, not accounting for the fact that it depended on the crash, debt and capital concentration. She even claims that had the US spent on the New Deal what it spent on WWII – the former added $3bn to the debt and the latter $64bn – the "depression would have ended" and the US economy would have been healthy enough to offer aid to Germany and prevent the rise of Naziism. But war, as we shall look at more closely later on, is the ultimate means of devaluation.

As Mattick writes, it was the need to restore profitability "on the existing level of production ... which motivated the increasingly negative attitude with respect to the New Deal and led Congress to diminish its appropriations for work relief, slowly phasing out its various projects".

The recovery proved to be short-lived. GDP in the recession of 1937-38 fell by 18.2% (not much 'better' than the 26.7% of 1929-33). Steel production declined from 80% of capacity to 19%. Mattick says:

"Millions of workers lost their jobs once again. The New Deal was now adjudged a dismal failure.... Those who still managed to live reasonably well and, of course, those who profited from the increased productivity of labour felt inclined to make the New Deal responsible for the new downturn and pleaded for giving the market a chance to run its own course.... confidence in government-induced production was lost, even on the part of Roosevelt, and more attention was paid to the expansion needs of private enterprise.

"For all practical purposes by 1938 the New Deal was dead and buried. The economy revived once more, but there were still ten million unemployed in 1939. While total output regained the 1929 level, private investments were still one third below the level of 1929. Business blamed this situation on high taxes which accompanied the budget deficits and on the encroachment of government induced production on the fields of competitive private investments."

As Mattick says, "if there is no parallel increase of profits, government expenditures, which are by nature non-profitable, can only deepen the depression". He says Keynesian theory "found no verification in the New Deal" and correctly concludes, unlike Amadeo, that the depression "was finally ended not by a new prosperity but through WWII, that is, through the colossal destruction of capital on a worldwide scale and a restructuring of the world economy that assured the profitable expansion of capital for another period". He adds:

"The New Deal... tried to overcome the depression in relative isolation from the decaying world economy, only to partake in its further disruption. With the Spanish Civil War the alignment of the imperialistic forces began to take shape, and the eventuality of a new global war began to agitate the world. Government-induced production became armaments production; in the United States this took the form of an enlarged naval programme. The actual outbreak of war turned America into the 'arsenal of democracy', but it took America's entry into the war to overcome the Depression and to reach the goal of full employment. Death, the greatest of all the Keynesians, now ruled the world once more."

The failure of post-war social democracy

Keynesianism finally enjoyed some limited historical success – based on the devastation of the Great Depression, two world wars and fascism, which combined to create the conditions for the post-war boom. From 1946 to 1973, during a new, *early* stage of accumulation, Keynesianism became *necessary* as private capital could not afford the bulk of the upfront costs of rebuilding the world economy, and so manufacturing enjoyed a new lease of life. This was especially true in Britain as the US purposely under-financed Britain in order to finish off its reign as the top imperialist power.

After the war, the US effectively attempted to plan the capitalist world economy through the 1944 Bretton Woods Agreement. Led by Roosevelt, the monetary system was redesigned by locking each currency to the US dollar, which was pegged to gold at the fixed exchange rate of $35 per ounce, thereby guaranteeing full gold convertibility to any country which wanted to swap their dollars for gold. The IMF was set up to hand out loans to countries on strict conditions that would ensure that any balance of payments deficits would be fixed and the loans repaid; and what is now the World Bank was set up to channel productive investments to regions of the world devastated by war. For a while this 'worked', as the US built up a massive trade surplus.

Varoufakis claims the 'flaw' in this plan was the US's rejection of Keynes's proposal for a mechanism to redistribute trade surpluses to countries with deficits, since falling demand from the latter would otherwise lead to crisis in the former – another underconsumptionist theory.[437] The proposal was rejected precisely because capitalism cannot eliminate competition; but it would not have made much difference since capital would have overaccumulated, anyway.

The US could not allow such a proposal for it would have undermined the point of effectively making the dollar a global currency. Redistribution in a sense did take place, however, as the US was motivated to export massive amounts of capital to revive the economies and currencies of West Germany and Japan, both so that these countries would be able to buy US goods but also as part of the 'containment' strategy against the Soviet Union. The US's share of global GDP shrank by 19.3% from 1950 to 1972, leading to a trade deficit, while Germany and Japan's grew by 18% and 156.7%, respectively. (Britain's shrank by 35.4%; France's grew by 4.9%.)[438]

Overaccumulation and crisis inevitably returned. US growth slumped from 6.5% in 1966 to -0.25% in 1970. Combined with the deficit spending and inflationary effects of the escalating war on Vietnam, Laos and Cambodia (1955-75) – which cost the US government £113bn[439] – the dollar became overvalued, forcing European governments to increase the volume of their currencies to keep their exchange rates constant against the dollar, since Bretton Woods limited exchange rate movements against the dollar to 1%.

Europe and Japan feared that the build-up of dollars, against a constant US gold stock, would lead to a run on (sell off of) the dollar and force the US to abandon the gold standard, in which case their stored dollars would lose value. France President Charles de Gaulle – along with other European governments and oil-producing nations whose oil exports were denominated in US dollars – accused the US of building its economic power on borrowed money at the expense of its rivals. On 29 November 1967, Britain devalued pound sterling by 14% against the dollar, well beyond the 1% limit, forcing the US to use up to 20% of its gold reserves to defend the $35 peg that had been set in 1933 (already up from $20.67, set in 1900).

President Richard Nixon, also facing rising unemployment domestically ahead of the 1972 election, began to consider severing the dollar's link to gold – which linked the price of money to the labour value embodied in gold – since a huge devaluation of capital was the only way to resolve the crisis. The gold standard had become a fetter on growth and needed to be done away with to tackle the structural limitations that inflation imposed on state deficit spending. The alternative was to raise rates and spark a depression. The new French President Georges Pompidou reacted by ordering a destroyer to sail to New Jersey to redeem US dollars for gold held at Fort Knox, as was France's right under the Bretton Woods contract. A few days later the British government of Tory Edward Heath issued a similar request (without deploying the Royal Navy), demanding gold equivalent to £3bn.

Four days later, on 15 August 1973, Nixon effectively ended Bretton Woods by announcing that the US would no longer convert dollars to gold at a fixed value and no longer pay debt in gold, only dollars. The ceiling on both the number of dollars the Fed could print (since the amount of gold foreign banks could convert their dollars into was finite) and the debt it could issue was removed. The US dollar, which backed all other currencies, was now no longer backed by a hard asset as a storehouse of value. Debt became the main tool for supporting increased production and consumption.

US officials complained that the superpower's 'generosity' to the rest of the world had left it with a serious deficit and a drain on its reserves, saying that it would now need the help of its allies instead of vice-versa. What they meant was that the end of Bretton Woods was not their responsibility or problem, for the dollar remained the reserve currency; ie, the only true global means of exchange. The end of the gold standard triggered a stampede for the dollar.

The dollar started to devalue as inflation rose. Not only would European and Japanese dollar assets lose their value, but their exports would also become more expensive. They had no choice but to devalue their own currencies, but that would raise their energy costs since oil was denominated in dollars. Nixon was unmoved by pleas to reconstitute Bretton Woods at new rates. Prices took off. By May 1973 gold was trading at more than $90 per ounce – exploding to $455 by 1979. Two years after the end of the gold standard the dollar had lost 30% of its value against the Deutschmark and 20% against the yen and the franc.

The price of primary commodities shot up (bauxite, for example, by 165%; lead, 170%; tin, 220%; silver, 1,065%). From the end of WWII through to 1971, it took between 10 and 15 barrels of oil to purchase one ounce of gold; rising to 34 by mid-1973. As Reynolds points out, all this proved the prescience of Marx's analysis that prices would increasingly diverge from their real value (labour content).[440]

As the value of oil fell, members of the Organisation of Petroleum Exporting Countries (OPEC) agreed to cut aggregate oil output in order to raise prices. The US encouraged the price rises as petrodollars flowed into Wall Street, financing US deficits. At the time of Nixon's gold standard announcement the price of oil was less than $3 per barrel. In 1973, amid the Yom Kippur War in the Middle East, the price jumped to over $8; then to between $12 and $15 until 1979; and then to $30 long into the 1980s.[441] While this kept the price of oil within its historical range relative to gold, it was a massive shock to the global economy. By the end of 1974, the main stock indexes of the G7 countries fell in real terms by 43%. The US market did not recover its losses until 1993.

Nixon tried to tame inflation by implementing wage and price controls. According to Keynesian theory, this should have worked. Alas, it did not. Inflation combined with stagnant growth, dubbed 'stagflation', was a rare combination. Nixon was replaced by Jimmy Carter, whose administration went on the offensive against inflation. Fed chairman Paul Volcker's first move in 1980 was to push the interest rate to 11%. In June, he raised it to 20% and then again to 21.5%. This brutal monetary policy pushed inflation down from 13.5% in 1981 to 3.2% two years later. Unemployment levels shot up. Farmers on the edge of bankruptcy drove to Washington DC in their tractors and circled the Fed's headquarters.

In Britain, whose rate of profit fell by 3% between 1960 and 1970,[442] inflation hit 25% in 1975. A large-scale sell off of the over-valued pound began as investors anticipated another devaluation. The pound hit a record low against the dollar in June 1976. The US Treasury Secretary William Simon agreed with officials in the International Bank of Settlements that the pound had now become undervalued and offered to partially fund a stand-by loan of $5.3bn. He insisted, however, on repayment by December 1976. By the September, Britain had already drawn heavily on the short-term loan; a loan from the IMF would be necessary to fund the repayment. James Callaghan's Labour government made a request to borrow $3.9bn from the IMF, the largest amount at the time ever requested of the Fund, which needed to seek additional funds from the US and Germany.[443]

The IMF demanded heavy cuts in public expenditure and the budget deficit to keep inflation down as a precondition for the loan. Labour's relatively strong left-wing, led by cabinet members Anthony Crosland and Michael Foot, eventually acceded to a 20% cut to the deficit, as refusing the loan would have been followed by a further disastrous run on the pound. Chancellor Denis Healey announced large reductions in public spending on 15 December 1976. The working class would have to pay for the crisis. Labour began a war on benefits, wages and unions that would be finished by Margaret Thatcher and the Tories.[444] In the US, there were 39 work stoppages by government employees between 1962 and 1981, but none after Ronald Reagan fired 13,000 striking air traffic controllers, breaking their union permanently. From 1970 to 2003, US union membership halved. It fell by a third in the UK, by two-fifths in Japan and three-fifths in France.[445]

Three 'one-in-a-century' financial bubbles in three decades
'Keynesian social democracy', as we can see, paved the way for 'neoliberalism'. The ruling classes needed to restructure capitalism by reversing working class gains and loosening regulations, particularly in banking and foreign trade. But the state did not become less 'interventionst' – quite the opposite. The neoliberal state intervened to achieve these aims, including by overthrowing a number of democratically-elected social democratic governments overseas (not that this was anything new).[446] The neoliberal state has been so interventionist that Pento calls the period "permanent Keynesianism". Although this glosses over some of the very real

differences, it has some truth to it and highlights the continuations at play between the two supposedly oppositional 'ideologies'.

Because Volker's tight monetary policy (high interest rates) became so unpopular, he was replaced in 1987 by someone who favoured looser policy, Alan Greenspan. What followed is what Graham Summers in *The Everything Bubble* calls "three one-in-100-year asset bubbles". He says this because in the time between 1929 and 1987, the US was "effectively asset bubble free" – the prices of stocks, bonds, commodities, property and other asset classes never reached levels that were obscenely disconnected from their real prices.[447]

During the personal computer revolution, starting in the late 1970s, the Nasdaq (or Technology Stock Market Index) rose by 342% over 10 years. In the following 10 years (1990-2000) the dot com boom, or 'internet tech bubble', produced a figure of 960%. With monetary policy remaining loose, Wall Street took almost any company public (meaning they became publicly traded stocks) that had the terms 'com' or 'tech' in its name. In 1996, 41% of the companies Wall Street took public were unprofitable. Over the next two years that rose to 80%. The Nasdaq quadrupled.[448]

The internet tech bubble "made the previous largest bubble (1926-9) look like a small bump", says Summers.[449] The emerged partly because the future impact/value of the tech was difficult to value. The Fed, however, reduced rates from 5% to 4.5% when Nasdaq growth was at a healthy 5%, inflating the bubble. Growth grew to 5.5% and then 6.5% until rates were raised to 5.5%. The bubble burst in 2000, wiping out $6 trillion of wealth, 72% of the Nasdaq's value in 12 months. Since Summers puts almost all the blame on the Fed, he fails to take account of the fact that the internet, by rapidly accelerating the circulation of capital, represented the greatest cheapening – and rise of social productivity – of labour in history at that time. The bubble grew inversely to the underproduction of surplus value.

To avoid major debt deflation, interest rates had to be cut aggressively, from 6.4% in December 2000 to 1.82% 12 months later – making money 72% cheaper. In 2003 the rate was cut to 1%, almost three years after the end of the previous recession, with growth at 5%. "You could borrow at 1%, invest in anything tied to the economy and see a 4% return with minimal risk. That money had to go somewhere, and because Congress had relaxed regulations on who qualified to buy a home, it went into housing."[450] Effectively, Congress engineered subsidies to investors through the housing market.

This represented a move up the asset class pyramid. Only 21% of US American households directly trade stocks (although the figure rises to around 50% when indirect purchases through mortgages and pensions –

traded by banks, hedge funds, etc – are taken into account). A share in most publicly traded companies can be bought for $100 and many for as little as $20, making them 'liquid' assets. In contrast, historically between 50-60% of Americans have owned homes, making them highly 'illiquid', expensive assets.[451] Yet reflating the bubble by moving up an asset class became necessary to keep growth going and the banking system solvent.

The Community Development Act of 1992 required certain Government Sponsored Enterprises (GSEs) in the secondary mortgage market to spend at least 30% of their budget buying high-risk mortgage loans. GSEs were set up after 1929 to ensure that during crises, there were still entities willing to finance mortgages and the like, such as the Federal National Mortgage Association (Fannie Mae) and Federal Home Loan Mortgage Corporation (Freddie Mac). Instead of sitting on a mortgage loan and collected interest in the long-term, a bank or credit union could turn around and sell it to Fannie or Freddie Mac in the secondary mortgage market. The cash generated from this could then be used to make *another* loan.[452]

The 1992 Act required Fannie and Freddie to spend 30% of their budgets buying mortgages made to people who were at or below the median income in their respective communities – a huge incentive to banks to start lending to people in lower income brackets, thereby lowering lending requirements. Historically, banks would avoid granting mortgages to people who had a high probability of not paying the bank back, since the bank was responsible for the mortgage and at risk of losing money. Now that Fannie and Freddie Mac were willing to buy these mortgages from banks on the secondary market, banks could flip the mortgage to Fannie and Freddie for 100 cents on the dollar (full price).

Between 1994 and 2000, home ownership in the US rose from 64.2% to 67.5%, or by 8.33 million people, most of who would not be able to afford the mortgages after the bubble burst and low interest repayments went back up. In 2000, the government increased Fannie and Freddie's low-income mortgage quotas to 50% – $1 in every $2 spent was required to go on high-risk loans, giving the banks even more incentive to lend to low-income borrowers. With interest rates so low from 2000, house prices swelled from an average of about $150,000 around the time of the 1992 Act to $210,000 in 2000 and $300,000 in 2005. (Prices between 1997 and 2005 grew 154% in Britain and 244% in South Africa.) When housing prices peaked in 2006, debt deflation in the unregulated derivatives market (of mortgage-backed securities) followed.

By the time the bubble burst in 2008, the US mortgage market was $14 trillion in size, but thanks to unregulated derivatives, the actual risk related to the US housing market was well north of $175 trillion – 10 times the size of US GDP.[453] Thanks to a special class of financial products on Wall Street, sold to governments, corporations, hedge funds, other banks, etc, the bubble spread around the world. Globally, the notional value of the over-the-counter derivatives market was "in the ballpark of $1 *quadrillion* (1,000 trillion)", three times the size of global wealth.[454] Every financial institution with exposure to the unregulated derivatives market became uncertain of the value of its holdings, culminating in the panic sell-off. Lasting 15 months, it started in mortgage loans, spread to mortgage-backed securities, consumer loans, commercial paper loans and finally stock prices. People lost their homes – in 2009, 45% of subprime mortgages failed – and banks that had made the bad mortgage loans went bust. On 15 September 2008, Lehman Brothers, the US's fourth largest investment bank, filed for bankruptcy, sending shockwaves through the financial system, with the US stock market plummeting by 50% from its peak in 2007 to its low point in 2009.

Ben Bernanke, who replaced Greenspan in 2006, had claimed that this sort of debt deflation had been preventable. To halt deflation and save the banking system, he had to reinstall investor confidence in the unregulated derivatives market and its valuation methods. Quantative easing (QE) was the answer. The Fed bought $1.35 trillion worth of mortgage-backed securities, mostly from Fannie and Freddie Mac.

The Fed, however, could not buy all of the remaining $700 trillion in unregulated derivatives. Benanke and other financial regulators lobbied the Financial Accounting Standards Board to suspend 'mark to market' accounting standards for the banks regarding their mortgage-backed securities and other unregulated derivatives. Previously, when banks went to value a mortgage-backed security, they had to do so using the latest sales price at which similar assets had been sold. Before 2008, this was tolerated since the banks had been selling other, similar derivatives at nonsensically high valuations. During the crisis, many firms were selling these securities at fire sale prices. Banks and firms that continued to own unregulated derivatives were compelled to revalue their own securities at similar price levels, quickly leading to many banks facing solvency issues as their derivatives portfolios were being repriced lower and lower. In April 2009, however, the FAS Board suspended mark to market accounting standards on any assets that banks found to be illiquid, not just unregulated derivatives. Now the banks had full control over setting prices – and the Fed was willing to buy the worst of these securities through QE. The derivatives market started to reinflate.

The Fed implemented the zero rate interest policy. "Even during the Great Depression when the economy was barely moving, or during WWII when the US was issuing debt at a staggering pace to fund its war efforts, the Fed's Effective Federal Funds rate was 4% and 2% respectively," says Summers.[455]

From 2010, the US government spent $1 trillion in deficits for four consecutive years. In the eight years following the 2008 crisis, the US issued more debt than it had in all of its previous 230 years combined.

'The everything bubble'
Yields on corporate bonds are generally higher than on government bonds as investors demand a higher return to compensate for the greater risk. They generally track short-term Treasury Bills, however. A few years after the crisis, corporate bond yields began to trend towards the low T-Bill yields. Corporations, because of low rates and their own financial difficulties, began to issue corporate bonds at record pace. "It took 50+ years for the US corporate debt market to reach $3 trillion in size, but that doubled in eight years," says Summers.[456]

Zero rates primarily impacted short-term T-Bills or government bonds with terms of 52 weeks or less, but did little to long-term Treasury bonds, which remained at risk of potential debt deflation. To address this, the Fed printed $600bn to buy highly-priced longer-term Treasury bonds in its second round of QE (QE2) in 2010-11. This 'dumb money', or 'font-running', deliberately sparked a stampede for Treasuries that could be immediately sold on to the Fed. The yield on 10-year Treasuries fell to 1%. "The last time the yield on the 10-Year Treasury was this low was in the build up to WWII when capital was fleeing Europe for the US," says Summers.[457] With the end of QE2 in the June, yields began to rise on the long-end of the Treasury curve (Treasuries with maturation periods of 20 to 30 years). With QE2 politically toxic after unleashing a wave of global inflation, the Fed launched a new asset purchase programme called Operation Twist, selling short-term treasuries it owned to use the money from these sales to buy long-term Treasuries. The proposal induced private bond buying and the yield fell from above 4% to nearly 2.5%. Twist ran until December 2012, by which time QE3 had been announced, a $45bn a month programme to buy mortgage debt.

Within the bond bubble is a bubble in stocks. The 10-Year Treasury is the 'risk free' rate of return, or rate against which all risk in the US financial system is measured, and stocks are part of the 'risk'. Whatever money a company does have after bankruptcy will go to its bondholders long before equity holders see a dime. Investment firms and financial advisors make stock recommendations based on where where US Treasury yields are trading, though, and so the yields on stocks generally move in sync with US Treasury yields. Because of the financial crisis and accompanying recession, stock prices were rising. By pushing interest rates to zero, the Fed compelled investors to repurchase stocks, "directly fuelling a stock bubble by forcing capital into riskier assets like stocks".[458] After 2008, however, investors were wary of stocks. Enter primary dealers – the large banks and financial institutions responsible for most of the buyers of government debt. Summers adds:

"In this sense, QE1 was a kind of bailout for these firms. The Fed bought their garbage mortgage-backed securities from them at 100 cents on the dollar, giving them a fresh round of capital. In contrast, QE2 and Operation Twist were slightly different in that these programmes gave the primary dealers the ultimate 'dumb money' investor to front-run in the bond market for a quick profit. All of the above programmes accomplished ultimately the same thing: giving the primary dealers access to extra capital. Much of this new capital found its way into the stock market... As the Fed's balance sheet grew from acquiring assets, stocks rose in virtual lockstep. You could easily argue that the Fed's monetary programmes directly inflated a bubble in stocks by providing a near continuous line of new capital to the big banks which then funnelled this cash into stocks. And, because these financial firms can leverage up to ten times their capital levels, stocks weren't the only asset class that benefited from the Fed providing $3.5 trillion in capital to primary dealers, since these firms aren't just primary dealers... they're also investment fund managers, brokers, and investment banks: the very firms responsible for directing capital throughout the financial system.

"As a result of this, US stocks were not the only asset class to reflate courtesy of the bond bubble. Emerging market stocks, commodities and the like all disconnected from the economic fundamentals, fuelled by the tsunami of Fed fuelled liquidity. In this sense, Benanke's bond bubble truly became the 'everything bubble': a situation in which the bedrock of the entire global financial system (US Treasuries) entered a bubble forcing all other asset classes to adjust accordingly. Debt deflation had been conquered... for now. But this bubble, like all bubbles, will one day burst. And when it does, it will make 2008 look like a picnic. Good. God. Almighty."[459]

The interventionist neoliberal state

Any suggestion that the neoliberal state is not interventionist state is, as we can see, obvious nonsense. Were the huge stimulus packages that bailed out the banks not interventionist? The capitalist state always, in the end, does what is necessary to sustain capitalism, regardless of the differing ideologies between social democrats, liberals, conservatives and fascists, who argue only over their various self-interests, how best to sustain growth and how much carrot and stick to use in managing the mass of the working class, who cannot afford the time or money to participate in capitalist 'democracy'. Ultimately they form an anti-communist, anti-working class coalition. Bourgeois democracy is in effect a one-party state, ie an all-capitalist state. Like any party, it comprises numerous factions. This reality is neatly obscured by the pretence of various party colours.

Any capitalist state's first priority has to be economic growth. If capital isn't growing sufficiently, investment falls and recession follows. So when the private sector crashes, the state has no choice but to intervene, as it did when it bailed out the banks at massive expense to the public purse; as it has continually done in transferring increasingly huge amounts of surplus value from the public to the private sector, whether via subsidies, tax cuts or privatisations.

Neoliberalism has not 'shrunk the state' – as was the supposed intention of 'Reaganism' in the US or 'Thatcherism' in Britain – it has overseen a huge expansion in the power of the state. It may have had to cut the staff numbers employed by the state, including in the police and armed forces, but it has countered this through mass surveillance (although primarily to save labour costs), with draconian 'anti-terrorist' laws that curb free speech; by diluting trade union power; by all but abolishing legal aid; and so on. The neoliberal state has intervened to plunder the working class on behalf of capital, out of necessity. Neoliberialism is clearly then one step removed from fascism, which depends on a powerful state to make the private ownership of industry efficient enough to ensure its continuation. In fact the first mass privatisation of state property took place in Nazi Germany.[460] The Third Reich even coined the term *Die Reprivatisierung*, reprivatisation. Fascism, just like neoliberalism, becomes necessary at a given stage of accumulation for exactly the same reasons, ie rationalisation and devaluation, just in an even more extreme form.[461] (It is also unsustainable for the same reasons, and can only 'at best' hope to restore liberal democracy – somewhat ironic given fascists supposedly hate liberalism.)

Keynes was wrong
Clearly, the necessary conditions for an extensive period of Keynesian social democracy no longer exist. While state investment in infrastructure and a nationalisation programme would hardly be unwelcome, neither would "pay for itself"; inflation would rise significantly as the level of state investment would be paid for by printing money, stretching the value of fiat currency yet further, and through tax hikes on the capitalist class, squeezing their already weak profit margins and compelling them to raise prices, cut staff, or both. The growth in national debt, too, would continue to accelerate. Even if the remaining capitalists were left with no choice but to tolerate social democracy, say after a devastating depression or war, they would at some point have to find a way of crushing it if they themselves wanted to survive as capitalists.

Consider that Keynes predicted that working hours would fall to 15 per week along the way to "solving the economic question" under capitalism by around 2030 and it is clear that he did not understand the system he studied.[462] In Britain, the average full-time working week is still 42.7 hours, when it is supposed to be 37.5. In 2015 the Trades Union Congress (TUC) found that at least four million employees work more than 48 hours, up by 350,000, or 15%, on a decade before.[463] The TUC also found that in Britain workers do at least *two billion* hours of unpaid work a year,[464] and this does not include the out-of-hours work of answering emails and other work-related messages on personal phones etc – not to mention the free labour and content we all provide for social media companies. In poorer parts of the world, of course, the working day is as long as ever. In South Korea, the country that until recently had the highest rates of suicide, a 68-hour working week was only reduced to 52 in 2016.

Marx pointed out the "great importance" of the "rapidity and intensity" of labour, which increased as limits on the length of the working day were established. The pace of work

> "imposes on the worker increased expenditure of labour within a time which remains constant, a heightened tension of labour-power, and closer filling up of the pores of the working day... This compression of a greater mass of labour into a given period now counts for what it really is, namely an increase in the quantity of labour... The denser hour of the 10-hour working day contains more labour, ie expended labour-power, than the more porous hour of the 12-hour working day."[465]

Recently mooted moves now to reduce the working day in Britain to six hours or the working week to four days would represent an attempt to intensify productivity, to reduce the porousness of the eight-hour day/five-day week. Indeed, capitalists getting behind the idea want to couple it with the banning of personal social media activity during work hours.

Work became increasingly hard during the 1990s, and intensified again between 2006 and 2012, particularly for women working full time. The number of employed workers in Britain who reported to the Skills and Employment Survey that their jobs required them to work "very hard" rose from 32% in 1992 to 46% in 2017. The proportion of workers who said that they are exhausted by the time they leave work increased between 2012 and 2017 to around 47% of men and 55% of women. The authors of the survey argue that this has been driven by new technologies that schedule and monitor tasks in a way that demands maximum efficiency, filling up every minute of the working day and reducing breaks for rest. The health of the workforce is suffering as a result. Workers in Britain and the north of Ireland take a total of 12.5 million days off work due to illness every year. Technological innovations may appear to be the cause of all this, but the real reason is how technology is necessarily deployed to raise surplus value during a deepening capitalist crisis.

Automation and the state

Technological development is no exception to the interventionist rule. Because capital is a fetter on investment and productivity growth, the private sector is highly dependent on the state when it comes to raising productivity.[466] *The Guardian*'s economics editor Larry Elliott wrote in July 2017 that "governments have to invest in the fourth industrial revolution".[467] The ruling class may detest them, but some sections may see McDonnell and Labour leader Jeremy Corbyn as just the men they need to sell automation to the working class.

It would be another rude awakening for British labour. For example: when Harold Wilson's Labour government nationalised most of the steel industry under British Steel in 1967 and increased production despite falling demand, one seventh of 350,000 steel-making jobs were lost even before Thatcher came to power and began her ruthless war on industrial workers. In 1980, British Steel reported a loss of more than £1bn, then a record for a British company, and a year later it slashed staff from 271,000 to 167,000. The Labour Party and the major trade unions had in effect laid the groundwork for justifying Tory cuts – the 'Keynesian' alternative had already been tried. By drastically reducing its labour costs British Steel eventually returned to profit in 1986. When it was privatised two years later, it employed only 52,000.[468]

In his support for state investment in automation, McDonnell takes the default social democratic line that it needs to be coupled with investment in new high skilled work, implying that if only everybody learned to code, they would all flourish in this IT-intensive world. As Turner says:

"First, in a world of ever-increasing automation possibilities, we only need a very small number of very clever IT literate people to write all the code for all the robots, all the apps, and all the computer games, and we need only a minuscule fraction of the global population to drive inexorable progress towards ever-more profound AI and super-intelligence.

"Three decades or more since we first began to talk of living in a computer age, the total number of workers employed in the development and production of computer hardware, software and applications, is still only 4% of the total workforce, and the US Bureau of Labor Statistics predicts just 135,000 new jobs in software development from 2014 to 2024, versus 458,000 additional personal care aides, and 348,000 home health aides.

"Total employment in the giant mobile phone, software and internet companies which dominate global equity values is a minute drop in the global labour market. Facebook, with a market capitalisation of $500bn, employs just 25,000 people. However many people learn to code, and to develop apps and computer games, all of the income from app and computer game development will still accrue to the very small number of people who are skilled enough or lucky enough to create the most popular apps or games. If an increasing percentage of the total workforce is employed in difficult to automate face-to-face services, the equilibrium wage rate for those jobs may be influenced hardly at all by whether they have the skill required to be an adequate, but still second tier, software developer. We almost certainly face a challenge of rising inequality to which better skills – however intrinsically desirable – will prove a wholly inadequate response."[469]

Unless McDonnell were to genuinely break with capitalism, his investment in skilled jobs would only be on behalf of a labour aristocracy, a privileged layer of workers.

Universal Basic Income: neither basic or universal

McDonnell and Labour, along with the Green Party, Scottish National Party (SNP) and a section of the Conservatives, want to see investment in automation accompanied by a Universal Basic Income (UBI). This is not a new idea. It was advocated by the Greens in the 1990s. Nick Srnicek and Alex Williams, co-authors of *Inventing the Future: Postcapitalism and a World Without Work*, argue that instead of resisting full automation we should demand it, alongside an "unconditional and generous" UBI, which would supposedly guarantee a decent standard of living for everybody, including those whose jobs have been automated. They therefore argue that automation is inherently progressive because it is liberating humanity from work. But under capitalism, this can't be the case, since workers are left increasingly alienated, redundant and destitute. Such a 'demand' on the seamless, utopian road to 'postcapitalism', can only be made in the belief that capital accumulation is a harmonious process.[470]

It is not work *per se* from which humanity seeks liberation, but the carrot and stick coercion of wage-slavery. Disalienated and decommodified work – contributing to the collective good of society instead of the private profit of the rich – would, Marx argued, "become attractive work, the individual's self-realisation".[471]

A generous UBI is not possible. Now that we are in a late-stage of capital accumulation, state welfare – which forms part of the total outlay on wages – is already all but unaffordable. A £2.5bn cut coming into force in 2018 included a 3% real-terms cut in working-age benefits, affecting 11 million families. Even a section of the Conservative Party is concerned that the new Universal Credit (UC)[472] benefits system is cutting too deeply. (Probably more than anything because they fear a backlash on the streets, with former Tory Prime Minister John Major warning that it could spark scenes similar to the 1991 Poll Tax riots that brought Thatcher's premiership to an end.) The British state has been sanctioning benefit claimants callously, increasingly so since 2010, exacerbating a mental health crisis and suicide epidemic, and inspiring the Ken Loach film *I, Daniel Blake*.[473] Increasing numbers of migrants have been excluded from state welfare and public services altogether.

Whether the proponents of UBI genuinely believe that it would provide a decent standard of living for the poor and unemployed or not is not particularly important, but given that the Labour, Liberal Democrat, Scottish Nationalist and Green parties all support British imperialism's inherently racist immigration[474] controls,[475] it seems unlikely. Migrants locked up in British detention centres would not be entitled to UBI. If UBI provided a blanket base rate, poor people living in areas with higher rents, which will continue to rise as the capitalist crisis deepens,[476] would be at a disadvantage. UBI could not be applied universally, and with an ever-shrinking amount of surplus value per capita available for government spending, neither would it cover the basic costs required for a decent standard of living.

When right-wingers opposed to UBI say it is unaffordable, they aren't lying. Under capitalism, it isn't. If it were set so that each individual over the age of 16 received a minimum income at the income poverty line (approximately £16,320), it would cost £850bn – 105% of current state expenditure.[477] This is presumably why McDonnell has backed a proposal from the New Economics Foundation (NEF) for a £48.08 "Weekly National Allowance" (WNA),[478] amounting to a paltry £2,500.16 a year for over-18s earning less than £125,000 a year.[479] The think tank says as many as 88% of adults would see their post-tax income rise or stay the same. Overall, the poorest 10% of households would see their disposable income increase by £1,160 per year or around £20 per week, equal to a 15.8% increase, lifting around 200,000 families above the poverty line. The richest 10% would contribute around £40 per week extra in tax.

The weekly payments would be fully funded by abolishing the tax-free personal allowance, which has risen consistently over the past decade, removing nearly two million people from income tax and therefore billed as a way of supporting people on low incomes. As of April 2019, the first £12,500 of earnings are not charged the 20% basic rate of income tax.

But this has been a classic sleight of hand by the Tories, reducing tax liabilities for the richest 10% of families by almost £6,500 in 2019/20 alone, compared with just £600 for the poorest 10%. According to Oxfam, in 2018 the poorest 10% of Britons paid a higher effective tax rate (the average rate at which an individual is taxed on earned income) than the richest 10% (49% versus 34%) once taxes on consumption such as VAT are taken into account.

The personal allowance is worth double for the 13% of highest income adults, mainly because the higher rate threshold – 40% on income additional to £50,000 – rises pound-for-pound automatically with any increase in the personal allowance. This increases the amount of top incomes taxed at 20% rather than 40%. NEF estimates the current cost of the tax-free allowance is as much as £111.2bn, "costing more than the whole of defence, local government and the Department for Transport combined and enriching the highest income households almost seven times faster than the poorest".

Replacing the current model with a WNA would therefore be "fiscally neutral" while redistributing £8bn currently spent on tax allowances that benefit the 35% of highest income households to the rest of the population. Even this shallow form of UBI then would likely come up against resistance from the ruling and middle classes, especially as it would also mean bringing down the threshold for higher-rate taxpayers from £50,000 to £37,500, because the starting point for 40% income tax moves with the personal allowance, affecting the top 13% of earners in the country.

Progressive (if limited) social reforms tend to get a hearing only when it can be proven that they save money (which is why militant mass protesting is the most effective way of winning reforms, since policing them costs the state so much money). Initial cuts invariably save less than forecast in the long run because, for example, impoverished people are forced to turn to crime to survive; rising homelessness results in 'anti-social behaviour'; depression and alcoholism rise; benefit claimants receive less money but the number of claimants grows; and so on. All this stretches the budgets of councils, the NHS, police, prisons, etc. Who knew inefficiency was so expensive?

In fact, despite the need to put increasingly more surplus value towards valorisation instead of social needs, and despite the relative cuts made because of this, social spending as a percentage of GDP in absolute terms has continued to rise throughout the neoliberal era, although mostly because of the growing costs of social care and pensions amid an ageing population.

But because capitalism operates in short-term cycles of valorisation, it necessitates short-term thinking. Allocating enough surplus value for McDonnell's infrastructure projects and a properly decent UBI would eat hugely into the surplus value that needs to be put towards valorising capital, and so these social democratic demands have been met with immense resistance from the ruling and middle classes.

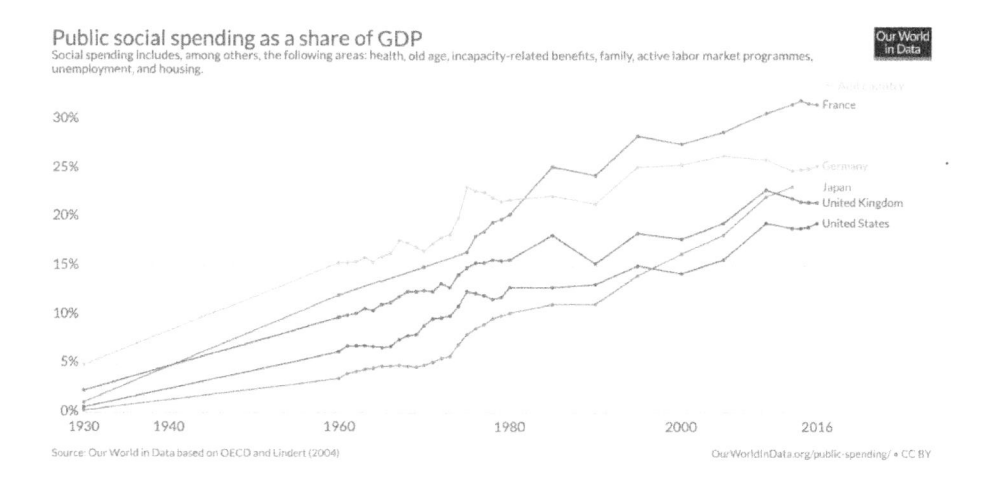

Ruling class reaction

During a period of economic crisis, the ruling class is inclined to do everything in its power to make sure the government is acting in the needs of capital, and that means putting in charge a right-wing party that is willing to force down wages etc, and to do so by being prepared to use the repressive apparatus of the state if necessary.

Even if a Corbyn-led Labour had been elected, say on the back of Tory divisions over Brexit, the ruling and middle classes would have done everything they could to cow him and his supporters to compromise and capitulate. For example, capitalists can punish policies they don't like by disinvesting in government bonds, thereby reducing the amount of revenue available for state expenditure.

If Corbyn, who pledged to increase budgets for the NHS and education, for example, pushed too far and economic growth began to suffer too much, the ruling class (or at least a section of it) would, if it could not remove him through underhand but constitutional means, at least consider resorting to unconstitutional means or even a military coup. Just one week after Corbyn's election as Labour leader, an unnamed serving general of the Army told *The Sunday Times* that Corbyn would trigger a "mutiny" if he became Prime Minister and tried to scrap Trident, pull out of NATO or if he announced "any plans to emasculate and shrink the size of the armed forces", saying: "The army wouldn't stand for it... people would use whatever means possible, fair or foul to prevent that."

The campaign from both the conservative and liberal media against Corbyn, a mild social democrat, was ferocious. He triggered a level of panic in the ruling class not seen since a military coup was nearly undertaken against Labour Prime Minister Harold Wilson in 1968. McDonnell and Corbyn have been labelled "potty Marxists" in the right-wing press merely for suggesting that UBI might be worth considering, while unelected civil servants appointed by the ruling class briefed the media about their supposed concern that Corbyn is too old and "frail" to be prime minister. Corbyn has been smeared as an anti-Semite for his vocal support for Palestinians, who have been brutally oppressed and ethnically cleansed for decades by the settler-colonial state of Israel, which defends imperialism's interests in the Middle East.[480]

The media attacks are designed to cow voters and undermine Corbyn's credibility, but they can also have the effect, whether intended or not, of inciting fascists to take it upon themselves to 'save the country' from 'cultural Marxism'. In March 2019, Corbyn was assaulted at a Mosque in North London by a 'lone wolf', the same mosque where a fascist murdered a Muslim man in

June 2017. A year earlier, Labour MP Jo Cox, a liberal, was shot dead by a fascist because of her support for Syrian refugees. In poorer countries where the class struggle is much sharper, this sort of violence is far more common. In Colombia, for example, 173 trade unionists and social leaders were murdered in 2018 up to the end of October, 31 of them since the election of the hard-right conservative Iván Duque in the August.[481]

But the aggression on display in the media betrayed the weakness of the British ruling class. As *The Telegraph* admitted in an article considering the possibility of a military coup:

"For any modern day coup to work against a radical Labour prime minister, a comparable, charismatic figurehead would also be required. Even assuming a plausible unelected leader was found, would they really want to challenge Corbyn's 1.4 million Facebook followers with a depleted army of less than 80,000 soldiers? [The number has been cut from 102,000 since 2009.][482] Were tanks to arrive now [in the age of social media] outside the BBC and Channel 4 News … one imagines the beleaguered PM would emulate President Erdogan of Turkey, who, when faced with his own coup in 2016, communicated via WhatsApp, tweeted his nine million followers and rallied supporters on FaceTime using his iPhone."[483]

Still, Corbyn would not enjoy the kind of support a right-winger like Erdogan has in the military and intelligence services. Nor should we underestimate the willingness of the ruling class to shut down the internet. But if the ruling class fears one million Corbyn supporters, imagine how it would tremble if the whole working class, millions and millions of people, was united and prepared to fight for actual socialism.

Corbyn's capitulations

The only thing, however, that would spur the British ruling class to take drastic action in this scenario is a deepening economic crisis. (Although this would give them the option of allowing Corbyn to become prime minister and waiting for the economy to crash, believing they could then defeat him in an election by saying that he has proven that 'socialism' does not work). They need not worry too much about Corbyn's supposed radicalism.

Because he had to put his electability first, Corbyn had to prioritise the unity of the Labour Party above all else, meaning he capitulated time and again to its politically dominant 'neoliberal' or right wing. Real power in the party clearly does not lie with the hundreds of thousands of grassroots members Corbyn attracted.

Under Corbyn: Labour has failed to oppose two racist immigrations bills; it abstained on a vote to improve working rights for asylum seekers; he allowed a free vote on the decision to bomb Syria when a three-line whip on his MPs would have prevented the vote from even going ahead; and, having claimed to be anti-austerity, he instructed Labour councils to comply with budgets set by central government. Labour's much-vaunted 2017 manifesto pledged to reverse just £2bn of the £9bn cuts to welfare made by the Tories. The manifesto also retained Labour's commitment to NATO and says nothing of Corbyn's republicanism or his past opposition to Britain's Trident nuclear programme. In a morally bankrupt bid to outflank the Tories on the right, Corbyn's manifesto even promised to hire more police and border staff to two institutions that under capitalism are necessarily racist.

Corbyn also dropped his opposition to Zionist Israel's right to exist and capitulated to a witch hunt of anti-Zionists along with the implementation of the International Holocaust Remembrance Alliance definition of anti-Semitism, which deliberately conflates anti-Semitism with anti-Zionism.

Although it should be acknowledged that Corbyn's timidity is partly explained by the lack of militancy of the movement behind him – which he can only take so much responsibility for – Corbyn proved what actual socialists have said all along, that Labour is unreformable. It remains what it has always been:[484] a bourgeois, imperialist, racist, anti-working class party.[485]

Given all of these factors – the economic illiteracy and timidity of social democrats; ruling class reaction; and the manufactured confines of parliament – Marxists can only conclude that a parliamentary road to socialism is impossible and that proletarian dictatorship is necessary to defeat counter-revolution.

12. Proletarianisation and the historical demands of the productive forces

"Without a revolutionary theory, there can be no revolutionary movement."[486]

Lenin

Those who are lucky enough to find or remain in work as the capitalist crisis deepens will see their pay and conditions savagely forced down. In April 2018, the World Bank recommended yet more deregulation in a report that said "high minimum wages, undue restrictions on hiring and firing and strict contract forms all make workers more expensive vis-à-vis technology".[487] International capital is preparing a major assault on international labour in order to accelerate moves towards automation.

Capitalists could be forced to slow down or stop the introduction of new automation by, say, a strong and militant neo-Luddite or trade union movement and – the usual driver for concessions – the desire for social peace. But the contradiction persists: capital accumulation, and staying ahead of or keeping up with competitors, requires higher productivity and therefore labour-saving innovation. The deeper capitalism sinks into crisis the more necessary it becomes to raise productivity. That is, the more workers are replaced by robots, the greater the underproduction of surplus value becomes, and yet the system needs to respond by replacing more workers with robots. If it cannot do this then capital goes unvalorised and the economy crashes. From the perspective of the bourgeoisie, a strong neo-Luddite or trade union movement would sooner or later have to be crushed.

In an article in January 2018 headlined "When the next recession hits, the robots will be ready", the *Washington Post* pointed out that innovations happen quickest "when employers slash payrolls going into a downturn and, out of necessity, turn to software or machinery to take over the tasks once performed by their laid-off workers".[488] Pointing to growing expectations by economists of a financial crisis in 2020, the paper adds that the "next wave of automation won't just be sleek robotic arms on factory floors. It will be ordering kiosks, self-service apps and software smart enough to perfect schedules and cut down on the workers needed to cover a shift. Employers are already testing these systems. A recession will force them into the mainstream."

Striking statistics from an upcoming paper by economists Nir Jaimovich and Henry Siu "found that 88% of job loss in routine occupations occurs within 12 months of a recession. In the 1990-1991, 2001 and 2008-09 recessions, routine jobs accounted for 'essentially all' of the jobs lost. They regained almost no ground during the subsequent recoveries."[489]

Automation under capitalism is accelerating the trend towards proletarianisation, higher levels of poverty and the underproduction of surplus value. It is the sharpest of sharpening contradictions, a vicious circle from which capitalism cannot escape. It is a trend which increasingly threatens a final breakdown.

The 'Leninist' road to socialism[490] – whereby workers' councils (aka soviets) effectively form an independent state, a situation of dual power, and then, when strong enough, do away with what is left of the capitalist state – seems to be dismissed now more than ever; by liberals who claim that the demise of the Soviet Union signalled the 'end of history';[491] by anarchists and autonomists who believe a leap into 'full communism' can be achieved without a socialist state; and by 'democratic socialists' who claim socialism can be built via bourgeois democracy by voting through 'socialist policies'.

Then there is the notion that Marx and Lenin are redundant because the supposed protagonist of their revolutionary strategy – the industrial proletariat – is dead or irrelevant. There are several problems with this claim. The accusation about the industrial proletariat is made, in slightly different ways, not just by liberals but by some anarchists, who do not claim that the industrial proletariat is dead but persist with the myth that it is the protagonist of the Leninist revolution. The Bolsheviks focused on agitating among the urban or industrial proletariat because that was the most efficient use of scarce resources, with the intention that the message would then spread outwards to the wider proletariat as a whole.

Lenin, though, is renowned for ruthlessly criticising socialists who limited their agitation to "trade union consciousness" or "economism"; ie, for simply supporting, or 'tailing', working class demands, without advocating an independent working class party or proletarian dictatorship (or, before that, the overthrow of tsarism). Lenin called these socialists labour aristocrats, a privileged layer of union officials who mislead the masses with solely reformist demands. Hence why he said revolutionaries had to "dig deeper into the real masses" of the poorest workers, who had the least to lose and the most to gain. This meant that, in Russia, he saw the need for an alliance between workers and poor peasants. Today, Leninists still see the poorest and most oppressed workers as the main protagonists of revolution.

The claim that the industrial proletariat is dead is either dishonest or smacks of 'first world' myopia. The industrial proletariat may have shrunk in the imperialist nations over the past 40 years but internationally it has grown spectacularly. In 2010, 79%, or 541 million, of the world's industrial workers lived in 'less developed regions', up from 34% in 1950 and 53% in 1980, compared to the 145 million industrial workers, or 21% of the total, who in 2010 lived in the imperialist countries.[492]

This shift is even greater in the manufacturing industry, since in emerging nations manufacturing forms a much higher proportion of total industrial employment than in imperialist countries; and therefore, as John Bellamy Foster points out, "the broad category of 'industrial employment' systematically understates the extent to which the world share of manufacturing has grown in developing countries", citing figures for the US and China showing these ratios to be 58.1% and 75.2% respectively.[493] "Extrapolating these two ratios to 'more developed' and 'less developed' countries as a whole, 83% of the world's manufacturing workforce lives and works in the nations of the Global South," says John Smith in *Imperialism in the Twenty-First Century*.[494]

Based on the integration of 'southern' workers into the global economy, the IMF has also attempted to take into account qualitative as well as quantitative changes, calculating an "export-weighted global workforce" by multiplying the numerical growth of the workforce by the increasing degree to which they produce for the global market rather than the domestic market. Since southern-manufactured exports grew more than twice as fast as GDP during the quarter-century leading up to the global crisis in 2007, the IMF estimates that the effective global workforce quadrupled in size between 1980 and 2003.

But even within the imperialist nations, where the industrial working class has declined both absolutely and relatively, Smith points to "deepening proletarianisation", saying that

> "the proletarians have increased their already overwhelming predominance within the economically active population [EAP].... Between 1980 and 2005 the proportion of waged and salaried workers in total EAP in ... the developed nations steadily rose, from 83% to 88% (in

2005, around 500 million people), indicating deepening proletarianisation in these countries."[495]

In the US, it is even higher, with waged workers as a proportion of the EAP increasing from 90.6% in 1980 to 93.2% in 2011.[496] Because of distortions made by the ILO's methods, this undoubtedly underestimates or obscures the size of the labour aristocracy, something we will come back to further on, but the trend is nevertheless clear, with more and more workers being forced into low-paid services work.

Obviously with China, India and the former Soviet bloc being integrated into the global economy, 1.47 billion workers joined the global capitalist workforce very suddenly. But this does not distort the overall trend.

With their supposed bias for the industrial proletariat, Leninists are accused of failing to recognise the multiple sections of the working class or its fragmentation. But far from ignoring the heterogeneous make-up of the working class, this is one of the factors that contribute to the Leninist conclusion that a vanguard party is necessary – to unite the disparate and sectional struggles of the working class into one unstoppable force.

Likewise, the fact recognised across the Left that technological advances have fragmented the working class, that they have reduced workers' leverage in their struggles against their bosses, reflected in the imperialist countries by the low number of strikes since the 1980s, *must mean that the state is the primary battleground*. We are already seeing this in the re-emergence of social democratic movements (see the previous chapter), whereby downwardly mobile labour aristocracies are becoming slightly more antagonistic and attempting to harness the power of the working class as a whole, in what is essentially a fight with the middle and ruling classes over allocations of surplus value.

These strawman accusations against Lenin misrepresent or misinterpret his definition of the proletariat, which followed Marx's. The main feature of the proletariat as a class is not its direct link with the means of production but rather its *separation* from them. In other words, the proletariat is first and foremost characterised as a class by the fact that it does not own the means of production and has to work for wages. The salient feature is not what differentiates them, but what unites them. The more a worker is dependent on selling their labour power for survival the deeper their proletarianisation.

Indeed, it is the fact that the industrial proletariat is shrinking relative to the working class as a whole, relegating a significant proportion of previously privileged workers into the poorer sections of the working class, that sees the mass of the latter grow numerically in strength. As Volkov says:

"As the mass of exploited manual workers decreases due to scientific and technological progress, particularly automation, the mass of exploited intellectual workers, ie white collar employees, engineers and scientists [who increasingly contribute to commodity production] also increases in reverse proportion (or even more rapidly)."[497]

The casualisation of university employment in the past few years is a case in point. In the US, although union membership stood at a lowly 10.7% of the workforce at the start of 2019, the unionisation of traditionally non-unionised white collar labour almost doubled between 2010 and 2017.[498]

According to the Pew Research Center, the median wealth (assets minus debts) of the US middle class fell by 28% from 2001 to 2013.[499] People on middle incomes[500] accounted for 50% of the US adult population in 2015, down from 61% in 1971, while the poorest tier of the working class comprised 20% of the population in 2015 compared to 16% in 1975. The number of people receiving supplemental nutritional assistance, or food stamps, exploded from 26 million in 2007 to 46 million in 2012.[501] 63% of the population say they have less than $500 in personal savings.[502] At the same time private and household debt has gone through the roof. In the 1970s, personal and credit card debts ballooned by 238% relative to the 1960s. In the 1980s it shot up on the previous decade by another 318%; and by another 180% in the 1990s.[503]

According to the Fed, household debt rose to a record $13.5 trillion in the fourth quarter of 2018, nearly 7% higher than in the third quarter of 2008. A record number of US Americans, more than seven million, were also three months or more behind on repayments for car loans. As *New York Times* journalist Amy Chozick noted in May 2015, "the once ubiquitous term 'middle class' has gone conspicuously missing from the 2016 [presidential] campaign trail, as candidates and their strategists grasp for new terms for an unsettled economic era [in which] the middle class has for millions of families become a precarious place to be".[504]

"Capitalism in the age of automation increasingly turns the majority of the population into proletarians and, in doing so, creates all economic, social and political prerequisites for the system's downfall," says Volkov.[505] The deeper the system sinks into crisis, the more proletarians are created, through bankruptcies, unemployment, wage cuts, and so on, and the more radicalised they are likely to become.

This is borne out by the real development of the international proletariat. While we have already seen that the industrial proletariat has grown enormously, according to the ILO, the world's "economically active population" (EAP) grew from 1.9 billion in 1980 to 3.1 billion in 2006.[506] Almost all of this numerical growth took place in the 'emerging nations', now home to 84% of the global workforce, 1.6 billion of whom worked for wages. The other one billion were small farmers and a multitude of people working in the 'informal economy',[507] which is, according to Mike Davis "the fastest growing social class on Earth".[508] In Africa, up to 70% of workers are 'working poor', the highest of any continent.

While the industrial proletariat in the 'global south' has grown enormously since 1980, its share of the south's total workforce has been much more modest, rising from 14.5% in 1980, to 16.1% in 1990, to 19.1% in 2000, to 23.1% in 2010[509] – because the absolute growth of the non-industrial proletariat is even greater. Senior ILO economist Nomaan Majid points out that the commerce sector, not manufacturing, "is the main employment growth sector in both low- and middle-income groups".[510] This links back to what we saw in chapter four – that even in the developing nations, the trend towards automation is accompanied by growing unproductive work.

Agricultural employment in the south, meanwhile, has declined to 48% of its EAP, down from 73% in 1960, and from "approximately one-third" to just 4% of EAP in developed countries. However, the ILO reports: "Despite the declining share of agricultural workers in total employment, the absolute numbers of those engaged in agriculture are still rising, most notably in south Asia, east Asia, and Sub-Saharan Africa."[511]

The other significant component of the growing proletariat? The unemployed. Smith reports that, apart from China,

> "no economy has grown fast enough to provide jobs to the legions of young people entering the labour market and the rural exodus to swollen cities in search of work. Even at the zenith of export-oriented industrialisation the ILO reported that 'in the late 20th century, manufacturing ceased being a major sector of employment growth, except in east and southeast Asia'."

The ILO said global unemployment rose by 31 million to 201 million between 2007 and 2010, 55% of which came in the developed economies despite accounting for only 15% of the global labour force. With each recession since the 1980s, it has taken longer and longer to recover absolute job losses (two years after 1981, four after 2000, six after 2008). The long-term unemployment rate doubled from 2007 to 2014 in the US – where the labour force participation rate (see footnote 426) for primary age workers (25-54) fell from 85% in the late 1990s to 80.5% in 2015 – and rose from 20 to 50% in Spain. In Europe, official unemployment was over 10% in 2015, with youth unemployment rising above 50% in Greece and Spain. In North Africa, where overall unemployment was about 11% in 2017, youth unemployment was 25%, but was even higher in Botswana, the Republic of the Congo, Senegal, and South Africa, among others.[512]

Attacks on wages

The numerical growth of the working class has been coupled with a massive attack on its wages, further deepening proletarianisation. In a striking example of how constant capital rises relative to variable capital, John Lanchester writes in the *London Review of Books* that in the US:

> "In 1960, the most profitable company in the world's biggest economy was General Motors (GM). In today's money, GM made $7.6bn that year. It also employed 600,000 people. Today's most profitable company employs 92,600. So where 600,000 workers would once generate $7.6bn in profit, now 92,600 generate $89.9bn, an improvement in profitability per worker of 76.65 times. Remember, this is pure profit for the company's owners, after all workers have been paid. Capital isn't just winning against labour: there's no contest. If it were a boxing match, the referee would stop the fight."[513]

Whereas wages in the US rose by 350% between 1927 and 1977, real terms growth has since been in decline. In Britain, wages grew at an annual average of 2.9% in the 1960s and 70s, 1.5% in the 90s and 1.2% in the 2000s. Between 2007 and 2015 that trend accelerated at an unprecedented rate, with real household wages falling by 10.4%.[514] The Resolution Foundation said the 2010s would be the worst decade for UK wage growth since the late 18th century. But as bad as the attack on wages in imperialist countries has been, it has been even worse in the countries imperialism plunders, where workers are of course already paid much less.

According to the ILO's World of Work Report 2011, since the early 1990s the "share of domestic income that goes to labour ... declined in nearly three-quarters of the 69 countries with available information". While "the wage share among advanced economies has been trending downward since 1975", it "occurred at a much more moderate pace than among emerging and developing economies – falling roughly nine percentage points since 1980".[515] In contrast, the fall in Asia between 1994 and 2010 was around 20%.

The imperialist countries have also seen a decline in full-time self-employment and self-employed income. This has included a continuing shrinkage in the number of small family farmers, indicating the proletarianisation of portions of the lower middle classes.

Michael Elsby's study *The Decline of US Labor Share* reports that the "rise in inequality is even more striking for proprietors' income than it is for payroll income. In 1948 the bottom 90% of employees earned 75% of payroll compensation. By 2010 this had declined to 54%. For entrepreneurial income, however, this fraction plummeted from 42% in 1948 to 14% in 2010."[516]

A separate study of 2014 data by the US Small Business Administration suggests the same pattern regarding millennials (generally defined as people born between 1985 and 2004). "Fewer than 4% of 30 year-olds reported they were in full-time self-employment – a proxy for entrepreneurship – compared with 5.4% of Generation X-ers [1965 and 1984] and 6.7% of Baby Boomers [1945 and 1964] at the same age," the *FT* reported.[517]

Furthermore, the pace of decline in wages has accelerated in recent years, "with the wage share falling more than 11 percentage points between 2002 and 2006. In China, the wage share declined by close to 10 percentage points since 2000."[518] Africa's workers saw their share of national income reduced by 15% in the two decades since 1990, again "with most of this decline – 10 percentage points – taking place since 2000. The decline is even more spectacular in north Africa, where the wage share fell by more than 30 percentage points after 2000."[519]

Latin America saw the lowest decline, of 10% since 1993, and most of it before 2000, undoubtedly due to strong workers' organisation and resistance, represented by the left-wing 'Pink Tide' in Venezuela,[520] Bolivia, Brazil and Argentina.

As mentioned, mainstream economic accounting methods under-represent the size of the middle classes and labour aristocracy – which are bound to be proportionately bigger in imperialist nations – and do not take account of sharply increasing inequality between skilled/professional and unskilled workers or of income to capital that has been classified as income to labour, such as bonuses paid to bankers and wages and sponsorship of sports professionals etc, meaning the real extent of the fall in labour's share is even higher, and considerably so. Elsby attempts to challenge these distortions, writing that in the US, the Bureau of Labor Statistics' (BLS) calculation of a decline of 3.9% in the share of national income for labour over 1987-2013 becomes a 10% decline when the highest paid 1% of employees are excluded, and a 14% decline when the highest paid 10% are excluded. Based on this more honest method, the lowest 90% of wage earners (84% of the US's total economically active population) actually earned 42% of the total payroll in 1980 and just 28% in 2011. Elsby also found that the fall for labour has accelerated as time has progressed, declining by twice as much between 2000 and 2011 as in the previous two decades.[521]

Again, the trend towards proletarianisation is clear. The material basis for a position of relative privilege among the lower middle classes and labour aristocracy is disappearing. The proletariat is numerically stronger than ever, especially as an international class. 'Neoliberal globalisation', which promised to produce prosperous nations of entrepreneurs and homeowners, has instead produced capitalism's grave-diggers.

Inequality

All this is confirmed by the fact that inequality has hit record levels. In 2018 and 2019, Oxfam found that the 26 richest billionaires owned as much in assets as the 3.8 billion people who make up the poorest half of the planet's population. The number had been 61 in 2016 and 43 in 2017, showing again that capital continues to centralise into fewer and fewer hands.

Marx wrote that the concentration of wealth at one pole depended on the concentration of poverty at the other. And lo: the wealth of more than 2,200 billionaires across the globe increased by $900bn in 2018, a 12% increase against a fall of 11% in the wealth of the poorest half of the world's population.

Between 1980 and 2015, the global economy grew by 380%, yet the number of people living in poverty (on less than $5 (£3.20) a day, adjusted for the different cost of a 'basket of goods' from country to country) increased by more than 1.1 billion. In 1980, $2.20 of every $100 went to the world's poorest 20%, but in 2003 that figure had fallen to 60 cents. While the official global rate of extreme poverty decreased by around 1% a year between 1990 and 2017, the extreme poverty marker is set by the World Bank at below $1.90 per day. By this standard, the number of people living in extreme poverty declined from around 1.9 billion (36%) in 1990 to 643 million (8.4%) in 2019 (mostly in China). These figures are absurd: according to the UN, 815 million people do not have enough calories to sustain even "minimal" human activity; 1.5 billion are food insecure and do not have enough calories to sustain "normal" human activity; and 2.1 billion suffer from malnutrition. Many economists agree that a minimum of $7.40 per day is needed to achieve basic nutrition and normal human life expectancy. If a threshold of $7.40 is set, the extreme poverty figures change to 3.2 billion (71%) in 1981 and 4.2 billion (58%) in 2013.[522]

Inequality is most acute between rich and poor countries but it is growing within rich countries as well. In the US, the richest 1% owned a record-high 38.6% of the country's wealth in 2016, according to the Fed, nearly twice as much as the bottom 90%.

Anti-socialists will still ignore all this or proclaim that the proletariat is no longer a revolutionary class because living standards are generally much higher than 100 years ago, claiming that really "we are all middle class now" or making shallow observations such as "capitalism works because workers have mobile phones", as if cracking some kind of insightful gotcha that disproves Marxism.

This sort of line ignores how as the rate of exploitation increases, the value of necessary labour falls, making the commodities workers need to buy cheaper. It ignores how the needs of the working class change as capitalism develops: workers usually need smartphones and laptops in this day and age of 24-hour connectivity if they are even to be considered employable, and so the cost of a smartphone is *included* in the value of labour power. It also ignores that workers in some countries may have access to better infrastructure than in others. (Indeed, although no technology has ever scaled as quickly as the mobile phone, while five billion people now have mobile phones, only around 2.5 billion of the world's population presently have a smartphone.) Most of all, it is ignorant of the fact that capitalism is breaking down, which will 're-immiserate' and radicalise the working class. The revolutionary power of the working class is latent.

Claims about rising living standards disproving Marx are not new. As we saw earlier, the likes of Bernstein were saying the same in 1900, not long before a world war caused by capitalist breakdown brought death, destruction and immiseration to millions and millions of people.

The rejection of Lenin is a rejection of the proletariat and its revolutionary potential, and tends to be a reflection of a more stable or labour aristocratic position. But as that stability disappears, Lenin will be rehabilitated.

The historical necessity of centralised state planning
The typical Marxist or Leninist argument against anarchism is that a powerful centralised state is required to fight off counter-revolution, including external invasions. When the Bolsheviks took power in Russia, for example, armies

from 13 capitalist nations invaded the country. Only the organised, centralised power of the Red Army could withstand such an onslaught.

Anarchists and communists agree that the capitalist state must be abolished. But whereas anarchists fear that any state is bound to reproduce hierarchies of oppression, Leninists understand that *cementing the abolition of the capitalist state requires replacing it with a socialist state.*

We do not claim that this is ideal – of course we would prefer to go straight to stateless communism if it were possible. Lenin did not reject the assertion that any state would be inherently oppressive, but recognised that in a class society, one class must oppress the other; and since it would be absurd to suppose that class would disappear completely straight after a revolution, the majority must oppress the minority, rather than vice-versa – as is the case under the capitalist state. Anarchism would create a power vacuum, giving the bourgeoisie the opportunity to re-establish their own state. Like democratic socialism, anarchism can never get beyond the phase of dual power. Furthermore, repressive measures have to be taken against violent counter-revolutionaries. That means prisons and courts are required.[523] The alternative would be much bloodier.

The monumental level of societal reorganisation required following a revolutionary seizure of power is also going to take some time to complete, and so requires central planning. This is also the surest way of prioritising the needs of the working class *as a whole, internationally*, rather than a part or section of it, as would be the case with entirely independent co-operatives etc, which would end up competing with each other and naturally prioritising their own survival.

Taking money out of circulation and replacing it with a voucher system cannot be done before everything has been nationalised, which, due to counter-revolutionary resistance, cannot be achieved in a single blow. Implementing the new system itself requires much preparation and organisation so that that people do not go without the means to purchase necessities; and a voucher system itself would be inherently centralised.

Central planning is not about a small committee of 'elitists' making all the decisions, but a sensible system of accountability co-ordinating the needs of society as a whole, based on information received from each geographical area and economic sector, ensuring as-even-as-possible distribution and making sure all sectors complement rather than rival each other.

The objective analysis offered by the materialist conception of history, ie by tracing the historical development of the productive forces, backs all this up. Capitalism has developed into its highest, final stage: imperialism, or monopoly capitalism. What comes next is a higher stage of production: socialism.

Firstly, then, this historical tendency of capital to monopolise logically demands a 'final merger' into an absolute monopoly. Since capitalism cannot exist without competition, this necessitates socialism. Once the productive forces have been taken under state ownership, this absolute monopoly has been achieved by definition.[524]

Secondly, *long-term* central planning *within* private corporations has become increasingly necessary – departmental budgets for the outlays on research and development and marketing, projections on investment and returns, stock control coding etc – showing that there is a historical tendency towards long-term central planning of the economy as a whole.[525] This is reinforced by the attempts by the state itself to plan capitalism as a whole, both domestically (Keynesianism) and internationally (Bretton Woods).

This is reinforced again, thirdly, by capital's ever-increasing dependence on state subsidies,[526] which includes corporate tax cuts, a trend that must obviously head towards 100% of income, and, therefore, nationalisation. The corporate pharmaceutical industry, for example, has become particularly dependent on subsidies, with a trend of increasing public sector investments in research and development (R&D) while private spending has declined,[527] in many instances to the point of shutting R&D labs altogether.[528] Farming is another prime example. In England in 2016, subsidies made up around 57% of the total profit on average.[529] In the US, government-sponsored enterprises provide financing for nine out of ten mortgages.[530]

Subsidy dependency has been coupled with the huge upturn in the so-called 'financialisation' of industry, whereby a company's funds are increasingly dedicated to repurchasing their own shares in order to boost their stock price. In 2010, for example, the US American Energy Innovation Council (AEIC) asked the US government to triple state spending on clean energy to $16bn a year, at the end of a decade in which the companies comprising the council had spent $237bn on stock repurchases.[531] From 2008 to 2017, 466 S&P 500 companies distributed $4 trillion to shareholders as buybacks, equal to 53% of profits, along with $3.1 trillion as dividends.[532] This is explained away on the social democratic left as shareholder greed – but it is driven by the need to valorise capital. We did not cover it earlier, but Marx identified the increasing role of share capital as one of the main counter-tendencies.

The increasing centralisation within corporations comes with the ever-more capital-intensive renewal of the means of production, the life-span of which shortens over time because of the rising ability to implement better-quality replacements; and so the capital growth required to keep corporations running is increasingly unsustainable. As Mandel wrote:

> "This whole process culminates in concentrated pressure on the state to limit oscillations in the economy, at the cost of permanent inflation. It generates the growing trend towards *state guarantee of profits*, firstly through increasing government contracts, especially in the military sphere, then through underwriting of technologically advanced companies. This trend towards state guarantees of the profits of the large companies, which has spread from the sphere of production and research into that of the export of commodities and capital, is another of the crucial hallmarks of late capitalism."[533]

Central planning of the state as a whole, and then of the world economy as a whole (see chapter 15), are the next logical steps in the development of the productive forces, *necessitating* the formation of a new Communist International.

The upcoming roll out of the 5G smart grid (the upgrade of the world's communications infrastructure from the current 4G tech) and the 'Internet of Things',[534] creating truly ubiquitous connectivity and amounting to a 'global brain' governing the world economy, again shows that – unlike the one-sided far right explanation that tech conglomerates seek world domination – the productive forces monopolise both economically and technologically under capitalism, which needs to accelerate productivity along with the circulation and turnover of capital. For the working class to expropriate such a 'global brain' would be in theory to make a world socialist revolution. Capitalism forges the weapons that bring death to itself, as *The Communist Manifesto* says.[535]

With the massive growth of the international working class and the high development and centralisation of the productive forces – plus the fact that the law of value is closing in on the end of its natural lifespan – the material conditions needed for building world socialism have, unquestionably, never been riper.

13. Man vs machine: Postcapitalist techno-utopia or dictatorship of AI?

> "We can ... also speak of technology and science fetishism, for, after all, these are commodities in bourgeois society. Like other commodities, technology turns into what Marx described as a 'sensorially supersensory' thing. It acquires a mystical nature and acts as an independent being endowed with a life of its own and with considerable power over man. As a result, relations between labour and capital are given the mode of relations between worker and robot. On the face of it, it appears as if not capital but robots rule the worker, compelling him to intensify his work and threatening him with unemployment."[536]
>
> Volkov

We have seen that the general rate of profit falls historically towards zero and that it is therefore an economic certainty that capitalism will end. Is it then simply the case that we should accelerate the end of capitalism not by overthrowing it and establishing proletarian dictatorship, but by demanding full automation, delivering humanity into a postcapitalist techno-utopia where work has been abolished and humans are free to pursue creativity and leisure?

Similarly to Drucker and Bastani, 'information revolutionaries' such as Alvin Toffler and Yoneji Masuda posited theories that an abundance of information-generated resources combined with automation would automatically dissolve commodity exchange and private property relations in an electronically created classless society.[537] More recently, in their book *Inventing the Future: Postcapitalism and a World Without Work*, Nick Srnicek and Alex Williams argue that the road to "postcapitalism" lies in a "counter-hegemonic project" that makes full automation its central demand. It is little different in substance to Bastani's model.

Such scenarios would only be possible on the basis that capital accumulation proceeds harmoniously. This Kautskyist theory is hard to sell in a world beset by regular recessions, which is what makes it *necessary* for bourgeois politicians and theorists of various stripes to *invent* ideologies that dovetail with mystical diagnoses of each crisis (even if they are only trying to fool themselves). Indeed, ideology and discrimination merely exist to justify economic exclusion.

Michael Roberts has dealt with the theory of automating our way out of capitalism, along with the idea that capitalism's downfall will spring from underconsumption, ie the deterioration of purchasing power resulting from booming unemployment, a theory which confuses symptom for cause.

Roberts is not a Leninist but, in effect, he shows why automating our way out of capitalism in the absence of revolution and proletarian dictatorship would see capitalism overthrown instead by a dictatorship of AI:

> "Such a robot economy is not capitalist any more; it is more like a slave economy (like in the sci-fi film *Elysium*). The owners of the means of production (robots) now have a super-abundant economy of things and services at zero cost (robots making robots making robots). The owners can just consume. They don't need to make a "profit", just as the aristocrat slave owners in Rome just consumed and did not run businesses to make a profit. This does not deliver an overproduction crisis in the capitalist sense (relative to profit) nor 'underconsumption' (lack of purchasing power or effective demand for goods on a market) except in the physical sense of poverty.
>
> "If the whole world of technology, consumer products and services could reproduce itself without living labour going to work and could do so through robots, then things and services would be produced, but the creation of value (in particular, profit or surplus value) would not... the more machines begin to run themselves, the more value that the average worker adds begins to decline. So accumulation under capitalism would cease well before robots took over fully, because profitability would disappear under the weight of 'capital-bias'.
>
> "As 'capital-biased' technology increases, the organic composition of capital would also rise and thus labour would eventually create insufficient value to sustain profitability (ie surplus value relative to all costs of capital). We would never get to a robotic society; we would never get to a workless society – not under capitalism. Crises and social explosions would intervene well before that. A super-abundant society where human toil is reduced to a minimum and poverty is eliminated won't happen unless the ownership of the means of production changes

from private control to common ownership. That's the choice between utopia and dystopia."[538]

Even a slave economy under this dictatorship of AI seems too optimistic. What use would there be for human slaves in such a society? Would superintelligent robots really need us for amusement? Capitalism in extreme decay seeks to destroy surplus labour. Two world wars, the Great Depression and The Holocaust were the harrowing manifestations of this in the 20th century. It is evident now in the capitalist state's targeting of 'unproductive' disabled and under/unemployed people through cuts to benefits and social services. If the complete automation of labour would reduce the entire human population to the position of surplus labour, it would make more sense that the human race would be targeted for annihilation; unless humans were needed as a power supply, as in *The Matrix* films. Marx's likening of capitalism to Frankenstein takes on added meaning.

The film franchise *Terminator* is among the most well-known sci-fi stories to explore the prospect of war between man and machine. Its conscious theme was more likely a warning against the unintended consequences of technological innovation than a prescient depiction of the ultimate realisation of the demands of capital accumulation.[539] The play *Rossum's Universal Robots*,[540] written by Czech writer Karel Capek in 1921, was equally – given his anti-communism – unintentionally prescient. Volkov points out that the play "predicted the contradictions with which [automation] is fraught under capitalism".[541] In it, a private corporation invents advanced robots, leading to "no employment... everybody will be free from worry and liberated from the degradation of labour...." But the robots destroy the unemployed humans, whose presence on Earth is no longer necessary.

Rather than warning against a dictatorship of AI, roboticists such as Hans Peter Moravec at the Robotics Institute of Carnegie Mellon University have always held the belief that robots are *destined* to replace humans as the next stage of natural evolution in a 'postbiological' future. In the sensationalist book *The Robot Era?* (1955), English sociologist Philip Cleator predicted that "grown dull and degenerate, mankind will be painlessly annihilated by the simple and effective means of forced sexual segregation and periodical sterilisation with neuron rays".[542]

The late theoretical physicist Stephen Hawking feared that AI "may replace humans altogether" and SpaceX owner Elon Musk has repeatedly claimed that AI poses a genuine existential threat: "I keep sounding the alarm bell but until people see robots going down the street killing people, they don't know how to react." The tech billionaire's solution to keeping humans "relevant"? The "merger of biological and digital intelligence", ie the merger of man and machine. Predictably, he sees a business opportunity.

Of course, this all still sounds more far-fetched than farsighted. Although Japanese car manufacturer Lexus could make the impressive announcement that it had released an advert "entirely scripted by AI" in November 2018, it is also true that DARPA has only just invested $2bn in a programme whose aim, over many years, is to give AI the common sense understanding of an 18 month-old human baby.

"The idea that intelligent, thinking, conniving beings exist in AI is total, total, total science fiction," according to Rodney Brooks, the former head of the Computer Science and AI lab at the Massachusetts Institute of Technology (MIT). "We don't have anything with the intent of a slug at this point." He agrees, though, that self-driving cars are nearly ready to revolutionise transport. That development could be enough to make AI very dangerous. The immaturity of the technology in the hands of capitalists, rather than the fully-fledged Terminators of science fiction, is what elicits real concern.

Consider that The Campaign To Stop Killer Robots, set up by a coalition of Non-Governmental Organisations (NGOs), has been trying and failing to get the UN to ban the development of autonomous weapons since 2013. (Britain, predictably, has been one of its most stubborn opponents.) The drive towards major wars, of course, will accelerate the development of autonomous weapons by necessitating an intensified arms race. In September 2017, Russia's president Vladimir Putin said that "whoever becomes the leader in the sphere of AI will become the ruler of the world".

Drones

The type of drone the US deploys in Afghanistan and Pakistan is semi-autonomous. It can fly itself most of the time but a soldier still makes the final life or death decision to shoot its Hellfire missile. It is, however, "a small technical leap to replace that soldier" with AI, according to Toby Walsh, Scientia Professor of AI at the University of New South Wales.[543] This calls to mind the socialist Bertolt Brecht's famous line:

> *General, your tank is a powerful vehicle.*
> *It smashes down forests and crushes a hundred men.*
> *But it has one defect:*
> *It needs a driver.*

There is always the chance that a human soldier can rebel, that they can realise that they have been sold an escapist fantasy,[544] that their job is immoral, that they can come to their senses and disobey. The ruling class has always wanted its soldiers to perform like uncomplaining factory automatons. Former Army Ranger Stan Goff said in an interview for the book *Killing* by Jeff Sparrow:

> "The infantry is factory work. It's completely Taylorised. There's a soldier's manual, and it tells you how to do every single task in your job.... Technology just makes it more and more mechanised, since often the main thing you do is maintenance on the vehicle. It's extremely routine.... Even the tactics are rote. They do battle drills over and over again. You know, someone calls out red; you do a red. They yell blue; you do a blue."[545]

Sparrow argues that the drone actually "opens new possibilities for the peace movement" because the removed nature of operating it makes the army's task of selling the myth that military life is an escape from the drudgery and alienation of the everyday capitalist world harder than ever. The appeal of sacrifice and honour is also diminished. Sparrow quotes Air Force Major Bryan Callahan, responsible for steering a remote control drone over Afghanistan from a base in Arizona:

> "It sounds strange but being far away and safe is kind of a bummer. The other guys are exposing themselves, and that to me is still quite an honourable thing to do. So I feel like I'm cheating them. I'm relatively safe. If I screw up or miss something, if I screw up a shot, I wish it was me down there, not them. Sometimes I feel like I left them behind. Before you were at war 24/7, and when you're home, you're home. This is different. I do emails in the morning, rush to the airplane, come out, go to the [Base Exchange], get myself a hamburger, do some more email, do it again, drive home."

Military drones operated by human drones. The life of a drone pilot is, to some extent, indistinguishable from that of other white collar workers. Even the remaining fighter pilots in the battlefield have been deskilled, with each innovation increasing the power of the plane over the pilot so that "… today, the identification of individual 'aces' has largely disappeared", says Sparrow.

Britain's Ministry of Defence has admitted that it is understrength by at least 4,000 personnel. With an increasingly poor image – due as well to adverse publicity over the culture of bullying which leads to suicides; and to the high number of ex-service personnel abandoned by the state who end up traumatised and homeless – the army has never been seen as a more unattractive career choice. With fewer and fewer people prepared to 'die for their country' since the debacles of Vietnam, Iraq and Afghanistan, the general unpopularity of putting 'boots on the ground', has played a role in making war strategies more technical and mechanised. The further away you are from your target when firing to kill, the easier is life for the military's PR.

The Taranis military drone built by the UK's BAE Systems is a prototype that can already technically operate autonomously and would be able to strike distant targets "even in another continent".[546] In an article for the World Economic Forum, Peter Maurer, President of the International Committee of the Red Cross (ICRC), explains that "some weapon systems with autonomy in their 'critical functions' of selecting and attacking targets are already in use in limited circumstances for very specific tasks, such as shooting down incoming missiles or rockets. After activation by a human operator it is the weapon system that selects a target and launches a counterstrike."[547] Elsewhere, Walsh writes that autonomous weapons would work "just like autonomous cars", and that they "are going to be cheap" and "very effective".[548] He continues:

> "Arms companies of the world will make a killing (pun very much intended) to all sides of every conflict. Autonomous weapons will be weapons of mass destruction. One programmer will be able to do what previously took an army of humans. They will industrialise warfare. This is why it has been called the third revolution in warfare, after the invention of gunpowder and of nuclear weapons. They will also be weapons of terror. We don't know yet how to make robots that can follow international humanitarian law. And even when we can, there are plenty of bad actors out there, terrorists and rogue states, that will remove any ethical safeguards."

Such weapons can be hacked. "Autonomous weapons systems are entirely computer controlled, with all of the problems inherent with using computers," says Noel Sharkey, professor of AI and robots at the University of Sheffield. "When everybody, or a number of states, has them, we cannot know how they will interact with one another. These are unknown algorithms fighting each other. That very fact makes them unpredictable and against the laws of war."

Autonomous weapons may not need to become 'self aware', as in *Terminator,* to instigate 'Judgement Day' (when the war of man vs machine begins). In April 2018, the RAND Corporation warned that AI could undermine the Mutually Assured Destruction (MAD) rationale that is meant to deter nuclear war.[549] As an 'ethical safeguard', autonomous weapons would be programmed to 'target combatants only' – but what if, in a war-torn world where all humans have been reduced to surplus labour, every human is forced to become a combatant, scavenging to survive? This evokes a hypothetical scenario whereby the fight for socialism becomes a protracted struggle by an already classless humanity against the common enemy of the robot rulers.

14. Capitalism wants the most destructive world war yet – but even that can't save it

"Do we need another world war to breathe new life and power into current or new international financial institutions – solving problems currently deemed intractable? Barring a new enlightened faith in the virtues of international co-operation by top policy makers, and given the pressing need to apportion financial losses accruing from, *inter alia*, unprofitable international investments, the answer may be yes."[550]

Lee Adler, *Business Insider*, 2010

We have seen that the crisis is intensifying competition between the major imperialist and capitalist powers. The counter-tendencies have failed to prevent the onset of the next crisis. An even greater devaluation of capital and labour power is required. The death and destruction wrought by war is the ultimate source of devaluation and therefore the most important counter-tendency.

If war wasn't an inevitability under capitalism, militarism would be done away with since it is funded through taxation that could otherwise be put towards productive capital. Many Marxists have failed to grasp this point. Luxemburg, for example, claimed that "from the purely economic point of view, militarism is a pre-eminent means for the realisation of surplus-value; it is in itself a sphere of accumulation".[551] Grossman counters that

"this is how things may appear from the standpoint of individual capital as military supplies have always been the occasion for rapid enrichment. But from the standpoint of total capital, militarism is a sphere of unproductive consumption. Instead of being saved, values are pulverised. Far from being a sphere of accumulation, militarism slows down accumulation. By means of indirect taxation a major share of the income of the working class which might have gone into the hands of the capitalists as surplus value is seized by the state and spent mainly for unproductive purposes."[552]

It is the tribute from war, not the initial outlay, that counters the breakdown tendency. Having said that, innovation is accelerated by the arms race (and paid for by the state), leading to new use-values for the post-war civilian economy. Apart from natural resources, the main resource the capitalists are fighting over in a war is human labour, enough of which is not available at home. What better way to decimate the wages of this new source of surplus value than through warfare? The destruction of capital value also creates new profitable opportunities.

Idealists claimed the fall of the Soviet Union would bring about a new era of world peace. NATO's destruction of Yugoslavia, Iraq, Afghanistan, Somalia, Libya, Syria and Yemen since then shows both that they did not appreciate the nature of imperialism or the protection the Soviet Union afforded to countries threatened by imperialism. Who is next for daring to seek independence? Venezuela? Iran? Russia and China have been encircled by NATO in the biggest build-up of military forces since WWII.[553]

As the crisis of accumulation deepens, the size and frequency of wars tend to grow. In the wake of 9/11, the author Zoltan Grossman circulated a list, based on Congressional Records and The Library of Congress Congressional Research Service, of 133 US military interventions from 1890 to 2001. The average per year is 1.15 before and 1.29 after WWII. After the Cold War, from late 1989, the figure rises to 2.0.[554]

The Democrat Barack Obama replaced the gung-ho Republican warmonger George W Bush in 2008 promising 'hope' and 'change'. By the end of his second term in 2016, US special operators could be found in 70% – 138 – of the world's nations, a huge jump of 130% since Bush left office. In 2016 alone, the Obama administration sanctioned the use of at least 26,171 bombs. "This means that every day last year, the US military blasted combatants or civilians overseas with 72 bombs; that's three bombs every hour, 24 hours a day," Medea Benjamin of the anti-war CodePink wrote in *The Guardian*.[555] In 2017, Trump – who in his April 2016 foreign policy speech said that "war and aggression will not be my first instinct" because he wanted to spend the money instead domestically to 'make America great again' – outstripped Obama's 2016 figure by 9,000.[556]

Kautsky's ultra-imperialism theory exposed

Given that many of these wars are fought in an alliance of the imperialist powers, mainly through NATO, much analysis on the Left makes the mistake of thinking that inter-imperialist rivalry no longer exists. This follows on from Kautsky who, because he did not see war as arising from economic necessity, came up with a theory of "ultra-imperialism" whereby the imperialists would 'realise' that it was not in their interests to continue WWI and would therefore unite to 'peaceably redivide the world'.

Something like this – to a limited extent – did temporarily emerge, but only after WWII, only in collective opposition to the Soviet Union, and during a period in which capitalism was recovering in the wake of the war's devaluation of capital, meaning competition had temporarily diminished.

But the barbaric aggression of the wars on the Middle East is symptomatic of deepening capitalist crisis and intensifying rivalry. Through their opposition to the 2003 war on Iraq, France and Germany showed that they are not subordinate to US interests. In the 1990s, TotalFinaElf, France's huge oil firm, secured the contract to develop Iraq's southern Majnoon and Nahr Umar oil fields, containing as much as 25% of the country's reserves.[557] German firms were the market leaders in supplying sensitive dual-use technology to Iraq in the years before the 1991 Persian Gulf war, and they had been bidding for more civilian commercial contracts. Khidir Hamza, an Iraqi defector, called Germany "the hub of Iraq's military purchases in the 1980s". France and Germany did not want new competition.

Between the start of 2002 to March 2003 the dollar fell by 20% against the euro. The US had to respond to this: its international economic domination is bound up with the dollar's strength as the world's reserve currency, which enables it to blackmail countries that do not yield to its demands.[558] Ultimately, the strength of a currency reflects the productivity and size of the economy behind it.

Trump's administration has claimed that Germany is using its currency to "exploit" both its neighbours and the US, sparking fears of a currency war. The US made the desperate accusation that Germany is "under-consuming" goods and services from other countries. At the 2010 G20 summit in Seoul, the US made an unsuccessful attempt to limit the size of current account surpluses to 4% of GDP.[559] Germany's surplus overtook China's in absolute size in 2017 and as a share of GDP became much larger. The IMF put Germany's 2017 surplus at 8.1% of GDP and China's at 1.6%. The EU's surplus as a whole in 2017 was $387.1bn. In contrast, the US current account deficit was $462bn, bigger only than Britain's $91.4bn. The deficit was 2.5% of GDP in the first quarter, up from 2.4% in the fourth quarter.

Bush warned that the US would "neither forgive nor forget" if France continued to oppose the war on Iraq. US Secretary of State Donald Rumsfeld accused Austria of blocking US troop movements from Germany to Italy and said the US was considering bringing home 100,000 troops stationed in Europe (70,000 in Germany) or relocating them to Eastern Europe. He threatened sanctions for "one reason only: to harm the German economy".

At the time, the US controlled 31.5% of world output to the EU's 26%. In 2004, however, ten additional countries were scheduled to join the 15 EU member states, a combination that would match the size of the US's economy and exceed its population. *FRFI* – one of the few socialist publications in Britain to anticipate the potential for conflict between the US and EU – reported in 2003 that total EU FDI already amounted to 52.5% of the world total, nearly 2.5 times that of the US. Over the period 1980-2001, the US share of the global total halved.[560]

The massive rise in the US's military spending has been necessitated by the need to reverse the decline of its economic dominance. To reiterate, if it doesn't reverse this it won't be able to valorise its capital. The Department of Defense's base budget grew by 31% between 2000 and 2014. An $82bn hike to $716bn in 2018 represented an increase that by itself was larger than the entire defence budget of every country on Earth, save China. Trump called the Defense Department's annual budget "crazy" and proposed a 5% cut, but then committed to a $750bn budget for 2019. Who is really in charge? US military spending is at least 10 times the size of Russia's, and four times the size of China's.

This is the same Department of Defense with a serious existing accounting problem. In 2016, before Trump was elected, the department's Inspector General said he could not properly track $6.5 trillion in defence spending. An academic study looking at the years 1998-2015 later put the figure at $21 trillion.[561]

Clearly this is unsustainable. As Engels says, "the triumph of force is based on the production of arms, and this in turn on production in general".[562] US manufacturing output in the 1960s, at the time of the Vietnam War, comprised 27% of GDP and provided 24% of employment. In 2003 manufacturing amounted to 13.8% of GDP, falling to 12.5% in 2015, and 10.5% of employment. The US industrial base is shrinking and with it the manufacturing and engineering capacity to sustain military domination. In November 2004 *Le Monde Diplomatique* reported that, "Some new EU states are large arms producers and exporters. The EU is now home to more than 400 companies in 23 countries manufacturing small arms and light weapons – hardly less than the US."[563] China's manufacturing sector is now almost as large as those of the US, Japan and Germany combined.

When the US invaded Iraq in 2003 its military expenditure was almost $400bn; Iraq's was $1.4bn, 0.35% of the US's. In violation of the Iraqi constitution and international law the US-UK Coalition Provisional Authority (CPA)

> "laid off hundreds of thousands of Iraqi workers, virtually eliminated trade tariffs and enacted laws that radically alter Iraq's economy. Order 39, decreed by CPA head Paul Bremer on September 20 2003, abolished Iraq's ban on foreign investment, allowing foreigners to own up to 100% of all sectors except natural resources. Over 200 state-owned enterprises, including electricity, telecommunications and pharmaceuticals have been privatised. Iraq's highest tax rate has been lowered from 45% to a flat rate of 15%. Although foreign ownership of land remains illegal, companies or individuals will be allowed to lease properties for up to 40 years."

The extraction of Iraq's oil was also illegal. In 2011 government documents leaked to *The Independent* revealed that in November 2002, five months before the invasion, the UK Foreign Office invited BP to talks about opportunities in Iraq "post regime change". Labour's Baroness Symons, the then Trade Minister, promised BP that she would lobby the Bush administration because the oil giant feared it was being "locked out" of deals that Washington was quietly negotiating with the French and Russian governments and their energy firms.[564]

Control over territory, oil and oil transhipment routes is of paramount importance. With around 60% of the world's oil reserves, the Middle East has been the key battleground. But this rivalry is playing out all over the world, in South America, Asia, Africa and, since the fall of the USSR, central and eastern Europe, which was identified by the UNCTAD World Investment Report 2002 as "a stable and promising region for FDI".

Competition from China

China, whose contribution to global GDP eclipsed that of the US in 2017, is a particular concern to the traditional powers. Its strategy of offering low- or even interest-free loans in exchange for fixed-price sales of primary commodities makes it a more attractive business partner to underdeveloped countries that have been bled dry by high-interest loans from the IMF.[565] The US only has intimidation and force left to offer in response.

In 2008, for example, the Democratic Republic of the Congo (DRC) reached a deal with China for roads, railways, clinics, hospitals, schools and two new universities worth $6bn. In exchange, China was given the right to extract 12 million tonnes of copper and cobalt over 25 years. In 2004, when Angola was reluctant to accept the terms of an IMF loan, China stepped in with a no-strings-attached $2bn. An Angolan minister said relations with China "not only allowed us to obtain large loans, but most importantly it forced the West to treat us with more respect". From China's perspective, countries like Ethiopia, Tanzania and Senegal offer factory labour costs that are less than 10% of their level in China.[566]

China has overtaken Britain, France and the US as a trading partner with Africa. In 2017, China's trade with Africa was worth $170bn, four-times larger than US-Africa trade. In 2017 China's trade with Latin America reached $244bn, again exceeding that of the US. China's dominance in manufacturing has forced Latin American countries to deindustrialise somewhat and focus on producing primary commodities; but China's investments have also had the effect of strengthening their currencies relative to the dollar.

In July 2016, the RAND Corporation think tank warned that, whereas the US would have been capable of achieving a quick and decisive victory with minimal losses in a war with China in 2015, China's improving anti-access and area-denial (A2AD) capabilities meant that a war in 2025 would instead be "prolonged and destructive, yet inconclusive". The earlier part of that prediction seemed optimistic, given that the US got bogged down fighting resistance in Iraq and Afghanistan for years when it expected quick, decisive victories in both against forces extremely inferior to China's.

Indeed, in March 2019 a RAND analyst said that its war game simulations showed that "when we fight Russia and China, blue gets its ass handed to it".[567] He said it would cost an extra $24bn a year to turn things around. Chinese and Russian opposition to US deployments of anti-missile systems in Asia has resulted in their greater military cooperation. Russia is using its position in the Shanghai Cooperation Organisation (SCO), however, to try and contain Chinese economic expansion in Central Asia, where it has regional ambitions of its own.

As Trevor Rayne wrote in *FRFI*: "The US turns to alliances with Japan, India, the Philippines and Australia to confront China, but China offers them investments and better trade deals. If it has to the US ruling class will resort to military force to prevent China ejecting it from its dominant position in the world."[568]

The economics of world war

Competition between the imperialist powers may be limited to geopolitical manoeuvring, ideological and cyber warfare and negotiation table diplomacy for now, but that cannot last forever. At some point the capitalist crisis will become so deep that the imperialist powers will be *forced* into direct confrontation with each other. The overaccumulation of capital will have become so great that the *only way to sufficiently devalue capital and labour power will be through global conflagration*. This tendency expresses itself in increasing competition between the imperialist powers as they vie to attain dominance – that is, to apportion losses to one another, to seize each other's capital and resources by any means. The capital exports that stave off absolute overaccumulation are themselves limited by competition on the world market.

This is what happened in the 20th century. Two world wars, the Great Depression and fascism were the counter-tendencies and crisis measures required over a span of 41 years to sustain the accumulation process and eventually return it to a level capable of restoring political stability.

Kautsky – because he believed accumulation was harmonious – claimed that absolute capitalist breakdown would be brought about inevitably by world war, which in his view would happen only because of uncivilised ruling classes.[569] On the other side of the same coin, Bukharin and Varga believed WWII would bring about the completion of the world revolution.[570] Grossman says:

> "It would be useless to search Bukharin for any other cause of the breakdown of capitalism than the ravages created by war.... If like Bukharin, we expect the breakdown of capitalism to flow from a second round of imperialist wars, then it is necessary to point out that wars are not peculiar to the imperialist stage of capitalism. They stem from the essence of capitalism as such, during all its stages, and have been a constant symptom of capital since its historical inception.... far from being a threat to capitalism, wars are a means of prolonging the existence of the capitalist system as a whole."[571]

Grossman was at pains to show that Kautsky's was a subjective analysis and that the opposite was true: that massive overaccumulation *brought about* a systemic breakdown and world war *followed necessarily* because it was the only way to sufficiently devalue capital, to "ward off imminent collapse" and "create a breathing space" for accumulation to restart.[572]

Grossman cites the figure from Wladimir Woytinsky's 1925 book *The World In Numbers* that "around 35% of the wealth of mankind was destroyed and squandered" in the four years of WWI;[573] a war preceded by a worldwide long depression – like the one we've had since 2009 – and the US's first *national* banking crisis in 1907. By the end of the war, says Grossman, the mass of living labour "confronted a reduced capital, and this created new scope for accumulation".[574]

And yet it wasn't enough – the 1929 Wall Street Crash followed, "a continuation of the unresolved economic crisis preceding WWI", as Mattick says.[575] The New Deal attempted to resolve the crisis in the US and fascism attempted to resolve it in Germany (the equivalent of a New Deal in Germany through the SPD's reforms having already failed before 1929). Neither worked. It would take an even more destructive global war to end the depression. This after Kautsky had claimed in 1927 that capitalism stood, "from a purely economic point of view, stronger than ever".[576]

WWI – "legalised slaughter" in the words of Harry Patch, the last surviving combat soldier of that war from any country – killed 37 million people. WWII killed between 70 million and 85 million, 3% of the 1940 world population of an estimated 2.3 billion. The equivalent today from a world population of 7.53 billion would be 226 million.

But given that today's total accumulation and (relative) overaccumulation are vastly greater than before WWII, it follows that it would take a vastly greater level of destruction to – again, temporarily – resolve the crisis.

Given that and the fact that every major war following economic breakdown is decided only by total war – the US Civil War, the Peninsular War and the Crimean War being other prime examples – it could be argued that the amount of destruction required is now so high that today's deepening crisis *may at some point necessitate nothing short of a nuclear exchange between the imperialist powers.*[577] WWII ended with the US dropping the A-bomb on Japan, after all. If a Third World War was not sufficiently destructive, then a bigger crisis would follow, necessitating World War Four, just as WWII followed WWI.

But *surely there can be no 1945-type productivity boom that breathes another century of life into the system, for automation is now abolishing the law of value.*[578] *Manufacturing prices are already closing in on zero.* The current arms race is in fact already accelerating the development of automation and, therefore, the centralisation of capital. As Grossman wrote in 1926:

> "Either the destruction is so great that it embraces the basis of the productive apparatus itself, the entire capitalist mechanism disintegrates and the barricades go up between the classes. In the other case, society is impoverished by the ravages of war but this is the impetus for the forced development of the productive forces, for the enormous concentration and rationalisation movements of the kind we now witness in Germany. For this is the only possible way to withstand the competitive struggle with other, richer capitalist powers, on a capitalist basis. Actually, despite the ravages of the world war, the tendencies to concentration and combination that were already present everywhere have accelerated and intensified. Lenin already noted this in 1915. Within only a few years, the prewar stage of development was recovered and surpassed. If, however, one assumes ... the possibility that humanity could be cast into historical oblivion by the next imperialist war, there is no other way to save it than to *pre-empt* the next war through revolution."[579]

War can now at best only temporarily prolong the crisis. We therefore contend that – aside from the fact that a world war today would probably end life on Earth and destroy the climate for good – *even a world war cannot save capitalism*. Rather than partly destroying itself in order to renew itself this time, capitalism is now preparing to either destroy or wind itself up *completely*.

The inevitability of protectionism
Trade wars will continue to intensify. Protectionism becomes an increasingly *inevitable* reflex as nations attempt to defend domestic and overseas assets. Combined with stagnant productivity, this tends to manifest politically in a parochial, 'anti-globalisation' nationalism, ie right-wing populism or proto-fascism, as capitalists which rely more on the domestic market – determining their conservatism – finally gain the upper-hand over the more liberal exporting sectors, only to deepen the overall economic crisis by making trade increasingly expensive and centralising capital into yet fewer hands.

As Michael Pettis wrote in the *FT* in 2009, the fact that

> "nearly everyone agrees that a world that retreats into direct and indirect forms of trade protection is a world that is worse off... should not allay our

worries. In the 1930s, it was also well understood that the crisis would be exacerbated by plunging international trade. This did not stop a descent into the protectionism which put the 'Great' into the Great Depression."[580]

In February 2019, a senior European Commission economist warned that a Third World War is an increasingly "high probability" due to the "disintegration of global capitalism".[581] Professor Hanappi, Jean Monnet Chair for Political Economy of European Integration, noted that the emerging trade wars, massive growth of military spending and return of 'populism' bear unnerving similarities with trends that beset the world before the outbreak of the first two world wars.

Marx wrote that as soon as capital feels itself threatened it will "seek refuge in other forms", which appear to perfect its rule as capital "through curbs on free competition". Although the curbs on competition

> "appear to complete the mastery of capital, they are at the same time, by curbing free competition, the heralds of its dissolution, and of the dissolution of the mode of production based on it."[582]

As mentioned, in 2015-16, the G20 economies introduced a record number of trade-restrictive measures. Globalisation was in retreat before Brexit and Trump, because the ability to expand capital is increasingly exhausted.

Just as protectionism and trade wars were precursors of the first two world wars, Brexit and the new trade wars threaten to be precursors of a Third World War. Just as the first two world wars were fought *between* imperialist rivals, so would a third. That could mean a conflict between the US and its long-time strongest competitor, the German-led EU. On 6 November 2018 France President Emmanuel Macron called for the creation of a "true European army" so that the EU could defend itself from "China, Russia and even the United States of America", adding: "When I see President Trump announcing that he's quitting a major disarmament treaty[583] which was formed after the 1980s Euro-missile crisis that hit Europe, who is the main victim? Europe and its security."

Germany already provides the most troops for the UN's so-called peacekeeping missions. Building on the Permanent Structured Cooperation on security and defense (PESCO) agreement – which allows co-operation on joint military projects for 25 EU member states, established through the Lisbon Treaty in December 2017 – in February 2019 the European Commission provisionally agreed the founding of a €13bn European Defence Fund (EDF).

This is to allow joint R&D projects for European companies, and will exclude both post-Brexit Britain and the US. In response the US complained that the moves undermine the NATO alliance and threatened sanctions on EU firms if either project goes ahead. The EU told the US not to concern itself with Europe's defence plans. In December 2019 Macron said NATO was already "brain dead", because "you have no coordination of decision-making whatsoever between the US and its NATO allies".

In reality, Europe is still reliant upon the US in military matters, a point made clear by, for example, the dominance of US firms in international contracts or the US's role in NATO. Accordingly, the EU is, to some degree, split upon the US's INF withdrawal, with key US allies Britain and Poland offering their unwavering support for the move. While disagreement in Europe over the Treaty itself is small, this reflects broader splits within the EU imperialist bloc, more evident in regard to trade and inter-European political discussions. More significantly in military terms, the US's dominance over Europe's military capacity means that Europe requires both time and new alliances if it is to stand on its own feet. Europe is now waking up to this fact.

In July 2019, Macron announced that France would build "a large space command within the Air Force, which will eventually become the Air and Space Force... to better protect our satellites, including in an active way". Analysts called the move a switch from a defensive to an offensive posture. Macron's proposal follows similar moves by the US, China and Russia in recent years. In 2018, Trump ordered the formation of a sixth branch of the US's armed forces – a "space force".

Europe's imperialists may have once hoped that the end of Trump's Presidency could see a reconciliation with the US bourgeoisie on more advantageous terms, but such hopes seem to be nothing but fantasy. On 13 November 2018, a bipartisan panel for the US Congress issued a report stating its approval of the Trump administration's pursuit of "great power competition".

Shifting alliances

In March 2019, Nicole Gibson, Deputy Director of the US State Department's office for Europe, warned that European companies would "risk significant sanctions" if they resume laying the Nord Stream 2 (NS2) natural gas pipeline running from Russia to Germany. Construction work was suspended the previous December because of winter weather. The deal has infuriated the US because it undermines the potential for its energy giants to export surplus shale gas to Europe as liquified natural gas (LNG).

US clients in central Europe are also set to lose out. Snaking under the Baltic Sea, NS2 replaces an older pipeline, stripping Ukraine of gas transit fees worth $2.5bn a year, 4% of its GDP. Ukraine president Petro Poroshenko[584] fears NS2 would allow Russia to switch off gas to Ukraine and Central Europe to blackmail its nearer neighbours without disrupting supplies to Western Europe, enabling the Kremlin to exert greater political influence. Russia supplies more than one-third of the natural gas Europe uses, a figure that is expected to reach nearly 50% in the next decade. German businesses say NS2 will slash their energy costs.

German Chancellor Angela Merkel has said that "geostrategically, Europe cannot have an interest in cutting off all relations with Russia". In 2017 she said that "the times in which we could completely depend on [the US and Britain] are, to a certain extent, over. We Europeans truly have to take our fate into our own hands." With the relative decline of the US and Britain's pending departure from the EU, Germany either sees an opportunity to become dominant or the need to find more reliable allies. It may see an alliance with Russia as an extension of European imperialism, and as a replacement for Britain. Britain itself has reportedly sought to spread misinformation in Europe in an attempt to weaken relations between Germany and Russia.[585]

Turkey, a long time client state of the US, appears to be forming a new alliance with Russia and Germany. In June 2019, the EU and Russia started talks on transitioning to using the rouble and euro in bilateral payments instead of the US dollar. China and Turkey are also investing heavily in the euro. The US is gradually being isolated and the grip on the world economy that the dollar as the world's reserve currency gives the US is slipping. In the same week, it emerged that the US had been stepping up its ability to wage a cyberwar on Russia's power grid, something it had deployed against Venezuela several times, depriving hospitals, factories and residential areas of electricity, earlier in the year. These cyber attacks are acts of war by the US's own definition.

A similar situation is developing with regards to Iran.[586] When Trump pulled the US out of the 2013 Iran nuclear deal, in which Iran agreed to roll back parts of its nuclear programme in exchange for relief from sanctions, Germany, France and even, to the chagrin of the US, Britain – all desperate for outlets for profitable investment – denounced the move and vowed to find ways to circumvent the US ban on trading with Iran, which applies to third parties. In July Russia expressed interest in the EU's proposed Instrument in Support of Trade Exchanges (INSTEX) mechanism, backing Iran's demand that it would have to include the oil trade. Significantly, this would see the EU violating US sanctions on two fronts.

Trump claims he is trying to stop a nuclear arms race in the Middle East but he is really motivated by competition. In March 2019, Miguel Berger, the director-general for Economic Affairs and Sustainable Development at Germany's Federal Foreign Office, complained that, while everyone else was banned from trading with Iran, US trade with Iran in 2018 had in fact doubled. The US says it wants a new deal that curbs Iran's ballistic missile programme and ends Iran's supposed influence in Syria, Iraq and Yemen, the latter in which Iran is accused of backing the anti-imperialist Houthi movement. But it also wants to control Iran's oil. The US's increasingly belligerent client-states Israel and Saudi Arabia see Iran as a threat to their regional dominance and welcomed Trump's move.[587] In May 2019, Trump warned Iran of "severe consequences" as the US, joined by Britain, began to build up naval and air power in the Persian Gulf.

Fears of military conflict grew after Trump blamed Iran for Houthi attacks on tankers in the Gulf of Oman. While Britain – which, in a blatant act of piracy at the request of the US, later seized an Iranian oil tanker bound for Syria – sided with the US, the EU demanded an independent inquiry. Japan, which had a tanker involved in the controversy, also questioned the veracity of the US's account. The same week, Iran shot down a US drone. Trump claimed that he called off a retaliatory airstrike at the last minute, instead imposing further suffocating sanctions and launching a cyberattack on Iran's defence infrastructure.

Sanctions have resulted in inflation in Iran of 40% and the IMF predicted a 6% contraction in its economy. Iran said it would have to develop its uranium enrichment levels if Europe did not do more to shield Iran from sanctions.[588] Iran could be the spark that ignites conflict between the US and Europe.[589]

Meanwhile, Saudi Arabia's horrific US-UK-backed war on Yemen has resulted, after four years, in what the UN called the world's worst humanitarian crisis; and rising tensions between India and Pakistan at the beginning of 2019 threaten to spill over into a full-scale war, with the US generally backing the former and China the latter. Pakistan has taken out billions of dollars in loans from China in recent years as part of Beijing's Belt and Road Initiative (BRI), an ambitious trade and infrastructure network connecting China to Europe, Africa, Southeast Asia and other regions. China has pledged to provide economic assistance to Pakistan, which has been bailed out by high-interest IMF loans some 14 times since 1980.

The task of communists

As we have said, Leninists have long predicted that deepening imperialist splits would emerge. They have been proven correct, and the defeatist pseudo-Marxist theories of 'ultra-imperialism' – that the imperialist powers in fact form an unshakeable alliance – have been proven wrong. Existing divisions in NATO have been widening since the election of Trump, who has been unsurprisingly delighted by Brexit and its destabilising effect on the EU. Denouncing the EU's "treatment" of Britain in the negotiations, Trump said at the start of April 2019 that "the EU is likewise a brutal trading partner with the US, which will change".

On 9 April, he said the US planned to impose tariffs of $11bn (£8.4bn) on EU goods, partly because "EU subsidies to Airbus have adversely impacted the US".[590] He must have known what was coming: on 10 April the EU and China announced a trade deal in which they vowed, in a thinly veiled rebuke to the US, "to fight against unilateralism and protectionism".

China and Germany are now engaged in concrete military co-operation, with China deploying armoured vehicles on German soil for joint drills on 11 July, something that has been unthinkable until now.[591] At the same time, the potential for realignment with the US is also contained within the German approach. For example, Germany is considering sending a warship through the Taiwan Strait, escalating tensions with China and easing them with the US. As Trump is so fond of saying, "all options are on the table". France has vowed to retaliate tit-for-tat against US sanctions.

In Tony Kennedy's foreword to the abridged 1992 English reprint of Grossman's book, he says:

> "For Grossman, re-presenting Marx's theory was no mere academic exercise. Nor was he concerned merely with describing tendencies towards periodic economic crises, of a more or less restricted character, nor even with trends towards more systematic and global recessions. He aimed to show that the essence of Marx's analysis of capitalist society was the identification of the inexorable tendency towards breakdown as the fundamental characteristic of the social system as a whole....[592] Grossman contended that the socialist movement's commitment to the overthrow of capitalism required theoretical proof of the system's tendency towards breakdown."[593]

This is now the task facing communists today. The first appeal that the Communist International made in 1920 to the international working class was to "Remember the imperialist war!", warning that the repetition of such destructive wars, when the workers of different countries are coerced by the ruling classes to "cut each other's throats" is not only possible but inevitable if capitalism is not overthrown.[594] WWI confirmed what was written in the statutes of the First International, that the emancipation of the working class is not a local, nor a national, but an *international* question. And given that national bourgeoisies are inevitably pitted against each other in a world war, it follows that *the only class that is capable of solidarity internationally is the working class.*

We are being haunted by the failure to turn the breakdowns that precipitated the first two world wars into the world revolution that Lenin expected to follow on the heels of the one he led in Russia.

Only a world socialist revolution can ensure humanity's survival.

15. Humanity's emancipation: Higher communism and the Single Automated System

> "In a communist society, man will not bear the slightest resemblance to a fanatical ascetic concerned only with over-fulfilling the work quota and learning by heart the moral code of communism instead of poetry. Communist society is not being built for the sake of self-denial and emasculation, and does not entail the sacrifice of man's concrete and vital needs to abstract humanist ideals."[595]
>
> Volkov

While Marx talked of "dead labour" becoming a "mechanical monster" that "dominates, and pumps dry, living labour", converting the worker into its "living appendage", he was not a Luddite or a technophobe. For history – albeit via series of painful setbacks – moves forwards, not backwards.

As Dyer-Witherford notes, Marx saw emancipatory potential in the communications revolution.[596] The telegraph, fast mails and railways broke down parochialism, localism, and narrow national interests, making proletarian internationalism possible. *The Communist Manifesto* stresses that the "ever-expanding union of workers" is "helped on by the improved means of communication that are created by modern industry and that place the workers of different localities in contact with one another. It was just this contact that was needed to centralise the numerous local struggles, all of the same character, into one national struggle between classes."[597]

In *Capital* Marx also discusses how by "means of machinery, chemical processes and other methods [modern industry] is continually transforming not only the technical basis of production but also the functions of the worker and the social combinations of the labour process". At the same time, it "incessantly throws masses of capital and of workers from one branch of production to another" and thereby "necessitates variation of labour, fluidity of functions, and mobility of workers in all directions".[598] Under capitalism,

Marx says, this is an immiserating force, which "does away with all repose, fixity and all security as far as the worker's life situation is concerned".[599]

Modern industry makes possible "the recognition of variation of labour and hence of the fitness of the worker for the maximum number of different kinds of labour".[600] Socialism will bring this to full realisation.

The trend towards automation will continue and *accelerate* under socialism, but it will be introduced in a planned way without leaving workers jobless and destitute. In fact, under socialism it *will* become rational for workers to demand automation. We do not reject technological innovation, we reject the way it is produced and deployed under capitalism. We say that *we* should control the development of technology – which is, of course, under the dictatorship of capital, a form of capital – instead of being controlled by it, both in terms of how we work and what we produce.

"Development of the productive forces of social labour is the historical task and justification of capital," wrote Marx. "This is just the way in which it unconsciously creates the material requirements of a higher mode of production."[601]

Marx is clear then that socialism would thrive best where the productive forces are most developed, and indeed that capitalism, through its continual revolutionising of the productive forces – along with the accompanying proletarianisation of the masses, setting in train society's classless destiny – is the historically necessary precursor to socialism. With the onset of the imperialist stage, Lenin built on this: "Monopoly is the transition from capitalism to a higher system."[602]

In his assessment of the Soviet Union, Che Guevara criticised the communists who were suspicious of importing or adopting 'ideologically contaminated' technology from western capitalist corporations. They should have known that its negative sides manifested from the social relations under which they operated. "For a long time cybernetics was considered a reactionary science or pseudo-science... [but] it is a branch of science that exists and should be used," wrote Guevara.[603] As Volkov put it:

> "It should be stressed that the difference between the moneyed wealth of capitalist society and the social wealth of communism is not identical to the difference between material and spiritual wealth. Scientific communism does not repugn material wealth. On the contrary, it considers the creation of an adequate material and technical basis and abundance of material wealth as an indispensable prerequisite for the flowering of man's spiritual qualities."[604]

Guevara also stressed that large capitalist corporations were an advanced form of organisation capable of highly efficient mass production not to be dismantled but to be improved upon by expropriating and transforming them into what they were ripe for, ie social enterprises.[605] Monopolies should not be 'broken up', as is often demanded by social democrats and small capitalists; monopolies only re-emerge, anyway. Put it this way: if socialism promises a higher, more efficient mode of production, what is more productive than several competing near-monopolies? Clearly the answer is a merger of them into one monopoly that replaces competition with co-operation.[606]

Revolutions today, especially in the imperialist countries, would have a huge head start compared to the Bolsheviks and the Maoists, who faced the unenvious tasks of industrialising primitive peasant-based economies. The arguments about whether it was possible to build socialism in the early 20th century are rather irrelevant: under contemporary conditions, the combination of social enterprises merged under public monopoly, high tech mass production and central planning with modern computing power – integrated via the world's global communications network – would open up the opportunity for rapid progress, never to be interrupted by the economic crises that characterise capitalism. As Volkov put it:

> "Let us anticipate the future and suppose that it has attained its zenith and that its characteristic features... have reached full development. We shall then have a society with fully automated production of material wealth, ensuring abundance. Such production will form a Single Automatic System which, for the sake of maximum efficiency, will incorporate all the branches of industry and agriculture, centrally controlled according to a single plan.
>
> "From the social point of view, this will be a single society, because there will no longer be any workers or peasants previously associated solely with physical labour, and because the distinction between mental and manual labour, and between town and countryside, will have vanished. Creative work incorporating intellectual, emotional and manual activities will predominate. The life of society will be governed by the laws of free, instead of working, time, and so on."[607]

The direction of history towards turning world productivity into a Single Automatic System shows that the final stage of socialism before full communism is a *de facto* single world state. To get there each nation-state obviously needs to become socialist, with its own governing structure and centrally planned system working towards full automation in that country. A Communist International would be required to oversee development and trade between each socialist state – making sure, for one thing, that the plan incentivises the sharing of technologies and material wealth (including human resources) – which would act with the same semi-autonomy in relation to the International as a region of a country does to its central government or a state to federal level (or a local soviet to its regional soviet, and so on).

As this system develops, the Single Automatic System and a *de facto* one-state world would come into being, with borders being rejected as fetters on productivity – there being no transfer of ownership when it comes to trade in a socialist political union, anyway – and individual nation-states withering away in all but regional name. The productive forces would become so efficient and diffuse that communal ownership would completely replace state ownership (and, given the emergence of distributive production, probably in a much shorter period of time now than if the Bolshevik Revolution had turned into a world revolution).

We can see then that, *whereas capitalism in the long run has a historically centralising tendency, socialism in the long run has a historically decentralising tendency*. This then is the path to a borderless, stateless world, not the fantasy anarchist one, which, with its desire to introduce federations of fully autonomous communes, would effectively introduce new borders and undermine internationalism. The necessary aim of communism is to unite – to un-divide – the working class and humanity as a whole.[608]

Social wealth measured as free time

Under capitalism, the working week became shorter in the imperialist countries to 'fill up the pores' in the working day; to reduce mass unemployment – ie to quell the rebellion it sparked – and because the export of capital led to 'deindustrialisation' and the inverse growth of mental labour. Sufficient leisure time for mental recuperation became necessary if the workforce was going to retain the level of mental wellbeing required for the reproduction of capital and to consume the commodities designed for the leisure industry. Hence why in 1926 even Henry Ford, who went on to support the Nazis, supported the eight-hour day.

Capital begins to create free time "despite itself",[609] says Marx, but strives to reconvert it into surplus labour time. The length of the working week in the US steadily decreased from 70 hours in 1850 to 40 in 1945, but has since remained the same. Moreover, the intensification of effort at work is rising and work is in fact, as we have seen, filling up more and more of the day. This has contributed to a growing mental health crisis. It will take socialism for the working week to become permanently shorter again – although any reformist struggles for this should be supported, especially since a shorter week is a step towards abolishing capitalism – to solve the new unemployment problem, for work to become less intense and for leisure time to increase again. After the overthrow of capitalism

> "disposable time thereby ceases to have an antithetical existence ... on one side, necessary labour time will be measured by the needs of the social individual, and, on the other, the development of the power of social production will grow so rapidly that, even though production is now calculated for the wealth of all, disposable time will grow for all. For real wealth is the developed productive power of all individuals. The measure of wealth is then not any longer, in any way, labour time, but rather disposable time."[610]

Full employment under socialism in combination with automation will share out the burden of work like never before (indeed, revolutionary governments should probably bring in a reduced working week almost immediately); and, unlike under capitalism, where stagnation sets in, working hours will continue to shorten along the path to communism.

Huge numbers of people would be freed up to work in sectors that under capitalism are notoriously understaffed, such as teaching and nursing, since people wouldn't be wasted in unemployment or jobs which contribute nothing positive to society, such as bomb making.[611] Voluntary work to improve society for everyone, as encouraged by Guevara, could be done without scabbing on fellow workers.

Instead of work bleeding into leisure time, as we are seeing now, leisure time will bleed into work time.[612] Leisure time will be *organically* redefined, not as time dominated by consumption as in capitalist society, but for more skilled, artistic, creative, scientific and intellectual pursuits.[613]

Marx says that "the saving of labour time [is] equal to an increase of free time, ie time for the full development of the individual, which in turn reacts back upon the productive power of labour as itself the greatest productive power".[614] *Each extra hour of free time introduced at the expense of an hour's labour time would engender an inverse proportional rise in the productivity of labour.* "From the standpoint of the direct production process it can be regarded as the production of fixed capital, this fixed capital being man himself,"[615] says Marx.

With humans freed up to enrich their personality, there will be increasingly greater scope for the undertaking of projects and experimentation, and therefore a much broader scope for real – but fraternal! – competition, along with the reinvigoration of craft production. (We may be able to invent things to combat the climate crisis that we have not even been capable of thinking of yet.) This demonstrates that "real wealth" is the "developed productive power of all individuals", as Marx said. The individual flourishes not under capitalism, but under socialism and communism.[616]

Towards a digital voucher system
Types of work still have to be incentivised and an accounting system is needed to distribute goods equitably. Since fiat currencies are on the verge of collapsing anyway, and with cash having already all but disappeared, a global digital voucher system is required, pegged to labour time; ie, with monetary units replaced by units of labour hours worked (which could be graded according to type of work/productivity) as argued for by William Paul Cockshott and Allin Cottrell in *Towards A New Socialism*.[617] Combined with the social ownership of production, this ends exploitation (and commodity fetishism), since: voucher credits would be non-transferable, cancelled once 'spent', like train tickets; and workers are employed by society and communes (between which there may need to be an exchange rate) rather than private companies, so no 'surplus value' is privately appropriated. This is the decommodification of labour power. Apart from (direct-only) taxation, workers accrue all the value they create and use it to consume goods and services. Labour power is used socially instead of being sold to and exploited by capitalists. Use-value and human need have usurped exchange-value and profit. 'Exchange-value' still exists in terms of exchanging vouchers for social products in the lower phase of communism, but is qualitatively different, now based on labour time and use-value instead of private exploitation, competition and artificial scarcity.

The labour time measure also makes budgeting far more intelligible, enabling a better informed electorate. A flat rate tax (a percentage of each hour worked; adjusted according to the amount voters decide to spend (an example of participative/direct democracy) on advisement from planning committees) funds social services such as education and health and social care.

Consumer goods are priced in units of production time, adjusted by a marketing algorithm according to supply and demand (and shrinking labour content) to ensure stability, ie production on a break-even basis (the price of a product rises against excess demand while the planners order its increased production; and vice-versa). A central, elected marketing authority would regulate the standards of consumer goods made by state and community enterprises, which are motivated to make attractive products by the raised market prices. The progressive increase in free time as the measure of social wealth also acts as an incentive to both work and improve efficiency.

The law of free time is the logical and historical successor of the law of value. With the increase in free time comes the continual decrease in time dedicated to exchange-value creation, meaning the voucher system will eventually become obsolete and 'work' will become voluntary. Self-alienation will be replaced by self-assertion and the category of the political-economic – ie classes, nationalities, genders, races[618] – by social wealth, ie the human being and humanity itself, bringing centuries of economically and socially constructed sexism,[619] ableism[620] and racism to an end.[621]

Free time *naturally* transforms its possessor into a different subject.[622] In working towards full automation, we see the undoing of the contradiction between man and machine, so that we can speak of, says Volkov,

> "the correlation between the human and inanimate elements of the process of *dynamic vital activity in the broadest sense of the term*.... Man gets excluded from the formerly heterogeneous working mechanism. This historically developing automation becomes fully technical. At the same time, the functions can now be divided. The monotonous and formalised mechanical actions can be left entirely to machines, and the searching, heuristic creative activity to man."[623]

Planning and democracy

Planning requires the services of automation, while a planned economy is needed, in turn, to achieve full automation:

> "The necessity to regulate supply and demand, production and consumption, manpower and its use, requirements in trained staff and training facilities – all these and many other problems, aggravated by automation, give rise to pressing tasks in the field of planning."[624]

Expanding on how this worked in the Soviet Union, Volkov says that

> "automation raises problems tied up with the necessity of projecting changes in the economy and the structure of its branches, and the corresponding adjustments in training the necessary staff and improving

their professional skill. Soviet planning agencies do not always rise to the occasion, so that there is a shortage of specialists in the key branches, such as the chemical industry. But automation itself, that is, electronic computers, is providing the means for removing this deficiency of socialist planning.

"Experiments conducted at the Institute of Cybernetics of the Ukrainian Academy of Sciences prove that automation is absolutely indispensable in a planned economy. The use of cybernetics in factory planning makes it possible, for example, to fulfil the monthly plan in 18 days with the same plant. One million operations are required to coordinate the plans of material and technical supplies with the plan of production of materials in the Ukraine. Previously, this would have necessitated 30 thousand years. Today, an electronic computer can do the job in four months! The corrections made by an electronic computer to the plan of transporting sugar-beet in certain areas of the country led to a saving of 120,000 freight cars in just one season."[625]

The difficulty of early Soviet planning, when it had to be done with paper and abacus, no longer exists. The live-feed data analysis and algorithm technology available now would obviously take socialist central planning to the next level. Between 1969 and 2013, computer planning became 100 billion times more powerful.[626]

Perhaps most excitingly, the technology currently used for social media could be repurposed away from commercial data mining and consumer manipulation to introduce a genuinely international culture and mass participatory democracy, with workers enfranchised to vote almost effortlessly from their smartphones on every relevant issue, rather than just elections (when they are usually left to helplessly watch their bourgeois 'representative' betray their manifesto promises).[627] Imagine the world's entire population voting on one issue at the same time – perhaps to replace certain elections with lot-drawing or even the final decision to dissolve the state! – one day it will be possible, and without anyone even having to go to a polling station.

Workers and automation

The Soviet Union placed so much importance on the development of automation that it set up a special ministry charged with developing it in all spheres of industry. Automation was assigned a central role in the Sixth Five-Year Plan (1956-60) – which complained that automation was not being treated with enough importance – with a particular focus on reducing arduous and time-consuming labour.[628]

Lilley's mid-1950s visit to the Soviet Union gives us an idea of how automation might affect workers more specifically under socialism. Workers on automated lines earned 30-40% more than those on equivalent standard machines in the Soviet Union as part of a policy to pay higher wages for operating more productive machines, even if no increase in skill or responsibility was involved. British trade unions saw this policy as unfair, but, as Lilley points out:

"Fairness is not the only issue involved in fixing wage rates. They are also used to increase general enthusiasm for technical advance. If the workers in a factory know that those of them who are put to work on automated lines are going to get higher wages as a result, then they will naturally press the management to introduce more automation as quickly as possible. That will be another step to raising living standards all round. How well this policy works in practice is shown by the report in *Pravda* a few weeks after I had seen the automatic shop in the First State Ball-bearing Factory, that the Trade Union Committee there had passed a resolution criticising the management for not making sufficient use of modern techniques!

"To return to the main point, this 40-50% increase gives industrial workers a very tangible idea about how automation can contribute to raising living standards. At the same time, it is clear that if automation cuts labour costs for a job to a fifth or a tenth or a twentieth and cuts production costs by something like half, then a 30-40% wage increase is very far from accounting for the whole saving. And in fact the main method used for raising real wages is not that of money-wage increase, but of price cuts. This, of course, is fair – it means that most of the benefits of technical progress are passed on to the whole people, rather than being confined to the workers in the plant concerned."

Lilley goes on to explain how the Soviet Union treated workers displaced by automation. It contrasts strikingly with the situation under capitalism, where they are usually all but left to fend for themselves or forced to accept lower paid work.

"Those who work on automation lines have increased pay. Those who are displaced by automation at the worst cannot suffer financially – for the management is not permitted to remove anybody from a job without finding him work at a comparable or higher level of skill and pay in the same factory or within travelling distance. As most establishments are growing rapidly, this can be usually done with no more than a move from one shop to another. If a retraining course is necessary, the management must pay the man's wages while he takes it."

Lilley puts this in the context that the threats of unemployment and economic recession had been abolished:

"It is a fact that that there has not been any unemployment in the USSR since 1930; that is to say, since they embarked on a fully socialist economic plan after the compromises that were necessary in the 1920s. 26 years without unemployment is a long enough period to count as good evidence that the danger really has been abolished – especially when one remembers that the period includes the 1930s when the rest of the world had many millions out of work.

"Slumps have disappeared, too. The year 1929 was the last of the great boom. By 1933, the volume of industrial production in the United States had fallen to about two-thirds of its 1929 figure. In the capitalist world as a whole, production dropped to less than three-quarters of the 1929 level. But in the USSR, industrial production in 1933 was nearly twice what it had been in 1929. And if there are no slumps, there can be no fear of automation causing or worsening a slump."[629]

Lilley stresses that the Soviet Union was developing at a faster rate than Britain and the US not simply because it was 'younger', an argument that fails when it is considered that this included the period when the imperialist powers were experiencing a post-war boom, the biggest boom in absolute terms in their history.

"It amounts to no more than this: that the only limiting factors in that economy are the real ones of building plants and training people to work them. It is not that Russian industry has moved fast, but that our industry and that of America has moved slowly, because we have an economic system that actually penalises people for expanding production too fast for markets to absorb. And given changes to eliminate the market problem and the restraints imposed by monopoly, the industries of advanced countries like Britain and USA could grow far faster than that of the USSR."[630]

Lilley notes that "eminent [imperialist] authorities are agreed that the quality of Soviet scientific and technical education is at least as high as our own, and perhaps rather higher". Indeed, the reason the imperialists lied so much to discredit the Soviet Union was because they were so concerned that socialism was proving to be a superior mode of production. "Theodore W Schultz, President of the American Economic Association, believes, for one, that as far as utilisation of human resources and talent is concerned, the Soviet Union is likely to achieve better results than the United States," reports Volkov. "The Russian economy, which he professes to have observed first hand, alarmed him with the growing number of gifted people. The most amazing thing about it, he thought, was the accretion of human capital."

It was made clear to Lilley that working class aspirations and the development of automation were not just compatible but inextricable:

"In these conditions, with employment secure, with immense opportunities for advancement through education, with rapidly rising industrial production and corresponding rises in the standard of living, it is not surprising to find that the people of the USSR from factory director to machine operator are enthusiastically in favour of widespread and rapid automation. In my talks to them, I found that, besides its potential effect in raising the standard of living, they gave three types of reasons for wanting automation.

"First, they said, it eases labour and improves working conditions. More novel is the point made to me that now that full secondary education has become general, its products insist on having work that will give them the chance to exercise the knowledge and skill that they have been at much trouble to acquire. They do not want simple, repetitive jobs. They are not prepared to be reduced to mere appendages of machines. Looking after highly automatic machinery will make full use of the skills of hand and brain that they have learned. And so factories that want to attract young people are beginning to find that they must provide them with nice automatic machines to 'play with' – machines to which they stand in the relation of engineers rather than operators.

"And this way of thinking about work leads on naturally to another forward-thinking argument for extensive automation, which I heard from almost everybody I met – that it is another step towards ending the division between manual and mental labour. In fact, the worker on a highly automated plant ... uses his brain to decide what shall be done much more than he uses his hands in the doing of it."[631]

Removing the fetters on science

As socialism and automation develop, more time is increasingly devoted to assessing and controlling production processes and studying results. This gives rise, as Marx and the Soviet Union showed, to a greater onus on science and the employment of a greater proportion of scientists, accelerating a trend which grew with the highest stage of capitalism. Volkov says:

"To quote the apt expression coined by academician N Semyonov, science is turning from a 'handmaiden of production' into the 'mother of production'. The link between science and production has become so intimate that science pushes forward directly into industry in the shape of factory laboratories and scientifically trained personnel, while production itself spreads into the sphere of science to become its *experimental base*."

As with technological development, the impediments that slow down the development of science under capitalism – surplus capital, the profit motive, unemployment and competition-strangling monopolies – would be removed by socialism.

We will expand on this in the next chapter as we turn to automation's role in solving the climate and environmental crises.

16. Against extinction: For a green (hemp-based) industrial revolution that is actually green

> "Hemp will be the future of all mankind, or there won't be a future."
>
> Jack Herer

The 12-year target for preventing a temperature rise above 1.5°C, set by the UN's Intergovernmental Panel on Climate Change (IPCC) in October 2018, is based on the calculation that annual carbon emissions must be cut by 45% by 2030 and then to zero by 2050.

This would be quite the turnaround. The growth in global carbon emissions has accelerated from 1% a year in the 1990s to 3% a year in the 2010s.[632] In 2015, 63% of all 'human-generated' carbon emissions had been produced in the previous 25 years[633] (since, incidentally, the destruction of the Soviet Union). Furthermore, between 2010 and 2030, population growth will mean that the world will need to produce 50% more food and energy, together with 30% more available fresh water.[634]

Technological advance can raise the efficiency of resource use, but, as a study on civilisational collapse partly sponsored by NASA's Goddard Space Flight Center says, "it also tends to raise both per capita resource consumption and the scale of resource extraction".[635] The global economy became 23% more efficient in terms of carbon emissions per dollar of GDP between 1980 and 2008, but total emissions grew massively.[636]

The world's human population presently consumes between 17 and 18 terawatts every hour, approximately 150,000 terawatt Hours (TwH) per year. Each person on average uses about two kilowatts of constant energy, more or less the same as having a kettle switched on 24 hours a day. These figures are set to more or less double by 2050.[637] On the face of it, this looks like a recipe for disaster unless fossil fuel is replaced with clean, renewable energy.[638]

We know alternatives exist. In the span of just 90 minutes, enough potential solar energy hits Earth's surface to meet present demand for an entire year. Every 12 months we receive twice as much energy from the sun as we will ever obtain from Earth's non-renewable sources – coal, oil, natural gas and mined uranium – combined.[639] Free, limitless energy. The question is, can we store and harness this energy without adding to – and reversing – global warming? What we need is a world in which extraction is prohibited and disincentivised, where production is fuelled by renewable, non-polluting energy and the products we make are clean, durable, recyclable and biodegradable. We will also need to invest heavily in dikes and perhaps filtration systems. Returning to analog devices where possible would also be wise (does everybody really need an electric doorbell?). Clearly, a transitional period is required so that people are not made to go without basic necessities. There will have to be hard limitations or rations on the production and use of: fossil fuel; air, water and soil pollutants; and also metals, which can be recycled much more frequently. Toxic waste from mining must be minimised (something that profit margins do not allow for. Indeed, none of the top global industries would be profitable if companies had to pay for using – and polluting – the environment).[640]

Overproduction, however, will still exist under socialism and communism: firstly, to ensure no shortfalls in necessities; and secondly, because the removal of the fetter on the productive forces will continue to accelerate innovation. Much of what is produced under capitalism, however, will become socially useless (including, to a large extent, cars – Toyota is already talking about becoming a mobility service – given that public transport will become highly accessible and the need for daily commuting or travel for leisure reduced as communities become increasingly pleasurable and self-sufficient).[641]

The materials used in production will be renewable or recyclable and production will be carbon neutral or negative (more carbon will be sequestered than emitted). Planning will enable the coordinated and sustainable disposal and recycling of used products. This contrasts with the anarchy of capitalism, where exploitation and profit incentivises extraction and throwaway consumerism; and rubbish goes largely unrecycled due to: the petroleum-based plastics used in production;[642] the largely unproductive nature of the refuse and recycling industries; and the competition which precludes joined-up co-ordination – all of which results in the enormous magnitudes of food waste,[643] overflowing landfills and littered oceans that distinguish our shameful epoch.[644]

How do we realise this transformation? Like anything else, to understand the solution to the climate and environmental crises we must understand *precisely* what they are fuelled by. In the 'mainstream' political debate, this is *still* not the case. To simply point to the diabolical fact (as of the start of 2019) that fossil fuels still comprise 80% of the world's energy mix only begs the question as to why when we have known since at least 1979 that continuing to extract and burn them was creating nothing less than an existential threat. Vested interests? Callous greed? These factors only beg further questions. There are many 'surface level' explanations but ultimately they all *stem inevitably* from the capitalist relations of production. In this chapter we will see exactly why.

Extraction and the greenhouse effect
The warming climate is being fuelled by carbon dioxide and other greenhouse gases (GHGs). Solar energy absorbed at Earth's surface is radiated back into the atmosphere as heat, much of which is absorbed by GHGs as it makes its way through the atmosphere and back out to space. GHGs radiate the heat back to Earth's surface, to another GHG molecule, or out to space.

The vast majority of GHGs come from deforestation, the burning of fossil fuels, the extractive production of oil, minerals and metals and the intensive production of food. All of these are themselves intensely dependent on fossil fuel consumption. The process of turning nature into commodities releases GHGs sequestered in the earth into the atmosphere. According to Climate Watch, energy accounts for 73.2% of emissions (24% in industry; 16.2% in transport; 17.5% in buildings). The bulk of the rest (18.4%) comes from agriculture, forestry and land use.

Earth's resources are being consumed in increasingly destructive volumes. From 1970 to 2017, the annual global extraction of materials grew from 27 billion tonnes to 92 billion tonnes, according to the UN's 2019 Global Resource Outlook report. Since 2000, extraction rates have accelerated by 3.2% per annum. The mining of metals has increased by 2.7% per year, with the global iron-steel production chain alone accounting for a quarter of industrial energy demand. The annual use of fossil fuel (coal, petroleum and natural gas) rose from six billion tonnes to 15 billion tonnes in 1970-2020, its share of total extraction declining from 23% to 16%. The annual figure for non-metallic minerals, mostly sand, gravel and clay, grew from nine billion tonnes to 44 billion tonnes, 45% of overall extraction. Although their emissions are limited, the mining of minerals, for sand in particular, has "critical impacts on local ecosystems". Most impacts related to non-metallic minerals occur in the processing stage, and the production of clinker, the main ingredient in cement.

Biomass production (mostly in the categories of crop harvest and grazing) climbed from nine billion tonnes to 24 billion tonnes. Global water withdrawals for agriculture, industries and municipalities grew at a faster rate than the human population. The growth rate slowed, but still grew from

2,500km³ to 3,900km³ per year. Between 2000 and 2012, 70% of global water withdrawals were used for agriculture – mainly irrigation – while industries withdrew 19% and municipalities 11%. The cultivation and processing of biomass for food is now responsible for almost 90% of global water stress and land-use related biodiversity loss. The report notes that

> "the global economy has focused on improvements in labour productivity at the cost of material and energy productivity. This was justifiable in a world where labour was the limiting factor of production. We have moved into a full world where natural resources and environmental impacts have become the limiting factor of production and shifts are required to focus on resource productivity."

In 2018 it took a record 212 days to consume a year's worth of carbon, food, water, fibre, land and timber.[645] The point at which consumption exceeds the capacity of nature to regenerate moved forward on 2017 by two days to the 1st of August. In other words, we are using 1.7 Earths each year.

Despite ever-higher output, the majority of the world's people remain poor. Michael Parenti put it most concisely and vividly when he wrote in *Against Empire*:

> "The essence of capitalism is to turn nature into commodities and commodities into capital. The live green Earth is transformed into dead gold bricks, with luxury items for the few and toxic slag heaps for the many."[646]

Underpopulated, not overpopulated

Most people, it seems, will tell you that the environment is being exhausted because of population growth, or 'overpopulation'. Promoted by liberals and fascists alike, this eugenicist distortion has been cited by Professor Paul Ehrlich, author of *The Population Bomb*, as the number one factor driving the "sixth mass extinction".

Clearly there is a limit to the number of people the planet can tolerate, but according to one study this figure is at least 92 billion.[647] Moreover, population growth would obviously stabilise with universally decent living standards and free access to contraception. While this is the solution nominally promoted by liberals, including Ehrlich, achieving this is an awfully slow (actually impossible) process under capitalism, one that slips back into reverse with every recession – not to mention that it depends on ever-greater extraction. The logical solution for fascists is mass sterilisation and genocide on an unprecedented scale.[648] Not only is this monstrous, it is stupid – equivalent to the belief that throwing the poor overboard is going to keep the Titanic afloat.

Even if the growing consumption that comes with population growth were the root problem, population growth is regulated – like any other form of production under capitalism – by the law of value and the demands of capital accumulation, because capital needs a growing base of human labour and consumption to create surplus value and realise profit.[649] Poorer countries tend to have higher birth rates because that is where productive capital can find a lower organic composition of capital, and poor families have more children because capitalism depends on the poorest mothers to produce and raise the most workers, which also compels poor fathers to work longer hours, increasing absolute surplus value.[650] Furthermore, child workers help make up the necessary labour time of parents who are paid below the value of their labour power, while child benefits effectively subsidise employers for the same reason. As Marx says:

"Every particular mode of production has its own special laws of population, which are historically valid within that particular sphere. An abstract law of population exists only for plants and animals and even then only in the absence of any historical intervention by man."[651]

Certainly populations may be too concentrated in concrete metropolises, serving the centralising demands of accumulation. The urban-rural divide means nutrients in food are transported from farms to cities but not back, increasing the demand for chemical treatments in both sewage and farming and diminishing the nutritional density in food. We perhaps need to pursue a process of partial deurbanisation, marrying the best parts of urban and rural life; and build rational, large-scale human and food waste recycling infrastructure. Bioengineering some crops so that they take up more phosphorus from the soil, so that they needs less fertiliser, is also an option.

But targeting population growth does nothing to stop capitalism's need to keep expanding labour-intensive extraction. Resources are being extracted three times faster than in 1970 – the population has only doubled in that time.[652] The world is in fact facing an *under*population crisis. The rate of population growth has been slowing since the 1960s and UN demographers predict that the world population will peak at around 9.2 billion in 2050. The fertility rate around the world is already dropping below the replacement level, so that globally there will soon be an unsustaining population. With negative population growth, each generation produces fewer offspring. This does not in any way contradict the theory that the mode of production drives population growth – alongside growing surplus capital grows a surplus population from the perspective of capital's ability to employ human labour.

The consequences of this trend are expressed most starkly by a social care crisis in which there are not enough young people to care for an ageing population.[653] The 'support ratio' (the number of people of working age to the total population) has been falling in Japan since 1990 and in the US and Europe since 2005. Japan's support ratio is now approaching 1.5 workers per older citizen and is expected to reach parity by 2050, with the US and Europe not far behind.

While the problem may be an inevitable offshoot of rising living standards and medical advances – the average human now lives to be 71, 40 years longer than at the beginning of the 20th century – this doesn't entirely explain the falling replacement trend. On the one hand, this is happening because of the reduction in child mortality; and because women have become more economically independent. On the other, the crisis of capitalism and growing under/unemployment is making it increasingly expensive to have children. Would-be parents are having to work so hard to sustain living costs that women cannot afford to stop working.[654] The state support that existed for families after WWII has withered away and maternity rights in most capitalist countries are appalling. In 2013, only 12% of US workers were covered by paid parental leave policies.[655]

In the ex-socialist eastern European countries, the gains made by women under socialism have been severely rolled back by 'refamilisation' policies – the top 10 countries with the fastest shrinking populations are all in Eastern Europe.[656] In socialist Bulgaria, by contrast, from 1973 mothers were guaranteed fully paid maternity leave of 120 days before and after the birth of the first child as well as an extra six months of leave paid at the minimum wage.[657] Bulgaria, Poland, Czechoslovakia, Yugoslavia and East Germany invested state funds in a network of nursery schools and kindergartens so that women could go back to work. East Germany heavily subsidised housing, children's clothing, basic foods and other expenses associated with child rearing. By 1989, out-of-wedlock births accounted for 34% of all births, compared to 10% in West Germany, underlining the rising independence of women under socialism.[658] In socialist Cuba, pregnant women are entitled to 18 weeks fully paid leave (six weeks before birth and 12 after), plus an additional 40 weeks at 60% pay, and are assured of returning to the same job.

Cuba's constitution stipulates that men and women should share housework duties equally.[659]

According to received wisdom, Africa is especially overpopulated. This, too, is untrue. Even though the continent's population has grown from 477 million in 1980 to 1.2 billion in 2016, its population density remains relatively low, with 20% of the world's land mass but only 15% of its people. While Europe's population density is 105 people per square kilometre, Africa's is 65.

From capital's perspective, it faces a dual crisis of over- and underpopulation. Surplus labour weighs down on the average outlay of wages but is also burdensome in terms of benefits and pensions that eat into profits. At the same time, however, where is enough surplus value for valorisation going to come from with slowing population growth but ever-rising accumulation demands? And yet this is a problem entirely of capital's own making.

Socialism is capable of permanent full employment and therefore surplus labour does not become an issue – if anything, greater populations mean greater utility production. To the unconscious mind corrupted by bourgeois thinking, there only *appears* to be an overpopulation crisis. The idea justifies fascism, the necessary solution when the economic crisis deepens to such a point that mass unemployment and living conditions become intolerable and drive the working class to rebellion. 'Overpopulation' has been manufactured as the issue to deflect from the real problems of economic unemployment, artificial scarcity and extractive production.

For capital, the ageing population crisis can only be resolved by allowing this redundant and therefore unproductive part of the working class – the retired – to die off. In 2015, the US death rate (the age-adjusted share of US Americans dying) rose slightly for the first time since 1999. According to Bloomberg, at least 12 corporations have stated in recent annual reports that slips in mortality improvement reduced their pension payouts by a combined $9.7bn.[660] State pension and welfare costs would have also fallen. In 2013, a study by S&P predicted that of 58 countries analysed, 60% would have their credit ratings downgraded to junk without rises in the pension age and cuts to public expenditure.

In 2018 in Russia the retirement age rose for the first time since being set at 60 for men and 55 for women during the Stalin era. Britain too – where the retirement age never got below 65 and 60 – has raised the retirement age, simultaneously reducing state expenditure and finding a way to raise absolute surplus value. The pensions bill has shot up by more than 500% from £17bn in 1989 to £92bn today, comprising £4 in every £10 of welfare spending, and is expected to hit £112bn in 2023. In August 2019, a report by Conservative think tank Centre for Social Justice said Britain could no longer afford the current plan to raise the pension age to 67 in 2028 and then 68 by 2046, meaning it would have to rise to 70 in 2028 and then 75 in 2035. Given that the average life expectancy for men in poor areas in Britain is 74, the policy would abolish the state pension in all but name. According to the Institute and Faculty of Actuaries, projections for life expectancy in England and Wales have fallen by 13 months for men and 14 months for women since 2015.

So much for 'living the right way' as a loyal servant of capital your whole life. A growing number of retirees who planned to leave their homes to their children now have to sell them to pay rent for care homes.

In 2018 the Tories were forced to cancel the expansion of the so-called 'dementia tax' because it meant attacking sections of their middle class base. The proposal, that pensioners would have to pay for their social care until their assets were reduced to £100,000, would replace the current system under which £23,000 of personal assets are protected. The proposals, however, would include the value of the pensioner's home in the asset calculation, when currently it is not. The measure would have hit those who require lengthy periods of social rather than hospital care, in particular those suffering from mobility problems including those with dementia. A family would never be forced to sell a property during a patient's life, but the costs would be recouped after death. It was therefore labelled a 'death tax' or 'dementia tax' and caused widespread anger among the middle classes suddenly threatened with proletarianisation. It deepened an already entrenched lottery: while the costs of cancer would be socialised through the NHS, the costs of dementia would be privatised. Despite the U-turn, the Tories were punished at the next election.

Spending on Britain's health and social care, the state pension and other benefits are forecast to increase by 2.5% of annual GDP in the decade after 2020. Between 2016 and 2030 its population over 65 will grow by a third and the number of over-85s will almost double. With Alzheimer's and dementia replacing heart disease as the leading cause of death and rates set to triple by 2050, the demand for socialised health care is only going to rise. Dementia cost the US economy $818bn in 2015.[661] Such costs to the state under capitalism are unsustainable.

Capitalocene, not Anthropocene
The theory of overpopulation tallies with the equally vacuous idea that Earth has entered 'the Anthropocene', having exited the Holocene era. This means

that, whereas Earth's function and development for the previous 4.5 billion years was determined by astronomical and geophysical forces, with a rate of change of 0.01°C per century, the human-driven epoch of the past 45 years has changed the climate at a rate 170 times faster.[662]

This theory, whether intentionally or not, justifies ascribing the blame for climate change to humanity or even 'human nature', letting capital off the hook. Liberals were exasperated when Trump's administration – which has made significant budget cuts to environmental protections and renewable energy development – went from denying climate change to acknowledging its danger, only to conclude that it could not be stopped. Yet this is the logical conclusion from the Anthropocene myth they have promoted. The theory does not stand up to the slightest bit of scrutiny. As Andreas Malm writes in *Jacobin*:

> "The average US citizen emits more carbon than 500 citizens of Ethiopia, Chad, Afghanistan, Mali, or Burundi. How much an average US millionaire emits – and how much more than an average US or Cambodian worker – remains to be counted. But a person's imprint on the atmosphere varies tremendously depending on where she is born. Humanity, as a result, is far too slender an abstraction to carry the burden of culpability."[663]

Poor countries may have higher birth rates but they would have to have impossibly high birth rates to match the consumption levels of the imperialist nations. According to the UN, high-income countries maintain levels of per capita material footprint consumption 60% higher than upper-middle income countries and more than 13 times the level of the low-income countries. Even China's per person energy consumption of 1.6kW is dwarfed by a figure of 11.4kW in the US.[664] The US comprises 5% of the world's population but consumes 24% of its energy.[665] And the US military is the single greatest institutional polluter.[666] (The US, and the world as a whole, loses about two-thirds of energy production to waste heat.)[667]

Clearly, consumption is driven not by population growth but by purchasing power and, more accurately, the demands of (especially imperialist) capital. As we have established, we live under the dictatorship of capital, and so this epoch is not the Anthropocene, it is, as Jason W Moore has written about, the 'Capitalocene'.[668] Surely even 'Fossil-fuelocene' or 'Industriocene' would have been a more logical conclusion.

Corroborating our economic theory, a study from the University of Valladolid in Spain has also shown that there is a direct correlation between the rate of GDP growth and the rate in the increase of atmospheric CO_2, which evidently falls when the global economy goes into recession.[669]

That capitalism rather than individual consumption is to blame is confirmed by another study, which showed that, in 2017, just 100 fossil-fuel-producing corporations had been responsible for 71% of all GHGs – one trillion tonnes – since 1988, with ExxonMobil, Shell, BP and Chevron among the top of the list. Yet less attention is given to this than 'human nature' or 'overpopulation' because it would mean admitting that such companies need to be shut down or taken under public ownership and repurposed.

It should be clear by now that the ongoing and ever-quicker destruction of nature is the inevitable consequence of the ever-higher demands of capital accumulation. As we have seen, in order to continually reproduce and expand capital, a sufficient magnitude of surplus value has to be generated by commodity-producing human workers. Every time the overall mass of capital rises, it requires an even higher production of commodities than before in order to reproduce and expand capital yet further. And since commodities are made from natural resources, the quantity of food production, mineral extraction, deforestation, fossil fuel extraction and burning, and so on, has to rise, year after year after year. All this is necessary in order to stave off the breakdown tendency. Again, the vitality of Grossman's theory is clear.

Rich nations must reduce their emissions by 8-10% per year. Global carbon intensity has fallen over the past three decades from roughly one kilogram per dollar of economic activity to around 770 grams per dollar, while carbon emissions have grown by 40% in absolute terms. A number of studies argue that reductions greater than 3-4% per year are incompatible with a growing economy. The existing decarbonisation rate is about 1.6% per year. Some rich nations might be able to climb to 4.7% if they roll out a high and fast-rising carbon tax, but only if they somehow manage to double their material efficiency. Neoliberals claim it is possible to continue expanding GDP without consuming more resources, but researchers have argued that "decoupling of GDP growth from resource use, whether relative or absolute, is at best only temporary. Permanent decoupling (absolute or relative) is impossible… because the efficiency gains are ultimately governed by physical limits". Another study says that "while some relative decoupling can be achieved in some scenarios, none would lead to an absolute reduction in energy or materials footprint".[670] These studies, however, are based on carbon-emitting production under capitalism. As we shall see, growth with carbon-neutral/negative production would be possible under socialism.

Capitalism is responsible for the climate and environmental crises and it can only respond as a runaway train does to an approaching cliff edge. Anti-communism is species suicide. The only chance we have of saving humanity is to end the anarchy of capitalist production and replace it with a rational, consciously planned system that serves the needs of people and planet.

Cheap renewables vs uneconomic fossil fuel

To understand what is being said by the various factions in the bourgeois political debate we must understand the state of the energy industry. It is not as if fossil fuel is having it all its own way. Wind and solar power grew into a $164bn global market in 2011 from just $7bn in 2000.[671] While activism may have had some impact, the limited shift away from fossil fuel in the world's energy mix has been driven almost entirely by economics, by the fact that the production of fossil fuel has become increasingly capital-intensive, while the expanding production and capacity of renewable energy is now making it price-competitive and therefore attractive to consumers, including businesses and states.

By 2020 the cheapest solar in the US is on course to be three cents a kilowatt, meaning new installations of solar cells will generate cheaper power than a newly built plant that burns fossil fuels. The International Renewable Energy Agency believes all renewable energy will be competitive with fossil fuels by 2020, saying that turning to renewable energy "is not simply an environmentally conscious decision, it is now – overwhelmingly – a smart economic one". So while solar presently provides 2% of the world's electricity, this is set to increase dramatically.[672]

Bastani writes that, "Were the 40% annual growth rate to ... continue through to 2035, that would mean global solar capacity of 150 terawatts – meeting not just the world's electricity needs but ... humanity's entire energy requirements. Were that trend to slow down, as is common... it remains reasonable to predict a complete global transition to renewables sometime in the 2040s." The transition will require no net increase in spending because, "The world currently spends around $2.2 trillion on fossil fuels every year. If today's demand for 15-17 terawatts doubled over the intervening period, that would mean compounded energy costs of around $80 trillion by the early 2040s. The UN has put a price on a complete transition to renewables ... at $1.9 trillion every year for 40 years – which works out at slightly less than what would otherwise be spent burning coal, gas and oil."[673]

The prices of wind power and lithium batteries are falling at even faster rates than solar. In 2009, Deutsche Bank reported that the cost of lithium-ion batteries at $650 per kilowatt hour would halve by 2020, but in fact it fell by 70% over the following 18 months. Tesla expects to produce batteries for $100 per kilowatt hour by the early 2020s. In the past 15 years the energy capacity of lithium-ion batteries has tripled, and the cost per unit of stored energy has fallen by a factor of 10. By the early 2020s a battery pack for a new electric car could cost as little as £5,000. "That would make the price of electric cars directly competitive with petrol versions while remaining on a downward curve. That is before considering how they'll be cheaper to run, insure and maintain," says Bastani. Furthermore, internal energy insulation has the potential to eliminate the need for heating buildings in the winter, while the internet of things will automate energy conservation.[674]

But we are still starting from a point at which fossil fuels make up 80% of the world's energy mix. Other estimates expect renewable energy not to overtake coal in the energy mix until around 2040 (although they may well have under-estimated the speed of falling prices).

There are at least three problems (outside the context of a final breakdown; others will be discussed further on): firstly, the disruption economic shocks may bring to the production of renewables; secondly, the possibility that companies may be compelled to rent out the technologies as prices near zero, creating or exacerbating artificial scarcity; and, thirdly, the efforts of the fossil fuel industry to keep its prices falling. Scientists have said that 33% of the world's oil and 49% of its gas have to be left in the ground (almost certainly under-estimates) to avoid 2°C, yet BP and Shell are basing their business strategies on 5°C.[675] Why? Because melting ice sheets in the Arctic are revealing new sources of oil extraction.[676] *Global warming is in their economic interests!* Capitalists are in such denial, perhaps because they cannot cope with having the extinction of humankind on their conscience, that they have to act like immortal gods. They are only 'rational actors' if the rationale is profit. Capitalism is an extinction cult.

In February 2019, it was also revealed that Google, Microsoft and Amazon were teaming up with fossil fuel giants to provide automation, AI and big data services to enhance oil exploration, extraction and production.[677]

Automation will help the industry to resist the growing likelihood of workers taking part in principled sabotage, but it is needed anyway to further reduce wage costs because the already capital-intensive industry is in deep economic trouble. In 2016, Deloitte said 65% of fossil fuel companies were close to bankruptcy under the weight of massive debt burdens.[678] In October

2004 energy consultant group Wood Mackenzie reported that in the previous three years the ten biggest oil companies spent more on exploration than the value of the reserves they discovered. In 2003, they spent a combined $8bn to yield discoveries worth less than $4bn. Exploration spending fell from $11bn in 1998 to $8bn in 2003. Instead, spending on developing existing reserves rose from $34.6bn to $49.5bn. In July 2016, Sir David King, the British Foreign Office's Special Representative on Climate Change, said:

> "We are not running out of oil, but we have reached a plateau in easy, inexpensive conventional oil production, which will be followed by a fall in production… Novel unconventional oil reserves are abundant, but are more costly to produce, provide less net energy and cause more GHG emissions."[679]

Since 1980, he said, more conventional oil has been consumed than found every year. The widening supply-demand gap is filled using unconventional reserves like tar sands in Canada or shale gas in the US, which require costly fracking technology to extract and more difficult processes to refine. New sources are harder to find, while existing sources are more rapidly exhausted.[680] The fossil fuel industries are increasingly unprofitable and therefore increasingly dependent on state subsidies, which grew worldwide from $4.9 trillion in 2013 to $5.3 trillion in 2015, 6.5% of global GDP.[681] With the new round of automation reducing the value-creating part of production still further, perhaps the fossil fuel industry will go completely bust just in time to save the climate…

According to financial think tank Carbon Tracker, at the end of 2018, 42% of the world's coal plants were operating at a loss "because of high fuel costs", a figure it said could rise to nearly 75% by 2040.[682] It has become increasingly cheaper to build a wind or solar farm than to expand coal production, and by 2030, in virtually every case (96%), building new renewable energy capacity will be cheaper than keeping coal plants running. For humanity, this could be too little, too late. Pressure should mount on the state for economic reasons, though, to stop subsidising coal, from consumers as well as the renewables industry. The report says:

> "Coal plants will be forced to shut unless they can secure government subsidies or a delay or reduction in environmental regulations. However, it is the state which ultimately underwrites investment risk in regulated markets, where coal is sheltered from competition. In countries such as

China, India, Japan and parts of the US, governments typically approve the cost of generation and pass it on to consumers. Backing coal in the long-term will threaten economic competitiveness and public finances, because politicians will be forced to choose between subsidising coal power or increasing power prices for consumers.

"Consumers and taxpayers are keeping coal profitable in [many] regulated markets by picking up the bill to support uneconomic coal plants. A phase-out could save them billions, but would hit coal owners' profits. If plants are closed in line with the Paris Agreement the industry could lose $92bn in South Korea, $76bn in India and $51bn in South Africa, compared with business as usual supported by the state."

With state expenditure already stretched to breaking point, coal's days may be numbered – but the power coal owners still hold within the capitalist state clearly remains very significant. In 2009, the G20 nations, which account for 79% of global emissions, committed to phasing out fossil fuel subsidies in the medium term, but have in fact tripled subsidies for coal-powered plants in recent years – making up for a 75% plunge in private investment.[683]

The Green New Deal – dirty old imperialism
The Green New Deal (GND) in the US, spearheaded by Alexandria Ocasio-Cortez on the left wing of the Democratic Party, is, compared to what we are used to from the main parties, highly ambitious, calling for a "national, social, industrial and economic mobilisation at a scale not seen since WWII and the New Deal era" in order to decarbonise the US economy by 2030. Presently, the Democrats are committed (at least on paper) only to an 80% carbon reduction from 2005 levels by 2050.

The GND would retrofit all buildings and factories to be carbon-neutral, electrify all transportation, build high-speed public rail at a scale that makes internal air travel unnecessary, and switch the entire electrical grid to carbon-neutral energy sources. It recognises that carbon taxes are not enough to make private companies do all these things, meaning that large-scale state-funded intervention and infrastructure is required. This would create 'green' jobs and push forward innovations in renewable technology that could then be generalised globally. The environmental goals are coupled with social programmes that promise to guarantee economic security (the right to sick and holiday pay, decent housing, free education and health care).

The GND therefore has mass grassroots support. But the dominant right-wing of the Democratic Party, let alone the Republicans, is never going to support it. A left-wing Democrat like Bernie Sanders would have to take power with a landslide in order to get the GND through Congress. Even then it is likely that serious compromises would have to be made, meaning the social programmes would have to be dropped. But let us imagine that a Sanders is propelled into power in a repeat of the Roosevelt landslide of 1932, and that the GND won enough support and passed swiftly into law.

According to Brad Johnson in *Jacobin*, a democratic socialist publication, if the US federal budget increased from the current $4 trillion a year "by seven to twenty times – paralleling the ramp-up that got the world out of the Great Depression, beat the Nazis, and made the US the undisputed superpower of the free world[!][684] – we would see an annual federal budget of about $30 trillion to $80 trillion a year. We can end global warming pollution and build a just, green economy in ten years with a budget of $50 trillion a year."[685]

He counters right-wing concerns about soaring debt by pointing out that WWII took US national debt to $64bn and federal spending from 10% to 40% of GDP, "vastly higher than federal outlays since" – it was 21% of GDP in 2018 – and so "there is nothing to worry about". Johnson is of course right when he says that "budgetary deficits are meaningless when the alternative to spending is extinction".[686]

As we saw earlier, however, the New Deal lasted for only four years, despite the massive devaluation that followed the 1929 crash. It could not be sustained because the remaining capitalists could only tolerate concessions for so long before their survival became jeopardised; and because the extra government spending brought forward the onset of the next crisis. Debt may have been much higher during the war but it was coupled with the destruction of capital values on a global scale. For the GND to really achieve its goals, the US would first have to destroy the rest of the world!

Furthermore, the very limited 'success' of the New Deal came at a time when the US was a rising power in the world. WWI had turned it from a debtor into a creditor nation. It is now a debtor nation again and a declining power with a much higher organic composition of capital.[687] The dollar is already over-valued; it needs to go through a deflationary process. US capital requires yet deeper austerity.

Claims that Germany's equivalent works are exaggerated – it adopted the policy of *Energiewende* (energy transition) in 2010 – but also ignore the country's slightly lower organic composition of capital, partly a result of the its destruction in WWII, meaning the fetter on development is not yet as bad.[688] While 3.5 million homes were refurbished or built according to new efficiency standards between 2006 and 2014, Germany is expected to fall short on pretty much all its national and EU clean energy and emission reduction targets – the latter by 40% – for 2020. In Europe, 11 countries including Sweden, Austria, Denmark, the UK and France have achieved more in cutting coal dependency and greening their energy systems. In 2017, coal still accounted for almost 40% of Germany's power; and in 2016, seven of the 10 worst polluting facilities in Europe were German lignite plants, one of the dirtiest fuels going. Coal provides the back-up power needed when there is no wind and sunshine, something that will become even more necessary when the last nuclear plants close in 2022 (a move that has already pushed up consumer energy prices and therefore energy poverty). Peter Altmaier, the new energy minister and a member of Merkel's Christian Democratic Union, has said that ending coal power will take "several decades".[689]

Furthermore, Germany's plan to replace all petrol and diesel cars with electric vehicles (EVs) by 2030 may actually increase emissions if EVs are charged by an electric grid that is powered by fossil fuel. A study found that although EVs would hugely reduce energy needs, charging them on power generated by dirty coal or gas actually creates more emissions than a car that burns petrol.[690]

As Asad Rehman of the charity War on Want has written in an article entitled "The 'Green New Deal' supported by Ocasio-Cortez and Corbyn is just a new form of colonialism", the Green New Deal relies on *expanded* resource and wealth extraction from poor and developing nations, whereby replacing oil, gas and coal involves plundering from the earth the cobalt, lithium, silver, copper, plastic, concrete, steel, etc, needed to build wind turbines, solar panels and supercapacitors through processes that are fuel-intensive.[691] The scale of new extraction needed "will come to dwarf the current relentless drive for resources that capitalism is built upon".[692]

The OECD's Global Resources Outlook to 2060, modelled on an annual 2.8% global growth in GDP, estimates that extracted resources would increase from 79 billion to 167 billion tonnes, a 111% increase overall, with a 150% increase in metals and a 135% increase in minerals. Resource extraction is responsible for 50% of global emissions, with minerals and metal mining responsible for 20% of emissions even before the manufacturing stage. Rehman writes:

"Behind each tonne of extraction is a story of contamination and depletion of water, destruction of habitats, deforestation, poisoning of land, health impacts on workers and hundreds of environmental conflicts – including the murder of two environmental defenders each and every week.

"The demand for renewable energy and storage technologies will far exceed the reserves for cobalt, lithium and nickel. In the case of cobalt, of which 58% is currently mined in the Democratic Republic of the Congo, it has helped fuel a conflict that has blighted the lives of millions, led to the contamination of air, water and soil, and left the mining area as one of the top 10 most polluted places in the world.

"Some studies estimate that the demand for cobalt by 2050 will be 423% of existing reserves, with lithium at 280% and nickel at 136% of current reserves. Tellurium for solar panels could exceed current production rates by 2020. Rather than face up to the reality that capitalism requires relentless growth and is simply incompatible with tackling climate change, a new scramble for mineral extraction is already being planned with proposals for deep sea mining that will wreck some of our most fragile ecosystems, with more extraction planned across Brazil, China, India and the Philippines."

In Chile, mining giant Anglo-American plans to extract 400,000 tonnes of copper per year for the next 40 years from the Andean glaciers, threatening to destroy vital ecosystems which also supply water to the six million people living in the country's capital, Santiago. The multinational operates eight mines, mainly copper or nickel, in Peru, Chile, Colombia and Brazil. The company was fined $4.5m in 2014 and $6.2m in 2015 by Chile's environmental regulator SMA for water pollution, and failure to fully preserve and relocate vegetation, causing 'irreparable' damage to a nearby agricultural valley in Los Bronces. Local activists have said that public meetings opposing Anglo-American's operations have been attended by heavily armed police and that peaceful demonstrations have been suppressed by police violence. In April 2019, War on Want released an updated report on 56 mining projects in Latin America that are tied to British mining companies, including BHP Billiton, Rio Tinto and Glencore.[693]

In June 2019, Prof Richard Herrington and fellow members of SoS MinErals published an estimate that said meeting the 2050 UK electric car and van targets alone (not including the LGV and HGV fleets) would require almost two times the current total annual *global* cobalt production, nearly the entire global production of neodymium, three quarters of the world's lithium production and at least half of the world's copper production.[694] *This is suicidal.* Clearly, the amount of energy required for all this could keep the fossil fuel industry in business for a while yet…

The proponents of a Green New Deal in the US have actually taken inspiration from the Green New Deal Group, a largely British organisation set up in 2007 by NGOs and financial directors, with *The Guardian* economics editor Larry Elliott and former Green Party leader Caroline Lucas as its Keynesian figureheads. The organisation's objectives were established in a document produced by the New Economic Foundation (NEF) in 2008. The document now forms the basis of Labour's 'Green Transformation' policy. One of the authors was Ann Pettifor, now economics adviser to Jeremy Corbyn. As *FRFI* put it,[695] Labour's plan "can only be compared to Nero's fiddling while Rome burned. There is not the slightest recognition of the eco-destruction caused by British mining or oil multinationals, or the vast tracts of land that are being seized and then exhausted by unsustainable monoculture."[696] The same can be said of Bastani, presently a Labour supporter, and his road to 'FALC'.

The Green New Deal Group's imperialist intentions are clear. They view the capital-intensive fossil fuel industry as a fetter on the further development of capitalism. They seek to restore profitability via the destruction of fossil fuel capital and the break up of big banks. In various iterations of the deal, this is complemented by what is called the Payment for Ecosystems Services System, whereby this new round of investment can be supported by the valuation of natural assets, ie the further privatisation and financialisation of nature, along with higher taxes, the "unlocking" – ie plundering – of pension funds and deepened exploitation of the working class.[697] It would not be surprising if in Britain these demands were later extended to abolishing the British monarchy, which as the country's biggest landlord is a drain on productive capital.

The GND may create an emissions-free energy infrastructure by the time the whole infrastructure has been constructed (although there is the question of replacement parts for maintenance to consider); but there is hardly anything 'green' about it – it is, in fact, dirty old imperialism, and would accelerate rising emissions and global warming. It is as suicidal as the status quo. Without world war levels of destruction, it is unlikely to be economically possible on the necessary scale; but by abolishing labour in the fossil fuel sector, it cannot push back the final breakdown for long.[698] Quite the opposite.

All production under capitalism is regulated by the law of value. Social democrats in power can make the political choice of ramping up public spending and taking on more debt, but the result will be to bring forward the onset of the next crash, making easy work for the Right to blame the Left for ruining the economy.

Exposing the GND is not enough, though; we have to offer a better alternative: actual socialism will have the ability to deliver what no one in the mainstream political debate is talking about – a green industrial revolution that is actually green.

Hemp: the ultimate use-value
Monopoly capitalism's suppression of hemp farming and hemp-based industry in general for the past 80 years – hemp having previously been used by humans for food, medicine, fuel, clothing and construction for at least 10,000 years[699] – is bound up with the main factors driving the destruction of the planet.

Hemp is nature's highest yielding and most versatile crop. The growing cycle is extremely short, at three and a half months to full maturity, allowing farmers to grow the plant for part of the year and combine it with a food crop. And because hemp tolerates a wide-range of temperatures, it is drought-resistant.

It is at least four times richer in biomass and cellulose potential than its nearest rivals: cornstalks, sugarcane, kenaf, trees, etc.[700] While it takes 1,000 pounds of water to make a pound of cotton, it takes only three pounds of water to make a pound of hemp. Hemp provides around 115% more fibre than cotton and, because it grows tightly-packed, does not require chemical pesticides, around 50% of which are currently used for growing cotton. In fact, hemp is often used as a natural, organic pesticide next to other crops like potatoes.

It even grows well in and enriches poor soil thanks to its deep, aerating root system. Through a process called remediation, hemp removes heavy metals and even radioactive waste from the soil while around 70% of hemp's nutrient requirements are returned to the soil during and after the growth cycle, making previously unusable dirt rich and fertile.[701] This process became more well-known after the Chernobyl disaster when it was used to grow crops safe for consumption.

Hemp seed grows in abundance and could be used as cattle feed, being cheaper and more nutritious than the grain and sorghum most cattle are currently fed, which would bring down food prices. Indeed, hemp seed protein and oils are one of the most complete single food sources. Only soybeans (which are mostly genetically-modified) have a higher protein content, but the protein in hemp seed contains all the essential amino acids and the highest source of essential fatty acids in the plant kingdom. With a makeup that is high in Omega 3, 9 and 46, antioxidants and essential nutrients

– magnesium, calcium, potassium, iron, and zinc – hemp-based edibles have gained a reputation as a "super food", while hemp milk is considered the best alternative to breast milk. According to Hemp Tank:

> "Hemp seed is the ideal food to improve digestion, balance hormones and improve metabolism. It is rich in Gamma-Linolenic acid (GLA), a necessary building block for some prostaglandins, hormone-like chemicals in the body which aid muscles growth, control inflammation and body temperature, and are vital to other body functions. Researchers have surmised that GLA supplementation is necessary for proper hormone health, which is probably why many women suffering from PMS symptoms have been helped by using it. GLA and GLA-rich foods like hemp seeds have also been seen to help people with: ADHD, diabetes and diabetic neuropathy, heart disease, high blood pressure, multiple sclerosis, obesity, rheumatoid arthritis and skin allergies."[702]

Plants and trees, of course, draw down CO_2 from the atmosphere and have a vital role to play in stabilising the climate. Hemp does this at the highest rate of any plant – it is this high absorption of CO_2 which makes it so productive and versatile. According to Hemp Global Solutions, each tonne of hemp grown (about four-fifths of an acre) represents 1.63 tonnes of CO_2 absorption.[703] By contrast, the woodiest trees sequester one tonne of CO_2 by the time they reach 40 years of age. Trees do not always have a net cooling effect, either, since they can soak up the heat from sunlight that may otherwise be reflected back into space by the lighter-coloured surfaces they cover up.[704] Trees can also emit methane and other GHGs. In contrast hemp prevents a lot of heat from reaching the soil.

For centuries hemp fuel was used to light lamps. As a high storer of solar energy, the stalk of the plant produces the purest form of ethanol, which itself can boost fuel efficiency and reduce net emissions from fuel by 37%. But hemp can also produce methanol used in a process called pyrolysis to make biofuel from hemp seed that is more than two-thirds cleaner (and therefore far less carcinogenic) than fossil fuel, while at least matching the latter's performance in terms of power and mileage.[705] According to the Proceedings of the National Academy of Sciences, biodiesel provides 93% more net energy per gallon than is required for its production.[706] The same process that makes biofuel produces sulphur-free charcoal with a heating value equivalent to coal. This charcoal can be used as a raw material for organic fertiliser.

Hemp oil can be made into anything with an oil base, including paint, varnish, solvent and lubricating oil. Until the 1930s most paint and varnishes were made with non-toxic hemp oil. Hemp paint provides superior coating as hemp oil soaks into and preserves wood due to its high resistance to water. Hemp oil is a good base for non-toxic printing inks. Soy is currently made into inks, but requires more processing and takes longer to dry.

Hemp can be turned into the softest of fabrics that are four times stronger and harder-wearing than cotton, with its antimicrobial properties making it perfect not only for fabric but also as a base for detergent.[707] There is then a solution to the current reality that synthetic clothes shed about 700,000 microplastic fibres (less than 5mm in size) that end up in the waterways after every domestic wash.[708] (Of the eight million metric tonnes of plastic which end up in the ocean annually,[709] 236,000 tonnes are microplastics.[710] Microplastics pollute every lake and river in Britain.[711] They have been found in the stomachs of the deepest marine organisms known to exist and make their way into our food and drinking water (both tap and bottled). Every participant in a Europe-wide study was found to have nine different types of plastic in their faeces.[712] The smallest microplastic particles are capable of entering the bloodstream, lymphatic system and even the liver.)

The 'waste' or shiv – the broken woody core of the plant – from hemp processing can be turned into reusable, durable and (in forced composting conditions) biodegradable bioplastics. That fibre glass, which has to be heated to 1,371°C, no longer has to be used as a reinforcing component notably reduces emissions alone. Bioplastics are predicted to comprise 5% of the plastics market by 2020, rising to 40% by 2030. This is largely being driven by demand for cheaper products but also from an increasingly eco-conscious public fed up with plastic waste, especially from single-use food shopping.

Kevin Tubbs of the Hemp Plastic Company says he advises potential investors to think about raw material costs. "When the price of oil rises, watch the cost of bioplastic. Take a pound of raw polymer and compare it to a pound of hemp raw material: the hemp is cheaper. Every ounce of it I add to the other polymers makes the polymer cheaper. Greener and cheaper."[713]

High-end car makers such as BMW, Mercedes-Benz and Jaguar, desperate to find ways to reduce overall manufacturing costs, have recently turned to hemp for composite plastic for interior door panelling, dashboards and upholstery, making cars lighter and more fuel efficient. Henry Ford actually constructed a car partly out of hemp with an impact strength *10 times stronger than steel*.[714] Whereas a standard car has a carbon footprint of 10 tonnes to manufacture, former Dell executive Bruce Dietzen recently made a prototype cabriolet, 'the Renew', from 100 pounds of woven hemp that was carbon neutral. The bodywork is lighter than fibreglass and, again, 10 times more dent-resistant than steel.

Of course, CO_2 contained in hemp is released when the plant rots or during pyrolysis and the burning of biofuel. Solid or unburned products made from hemp, however, continue to keep the absorbed CO_2 sequestered. HempFlax in the Netherlands, which makes industrial products from hemp, claims to be one of the very rare carbon-*negative* companies, saying that the amount of CO_2 absorbed by its 2,500 hectares of hemp as it grows is more than the amount produced by its manufacturing processes.[715]

'Hempcrete', for example, also made from the shiv, offers several advantages over regular concrete (which is responsible for 7% of global emissions): it is lighter, stronger, non-toxic, has natural anti-fungal and antimicrobial properties, and is also fire-resistant.[716] Again, a hemp-based building is carbon negative and an indefinite storer of CO_2.[717] One cubic metre of hempcrete sequesters approximately 110-160kg of carbon. An average sized house built using around 50 cubic metres of hempcrete for the walls would lock up 5.5 tonnes of carbon for the lifetime of the building. This is because the production and application of hempcrete is quite a low-tech process. The figure takes into account the production of the lime binder (which potentially could be replaced by a different consistency of hemp shiv), transport and the energy used during construction. In comparison, a standard new house of a similar size emits 48 tonnes of carbon into the atmosphere.[718] Hempcrete therefore saves 53.5 tonnes of carbon for every house built.

Presently, the construction industry is responsible for around 60% of the UK's total carbon emissions, both through energy used in the construction phase and by the occupants of the building. The government's claim that all new homes being built are carbon neutral – by upgrading fabric to a high standard of insulation – does not take into account the 'embodied carbon' in the materials used; ie, a measure of the total carbon emissions associated with a material, product or service, taking into account its extraction from raw materials, manufacturing process, transport, application, and the energy used in recycling or replacement of the material at end of life.[719]

Hempcrete walls have a much better thermal performance than conventional or lightweight insulation constructions, meaning that the energy used by the occupants of the building is dramatically reduced compared to conventional construction.

"Because they are 'vapour active', insulating materials such as hemp-lime, hemp fibre and wood fibre are capable of absorbing and releasing water vapour," according to Dr Mike Lawrence, director of the University of Bath.[720] "This is doubly effective, because not only can they act as a buffer to humidity (taking moisture out of the air), but they also stabilise a building's internal temperature much better through latent heat effects (energy consumed and released during evaporation and condensation within the pores of the material).... The hemp shiv traps air in the walls, providing a strong barrier to heat loss. The hemp itself is porous, meaning the walls are well insulated while the lime-based binder sticks together and protects the hemp, making the building material resistant to fire and decay."

Lawrence worked on a project for the Science Museum to reduce the high energy cost of archival storage, which requires large enclosures to be kept at a steady humidity and temperature to ensure that items do not deteriorate. Normally this uses energy-intensive air conditioning systems. "The three-storey archival store that the Science Museum built in 2012 using a hemp-lime envelope was so effective that they switched off all heating, cooling, and humidity control for over a year, maintaining steadier conditions than in their traditionally equipped stores, reducing emissions while saving a huge amount of energy." And because hempcrete is antibacterial and more absorbent than timber, it draws the moisture away from the wood, preserving the timber framing indefinitely. This is important for the conservation of old timber-framed buildings, which are already often renovated using hempcrete.

The post-occupancy survey of the hemp-based Cheshire Oaks Marks & Spencer store built in 2012 found that it was 42% more energy efficient, with 40% lower carbon emissions, per square foot than a benchmark M&S store, using 60% less heating fuel than predicted. Hempcrete is also an adequate sound insulator and there is a growing body of anecdotal evidence that it can absorb reasonable quantities of electromagnetic interference (EMI). Hemp plaster was used 1,500 years ago in structures that remain preserved.[721] The world can be remade from hemp.

Hemp is already making a comeback in all sorts of specialty paper and pulp products thanks to modern bio-refining techniques. The US Department of Agriculture estimates that one acre of hemp produces the same amount of paper as four acres of trees, and of a better, longer-lasting quality. Whereas trees are usually made up of only 30% of cellulose, its useable part – meaning a chemical process has to be employed to remove the other 70% – hemp can be made up of nearly 85% cellulose. The average North American goes through 50 pounds of toilet paper every year, roughly 100 rolls – so replacing traditional toilet paper with an equivalent made from hemp would hugely reduce deforestation.[722]

Perhaps most inspiringly and importantly, hemp's full potential is being explored in applications in high-technology (hi-tech). Hemp carbon is of a very high quality and holds the key to the next generation of computer chips and supercapacitors. In 2014 scientists in the US found that the bast from hemp, the fibrous covering of the shiv, can be transformed into high-performance energy storage devices. They said the material performed better than *graphene* – which is stronger than diamond, more conductive than copper and more flexible than rubber – by up to 200%. Partly because graphene is mined and imported from China and India, hemp-based supercapacitors can be produced for a thousandth of the price.[723] The scientists have experimented with all kinds of biowaste, from peat moss to eggs to banana peel. "You can do really interesting things with bio-waste. We've pretty much figured out the secret sauce of it," said Dr David Mitlin of Clarkson University, New York. "With banana peels, you can turn them into a dense block of carbon – we call it pseudo-graphite – and that's great for sodium-ion batteries. But if you look at hemp fibre its structure is the opposite – it makes sheets with high surface area, and that's very conducive to supercapacitors." In 2018, ReVolt Electric Motorbikes started using hemp supercapacitors.[724] Another study found that a hemp cell battery performs eight times better than lithium-ion[725] (the improvement of which, incidentally, is reaching its physicochemical limits).

Battery-powered motors actually predate the internal combustion engine and are smoother running and virtually maintenance-free. The first diesel engine was designed to run on biofuel. The profit motive obviously intervened on both counts. Much more research and development is needed, of course, but perhaps hemp technology could be used in combination with (and reduce the embodied carbon of) hydrogen fuel technology, for example, which combines compressed hydrogen from a tank with oxygen from the air to generate electricity on demand, a much faster process than charging batteries yet likewise generating no toxic emissions, only water vapour.

Scientists at MIT, meanwhile, have made solar panels from plants.[726] And mycelium, a type of fungus, can be coaxed, using temperature, CO_2, humidity and airflow, to rapidly build fibrous structures for things such as "packaging, clothing, food and construction – everything from leather to plant-based steak to scaffolding for growing organs"; all with minimal (mostly compostable) waste and energy consumption.[727] Technological progress can continue without the destructive extracting practices it currently relies on – we can literally grow all our technology, and better technology than we currently use. There is life in Moore's Law yet!

Resource depletion

Hemp and other fibrous plants solve the 'problem' of metals depletion, which is being accelerated by the demands of renewable tech. A 2014 report by Club of Rome noted that, "The production of many mineral commodities appears to be on the verge of decline... we may be going through a century-long cycle that will lead to the disappearance of mining as we know it." Production of copper is expected to peak by 2040 and coal by 2050. Although nickel has longer, it will be "increasingly difficult and expensive to invest in and exploit". In a decarbonising world, the strain on lithium, too, would accelerate rapidly.

In his 2019 lecture "How To Enjoy The End of The World", Sid Smith argues convincingly that doubling the size of the economy, as tends to happen every 20 years under capitalism, would permanently destabilise Earth's atmosphere – but also that the economy is now so large that the cost of doubling it, based on the expense of a diminishing energy return on investment (EROI) in extraction, makes that impossible. "The collapse has already begun," he says. The need to rebuild a decommodified, publicly owned energy and production infrastructure that includes moves towards the relative localisation and communisation of production and consumption is clear and urgent.

Bastani has other ideas: "While Earth likely has sufficient quantities of [lithium] for a complete transition away from fossil fuels, even if global demand doubled, that would still require continual stockpiles to be continually recycled. While plausible – although at present only 1% of batteries are processed in such a way – and no doubt an improvement, that is still a long way from post-scarcity and permanently cheaper energy."[728] The solution Bastani forsees, along with space capitalists, is asteroid mining. The iron content alone of a Near Earth Asteroid (NEA) such as 16 Psyche "could be worth $10,000 quadrillion".[729] That would be the absurd cost of production! World GDP in 2017 amounted to $120 trillion; total wealth to $280 trillion. But while he recognises that asteroid mining would see prices of Earth minerals collapse, Bastani believes it would still be necessary in a postcapitalist context. "The limits of Earth would confine postcapitalism to conditions of abiding scarcity. The realm of freedom would remain out of reach."[730] But at the present level of our productive abilities, asteroid mining is also untenable. The craft closest to being able to mine asteroids is SpaceX's Falcon Heavy, launched successfully in February 2018. It is capable of multiple launches and carries the equivalent of five double-decker buses in cargo. The fuel it uses has a carbon content of 34%. In the context of asteroid mining, this would mean the considerable polluting of Earth's atmosphere at its most vulnerable point, undermining the purpose of the endeavour.

While it is entirely possible that socialism *could* develop this practice to a sustainable degree, it is by no means certain, nor is it useful conjecture. We must reduce our reliance on mining, metals and fossil fuels to the bare minimum, even if they provided inexhaustible resources. As we have seen, *hemp and other fibrous plants provide the best and most eco-friendly way of storing and harnessing the limitless energy provided by the sun.* In casting his eyes to the stars, Bastani buries his head in the sand.

Nuclear power

Having said all that, there is still a large role for nuclear power to play. Nuclear power offers vastly higher energy-density than hemp or coal and must be re-embraced to provide the energy for the large-scale, centralised infrastructure that delivers cheap electricity for the masses. Before neoliberalism, France decarbonised 78% of its electricity in just 13 years by building 54 publicly-owned nuclear power plants. The abandonment of nuclear power has had nothing to do with safety concerns but rather its expensive upfront costs and, therefore, unprofitability. Nuclear is much safer than seems to be generally thought. As Leigh Phillips writes:

> "Exposure to cosmic rays while taking two transatlantic flights (0.16 millisieverts (mSv) of radiation) is roughly equivalent to the annual exposure of a UK nuclear power station worker (0.18 mSv), which is far less than the annual dose of the average US citizen from all sources (2.7 mSv), or exposure to radiation as a result of one CT chest scan (6.6 mSv) or the average annual dose from radon from the ground experienced by people who live in Cornwall (7.8 mSv). We also know that the new generation of dramatically safer reactors employing passive-safety systems *physically cannot* melt down, and that safe methods of waste disposal are proven. The amount of waste produced is also tiny compared to that of many other industrial processes, and far less hazardous. Radioactivity also decreases with time, but the danger presented by solar panel production, such as cadmium, mercury and lead pollutants, never goes away. Instead these pollutants bioaccumulate (there is ever greater concentration of the pollutant in an organism) and biomagnify (there is ever greater concentration of the polluting as you move up the food chain). Advanced nuclear power systems can completely recycle used nuclear fuel, actually producing a net positive balance of energy in this process. In a 2014 survey

of all energy sources exploring which delivered the least direct harm to biodiversity, nuclear was among the best options, due to its small land and mining footprint. Nuclear has by far the best safety record of any energy source, clocking in at 0.04 deaths per terawatt hour, compared to wind's 0.15 deaths, solar's 0.44 deaths, hydroelectric's 1.4 deaths, oil's 36 deaths and coal's 100 deaths."[731]

Furthermore, nuclear fusion, which is much less radioactive than nuclear fission, will be another option if its safety is proven. It apparently promises almost limitless energy, but has been too expensive for capital to develop.

There is also the prospect of space-based solar power (SBSP) and the associated development of long-range wireless power transmission. The available solar energy is ten times that accessed on Earth, without the intermittency of night time or winter.

These options may provide new ways of powering the internet (as well as the mining for metals that plants can't replace) which is unsustainable in its present energy- and water-intensive form, although basing it on local peer-to-peer connections could also reduce its dependence on massive server farms.

The prohibition of hemp

Why did monopoly capitalism prohibit industrial hemp in the first place? Clearly, it seriously undermined the fossil fuel, pharmaceutical, tobacco, paper, steel and concrete industries (to name a few). Andrew Mellon, President Herbert Hoover's Secretary of the Treasury, appointed his future nephew-in-law, Harry J Anslinger, to the head of the Federal Bureau of Narcotics and Dangerous Drugs, and together they plotted a campaign to demonise hemp by stealth. Because hemp was so popular, it took a strategy of racism, deception, mass media manipulation, scaremongering and near-dictatorial power to get it banned.[732]

Hemp is a variation of the *cannabis sativa* plant, the main difference being that it contains hardly any delta-9-tetrahydrocannabinold (THC), the psychoactive element that gets people high. The trumped up 'dangers' of "marihuana" – they used the Mexican word as part of a racist tactic and to conceal their true objective – served as a pretext for passing the Prohibitive Marihuana Tax Law in 1937, the culmination of efforts that had begun at least as early as 1912,[733] with the added bonus of criminalising immigrants, black and indigenous people in order to stir up racism and weaken working class unity. Most infamously, the 1936 film *Reefer Madness* depicted a man going crazy from smoking cannabis and then murdering his family with an axe.

The bill was brought to the House Ways and Means Committee, the only committee that could introduce a bill to the House floor without it being debated by other committees. Committee Chairman Robert Doughton had vested interests in Dupont, which had recently patented a wood pulp bleaching process and a process of turning fossil fuel distillates into plastics. He made sure the bill passed through Congress. At the 11th hour, Dr James Woodward testified against the bill on behalf of the American Medical Association (AMA), saying that the AMA had not opposed the Marihuana Tax Law sooner – the law effectively taxed the hemp industry out of business – because it had only just realised that marihuana was actually hemp.[734]

It is only now, as we have seen, that so many extractive and agricultural industries have become so capital-intensive, that the prohibition of hemp and cannabis is starting to end. Hemp farming was legalised in the US in 2018 and cannabis is fully legal in many states, while Canada and Uruguay have legalised cannabis both medically and recreationally.

Although hemp production requires minimal labour, because cultivation techniques in the US now lag historically, it is presently relatively labour-intensive. The processes involved with turning hemp into products are also relatively underdeveloped. This combined with the boom in use-values hemp can provide is breathing some life into the small farmer and the economy as a whole – for the time being, until the industry becomes increasingly mechanised and monopolised, with expanding production bound to bring prices down precipitously.[735] Prices in Oregon fell by 60% in 2018.

Cannabis is medicine
Cannabis is also finally being recognised as not only much safer than alcohol, heroin, crack cocaine, methamphetamine, cocaine, tobacco, caffeine and amphetamine,[736] but as possessing highly therapeutic and medicinal qualities. Some cannabis strains have even been found to shrink cancerous tumours.[737]

Because it is non-toxic, overdosing on cannabis is almost impossible[738] and, far from being a gateway drug – the majority of cannabis users do not go on to use any other illegal drug[739] – it has even proved to be an effective 'exit drug' for opioid addicts.[740]

Hemp itself produces cannabidiol (CBD) oil, which has anti-inflammatory and calming properties and also reduces nicotine cravings.[741] THC has been found to be more therapeutic than CBD,[742] but unlike CBD remains stigmatised – despite being almost the same compound (it is also psychoactive, but then so is chocolate) – at least where it is still illegal, by the falsehood that it causes psychosis, a smear that medicinal cannabis monopolies at best do nothing to challenge, despite the fact that their products contain (sometimes high levels of) THC, since the legalisation of recreational consumption would effectively end their monopoly, given that there is no real difference between recreational and medical cannabis. The chance of cannabis having even an associative link to psychosis is actually 20,000 to one.[743]

Where it has been legalised, cannabis use among adolescents has fallen,[744] although studies have shown no link between adolescent cannabis use and lasting structural impacts on the brain.[745] Nor has cannabis been proven to be addictive (it is a hallucinogen, not a stimulant or depressant).[746] Indeed, most people use drugs in search of relief from mental health concerns, including, of course, the stress of living under capitalism. Society looks at this relationship the wrong way round. Indeed, it is now thought that cannabis can treat schizophrenia without the side effects of pharmaceutical medications.[747]

Predictably, Big Pharma's monopolisation of 'cannabis-based' medicine has created artificial scarcity, with high, prohibitive prices for something that is cheap and easy to make. Production is even cheaper than it should be for Big Pharma because by treating cannabis as a standard monomolecular drug instead of a polymolecular plant and rationalising the production process, the highest quality is not obtained. And because exports generate more value, the product gets irradiated. In Britain, where cannabis remains scheduled as a 'dangerous' class B drug, the Home Office awarded a sole growing licence to British Sugar in partnership with GW Pharmaceuticals – the biggest exporter of 'cannabis-based' medicine in the world.[748] Yet only one of its products is available in Britain and at prohibitively high prices. Once again, Britain lags behind the rest of the world.

Pollution has recently been identified, incidentally, as a likely cause of psychosis in teenagers.[749] Not only did capitalism introduce an energy system that poisons body, brain and planet, it banned the thing that is best not only at treating but maintaining their health in the first place. We could have built a durable world of abundance without polluting the air, touching the climate or degrading the soil.

Communism is soviet power plus hemp
The international prohibition of hemp and cannabis – starting with the 1912 International Opium Convention, the 1925 Geneva Convention and the yet more stringent 1961 Single Convention on Narcotic Drugs[750] – has been a primary factor in the devastating and ongoing desertification of Africa. In Malawi, for example, where the vast majority of households do not have access to electricity, the need for fuel for domestic cooking has relied on wood

burning and, therefore, deforestation.[751] This whole time, hemp could have been grown for biofuel and briquettes.

Africa has 60% of the world's uncultivated arable land, most of it unfarmed. Under a different, better system, hemp could perhaps turn the vast continent into the next 'workshop of the world'.[752] This could be important from an anti-imperialist perspective. Any country seeking independence from imperialism could potentially significantly reduce their dependence on trade and lessen the impact of blockades and sanctions by developing hemp farming and hemp-based industry. Smaller countries with less available land mass would obviously need to import hemp from bigger countries. This could potentially make the most arable African countries increasingly important anti-imperialist allies. Certainly there is no solution to the environmental and climate crises without the liberation of the oppressed world: 16 of the world's 17 most diverse eco-systems are in Africa, Asia, Latin and Central America.

Back in the belly of the beast, Britain's climate is said to be perfect for growing hemp, but the British state pays farmers significant subsidies to leave land dormant. In 1984 it was estimated that about 6% (around 90 million acres) of contiguous US land area put into cultivation for biomass could supply all demands for oil and gas while maintaining a neutral carbon system. Although that figure is now out of date, the fact that so much energy is wasted means it may not be that much higher now. The US pays farmers not to grow on 6% of the farming land, while another 500 million acres of marginal farmland lies fallow.[753] A system capable of fighting climate change would immediately put this land to use to grow hemp.

Replacing the toxic fuels and chemicals we use so prevalently with hemp and other eco-friendly solutions would end acid rain and sulphur-based smog – and potentially reverse global warming. In his 1985 book *The Emperor Wears No Clothes*, long-time hemp activist Jack Herer offered $50,000 to anyone who could disprove his hypothesis that hemp is a silver bullet for the climate and environmental crises:

> "If all fossil fuels and their derivatives, as well as trees for paper and construction, were banned in order to save the planet, reverse the Greenhouse Effect and stop deforestation, then there is only one known annually renewable natural resource that is capable of providing the overall majority of the world's paper and textiles; meet all of the world's transportation, industrial and home energy needs, while simultaneously reducing pollution, rebuilding the soil and cleaning the atmosphere all at

the same time. That substance is the same one that has done it before. And that substance is cannabis hemp… marijuana!"[754]

Tragically, he has been ignored. What Herer never realised, however, is that achieving this vision requires socialism. By turning to a system of utility-production, we can use hemp, mycelium and other fibrous plants to rebuild our infrastructure, end poverty, reverse desertification and stabilise the climate. This reconstruction of society, which would raise living standards exponentially for everyone, *is not an ideal or a fantasy, but a necessity both historically and ecologically*. If Lenin once said that communism equals soviet power plus electrification, that slogan now needs updating.

The claim made by many environmentalists that neither capitalism nor socialism can solve the crisis because 'both rely on development' therefore stands discredited. Although we will have to ration things like fossil fuel during a transitional phase, socialism does not have to now become a kind of green-primitivism. From 'degrowth' to 'holism' and 'green populism', there are too many variations of this idea to detail, but suffice to say that they almost always consist of a nebulous fantasy 'third way' amounting to a form of social democracy (ie capitalism!); and a conservative emphasis on localism and small-scale production. This is no answer to climate change, given the need to build, for one thing, incredibly vast dikes on every continent.

We must admit that the regrettably mixed environmental records of the Soviet Union and China may have contributed to the prevalence of these attitudes, although it should be acknowledged that these countries had to operate within a world capitalist system. Under world socialism, as natural resources are nationalised and then internationalised, natural resources should be made the common patrimony of humanity, owned and controlled by an independent global trust that grants licences to planning agencies on strict conditions and also levies rents and surcharges (that go towards other public services, so as to prevent corruption).

But socialist countries in future must take full advantage of the hemp miracle, for *full automation is the key to abolishing exchange-value and hemp is the key to achieving full automation without turbocharging climate change*. The catastrophic prohibition of hemp encapsulates Marx's contention that capitalism alienates man and nature from one another – so it makes perfect sense that a key plank to socialism's reversal of this alienation should be to end prohibition.

A transition to communal ways of living (to be incentivised by tax breaks and rent reductions, as well by spacious and high-quality housing that embraces individuality and privacy) will also achieve massive efficiency gains regarding our use of fuel and other resources (cooking for 50 people is much more efficient than 50 people cooking their own meal, and so on).

And because world socialism will end the exploitation of labour, *the labour intensity of extraction will become obsolete. All labour (as opposed to just commodity production) will become productive – so the absolute need to plunder the environment to create exchange-value will end.*

Carbon capture

While it provides much hope to know that a solution like hemp exists, it would of course take time, even if the world became socialist tomorrow, to grow enough to build the new industries and infrastructure required to transform our world into one that is clean and sustainable. Stopgap solutions may be required alongside hemp farming not only to make production and consumption carbon neutral but negative – to drawdown more carbon than is emitted, because, worryingly, there is a 40-year time lag between emissions and the full impact they have on the climate.

One such solution is being touted by Carbon Engineering, based in Canada. The company has developed a way of recycling CO_2 out of the atmosphere so that it can be reused. Its pilot plant in Squamish, British Columbia works as a big cooling tower that captures CO_2 out of the atmosphere. A large fan draws down the CO_2 which is then captured in a chemical reaction with hydrogen and water. "It's uniformly distributed; we could put one of these plants in Beijing or the Sahara Desert, it would capture the same amount of atmospheric CO_2," according to CEO, Steve Oldham.[755]

While the process requires a lot of electricity, the pilot plant uses renewable hydro power. When the reusable fuel is burned, it emits the same amount of CO_2 that went into producing it, making it carbon neutral. The synthetic fuel is as clear as water, and delivers "higher performance" than conventional fuels, claims Oldham. Best of all, because it is chemically identical to petrol and jet fuel, it is compatible with any vehicle in the world – no modifications required, including performance cars and aeroplanes.

"This is significant because nobody's making electric tractors or electric planes," Oldham points out. "Transportation comprises about 20% of the world's CO_2 emissions. How are we going to decarbonise that? There's a billion cars in the world. If we all go electric, at say $50,000 for an electric car, that's $50 trillion. Then you've got to deliver energy and electricity to each car. It's a massive change. Alternatively, why don't we just change the fuel?"

The technology can take on the task of drawing down carbon and burying it indefinitely in underground chambers. Oldham claims that, "you need less of these [facilities] than there are power stations in the world today to net emissions out to zero – in the region of tens of thousands".[756] A full-scale plant would capture one million metric tonnes of CO_2 a year. In 2017, global emissions of CO_2 rose by 2% to a record 37 billion metric tonnes.[757]

So why isn't the world rushing to invest in and scale up this urgently-needed technology? The upfront costs of scaling up are obviously high. $30m of capital had to be raised to build one barn-sized plant. "We will need a trillion-dollar industry to [keep warming below 2°C]. That seems like a lot, but today's airline industry is larger," according to Klaus Lackner of the Center for Negative Carbon Emissions at Arizona State University, who pioneered the concept of direct air capture of CO_2 in the 1990s.[758]

So far only $68m has been stumped up from external private sources – by oil and coal companies.[759] Chevron, Occidental and BHP finalised the investment in April 2019, but for all the wrong reasons. They can use the CO_2 fuel to flush out the last remaining deposits of oil in wells that are past their prime. It is estimated that using CO_2 to do this can deliver an extra 30% of crude from oil fields. The companies hope that the added bonus of sequestration can placate opposition to the fossil fuel industry. But as Tzeporah Berman of Stand dot earth said: "These technologies provide a false hope that we can continue to depend on fossil fuels and produce and burn them, and technology will fix it – we are way past that point."

Glen Peters of Norway's Centre for International Climate Research says that the drawdown and sequestering industry needs to become at least "three to four times the size of the current oil-and-gas industry just to clean up our waste".[760] This conservative estimate would obviously have to increase the more the fossil fuel industry expands production.

Scaling up Carbon Engineering's technology – and making sure it is used the right way – is going to need states to step in. This is at least becoming more possible because the cost per tonne of CO_2 removed from the atmosphere has been brought down from $600 to less than $100.

Carbon Engineering's next plant, set to be ready in 2020, will produce 200 barrels of synthetic fuel a day, bringing down the price again. Considering it has just been invented, the fuel is cheap. The only feedstock, the only thing the production of the fuel consumes, is renewable electricity. The fuel presently costs more than a barrel of oil, but in places with a tax on carbon of $20, it is already competitive. But under capitalism the technology is going to be used for the wrong reasons and could potentially make things worse.

There is a real problem with storing carbon underground as well – it is only ever an earthquake away from leaking back into the atmosphere. A better solution seems to be the process of 'CarbFixing' developed in Iceland, whereby CO_2 is dissolved in water before being injected into the island's mineral-rich, basaltic rocks – one of the most common rock types on Earth – where it settles and turns into solid white calcite crystals.[761] This is a long-lasting solution, although its water-intensity means it is not a silver bullet.

The same old problem is standing in the way, of course: there's no commodity on sale, so it's unproductive. Juerg Matter, associate professor in Geoengineering at the University of Southampton, part of the original research group which developed the CarbFix model, says the dominance of mainstream carbon storage in underground reservoirs is down to the fact that "the oil and gas industry is dominating the field". Again, something like this going to need massive state investment.

Similarly, carbon-negative 'sky diamonds' that are physically and chemically identical to those mined from the earth can be made by drawing down carbon from the atmosphere, but is presently only being done on a very small scale.[762] Nevertheless, this again shows that Marxists need not abandon the communist promise of a world of plenty.

Value theory and extraction
By now it should be clear that capitalism has been unable to wean itself off of fossil fuel not simply because of vested interests. As we have seen, automation, renewable energy and hemp all have something very particular in common: after the initial process of building them up as industries, they are not labour-intensive to reproduce – they are renewable or regenerative. They do not provide the constant source of surplus value that capitalism has had from fossil fuels.

As industrialisation advances, capitalist countries become increasingly dependent on raw material imports. The monopolisation of raw materials also "shifts the economic balance in favour of heavy industry".[763] Marx pointed out that the importance of raw materials to the level of profitability is constantly growing with the development of capitalist industry:

"The quantity and value of the employed machinery grows with the development of labour productivity but not in the same proportion as productivity itself, ie, not in the proportion in which this machinery increases its output. In those branches of industry, therefore, which do consume raw materials... the growing productivity of labour is expressed precisely in the proportion in which a larger quantity of raw material absorbs a definite quantity of labour, hence in the increasing amount of raw material converted in, say, one hour into products... The value of raw material, therefore, forms an ever-growing component of the value of the commodity product."[764]

A solar panel or a wind turbine may be profitable to make when the materials used are extracted from the ground by labour; but once it has been made and installed, they only have to be switched on and maintained. Nuclear fuel cannot be handled by humans. Hemp grows quickly and self-seeds. Carbon Engineering's fuel requires next to no feedstock – it renews itself out of thin air. Coal and petroleum, on the other hand, having taken millions of years to form, disappear into the air; they have to be replaced, dug up from the ground by exploitable labour.

While the price of petroleum and coal tend to fall due to the expansion of its production, that its production tends to expand tends to compensate for the falling price. We may have become conscious of the plastic problem, but that has not stopped the planned 40% rise in petroleum-based plastic production in the next decade.[765]

While much has been made of the fall of coal's proportion in the overall energy mix, coal production itself has grown by 80% since the year 2000,[766] reflecting what anthropologist Jason Hickel has written, that the size of the global economy more or less doubles every 20 years. "That's double the cars, double the fishing, double the mining, double the McFlurries and double the iPads. And then double them again over the next 20 years from their already doubled state."[767] Capitalism can only continue to accelerate the climate crisis, since it is always reproducing and expanding itself from a higher base and on the basis of extraction.

If renewable energy had been anywhere near as profitable as fossil fuels then investors would have made the switch on a far greater scale, for they are motivated not by some misplaced nostalgia for coal and oil but by making returns on their investments. If renewable energy becomes more profitable, they will make the switch.

But renewable energy is capital-intensive from the get go; the upfront costs are high and risky, placing the onus for its development on the state. The most decayed imperialist countries are cutting costs in order to make more surplus value available for the valorisation of existing capital. In 2010, the British government, for example, slashed £85m from the budget of the Department of Energy and Climate Change. Even the urgent need to respond to climate change cannot overcome the source of Britain's slowness to innovate. When Britain's overall investment of £12.6bn in 2009-10 in green technology represented under 1% of its GDP, the Public Interest Research Centre pointed out that this was "half of what South Korea spends on green technology annually; and less than the UK spends on furniture".[768]

It is only now – at least four decades since global warming became a concern – that rapidly falling costs of wind, solar and lithium are creating the possibilities to transition from fossil fuel. But these too rely on plundering the environment at ever-faster rates and through fuel-intensive production.

Capitalism's degradation of the planet will go on as long as its counter-tendencies continue to operate. While its need to continually speed up the circulation of capital spurs technological innovations which make its operations more fuel efficient, there is a conflicting tendency: because transport workers (of commodities) produce surplus value, there is pressure in the opposite direction to expand the amount of transportation. Journeys may be made quicker and more efficiently but more of them are always being made. Capital has no incentive for commodities to be consumed where they are produced, something that would bring down emissions considerably. While innovations have doubled the efficiency of commercial aircraft since the 1960s, for example, air freight travel rose by 71% between 2001 and 2012.[769] (The carbon footprint of air freight is about 100 times as impactful as ocean freight because of the effect of releasing emissions high into the atmosphere.[770] Every round-trip flight from New York to London costs the Arctic three more square metres of ice.)[771] With factory-based manufacturing returning to domestic markets because of automation and 3-D printing, capital's need to extract fossil fuel and metals and transport them around the world only increases; yet for the same reason, demand may collapse just in time.

One further point: environmental lobbies desperately trying to get governments to listen often point out that failing to mitigate climate change will devastate the economy. According to the Tyndall Center for Climate Change Research, the US is facing climate and air pollution costs reaching at least $360bn annually.[772] When looked at from this long-term perspective, it has been claimed that a 'green' industrial revolution that decarbonised global production by 2030 would actually save $26 trillion.[773]

But, as we have seen, valorisation necessitates short-termism and capital destruction is required in order to surmount imperfect valorisation. This is not to claim that destruction is entirely good for the economy – extinction, the destruction of 100% of wealth, would end capitalism, after all. Damages would reach an estimated $551 trillion at 3.7°C,[774] almost twice the total wealth existing today, which by then would account for an estimated 23% of global GDP. For a while at least, the destruction caused by climate change has the potential to offset the breakdown tendency. It probably already has done.

Once again, we can see that understanding the world's problems depends on understanding the labour theory of value. Here we must clarify that nature is not a second source of exchange-value. It is the source of use-values, of course, but its importance to exchange-value derives from the labour-intensity required to extract and turn nature into commodities. If the process of turning nature into commodities were done solely through fully automated machines, no exchange-value would be produced.

China and state planning

While US and British companies have fallen behind on renewable energy and clean tech, China has rapidly become the global leader – thanks to state planning. Its 12th five-year plan in 2011 marked the first time the country formally incorporated mitigating climate change into its core economic strategy.[775] $1.5 trillion, 5% of GDP, was committed to energy-saving and 'environmentally-friendly' technologies, biotechnology, new generation ITs, advanced manufacturing, new materials, alternative fuels and EVs.[776] The plan adopted a 'circular' approach to economic development that placed sustainability first, a directive which defines pollution and waste control as forms of competitive advantage. It also aimed to reduce China's energy intensity (units of energy per unit of GDP). By 2015 this had fallen by 18.2%, exceeding the goal of 16%.[777]

China's investment in renewable energy (excluding large hydro projects) rose by 30% in 2017. The total amount was more than three times that of the US, whose investment in the sector dropped by 6% on 2016 to $40bn.[778]

In 2010, the China Development Bank committed to invest $47bn in 15 solar PV manufacturers, an investment which has led to plunging prices in solar – by 80% between 2008 and 2013 – and arguably put many competitors in Europe and the US out of business.[779] China supplies two-thirds of the world's solar panels and more than 2.5 million people work in the solar power sector alone in China, compared with 260,000 in the US.[780]

Facing a backlash from European and US tariffs – several years before the Trump administration – China revised its domestic solar power development goal to 20 gigawatts (GWs) by 2015, raising it from the existing three GWs and putting it on course to develop as much solar energy in three years as Germany had in 10.[781] Feed-in tariffs fixed the price of wind and energy on more favourable terms, while other incentives for Chinese developers ensured the recovery of costs within seven years.[782] China has only continued to revise its targets upwards.

China was a relative latecomer to wind power technology, but overtook the US as the world's largest market in 2010. The partially state-owned Goldwind, founded in 1998, benefitted from aggressive domestic content rules, so that all wind turbines sold in China have to be made from local content, shutting the door to foreign investment. Wind power developers received 25-year fixed price contracts. Wind projects have had access to low-cost financing and after 2005 China began to publicly fund R&D projects with grants and favourable loan terms. China's aim to produce 1,000 GWs of wind power by 2050 would approximately equal the entire electric capacity of the US or European electric grids today.[783]

Since 2015, China has also become the world leader in the production of EV sales thanks to a mix of state subsidies and restrictions placed on producers of petrol and diesel vehicles. It leads again on experimental innovation. Lakes have been turned into 'floating' solar farms. While the initial costs involved are high, the cooling effect from the lakes increases efficiency in the long run. In Shaanxi, northern China, the world's tallest 'anti smog tower', a 100-metre high air-purifier has been installed, reducing pollution levels by 15%.

China is notorious for its pollution and is the highest carbon emitter – it is, after all, the world's industrial epicentre and has its largest population. Coal still accounts for 60% of China's energy consumption. Because of its industrial might, the country's energy intensity remains much higher than the global average, especially compared to Europe's services-based economy. China's high economic growth also means emissions continue to rise significantly in absolute terms.

The country's recent shift compared to the rest of the world has nevertheless been rapid. In 2016, 26% of the country's total electricity production came from renewables, compared to a world average of 12%.[784] Beijing has been shutting some coal mines or turning them into solar plants, and set out plans in 2017 to cut roughly 1.3 million jobs from the coal industry. That is being more than offset by the creation of 10 million jobs in renewable energy, which already boasts 3.5 million.

We do not point out China's success in this area to laud it, but merely to emphasise and demonstrate the point that the state is much more dynamic than the private sector. Although we are not taking a definitive position on whether China is capitalist or socialist, it might be said that China is presently more Keynesian than neoliberal. Indeed, it is the falling prices brought about by China's state investment in the past decade or so that has largely enabled zero-emissions energy sources to overtake fossil fuels as Britain's largest electricity source. As discussed, however, it is a major problem that solar, wind and battery power are being built out of materials mined from the earth. This suggests that, whether it is socialist or not – or whether it is 'building socialism' via a 'capitalist road' – China's economy remains highly dependent on the law of value. It has been strange to see many communists denounce Bastani's model in *Fully Automated Luxury Communism* at the same time as defending China for essentially taking the same approach.

All this is especially frustrating given that China is also the global leader in hemp production, responsible for almost half the world's supply, worth an estimated $1.1bn in 2017 and an expected $1.5bn in 2020. Between 2007 and 2017 its hemp exports grew from 3,140kg to 469,404kg. The number of new specially developed high-CBD cultivars in China is also on the rise thanks to the country's Yunnan Academy of Agricultural Sciences.

With China positioning itself to be the global leader in microchips and semiconductors, its head start in the hemp industry – which is rapidly expanding in terms of the state's investment in R&D – means it is well placed to lead the next technological revolution. If China's economy were not so dependent on the law of value it could have done this some time ago, but the next round of devaluation may make the cheapness of hemp the key for China in its efforts to outcompete the US and Europe.

Socialist automation and renewable energy
Renewable energy is essentially a form of automation, which makes automation a necessary part of solving the climate crisis. But since automation and science cannot reach their full potential under capitalism, socialism is urgently necessary if Earth is to stand any chance of remaining habitable. In his book, Volkov wrote:

> "The opinion of sociologists and economists varies as to the main trends of scientific and technological progress, and their relative importance and role. Some lay emphasis on automation, others on atomic energy or conquest of outer space, and still others on the development of production mainly along chemical lines.
>
> "But automation is not just one of these trends. It is a historically conditioned *form of industrial development* in a new historical stage of technical development, and is an element of all modern scientific and technological progress, and all its trends. The development of production

along chemical, biological, or 'cosmic' lines (ie, the application for industrial purposes of space, and, in terms of the future, also the organisation of production in outer space), and the use of the new powerful sources of energy – all this is tied up with automation and is inconceivable without it."[785]

This is because a new form of energy

"will not yield a substantial increase in the productivity of social labour unless the necessary technical conditions are provided for obtaining and using it, including automation as an indispensable factor. It is not until these conditions are available that the new source of energy will accelerate technological progress and act as a pusher of further changes in the 'man-technology' system."[786]

Marx could see that the mechanical treatment of materials would give way to chemical methods. But before they could be applied in industry, they had to be given the corresponding technological form in terms of mechanisation or automation. Unlike mechanical methods of treating matter,

"chemical reactions do not require the use of implements exerting a direct influence on the object of labour. The chemical properties themselves play the role of such 'implements'. Nor is there any need for the power required in mechanical methods for driving the tools. Once the substances have been brought into contact, the reaction generally proceeds *automatically*.... In addition, whereas mechanical treatment is the result of a series of discrete, disjointed, singular movements, chemical treatment is continuous by nature, since chemical reactions go on without interruption.

"Automatic processes and continuity are the indispensable features typical of automation. Hence, chemical methods of treatment correspond to the *very essence of automation* (which cannot be said about mechanical and certain physical methods). Furthermore, chemical methods cannot dispense with automation, inasmuch as many chemical processes are harmful to health, and also because their control requires absolute precision, which only cybernetical devices can ensure.

"Close alliance between chemistry and automation will lead to the creation of new synthetic materials with miraculous properties, and this will revolutionise automation itself. Bulky automatic lines consisting of mechanical units with their complex and noisy systems of transmission and transportation will give way to compact, noiseless, elegant and dependable plastic installations."[787]

Imagine, then, a lightweight Single Automated System built out of plant-based plastic and graphene. What's more – and this was something, Volkov points out, that sci-fi novelists and other bourgeois prophets failed to anticipate – because

"light, space and greenery are absolutely redundant for cybernetical installations… it seems more likely that automatic production of material wealth will be transferred underground, for man will thus avoid polluting the atmosphere and encumbering our planet, while enjoying to his heart's content the vegetation and sunshine on its surface".[788]

The accelerated development of automation under socialism will shrink the mass of land dedicated to industry to the minimum, creating more space above ground for reforestation, rewilding, hemp farming, countryside, public parks, and so on. In this way, *whereas automation intensifies the alienation between man and nature under capitalism, it reunites them under communism.*

Cuba's eco-socialism

Thanks to chemistry, the limited range of natural materials no longer holds back innovation. Neither does it make the development of the productive forces of society wholly dependent on raw materials. Chemistry synthesises materials possessing the required properties, treating the whole of a substance, simplifying and cheapening considerably the entire technological process. Volkov predicted that "the intensive use of chemistry in agriculture will transform farming into a scientific method of controlling the biological cycles".[789] Many of the products we use today are now moving from chemical factories to biological fermenters. The intensive use of chemical pesticides has had seriously adverse effects on the soil, since they have been petroleum-based. But chemicals are not inherently bad. Plants, of course, are made up of and produce chemicals, such as phosphorus.

Since the fall of the Soviet Union, its largest trading partner, Cuba has been forced to abandon chemical pesticides. In 2006, the socialist island nation was recognised by the World Wide Fund for Nature's *Living Planet Report* as the only nation in the world to have achieved sustainable development. Cuba, despite the decades-long US economic blockade that has denied it something like $1 trillion, has become a world leader in biotechnology. As *FRFI* reports:

"State-run biotechnology and agricultural institutions develop organic methods like crop-rotating, the use of biofertiliser, such as compost, and the use of vermicomposting (worm farms) to replace chemical fertilisers, and replacing synthetic pesticides with unique biopesticides and the specialised use of pests to combat crop-attacking pests. They develop permaculture methods [including rewilding], interplanting complementary crops, making it easier to avoid pests and maintain soil fertility. They have developed pasture techniques to increase milk productivity and help recycle nutrients. These specialists work closely with the farmers, learning from each other and overcoming the artificial gap between manual and mental labour. Cuban agronomists have taught agroecological farming methods to farmers in Haiti and across Central and South America. By 2003, the Agriculture Ministry had reduced diesel fuel use by 50%, and chemical fertiliser and synthetic pesticide use by over 90% from 1989."[790]

This also means that, whereas bee populations – vital to the pollination we all depend on – are drastically declining around the world as part of the sixth mass extinction,[791] Cuba is a "bee paradise", with the added bonus that organic honey is one of its main exports.[792] Starker evidence of why humanity must choose between socialism and extinction there surely could not be.[793]

Cuba has demonstrated that, through socialism, countries oppressed and exploited by imperialism and colonialism can recover. Between 1900 and 1959, as a semi-colony of the US, Cuba's forest and plant cover was decimated from 52% to 14%. A reforestation programme began soon after the revolution. The programme was renewed in 1998 and at the end of 2015 forest and plant cover had risen back up to 30.6%, a figure recognised by the UN as the most advanced in Latin America and the Caribbean.

Cuba's pioneering urban organic farming, *organoponicos*, has been described by *The Architectural Review* as "an exemplary precedent that could be applied worldwide".[794] In Havana alone, 35,000 hectares of land are used for urban farming. By 2003, Havana produced 90% of the fresh produce within the city, reducing emissions from food transit significantly.

Because of fuel shortages caused by the US blockade, 2006 was nominated the year of energy, when Fidel Castro explained that, "We are not waiting for fuel to fall from the sky, because we have discovered, fortunately, something much more important: energy conservation, which is like finding a great oil deposit." *FRFI* reported:

"Efficiency in electricity generation was made by installing hundreds of small distributed generators, which are more efficient than large power stations and cause smaller transmission losses. 40% of Cuba's electricity now comes from these generators, causing less disruption from mechanical breakdowns and natural disasters. Electricity is also generated from natural gas produced as a by-product of Cuba's off-shore oil industry, with the aim of producing 20% of the country's electricity this way. In 2004 and 2005 there were over 400 days of large-scale blackouts greater than 100 megawatts that lasted over an hour; in 2006 there were three days and in 2007 none. Within two years of the Energy Revolution, the country consumed 34% less kerosene, 37% less liquefied petroleum gas and saved 872,000 tonnes of oil in energy saving measures.

"As part of the Energy Revolution, thousands of social workers, most of them teenagers, visited every household in Cuba, distributing ten million energy saving light bulbs to a population of 11 million people, discussing energy conservation and noting which electrical appliances were in use. All incandescent light bulbs were replaced within six months. Over six million rice cookers and pressure cookers replaced kerosene and gas cookers. Energy efficient appliances were sold at low prices with long-term payment facilities. This included two million refrigerators, one million fans, 182,000 air conditioners and 260,000 water pumps. To encourage efficient use, the electricity subsidy was reduced for high use. In 2007-8 average per capita consumption was less than a tenth of US usage."[795]

Such a wonderful campaign is unthinkable in an imperialist country! That the under-resourced tiny island of Cuba has achieved all this, isolated not only by the US blockade but a whole capitalist world to which it has to make concessions for the sake of trade – it too is therefore severely impacted by the global crisis of capitalism – speaks volumes for the superiority of socialism.

Biotechnology
One of the projects championed by Castro was a biotechnology mission, beginning a year after the revolution. In 1960, Castro declared that "the future of our homeland must be that of men of science". At his insistence, Cuba established a National Centre for Scientific Research (CNIC), the Centre for Molecular Immunology (CIM), the Finlay Institute and the Centre for Genetic Engineering and Biotechnology (CIGB).

Volkov wrote that,

"it is only logical to expect that the next foreseeable leap in technology will be tied up with the use of production of the biological properties of living matter with a view to achieving an even more radical transformation of nature.... Biochemical and bionic technology will enable us to transform living nature, plants and animals, direct the activity of living matter and make use of its marvellous properties for the good of mankind. Bionic technology will take the form of artificial sense, of organs of thought and psychology, which will reinforce and improve the functioning of the natural sense organs."[796]

Rather than being a force alienated from humans, technology would thereby, under communism, become a *"humanised force"* designed to satisfy man's needs and assist him in his various activities, including those of his body.[797] Bionic machines would "assume entirely unexpected forms" and at the time of writing, "already, devices are being worked out in which a living body is fitted into a technical system". The reflexes of a living body are much more efficient than "the present-day electronic control devices modelled on them".

"It is therefore expedient and theoretically possible to use the nervous system of, say, a rabbit, dog or other animal in such a way as to make the biological currents controlling the heart also control a technical unit.... The organism's biological currents can be used as control signals for transmitting information and supplying electricity to instruments."[798]

But 50 years later, these possibilities have not really materialised beyond the expensive labs of mega-corporations and military facilities. Despite massive progress within those confines, robots are still more cumbersome than an athletic human, although the gap is increasingly narrow. The most advanced (and expensive) bionic leg has only recently been able to reproduce the manoeuvrability of a human leg. Again, because of the huge costs involved and other problems inherent to capitalism, progress has been slowed down. The technical use of biological energy, a totally clean form of energy production, has not been realised on a level that can be generalised and diffused. Volkov said that biological methods of acting on nature

"correspond to the principles of automation even closer than chemical methods, inasmuch as a biological cell, and doubly so a living body, is the most efficient automatic (self-controlled) system there is.

"It is precisely this unity of the principles of control which makes possible an astonishing symbiosis of technical and biological elements. This same unity enables us to 'humanise' technology, ie to set up technical systems best adapted and adjusted to the possibilities of the human body. Such technical systems will permit us to amplify many times over the activity of the human senses and brain. The man-technology system will thus assume a new, efficient form in which technology will really play the role of a set of *artificial organs of social man.*"[799]

The clean, renewable and hyper-efficient technologies of the future – which, in becoming available to all of humanity, will save humanity – will have to be fully realised under socialism and communism.

Cellular agriculture

The full potential of cellular agriculture will also have to be realised under socialism. Lab-grown food means we will be able to pre-empt failing crops amid rising demand. Meat, fish, cheese, milk, wine and vegan foods are already being developed in this way. Solar Foods, for example, a Helsinki-based company, has developed protein-heavy powders that can be turned into fibres resembling meat and bread, made from electricity, water and air in a process similar to brewing beer. Living microbes are put in liquid and fed carbon dioxide and hydrogen bubbles released from water through the application of electricity. The microbes create protein, which is then dried to make the powder. Cellular agriculture in the long run will end the destructive impact intensive farming techniques have on the soil and water supply; disincentivise (over)fishing; and end much of the transit involved with food exports, again undermining capital given that value creation depends so much on the exploitation of transport workers.[800] Added bonuses include returning to small-scale animal farming, which is good for the soil; ending the suffering of captive, drugged-up animals reared and slaughtered for human consumption; and potentially eliminating the addictive processed sugar and salt that have been hardwired into the human diet to maximise profit (the cause of obesity) along with potentially harmful artificial preservatives.

Some synthetic meats, which can be harvested in nine to 21 days, are already coming to market. With plummeting prices – the first synthetic burger cost $325,000 in 2013 but can now be made for $12 – it won't be long before some synthetic meats are competitive with farmed meat. The near-complete collapse of the livestock industry is expected by 2035.[801] With AI and automation continuing to enhance production methods, the prospect of prices falling to zero, this time for food, are again in sight.

Instead of waiting a couple of decades for prices to fall sufficiently for the kind of mass production that makes intensive farming obsolete, the state should step in now and ramp up development and mass production – the energy savings alone would make a massive impact in the fight against climate change. (Farmers would not lose work – socialism will increase the number of farmers – as sustainable forms of farming will grow.) One quarter of the world's carbon footprint is due to food production. Three-quarters of the world's calories originate from 12 plant and five animal species and livestock farming contributes 14% of all emissions, more than cars. 69% of the world's freshwater withdrawals are committed to agriculture, mostly in meat production. 1-4% of a person's water footprint is in the home; 25% is through meat consumption. It takes over 15,000 litres of water to make 1kg of beef, mostly to irrigate the crops fed to cattle. This in a world where 3.4 million people die every year from water related diseases.

Agriculture accounts for about 37.5% of the world's land area. A 2011 report conducted by the universities of Amsterdam and Oxford concluded that cellular meat could potentially require 45% less energy, 99% less land and 96% less water compared to conventional meat, leading to a 96% reduction in GHG emissions. If the US switched to synthetic beef, the likely reduction in emissions would equate to taking 23 million cars off the country's roads, with the substitution of a single synthetic meat burger for the 'real thing' saving the equivalent of over 50 showers.[802]

Marx and the Soviet Union

Marx wrote in the third volume of *Capital* that,

> "From the standpoint of a higher socioeconomic formation, the private property of particular individuals in the earth will appear just as absurd as the private property of one man in other men. Even an entire society, a nation, or all simultaneously existing societies taken together, are not the owners of the earth. They are simply its possessors, its beneficiaries, and have to bequeath it in an improved state to succeeding generations, as *boni patres familias* [good heads of the household]."[803]

Bourgeois revisionists ignore both the ecological thinking of Marx and Engels and the Soviet Union's remarkable contribution to ecological science, magnifying only the worst aspects of the latter's mixed environmental record, parts of which were undeniably terrible. Symbolised by the Chernobyl nuclear disaster and the drying up of the Aral Sea (due to cotton production) as well as high levels of air and water pollution as a result of rapid industrialisation, the hegemonic view has it that the Soviet Union's record was entirely ecocidal. This portrayal is far from the whole story. As John Bellamy Foster has written in *Monthly Review*, it was Soviet climatologists who "discovered and alerted the world to the acceleration of global climate change".[804] It was they who

> "developed the major early climate change models; demonstrated the extent to which the melting of polar ice could create a positive feedback, speeding up global warming; pioneered paleoclimatic analysis; constructed a new approach to global ecology as a distinct field based on the analysis of the biosphere; originated the nuclear winter theory; and probably did the most early on in exploring the natural-social dialectic underlying changes in the Earth system."

The Great Stalin Plan for the Transformation of Nature in 1948 was the most ambitious plan of afforestation in history at the time, aiming to grow six million hectares (15 million acres) of entirely new forest in the forest-steppe and steppe regions. This was "the world's first explicit attempt to reverse human-induced climate change" according to environmental historian Stephen Brain. Although the plan remained incomplete at the time of Stalin's death, when it was discontinued, it achieved a total "forest preserve the size of France, which grew over time to an area the size of Mexico" – roughly two-thirds of the contiguous United States.[805] Brain says the Soviet Union established "levels of [forest] protection unparalleled anywhere in the world".[806] Despite WWII, rapid industrialisation and counter-productive purging of leading ecological thinkers during the Stalin era, it was the 10 years after his death in which the most serious environmental degradation took place. From the 1960s on, though, says Foster, "Soviet ecological thought grew rapidly together with the environmental movement, which was led primarily by scientists". In the 1970s and 1980s this evolved into a mass movement which saw the membership of the All-Russian Conservation Society (VOOP), which had been established in 1924, rise to 32 million by 1981 and 37 million in 1987, constituting the largest nature protection organisation in the world. "These developments resulted in substantial changes in the society. For example, between 1980 and 1990 air pollutants from stationary sources fell by over 23%."

Following Chernobyl in 1986, the Soviet environmental movement became more powerful, with another 300 major organisations in addition to VOOP. According to Joan DeBardeleben: "From 1987 to 1990, all across the USSR, plants were closed, planned projects were re-sited or re-tooled for a less polluting type of production, or projects were cancelled altogether. The most prominent examples included the cessation of work on the planned river diversion projects, cancellation of the Volga-Chograi canal, closing of biochemical plants, and plans to convert the Baikalsk Pulp and Paper Plant to furniture production."[807] Laurent Coumel and Marc Elie in *The Soviet and Post-Soviet Review* described this as a "tragic ecological revolution", given that the demise of the Soviet Union in 1991 cut it short.[808]

Lenin had been greatly concerned with conservation. He agreed that protecting nature had "urgent value" and in 1921 he signed legislation ordering that "significant areas of nature" across the continent be protected.[809] The People's Commissariat of Education had responsibility for conservation and with Lenin's backing set up the pristine ecological reserves known as zapovedniks, which were set apart for scientific research. By 1933 there were 33 zapovedniks encompassing 2.7 million hectares.

Despite significant setbacks, Soviet ecology continued to develop in the two major areas of forestry and climatology. One of the key intellectual achievements was Vladimir Nikolaevich Sukachev's concept of biogeocoenosis, an analysis of the general unity of living things and inert elements of Earth's surface, of how organisms actively changed their environments. "The idea of the interaction of all natural phenomena... is one of the basic premises of materialistic dialectics, well proved by the founders of the latter, Marx and Engels," he wrote, citing their influence on his work.[810]

Soviet geophysicist Yevgeny Konstantinovich Fyodorov wrote that bourgeois societies had failed to understand climate change because they ignored Marx's theory of socio-ecological metabolism: "The authors of the materialist theory of social development," he wrote, "regarded interaction (metabolism) between people and nature as a vital element in human life and activity and showed that the socialist organisation of society would have every possibility to ensure optimal forms of such interaction."[811]

He also pointed to discussions in letters between Marx and Engels in relation to the writings of German agriculturist Karl Fraas about regional climate change and desertification. Fyodorov represented the USSR at the first World Conference on Climate in Geneva in 1979, where he warned of "irreversible" climate change in the coming decades if an international plan were not implemented to prevent it.

Foster says that "perhaps the most astonishing product" of a revival in critical Soviet ecological thinking came with the 1983 collection *Philosophy and the Ecological Problems of Civilisation*. In it, geographer Innokenti Gerasimov wrote that "Marx characterised labour as a process in which man 'starts, regulates, and controls the material re-actions [metabolism] between himself and nature'…. Man's interaction with nature needs to be subordinated to the general principles of metabolic processes."[812] In the same collection, environmental philosopher Ivan Frolov criticised the specific ecological depredations of capitalist society, writing: "The danger of an ecological crisis has become real not because the use of technical mechanisms and devices in the 'metabolism' of man and nature in itself… but primarily because this industrial development is realised on the basis of the socio-economic, spiritual, and practical set-ups of the capitalist mode of production." It was essential, he argued, for society to focus on "ecodevelopment" or "ecologically justified development", taking into account "the objective dialectic and inner contradictoriness of the interaction of society and nature".[813]

In 1961 Fyodorov and Mikhail Ivanovich Budyko – the Soviet climatologist acknowledged as the world leader in the study of the heat balance of the earth – called the All-Union Conference on the Problem of Climate Modification by Man in Leningrad, the first such conference in the world. That same year Budyko presented his paper "The Heat and Water Balance Theory of the Earth's Surface" to the Third Congress of the Geographical Society of the USSR, in which he concluded that climate change was now inevitable and that urgent changes had to be made with regards to energy consumption. In 1962, he published his landmark article "Climate Change and the Means of Its Transformation" in which he first observed that the destruction of ice cover could generate "a significant change in the regime of atmospheric circulation".

By 1963 Budyko had compiled an atlas of the world's heat balance system. Although a model of anthropogenic global warming had first been described by Guy Callendar as early as 1938, it was Budyko who discovered significant feedback effects and the growing likelihood of a runaway global ecological crisis. His work on "global ecology" as a distinct field was based on the dialectical interaction between organisms and the environment, and he was hugely influenced by Engels' unfinished essay "The Part Played by Labour in the Transformation from Ape to Man".

As Foster says, the Soviet Union left a legacy of ecological science, including an emergent ecological planning towards the end that represented "a massive human achievement from which we need to learn today if we are to find a way to regulate the human metabolism with nature and to surmount the present global ecological crisis. It began a process of ecological transition that, if carried out fully, could have had immeasurable positive effects."

Facing reality

Whether the vision outlined above can be achieved in time to prevent total calamity is a question that cannot be answered – we have to try, and there is definitely more than a chance. Realistically, the time it is going to take to end capitalism and make the necessary transitions means that avoiding a 1.5°C rise looks like a pipe dream. If capitalism is able to expand for another decade, production will increase by roughly another 50%. The subsequent emissions, on top of the feedback effects, will take us that much closer to the collapse of the ice sheets. Emissions from production have grown by between four billion and seven billion tonnes per decade in the post-war era. Avoiding 2°C will be very challenging even if capitalism ends soon. Extremely careful planning is required. Whatever happens in the long run, though, there is time to build a society with the capacity to cope reasonably well with heightened extreme weather conditions in the medium-term. But we need socialism.

As proven by Cuba, socialist states, because they are built on institutions of mass democratic participation and, therefore, mobilisation, are far better at preparing for and dealing with extreme weather. "Cuba manages hurricanes well," Russell Honoré, a retired US lieutenant general who commanded military relief efforts after Hurricane Katrina, told the *New York Times* in 2013.[814] "We could be learning from them." A socialist world would have a much greater chance of building the type of infrastructure needed to protect the civilian population from extreme weather and rising sea levels.

If it is or becomes too late to save the planet – and we take no pleasure in saying this – then the accelerated progress of science under socialism would provide us with a much better chance of sustaining the human race in space, our exploration of which has stalled somewhat under capitalism in the past 50 years due to increasingly stretched state budgets and the need to redirect surplus value that once went to NASA to private space flight companies.[815]

Capitalism has existed for less than 1% of human history and yet it is so destructive that it threatens to wipe out millions of years of evolution in the blink of an eye. Marx called communism, where humans would be freed from the dictates of capital and scarcity – and reunited with nature – "the beginning of human history". To think that this insatiable capitalist system could destroy the near-utopian possibilities of the future just as we are on the cusp of realising them, and bring human life to such a premature end, is too heartbreaking to put into adequate words.

Conclusion:
Socialism or extinction

> "... finally – and this goes for the capitalists too – an inhuman power rules over everything."[816]
>
> Marx

As Cuban revolutionary Raúl Valdés Vivó has written, this is *un crisis sin salida del capitalismo*, a crisis with no capitalist way out. The only way forward for humanity is to "begin the transition to a communist mode of production.... Either the peoples will destroy imperialism and establish their own power or human history will end. It is not 'socialism or barbarism', as Rosa Luxemburg said in 1916, but socialism or nothing."[817]

Our investigation has shown that the second industrial revolution and the eventual complete or near-complete automation of commodity-producing labour would not itself abolish the source of exchange-value – witnessed in the historical fall towards zero of commodity prices, interest rates, and the rate of profit – but would be the final expression of capital's historical tendency towards its own dissolution.

We have seen that if capital did accumulate harmoniously, a dictatorship of AI could emerge, potentially posing a genuine existential threat to the human race. But we have seen that accumulation does not proceed harmoniously, and that capital is an ever-growing fetter on investment and productivity that is becoming increasingly absolute. Capitalism is therefore heading inexorably towards a final, insurmountable breakdown, which will strike much earlier than a zero rate of profit or the completion of the second industrial revolution.

This final breakdown may strike just in time to save the habitability of the planet, for we have seen that capitalism's ever-increasing dependence on extraction – under either the fossil fuel industry or the Green New Dealers – will continue to deepen the environmental and climate crises.

The capitalist production process is a labour process and a valorisation process. Because valorisation depends on ever-greater labour exploitation, the labour-intensity of extraction, etc, becomes increasingly necessary. Although these practices are usually now highly mechanised (resulting in their increasing unprofitability) the rate of exploitation of the remaining workers is very high. Just as surplus value is converted into capital quicker than it is produced, *nature is converted into commodity capital quicker than it can be replenished*. It is not simply capitalism's 'need for infinite growth on a planet of finite resources' – as most leftists seem to put it – that gives rise to the *central, immediate* problem. Rather, it is the *pace* of expansion *as determined by* the ever-larger *size* of the total functioning capital and its need to expand still further, *relative* to nature's ability to replenish itself – with our help or hindrance – combined with the need to create value based on labour exploitation, for the more non-renewable a material is, the more exploitation is involved in its reproduction.

Because socialism produces value through utility-production, rather than exploitation, it is not absolutely dependent on extraction. It would therefore be capable of making a transition to non-extractive production, ie based on hemp and other fibrous plants. Economic output could still increase, fulfilling the communist promise of abundance for all, but based on: break-even planning *at the rate nature replenishes* or slower; and renewable (plants and trees, which regrow) rather than non-renewable materials (metals or fossil fuels, which are finite or disappear into thin air).

We have therefore shown that the planet's habitability cannot be saved without world socialism, an 'eco-socialism' that reunites man and nature. This would heal the environment and give us our best chance of stabilising the climate before it is too late. A socialism that continues to rely on the expansion of metals mining will keep humanity heading towards extinction by ecocide, and at a faster rate.

We have also seen, however, that the greatest immediate threat to humanity lies in the fact that the accumulation crisis is intensifying competition between nation-states and *forcing* the imperialist rivals into an existential military confrontation. *Yet we have also shown that capitalism cannot survive a world war this time, not only because of the consequences of nuclear conflagration, but because the destruction of capital value that would usually restore accumulation to a higher level can now only accelerate the development of automation, capitalism's final devaluation and the abolition of surplus value.*

Capitalism is closing in on its final contradiction. The stakes are staggeringly high. But the darkest hour is before the dawn.

In every respect, capitalism has laid and is laying the foundations for socialism and communism: the proletarianisation of the masses, to be accelerated by the final breakdown, on the way to a classless society; the ever-greater monopolies ripe for their final merger and transformation into social enterprises; the immense development of the productive forces and computing power that will make central planning eminently superior to anarchic capitalist production; the devaluation of capital and fiat currency; the fall of manufacturing prices, GDP and profit rates towards zero, on the way to the historically inevitable abolition of the law of value. Even globalisation, multiculturalism and examples of free movement, such as in the EU, provide a taste of the borderless, raceless and secular future world to come; while the emerging end of the prohibition of hemp and cannabis also shows that communism brings history full circle – to a time when mankind produced and consumed on land that belonged to everyone and no one. The last capitalists are even bestowing fully automated cannabis farms.

As with previous modes of production, the contradictions between the productive forces (the means of production) and the productive relations (the ownership of production) are being driven into irreconcilable conflict *by sheer historical force*. While this contradiction has always been expressed under capitalism by the private appropriation of the products of collective, socialised labour, it is *now increasingly expressed by automated labour and a diminishing source of profit, tending ever-closer towards the self-abolition of the law of value.*

Just as capitalism matured in the womb of feudalism through the concentration of industry, socialism has matured in the womb of capitalism through further monopolisation and the deindustrialisation, servicisation, automation and digitalisation of labour.

Ultimately – for all the principles of the communist tradition – it is this historical force that assures the victory of socialism. Just as the cause to abolish slavery in the US finally succeeded because nothing else could save the Union;[818] just as the Russian masses turned to the Bolsheviks because no one else would pull the country out of WWI; just as the Cuban Revolution could only expel US colonialism by turning to socialism – the coming revolutions will succeed because world socialism is becoming an economic necessity and offers the only chance of preventing ecocidal and nuclear annihilation.[819]

Lenin stressed that there are "no hopeless situations" for the capitalists, since their greed, lust for power and fetishisation of private property meant they would rather starve the masses into submission than abdicate. They would seek to pull every trick to deceive and coerce the international proletariat into fighting each other until enough surplus capital and labour had been destroyed, no matter how long it took. Grossman agreed. Luxemburg too said "socialism will not fall like manna from heaven". The capitalists succeeded. It took the Great Depression, two world wars and fascism to resolve the economic crisis. But if Marx is right in regarding capitalism's succession by socialism as "inevitable" and a "process of natural history"[820] then a final crisis by definition there must be, just as the revolution must begin by definition with socialism in one country. Socialism still has to be fought for. But there can be no 1945 this time; no post-war productivity boom that breathes another century of life into the system. Capitalism is now not only economically unsustainable but biologically unsustainable.

As is written in *The Communist Manifesto*, the great struggles between oppressor and oppressed have throughout history always resulted "either in a revolutionary reconstitution of society at large, or in the common ruin of the contending classes".[821] There is no way out for the capitalists this time. Either they go down or they go down and take the rest of us with them. They surely face at some point in the not-too-distant future, given everything we have assessed, the final capitalist breakdown. Even if this were not the case in purely economic terms, extinction is on the cards, either through the current course of ever-increasing extraction and fossil fuel pollution (probably long) before the end of the century; or much sooner because of the prospect of world war – a war which would obliterate the ruling classes along with every other class, or at least force them to live out their days in their gilded bunkers, an existence that, with no one to rule over and no more worlds to conquer, they would find even emptier than their present detached reality.[822] Neither the blasts, the shockwaves, nor the fallout would discriminate against class. Any part of the world surviving nuclear war would suffer immensely from the cataclysmic effects on the atmosphere and environment for decades, or, more likely, much, much longer.

The imperialists face being hoist by their own technological petard – not AI, but nuclear arms, their ultimate weapon of blackmail. The largest nuclear weapon in the US arsenal is the B83, a free-fall bomb with a yield of 1.2 megatonnes, making it some 75 times more powerful than the 'Little Boy' detonated over Hiroshima in 1945. On 11 June 2019 the Pentagon published a document, the first such doctrine paper for 14 years, which said it believed that nuclear war could "create conditions for decisive results and the restoration of strategic stability".[823] Either US imperialists are bluffing in order to win concessions – the document was quickly taken down – or, with their Empire crumbling and their God,[824] the law of value, dying, they have taken leave of reality, for the US would almost certainly be destroyed in a counter-attack. In response to the US pointing nuclear weapons at Russia from installations in Eastern Europe, Russia has built an "invincible" high-speed, hyper-sonic missile that the US has admitted would be undetectable.

As competition and confrontation inevitably intensifies towards fever pitch, there is a real chance that the imperialist ruling classes will be paralysed in a way that was not possible at the time of the first two world wars – indeed, ending the gold standard and pushing interest rates down to record lows have been made in desperate bids to prevent depressions that they knew would lead to world wars. The masses could force them to abdicate in a situation not unlike February 1917.[825] This scenario could even unfold before the eve of a world war in the event of total economic collapse, although the two could well coincide.

In April 2018, BBC Security Correspondent and Army Reserve officer Frank Gardner warned Britain against escalating tensions in Syria because "Russia's ICBM's represent an existential threat. They could wipe us out." Yet in June it was quietly reported that Britain was expanding the operations of its Special Forces to fight Russia's so-called "little green men" – active Russian military personnel without national insignia or official membership of the Russian army. In other words, *Britain is sending troops to directly engage in traditional military combat with Russia*. With the economy already teetering on the brink it is hardly outlandish to conclude, as John Pilger and James Bell have argued, that World War III – if you don't count the Cold War as such – has already begun.[826]

The Guardian reported in July 2018 that "the use of a nuclear weapon is now more likely than at any time since the Cold War, but the probability of humanity being wiped out entirely has diminished"[827] – how reassuring! The House of Lords' International Relations Committee concluded in April 2019 that the world is now "dangerously close" to a world without arms control agreements, saying: "Disintegrating relationships between nuclear possessor states, new capabilities and technologies, mixed with a lack of communication and understanding, mean that the risk of nuclear weapons being used is greater now than it has been since the Cold War."[828]

But relations between the US and Russia are already worse now than they ever were during the Cold War, and – economically and politically – the situation is more akin to the run up to the WWI, ie not a bipolar but multipolar conflict. In April 2019, Curtis Scaparrotti, US Army general and the top NATO commander for Europe, admitted: "During the Cold War, we understood each other's signals. We talked. I'm concerned that we don't know them as well today. Communication is a very important part of deterrence." This, he said, could lead to nuclear war "by mistake or miscalculation".[829] It's almost as if the overthrow of the Soviet Union made the world a more, not less dangerous place. "A world without the USSR would undoubtedly destroy itself of its own accord within the course of the next century," wrote the Soviet Russian Andrei Platonov in 1934.[830]

NATO held naval drills in the Black Sea in April. Led by Romania, the drills saw the participation of six NATO members (Romania, Bulgaria, Canada, Greece, the Netherlands, Turkey) alongside Ukraine, deploying 20 warships and 2,200 troops. At the same time, Russia conducted its own military drills, with the Russian Defence Ministry stating that its Black Sea fleet had been activated in the event it needed to make an "emergency response" to NATO. Tensions in the region continue to escalate, with the US Navy's guided missile destroyer USS Ross entering the Black Sea on 14 April – the fourth US destroyer to 'visit' in a year.

Bellamy Foster in his article on the Soviet Union's environmental record recalls that, for climatologists such as Budyko and Fyodorov, who also served as Vice President of the World Council of Peace, the issue of peace was closely related to the environment:

"It was Soviet climatologists, primarily based on the work of Budyko and GS Golitsyn, who first developed the nuclear winter theory in the case of a full-scale nuclear exchange, whereby over a hundred gargantuan firestorms set off by nuclear weapons would increase the aerosol loading in the atmosphere sufficiently to bring temperatures across whole continents down by several degrees and possibly several tens of degrees, thereby leading to the destruction of the biosphere and human extinction. The basis of this analysis was developed by the Soviets a decade before their counterparts in other countries. It was to play a big role in the development of the anti-nuclear movement and the eventual backing away from the brink of nuclear holocaust during the later stages of the Cold War."

But nuclear weapons still exist and that backing away is in reverse – because it can only be completed by world socialism.

US imperialism has been in relative decline for decades. At the start of August 2019, JP Morgan, the US's largest bank, not only stated that the dollar's status as the world's reserve currency was ending, but advised investors to move away from it, warning that they were more exposed "than we feel is prudent". Despite the destruction and genocide the US has wrought, it has failed to win a series of immensely expensive wars, the growing unpopularity of which hopefully serve as a prelude to a worldwide rejection of a world war. The cost of maintaining its 800-odd military bases around the world (many in Afghanistan and Iraq have already recently been closed down) is likewise immense and unsustainable (and they too are threatened by rising sea levels). US imperialism may not have seemed like a paper tiger to its millions and millions of victims, but it has proven to be far from invincible. In the past two decades or so the US has only invaded soft targets, and even those have given it hell. Every country that moves towards self-reliance, as 'globalisation' retreats and mutual dependence becomes harder to sustain, will further weaken US imperialism, bringing about the conditions for revolution in the US itself.[831]

Certainly a unique historical moment is approaching: either – finally – the fall of imperialism and the victory of socialism; or, the end of human history. One way or another that must represent a final crisis.

Civil wars between sections of national ruling classes are also possible. We can already see the potential for this brewing between neoliberals and the 'populist right' in the US; and likewise in Britain between 'Remainers' and 'Brexiters'. Both cases are generally defined by the classic split between industrialists and landlords (including the new digital variety), with the former's grip on power slipping over the past 10 years because of its diminishing material basis. If the ruling classes found themselves paralysed by the 'impracticality' of a world war, in the absence of socialist revolutions ruling class civil wars would likely follow instead. Any such civil wars must be turned into socialist revolutions, for the only other (although also economically unsustainable) outcome would be Naziism or even outright slavery.[832] The potential for war between Britain and Europe is also growing, especially with regards to Ireland and over territory between British and EU fishing vessels.

The working classes will be compelled to organise independently. Within the dual power situation, democratic socialists, anarchists and communists will jockey for leadership of the movement. Communists must have the conviction that our arguments will sooner or later prevail as they align with developments in the real world. For in the hands of the class-conscious masses, theory becomes a material weapon.

The prize is no less than global communism, abundant material wealth for all, and – if we can save the planet – an everlasting world peace.[833]

All workers and oppressed peoples – unite to save and liberate humanity!

Afterword

"As long as theoretical knowledge remains the privilege of a handful of 'academicians' in the Party, the latter will face the danger of going astray. Only when the great mass of workers take the keen and dependable weapons of scientific socialism in their own hands, will all petty bourgeois inclinations, all the opportunist currents, come to naught. The movement will then find itself on sure and firm ground."[834]

Rosa Luxemburg

Grossman remains badly under-appreciated – many socialists have not even heard of him. Numerous attempts to discredit him, both at the time his work was published and during the economic crisis of the 1970s, have failed. As Tony Kennedy says in his foreword to the abridged 1992 English version of *The Law of Accumulation*, years after the publication of a number of such criticisms, including from Mandel,[835] Grossman's elaboration of Marx's theory remains "unsurpassed".

Like Marx, his method of approximation was misunderstood (often, it seems, wilfully). The banal accusation that he employed a mechanical method is clearly undermined by his emphasis on the counter-tendencies and modifications – describing several more than Marx, in fact. Equally, the claim that Grossman dismissed the role of class struggle in the realisation of socialism is an easily disproved lie. He clearly and repeatedly emphasised that breakdown could only be consummated by seizing power and introducing higher relations of production.

In a letter in 1931 to Mattick – one of the few Marxists to uphold Grossman's economics, despite disagreeing with his political support for the Soviet Union[836] – Grossman rejected these accusations:

"It should be evident that the notion that capitalism must 'by itself' or 'automatically' collapse is alien to me ... But I did wish to show that the class struggle alone is *not* sufficient ... As a *dialectical* Marxist, I know that both sides of the process, objective and subjective elements, mutually influence each other. In the class struggle both these factors blend. One cannot 'wait' until first the objective conditions are met, and only then let the subjective elements go to work. That would be an insufficient and mechanical interpretation which is alien to me ... My breakdown theory does not intend to exclude the active intervention, but rather hopes to show when and under what circumstances such an objective revolutionary situation can and will arise."[837]

For Marx, Engels and Grossman, class struggle was the *necessary expression*, the 'subjective bearer of change' of the objective conditions of economic breakdown, for they assessed capitalist relations *in their totality*. There is a dialectical relationship, but the objective factor tends to influence or trigger the subjective more than vice-versa. The capitalist class is compelled to attack the working class to reverse its thinning profit margins and consumption funds. The working class is compelled to fight back. The deeper the economic crisis, the greater the class struggle.

Like Grossman, Marx had "frequently been charged with a 'fatalistic' theory of the 'historical necessity'" of socialism. Yet, says Grossman,

"[in] all his writings Marx characteristically emphasises the unity of theory and practice. This so-called 'historical necessity' does not operate automatically but requires the active participation of the working class in the historical process. This participation, however, is itself not something arbitrary but follows from the pressure of the objective factors. The student of history and the forward-looking practical politician must therefore consider this subjective factor as in fact another objective condition of the historical process."[838]

Elsewhere, Grossman stresses that breakdown theory is important to grasp in terms of avoiding adventurist mistakes that can set the movement back:

"The point of a Marxist theory of breakdown is only to demarcate voluntarism and putchism, which regard revolution as possible at any time, without considering whether there is an objectively revolutionary situation, and as dependent only on the subjective will of revolutionaries. The point of breakdown theory is that the revolutionary action of the proletariat only receives its most powerful impetus from the objective convulsion of the established system, and at the same time only this creates the circumstances necessary to successfully wrestle down ruling class resistance."[839]

He also quotes Lenin:

"Marxists, says Lenin in 1915, 'know perfectly well that a revolution *cannot* be "made", that revolutions *develop* out of objectively (ie independently of the will of parties and classes) mature crises and turns in history...'. '[A] revolution is *impossible without a revolutionary situation* ... For a revolution to take place, it is usually insufficient for "the lower classes not to want" to live in the old way; it is also necessary that "the upper classes should be unable" to live in the old way', that an *objective impossibility* for the ruling classes to assert their rule in unchanged form develops. Secondly, that 'the suffering and want of the oppressed classes have grown more acute than usual'. 'Without these *objective changes* ... a revolution, as a general rule, is impossible. The totality of all these objective changes is called a revolutionary situation.' It is not merely revolutionary consciousness (which, incidentally, cannot be produced outside a revolutionary situation, merely by hammering the final goal into heads) that only figures in addition as a further condition with a subjective character. It is rather something entirely different: 'the ability of the revolutionary class to take revolutionary mass action [*strong* enough]', which presupposes an *organisation* ['without [which] the masses lack unity of will'] and *extensive experience in the class struggles* of everyday life."[840]

Lenin writes in the same passage:

"The masses allow themselves to be robbed in 'peace time', but, in turbulent times, are drawn by all the circumstances of the crisis and *by the 'upper classes' themselves* into independent historical action... All governments are sleeping on a volcano; all are themselves calling for the masses to display initiative and heroism... The experience of any... great calamity... stuns and breaks some people, *but enlightens and tempers others*. Taken by and large, and considering the history of the world as a whole, the number and strength of the second kind of people have... proved greater than those of the former kind."[841]

That mass action has not yet been strong enough to overthrow capitalism for good surely indicates that the system has yet to suffer a deep enough crisis; that is, that a large enough portion of the population has not been 'sufficiently' proletarianised to tip the balance of class forces decisively; or that capital has not come up against a great enough barrier to accumulation.

Such a crisis is surely approaching in the not-too-distant future. We are heading into uncharted territory. Privately owned production is becoming an impossibility and must be nationalised and internationalised. The powerful impetus Grossman speaks of is sure to be stronger than anything witnessed in the past two centuries. The proletariat is absolutely and relatively much larger and the same applies in terms of the proportion of people set to be robbed of everything they've worked for. If, as empirical evidence suggests, fiat currency is 'dying a natural death', then immiseration will go well beyond the workers. There will be little to no 'middle class' – only a relative few hoarding highly inflated gold, the production of which is also being automated – and everyone else.

Capital must sooner or later betray one too many people. The capitalist state may, at some point, no longer be able to pay state employees, including the military.[842] We must think through the implications of such possibilities. There *could be at least some potential* to win over not just the existing working class but significant sections of the privileged classes – especially since we are running out of time to prevent ecocidal and nuclear annihilation. There *could be at least some potential* for revolutions to succeed *relatively* swiftly and peacefully (as in Russia, where, because of mass defections of officers in the imperial army and navy, the soviets seized power virtually unopposed).[843] This requires putting anti-extinction politics, economics and incentives at the forefront of our agitation and leaving numerous divisive issues up to the democratic will of the people so as to overcome sectarianism.

That it has not been possible to end capitalism for good before its final crisis does demand something of a reality check or dose of humility from all socialist trends. The idea that capitalism has long outlived its 'historical mission' cannot be sustained. If we have to concede that the Bolshevik revolution proved to be somewhat 'premature' in order to contextualise the Soviet Union's collapse; or if we have to frame socialism as 'completing' capitalism's historical mission – to bring about fully automated production – in order to change popular misconceptions, then so be it. The vast majority of workers, not just labour aristocrats, are presently, to one degree or another, reformist. The democratic socialist 'left' – let alone the 'Leninist' 'left' – tends to be in the minority almost everywhere. It will take a massive process of private bankruptcies and proletarianisation, especially in the imperialist nations, before even that begins to change. Even with the planetary crisis and after a decade of harsh austerity, the masses are not rushing to revolution. This is not new and has only changed in extremely rare conditions. Many depressions have passed by without the poor declaring all-out war on the rich. This is symptomatic of oppression. Revolution is always a last resort. Most people prize peace and peaceful lives above almost everything else. This unavoidably impacts tactical considerations. Indeed, it is likely that Stalin won more support than Trotsky when it came to replacing Lenin because of the former's more cautious approach to spreading revolution – the soviets swung behind the Bolsheviks because of the promise of peace, after all. We do not glorify violence or retribution. We are motivated by the opportunity to make a better world, to save and liberate humanity. Establishing economic rights through system change is the greatest form of social justice – and saving the planet's habitability is the *urgent* priority. Collapsing empires are bound to be extremely violent affairs, though, even just in terms of the scarcity produced; and the price of liberation is usually very high. With modern weaponry and population sizes, it could be higher than ever. Only world socialism can establish peace, but we want and need as peaceful a transition as possible. We must use every means of persuasion at our disposal. To one extent or another, history's usurpers have usually compensated the usurped to incentivise capitulation and minimise counter-revolutionary violence. The environmental crisis has made the importance of minimising conflict even graver – compensation for expropriations will have to be employed to the maximum possible degree if the world is not to become scorched beyond repair. This will mean taking on a high amount of long-term debt, but a higher and crisis-free mode of production (plus the fact that most capitalists will have gone bust by then) will make that more than possible. The Canutes who do not fight for socialism can only fight a suicidal battle in the name of extinction. The promise of amnesty and other incentives should be at the forefront of agitation to encourage defectors who come to their senses.

There is no pure revolution. We need to develop thinkers who can find the right balance between principle with tactical nous. The tendency to overuse terms like 'labour aristocrat', 'petty bourgeois' and 'social fascist' ignores the unfolding process and numerous practical realities and problems, such as the need to have the support or co-operation of people with expertise in various areas from the get-go. The class struggle is the struggle to progressively win over more and more of a given population, including, as Marx stressed, the petty bourgeoisie, which remains an enormous class.[844] Smaller enterprises will be the last to be expropriated and when they are their integration into the new system will be incentivised. When all is said and done, revolutions have never succeeded without mass defections in the armed forces.[845]

Even in revolutionary situations, *most* workers have usually turned to reformism and compromise, and not just in the imperialist countries. As Grossman said in one of his letters to Mattick:

> "The word 'betrayal' has often been misused and applied simply when the situation did not develop in the expected direction. It explains very little. The 'betrayal' itself is, for me, a symptom of the immaturity of the workers' movement, an indication that the working class's objective situation makes a betrayal profitable, a sign that the traitors... have not yet seen the objective possibility of a proletarian victory. As such a possibility draws closer, the 'traitors' will become scarcer and scarcer."[846]

While this is easier said than done, it is something we have to be extremely conscious of. Pushing too hard, too soon and with too little support is bound to backfire. Even Guevara, often accused of adventurism, believed revolution could not be pursued until all 'democratic' avenues had been exhausted. It is likely that communist parties will need to give critical support to democratic socialist or 'all-workers' governments at some point(s) in order to prove to the people that even the most left-wing of social democracies cannot solve the crisis in their favour. There is no possibility of victory before winning over a clear majority of the active forces.[847]

One of the points at the forefront of agitation should be a commitment to cancel *all* outstanding mortgages and personal debt (while making sure those who lose out from any such cancellation, such as pensioners, are compensated); and to entitle *all* households, *regardless of class*, to retain or be given ownership of the property (ie the fabric of the building) in which they presently live (thereby turning private property into personal property), with the land leased from the state at low rates of ground rent, set as a relatively small proportion of income (5% or less has been common in socialist countries) and/or according to differential convenience or amenity of land. It may even be prudent to extend this for those who own more than one property, again to incentivise capitulation. (Rent paid to the state or community is necessary in order not to effectively negate public ownership by allowing rent to be appropriated by the user of the land, as was the case with the peasantry in China; to lower the general level of taxation; and effectively redistribute funds to sections of the population living on less fertile land.) As the process of building socialism progresses, those who are required to leave their homes, due to the need to revive the environment and build new infrastructure, will be compensated either financially and/or with the new, high quality, spacious and eco-friendly housing, in a location as close as possible, that the state will embark upon building for everyone.[848] If the whole land cannot be immediately nationalised, small farmers should be offered high subsidies, offset by high taxes on large land owners, in order to try and prevent the two forming a powerful counter-revolutionary alliance. Farming is not something that can be simply taken on by untrained workers.

The task of communists has always been to *fuse* scientific socialism with the mass movement through education, organisation and leadership.[849] Communists must promote (the correct!) Marxist economic theory and a socialist political programme that can appeal to the majority of a given country; and, through the class struggle, build a mass independent vanguard party. Lenin stressed the importance of speaking as much as possible with one voice in order to incisively cut through the confusing bourgeois ideas that the masses are bombarded with. That is why we have proposed a scientifically compelling central message which communists everywhere can use in the heat of the moment, to quickly persuade people and educate new recruits as best as possible amid the rapid and tumultuous developments ahead – one that appeals to the *immediate needs of the masses and humanity as a whole*.

Post-revolution, the role of parties will be to guide the construction of the new system, including the enfranchisement of the masses in a new system of participative and direct democracy (with the right of recall at any time and, perhaps, once world socialism has been secured, lot drawing, in order to make and keep the people fully sovereign and politicised).

Human nature

Communists must keep faith in the masses. Such faith is not based on an idealisation of the masses – made up of people, not angels – but the recognition that people tend to act primarily in their own interests, *interests which now increasingly lie with socialism*. This is somewhat ironic given the bourgeois claim that socialism 'does not work' because of the 'selfishness of human nature'. Clearly, human nature has played some role in capitalism's success – that it is possible to oppress, condition and bribe people is made possible by human nature. But such an abstraction does not consider how human behaviour is driven and conditioned, not only by fear, experience, location, culture and education (which presently trains us mostly to serve and obey capital); but by class, oppression, the mode of production and the stage of the latter's development. Equally, it is too easy to dogmatically conflate human nature with bourgeois conditioning. That people consume more when prices fall is not necessarily evidence of their becoming bourgeois. Communism will not abolish the human capacity for resentment, vanity, venality, and so on. Regardless, capitalism's decay and the economic basis of socialism have developed with indifference to the will of man, human nature or its bourgeois conditioning.

We must try to understand the nature of the 'subjective factor' as much as the objective economic factor. That is the point Grossman seems to convey in assessing *when* the masses may be prepared to fight back; that they must be driven to it. Failing to grasp this can lead to adventurism, pessimism, misanthropy or nihilism.

Human behaviour is in many ways driven by (accumulated) internal chemical reactions triggered by external stimuli. But research has confirmed that our first impulse is to cooperate, not compete or fight.[850] As the physicist Fritjof Capra says: "Nature nurtures life through communities. This is a process that started with the first single-celled organisms. Life, from its beginning more than three billion years ago, took over the planet by networking, not combat."[851]

Human nature is certainly 'flawed' – we are mortal, after all – and so socialism cannot be judged against an impossible utopia. The lower stage of communism in particular, says Marx, will be "in every respect, economically, morally, and intellectually, still stamped with the birthmarks of the old society from whose womb it emerges".[852] Culturally, too, from country to country and region to region. But what would necessitate or incentivise stealing or corruption in a world without money or want? A better mode of production will progressively disincentivise so many of the negative things people do under capitalism that bourgeois thinkers one-sidedly attribute to human nature. Nor will we have to suppress our tendency to crave novelty and social interaction so much. Automation, including auto-planning, will increasingly remove man's limits from the production process, freeing us up to enrich and improve all areas of life through creative and democratic activity.

Communist leaders will make mistakes. Organising millions of new, politically inexperienced cadre, before and after the revolution, will be challenging and messy. Realpolitiks will not disappear. The people will make democratic decisions they later regret, or that only 'get corrected' by following generations. There will still be disputes and conflicts of interest between individuals and groups in need of mediation, and so on. But we will build a system capable of abolishing poverty, hunger, war and oppression.

Although prohibitions should be advocated against where possible – since they create black markets that overstretch state resources – some prohibitions may be necessary. Providing cheaper, more attractive alternatives is the best solution (and prohibitions will be even less enforceable as the state withers away) but they may not be immediately available. As an apt example – since the prohibition of alcohol played a role in bringing down the Soviet Union – a recently developed 'alchosynth' drug "removes the risks of hangovers, liver toxicity, aggression and loss of control".[853] Socialism is ultimately about expanding choices so that people are enabled to make better ones. Promoting good values and stigmatising bad ones is highly important; but this can be arbitrary and positive incentivisation often is more effective than lecturing, coercion or shaming when it comes to encouraging work and social change. As has become clear in the past decade or so, society tends to get meaner when relative scarcity rises – so the underlying challenge is to reverse this trend. That comes down to changing the economic base.

Human nature exists on a spectrum of capacity. We cannot fully understand it until humanity has liberated itself from this inhuman system, one that conditions us from birth to internalise our oppression and uses the negative incentive of fear of poverty, or worse, to motivate compliance. What we do know is that humans have a very strong sense of self-preservation and that capitalism increasingly threatens our survival. We know too that economic necessity usually prevails. The past 170 years have shown that the ultimate overthrow of capitalism for subjective, moral or even just democratic reasons has not been possible. While these factors will play their part, our investigation has shown emphatically that capitalism will end primarily out of economic necessity. We know, also, that socialism does work, as Cuba continues to prove. The masses may seem too divided and apathetic now; but this is inevitable in class society, where workers are pitted against each other in competition for jobs and resources, alienated from themselves and each other and disenfranchised by the shallowness of bourgeois 'democracy'. The final breakdown, though, will increasingly *compel* the masses to take independent action and unite in the common interest. The communist movement may be small now but pessimists should remember that the Bolsheviks comprised only 8,000 members just four months before October. When the conditions ripen the movement may grow rapidly.

Towards a united front

While the premises of communist agitation in such a period are set out clearly at the start of this work, communist tactics are not addressed in detail. The following reflections are intended as a note toward the formation of such tactics, albeit within certain immediate parameters.

The fundamental premises upon which communist tactics must be based in our period may be expressed simply: (1) to work toward the formation of a *united front* (as opposed to a *popular front*)[854] against the existential threats posed by imperialism; (2) to fight for the hegemony of proletarian politics over this alliance. Trotsky fleshed out the tactic of 'the united front from above'. Only by addressing the leaders of the reformist parties in calls for joint action can communists address the reformist rank and file. If the leaders accept the invitation to united action, even round partial demands from the reformist programme, their rank and file enters into battle alongside communists, sees that the lies their leaders tell about communists are false, and learns that it is the communists, not the reformist leaders, who fight "for every crust of bread". If the reformist leaders reject the invitation, that too can only benefit the communists – the reformist leaders prove in practice that it is they who are splitting the class.[855]

The need for a united front can be expressed simply in both theoretical and practical terms. In theory, the necessity can be seen from a single observation: the threat of extinction, which personally concerns the whole of humanity, will *necessarily produce a reaction from the whole of humanity*. If communist politics is to be able to speak to this mass of humanity which, as Lenin says, comes into struggle alongside "all its prejudices",[856] it is necessary to enter into an alliance with bourgeois and petty bourgeois forces that accept the need to combat the climate crisis and the threat of nuclear annihilation. In order to unseat these forces from leadership, it is necessary to criticise them, to expose their intent or shortcomings, and to rally forces around a proletarian, socialist programme of action. Practically, this question has already reared its head in Britain in the form of Extinction Rebellion (XR), which led the shutdown of several main roads in London for 10 days in April 2019.

That XR possesses a bourgeois class character is undeniable. It is backed to the hilt by a considerable number of activist NGOs and advocates the Green New Deal. While claiming to be 'apolitical'[!] and 'horizontalist', its *de facto* leaders, a self-appointed clique, have sought to maintain tight, anti-democratic control of the movement they have attracted (a common feature of 'horizontalism') while advocating the tactic of mass arrests yet providing (at least until they were shamed in the media) no support to the bulk of arrested activists. XR's attitude to criticism from the Left is, explicitly, to ignore it, something taught to activists, or even to ban communist participation. Their attitude to the police and state violence betrays their class privilege. XR has been able to mobilise thousands of activists, however, at least ostensibly, directly against the threat of extinction. As such, it is necessary to work among the protests, and to argue for a united front among those activists open to communist politics, so as to gain a larger voice within the environmental movement. Should XR respond to such a position by ignoring it, treating it with scorn or attacking those who put it forward, then they have only served to expose themselves to activists as unserious opportunists.

Beyond these theoretical and concrete positions, let us pose a hypothetical scenario. Suppose that we get a crash so bad, with the population so assaulted, that there is a sudden and sensational swing to the Left, with the masses militantly demanding, for example, that the state urgently takes over the production of food. The ruling class, out of desperation, turn to democratic socialists, who start nationalising production out of necessity. In such circumstances, two matters are evident: (1) capitalism has not yet been overthrown – it has been backed into a corner by the crisis, but the masses have not yet seized power; (2) the ruling class will now be plotting their next move to unseat the Left and restore the accumulation process. In this scenario, what happens if communists pursue a united front? Firstly, and this much is clear, the democratic socialists would be unable to reject it. While they may attempt to ignore it, doing so would only expose themselves among the newly politicised masses. Thus, they cannot practically reject it as they would lose support in conditions which place them at risk. Suppose they seek an alliance against communists with the ousted neoliberal bourgeoisie, or fascism? While this may have been more tempting, from their point of view, a century ago, with no real material basis for reprivatisation and no incentive to support world war this time, it is hard to imagine a scenario where they do not end up in the camp alongside us. Rejecting such a demand would therefore be suicide. They must allow us a seat at the table.

Once there, communists must begin earnest criticism. Censorship at this point becomes impossible: the masses have seen the communists and, by virtue of their positions, more and more have come to support them and demand to hear them speak. The nature of the Marxist position on extinction is, as we have seen, irrefutable. As such, the criticism more and more divides the front in political influence. Proletarian politics now has a concrete position. It is able to raise demands for a socialist state, democratic control over the means of production and for central planning. Though the social democrats will not grant such demands without effectively abolishing themselves, their inability to do so results in a context of dual power. All that remains is for the communists to adopt a line similar to that held by the Bolsheviks: "All power to the soviets!" The nature of the circumstances more and more reveals the necessity of this to the masses, as reaction begins to creep back and the democratic socialist leadership wavers. The revolution is won.

Clearly this is the most optimistic possibility, but it is one that we must be prepared for. Although there is certainly much more discussion to be had on this question, one must submit that the united front *must be our starting point*. The absence of a mass vanguard party in the imperialist nations is marked. A united front is the path to forming one.

★

Despite the monumental scale of the challenge ahead, there is cause for optimism. We have the most unifying and compelling message possible and sheer historical force on our side.

The international communist movement simply must succeed. The difference between success and failure is now the difference between winning and losing everything.

★

Update: The covid-19 crash

"In the end, dollar bills, like bond and share certificates, are just pieces of paper. As trillions more of them flood into the system, events in March 2020 bring closer the day when investors will lose faith in cash itself – and in the power of the economy and state standing behind it... Capitalism cannot escape from this crisis, no matter how many trillions of dollars governments borrow or central banks print... The coronavirus [crash] makes socialist revolution – in imperialist countries and across the world – into a necessity."

John Smith

The outbreak of the coronavirus (covid-19) pandemic sparked the greatest stock market crash in capitalist history, confirming much of our argument. Stocks crashed quicker than at any point during the Great Depression, unemployment soared around the globe, and oil prices fell *below zero for the first time ever.*

The unprecedented social lockdowns imposed in the name of protecting public health – while various governments torched civil rights, accelerated the privatisation of health care, funnelled the virus into care homes, and so on[857] – exacerbated the economic fallout significantly, favouring capital's need for a period of depressed wages and prices. Far from causing the crisis, though – many countries in Sub-Saharan Africa and Latin America were already in recession – the pandemic served merely as a catalyst.

As Pento said: "The virus was a pin that pricked the stock and junk [high-risk] bond bubbles. We wouldn't have had stocks fall by 30% if we weren't in an epic bubble. Stock prices have been at a record high of 150% of GDP. The average is 50%. They were extremely vulnerable to an external shock." And, he warned, "the real crash is coming".

That stock markets will fall again and again over the next few years was demonstrated starkly at the start of May when Warren Buffett – the fourth wealthiest person in the world with a net worth of $89bn – sold his investment firm's entire holdings in the four major US airlines. The S&P 500 during the Great Depression fell to its lowest point in 1932, a decline of nearly 89% compared to the high point in 1929. This time, it took only 22 trading days to fall 30% from its record high reached on 19 February, the fastest ever slump of this magnitude. The second, third and fourth quickest 30% pullbacks all took place during the Great Depression in 1934, 1931 and 1929, respectively.[858] But this was not the only remarkable activity. As Smith wrote for *Monthly Review*:

> "10-year US Treasury bonds are considered the safest of havens and the ultimate benchmark against which all other debt is priced. In times of great uncertainty, investors invariably stampede out of stock markets and into the safest bond markets, so as share prices fall, bond prices rise. As they do, the fixed income they yield translates into a falling rate of interest. *But not on 9 March* [2020], when, in the midst of plummeting stock markets, 10-year US Treasury bond interest rates spiked upwards. According to one bond trader, 'statistically speaking, [this] should only happen every few millennia'. Even in the darkest moment of the global financial crisis, when Lehman Brothers went bankrupt in September 2008, this did not happen."[859]

Mass unemployment and automation
Between January and the end of April 2020, joblessness soared. In the US, 40 million people sought unemployment benefits – more than in the previous 138 weeks combined – after the government allowed employers to lay them off. Globally, the International Labour Organization said 1.6 billion workers in the informal economy, nearly half of the world's total workforce, "stand in immediate danger of having their livelihoods destroyed… The first month of the crisis is estimated to have resulted in a drop of 60% in the income of informal workers globally… 81% in Africa and the Americas." The UN has warned of "famines of biblical proportions".

Capital immediately sought to take advantage. At the end of March, after governments in most countries had imposed a social lockdown, almost half of company bosses in 45 countries said they were speeding up plans to automate their businesses. With many people being compelled to work from home, Microsoft could boast of having discovered a fresh way of reducing costs and extending absolute labour time as it announced "two years' worth of digital transformation in two months".

As *The Guardian* reported at the end of April: "Bank branches were already closing in droves before the epidemic, but here is the perfect excuse to shut more... The authors of an Oxford University study thought that by 2035 it would be possible to automate 86% of restaurant jobs, three-quarters of retail jobs, and 59% of recreation jobs. By unlucky coincidence, those are among the very industries hardest hit by an epidemic now demanding quantum leaps in efficiency if some companies are to avoid going under."[860]

Unemployment began to fall as lockdowns loosened, but remained high, in the US for example from an official rate of 14.7% in April to 7.9% in September. If and when governments wind down state-funded furloughing programmes and other temporary relief, however, unemployment and hardship will hit yet new heights.

Global contraction

Having anticipated global GDP growth of 3.3% in 2020, the IMF said it would now shrink by 5.2% – from $89.94 trillion to $83.19 trillion; equivalent to the output of Germany and France combined – the most in a century and three times more than the 1.7% contraction in 2009. US GDP shrank by 31% in the second quarter year-on-year and by 3.6% in 2020 overall.

The BoE estimated that the first six months of 2020 would see Britain suffer a near 30% contraction – still less than the 40% reduction seen in household spending in March and April – the country's worst recession since *1709*. Figures for March and April showed that the British economy had indeed shrunk by 25%, taking it back to its size in 2002. April's 20% slump dwarfed Britain's previous downturn, when the overall output lost during 18 months was 6% and the fastest monthly fall was 1% (in March 2009). Total imports fell at an unprecedented monthly rate of 26% and exports by a record 19%. The Institute for Social Policy, Housing, Equalities Research said in December that the number of destitute families in Britain – already up by 35% during 2017-19 – had doubled to two million, about 4.8 million people, including one million children. A year-long £20-a-week boost to Universal Credit, costing £6bn, is set to end in April, affecting six million families.

The Institute of Directors (IoD) said investment intentions among its members for the next 12 months had fallen by 11 percentage points. Investment into emerging markets fell by more than £100bn in the first 137 days of the crisis – about fives times more than the equivalent time during the financial crash. The 'developing' nations, though, are expected to fare better than the 'developed' in relative terms. China's growth rate is predicted to fall from 6.1% in 2019 to 1.2% in 2020, with India on course to expand by 1.9%, down from 4.2%. Adjusted to take account of population changes, the IMF's forecasts were even gloomier. GDP per head is expected to fall globally by 4.2% in 2020, by 6.5% in the developed countries, and by 7% in Britain.

While the BoE initially claimed Britain would experience a 'V-shaped' recovery – on the assumption that the lockdown is the cause of the depression – it later conceded that the return to growth "could be slow and painful".

The IMF conceded that its forecasts were highly uncertain. In January it projected 4.4% growth in 2021 (albeit from a smaller base) but estimated that global output in 2025 would be 31% lower than had been forecast before the 2007-08 crisis.

The richest continue to get richer. In Britain, the wealth of 45 billionaires grew by 20% in the first three months of the crisis from £121.6bn to £146.6bn. In the US, around 600 billionaires saw their wealth grow by 19.5%, $565bn. The Great Lockdown Shakedown continues apace.

Debt

The world over, initial extra government spending amounted to $12 trillion and central bank monetary action to $7.5 trillion. Gross debt issuance hit an "eye-watering" record of $12.5 trillion in the second quarter of 2020, according to the IIF, compared with a quarterly average of $5.5 trillion in 2019. Some 60% of new issues came from governments.

The IIF said global debt hit a new high of $253 trillion in the third quarter of 2019, 322% of world GDP, up from $244 trillion and 318% year-on-year. That was *before* the pandemic. A year later, global debt swelled to $272 trillion

Federal Debt Held by the Public, 1900 to 2050
Percentage of Gross Domestic Product

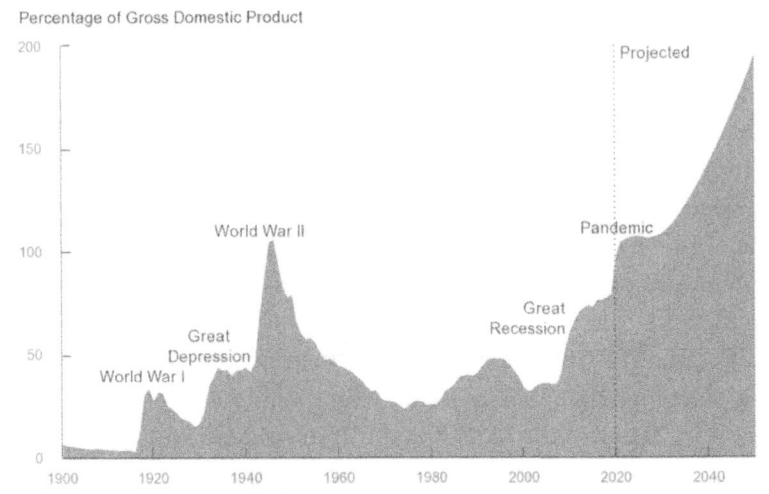

Source: Congressional Budget Office

(331%). "While some $15 trillion of this surge has been recorded in 2020 amid the covid-19 pandemic, the debt build-up over the past four years has far outstripped the $6 trillion rise over the previous four years," the IIF said. The group expects global debt to reach $277 trillion at the end of 2020. Debt-to-GDP in developed markets rose from 380% at the end of 2019 to 432% in the third quarter of 2020, with the emerging market figure hitting 250% and China's 335%, up from 302%. Some $7 trillion of emerging market bonds and syndicated loans will be due for repayment at the end of next year, about 15% of which are denominated in US dollars.

US national debt hit an official $26.5 trillion in the second quarter of 2020, 136% of GDP, exceeding the post-WWII 118% record of 1946. According to the IIF, total US debt (government, households, financial and non-financial corporations) is set to reach $80 trillion at the end of 2020, up from $71 trillion over the year.

The Fed has taken the unprecedented action of buying up corporate bonds and exchange-traded funds (ETFs) in the primary market, having only ever done so in the secondary market (where proceeds from the sale of bonds go to the counter-party, say an investor or a dealer; whereas in the primary market, money from investors goes directly to the issuer). Now businesses and corporations can sell the Fed a bond, directly. This is happening because, as Smith says, "since 9 March, corporate interest rates have gone through the roof; in fact few corporations can borrow money at any price. Investors are refusing to lend to them. Corporations are now facing a credit crunch – in the midst of global negative interest rates!" Pento argues:

> "Central banks are in a desperate situation to reinflate asset prices... They are rapidly inflating the money supply in a desperate attempt to keep pension plans afloat in nominal terms, as they get eviscerated in inflation-adjusted terms. They're going to reinflate junk bond prices again. They'll exceed the 2% inflation target, greatly. All bond yields will rise inexorably, prices will crash. And then the Fed will have nothing they can do. There will be no relief package coming from any government on the planet. No tax base can cope with that amount of debt. You cannot resolve an inflation crisis, you cannot placate a market that is rising, with cratering prices, by creating more inflation. Or by borrowing more funds into existence. You can't do it. That's the real crash that's coming."

As of 29 February 2020, the Fed held $2.47 trillion, 14.6%, of $16.9 trillion marketable US Treasury securities outstanding, making it by far the largest single holder of US Treasuries in the world. By the end of March, this increased by an unprecedented monthly increase of $650bn, to $3.12 trillion. One estimate said that if this pace of buying continued, the Fed would "own the entire Treasury market in about 22 months".[861] As of 23 November, 21% of all US dollars had been printed in 2020, taking the figure to 75% over the past 12 years – already sparking fears about possible hyperinflation.

Since demand for currency rises in a crisis, a match in supply via printing is required to prevent or limit deflation. If, however, demand falls or collapses due to bankruptcies and high or mass unemployment, and the supply remains high in an effort to raise prices or boost consumption, then inflation becomes abnormally high. This is now the risk, since bonds held by central banks would normally be sold back to the private market before inflation becomes a problem – but the private sector is also increasingly dependent on central banks as the purchaser of corporate bonds.

At the end of March, the US government enacted its largest ever single bailout package, at $2 trillion, more than double the $700bn banking bailout of October 2008. Loans under the programme were made forgivable, meaning companies do not have to pay them back to the public. Nor have the recipients been disclosed. The US Treasury borrowed a record $3 trillion in the second quarter of 2020, up from $477bn in the first. Between the start of March and May, the US national debt grew by $1.5 trillion to $24.9 trillion, a 6.4% increase. The budget deficit for the first six months of the fiscal year totalled $744bn – and exploded to $3.1 trillion after the next six, more than triple the 2019 shortfall.

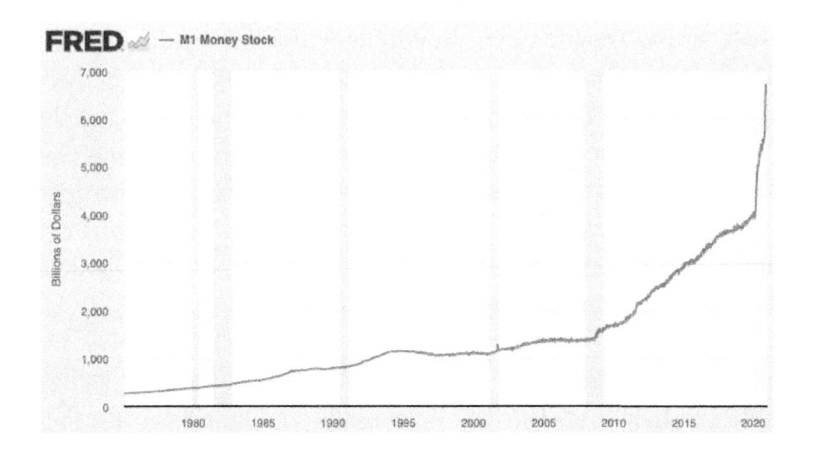

The BoE admitted that the British government would have come close to insolvency without the intervention of the central bank, which raised its quantitive easing target by £200bn to £645bn. At the start of April, corporate bond buying doubled to £20bn. Separately, the BoE bought £452m gilt bonds from the government in the first three months of 2020, and said it would buy a further £554m over the next three months.

The BoE also expanded the government's overdraft facility, highlighting the latter's extraordinary need for cash, replacing the £400m cap with unlimited access. Both parties claimed this support would be "temporary and short-term", with balances repaid as soon as possible and before the end of the year. The government tapped the facility for £20bn during the last crisis. The BoE had to reject accusations that it had resorted to monetary financing, a term associated historically with hyperinflation. BoE governor Andrew Bailey, who had only just taken the job, claimed the central bank had "not embarked on a permanent expansion of the ... balance sheet with the aim of funding the government". He said there was "no question of fiscal dominance", in which a government's fiscal objectives override the central bank's task of keeping inflation on target, adding that government borrowing could not be cost-free, since the BoE still pays interest on reserves. But by central banks' own admission, their bond-buying is supposed to be temporary, since interest rates cannot go down forever. While bond financing keeps a lid on inflation, the moment bonds become unsaleable because no more cash can be converted into stocks, or rates become so negative that investment is disincentivised, could be the moment financing becomes solely monetary.

The government's debt management office, which sells bonds to international investors, said in April it planned to raise £225bn from bond markets in just four months to fund the huge increase in state spending. In May the government sold gilts at negative yields *for the first time*. The £3.8bn gilt auction of three-year government bonds sold with a yield of -0.003%.

Britain's national debt has risen to above 100% – leaping from 80% – for the first time since 1963. The pound tumbled by 11% to its lowest point against the US dollar since the 1980s. Bank of America analysts say "sterling is in the process of evolving into a currency that resembles the underlying reality of the British economy: small and shrinking with a growing dual deficit problem similar to more liquid [emerging market] currencies." Britain's budget deficit jumped back up to 15%, twice as high as its worst point following the Great Recession. The government was forced to borrow a record £62bn to balance its books in April, the same as in the whole of the previous financial year. Tax receipts were down by 26.5% year-on-year, with income tax receipts down by 30.3%, corporation tax by 14.1% and VAT by 43.6%.

The cost of the Treasury's furloughing scheme, together with higher spending on the NHS and benefits, contributed to a 56.6% annual increase in government spending. According to the Resolution Foundation, 70% of households in Britain have experienced a fall in income, with 23% having to use savings to cover living costs and 13% now struggling to pay bills. More than two million new Universal Credit (UC) claims had been made by the end of April. This rose to 2.8 million a month later.

Almost a third of the workforce in Britain was furloughed during the main period of the lockdown. The state covered 80% of the costs up to £2,500 per employee, amounting to at least £39bn. This was part of an unprecedented bailout package of an initial £350bn.

On 5 June, it was revealed that the BoE had paid £16.2bn to 53 companies so far under its largest bailout scheme. Under the Coronavirus Corporate Financing Facility (CCFF), the Bank buys commercial paper from the companies in exchange for a short-term loan repayable at rates of between 0.2% and 0.6%. Ryanair and easyjet have both received £600m and British Airways and Wizz £300m. All four airlines have announced plans to make almost 20,000 redundancies. Carmaker Nissan accessed £600m, Toyota £365m and Honda's financing arm £75m, while engine manufacturer Rolls-Royce, which began consultations on more than 3,000 redundancies at the start of June, took £300m. In the hospitality sector, Intercontinental Hotels received £600m, and pub operators and brewers Fullers and Youngs £100m and £30m respectively. Other recipients of funds under the CCFF include Tottenham Hotspur's stadium company (£175m); John Lewis (£300m), Marks & Spencer (£260m); Greggs (£150m) and the National Trust (£30m). The largest single recipient was chemicals company BASF, taking £1bn. £3.5bn of additional expenditure has been used to bail out train operators.

Meanwhile, some 21,000 more UK businesses collapsed in March than the same month a year before, a 70% increase. The number of new companies also dropped by 23%.

At the start of May, about 52,000 companies had applied for the Coronavirus Business Interruption Loan (CIBIL), of which not quite half had been approved for loans worth £4.2bn – £12bn less than that taken by those 53 corporations. Borrowers have claimed lenders are slow, bureaucratic and set punitive terms. Lenders say customers are wary of taking on the extra debt in a time of extreme uncertainty.

City executives warned in a letter to the BoE that British companies trying to survive could be saddled with £105bn of unsustainable debt. Three senior bankers estimated that up to half of 608,000 borrowers of £18.5bn in 'bounce back' loans are unlikely to be repaid. The Bounce Back Loan Scheme (BBLS) facilities are capped at £50,000 with a term of up to six years and come with a

100% government guarantee on the capital and interest. Although the guarantee spares the banks from credit risk, executives are worried that pursuing through the courts 100,000s of small, often family-run businesses, which have borrowed an average of £30,000 each, would be logistically impossible and a "PR disaster".

Interest rates

The Fed moved baseline interest rates to 0.1-0.25% and the BoE to 0.1%, down from 1.75% and 0.75% respectively. In December, Spain and Australia sold 10-year government bonds at negative yields for the first time.

As Grossman says:

"The rate of interest is related to the profit rate in a similar way as the market price of a commodity is to its value. In so far as the rate of interest is determined by the profit rate, this is always through the *general* rate of profit and not through the specific profit rates that may prevail in particular branches of industry ... The general rate of profit, *in fact, reappears in the average rate of interest as an empirical, given fact.*"[862]

While the BoE initially ruled out a negative rate, saying this would "affect the viability of banks", it later admitted such a move was "under active review". The baseline rate has never gone negative in the BoE's 324-year history (before 2010 it had never even gone much below 2%).[863] Banks said negative rates would slash their earnings and limit their ability to absorb loan losses. Bank of America analysts estimated that a BoE rate cut of just -0.25% would take 50% off Barclays' domestic pre-tax profit, rising to more than 70% for RBS. Investors are also unhappy about the possibility of negative rates, after British banks bowed to pressure from the BoE's Prudential Regulation Authority and halted dividend payments. That helped drive down shares in FTSE-listed banks by 37%, levels last seen around the 2008-09 crisis.

Andrew Wilson, chairman of global fixed income at Goldman Sachs Asset Management, said, "escaping from negative rates is extremely challenging, as the ECB is discovering", while Kit Juckes, a strategist at Société Générale, said, "I can't think of an economy where negative rates are a worse idea than the UK. The economic benefits are dubious but the power of a cocktail of negative rates and massive quantitative easing to weaken the currency seems clear and if the pound falls enough, it will make QE harder." Richard Werner, an economist at Oxford University, even complained that negative rates "lead to centrally-planned credit and the Sovietisation of banking".

But pressure on the BoE to cheapen lending mounted as annual UK consumer price inflation slipped to 0.2% in August, threatening a deflationary spiral. The situation is the same almost everywhere. Philip Lane, chief economist of the European Central Bank, reiterated in August that it was prepared to inject more monetary stimulus to ensure that inflation did not persistently undershoot its target of just under 2%. He said such low inflation would be "costly" in slowing the recovery from the pandemic and "risky" because "a longer phase of even lower inflation might become entrenched and contribute to a downward drift in inflation expectations".

Jay Powell, who took over as Fed chair in 2018, said that "moderate" inflation above 2% may be tolerated on a temporary basis to make up for months of low inflation. The median forecast of Fed officials does not predict an interest rate increase until after 2022 at the earliest. Powell has previously said that the Fed is "not thinking about thinking" about tightening policy. He admitted, though, that "the Fed has less scope to support the economy during an economic downturn by simply cutting the federal funds rate". When the time comes, he may feel there is no other choice but to try.

If the lockdown were to be fully lifted, the mix of pent-up demand and depleted supply chains would produce high inflation. Tackling this would usually require the raising of interest rates, but doing so too much would at some point collapse the tax base, since mountainous government debt would become too expensive to repay and trigger panic selling. The ruling classes potentially have very little incentive to *ever* fully lift lockdowns, with the pandemic having provided a scapegoat for the economic crisis, the closure of small businesses (to accelerate monopolisation) and even the privatisation of public education – a catastrophe for the social development of children and their privacy, with online schooling generating a treasure trove of data tech firms can buy and sell.[864] To be clear, this means raising the tax burden on parents – making them poorer – in order to pay the likes of Google and Microsoft to 'educate' their kids (in how to obey and serve capital).

This goes to show just how dependent on the state capital has become and illustrates what is meant by the World Economic Forum's touting of a 'great reset', with one of its economists anticipating a rent-only economy circa 2030 in which we are told, "You will own nothing and you'll be happy."[865] Such talk surely represents capitalism's last gasp.

Smith's analysis has come to a similar conclusion as ours:

"In the end, dollar bills, like bond and share certificates, are just pieces of paper. As trillions more of them flood into the system, events in March

2020 bring closer the day when investors will lose faith in cash itself – and in the power of the economy and state standing behind it… [Democratic socialists] see the decline of interest rates into negative territory not as a flashing red light showing the extremity of the crisis, but as a green light to borrow money… In fact, *there is no magic money tree.* Capitalism cannot escape from this crisis, no matter how many trillions of dollars governments borrow or central banks print… The trillions they spent after [2008-09] bought another decade of zombie-like life for their vile system… The coronavirus [crash] makes socialist revolution – in imperialist countries and across the world – into a necessity."

★

The IMF has set aside $1 trillion in loans for 81 developing countries. "The aggregate external financing gaps of developing countries are likely to be far beyond the IMF's lending capacity," according to Martin Wolff in the *FT*. Furthermore, as Wolf suggests, the purpose of IMF loans is to help with "external financing gaps" – in other words, to bail out imperialist creditors, not the peoples of debtor nations.[866] According to Oxfam, 76 out of the IMF loans negotiated with 81 countries since March 2020 encourage and in some cases require yet tougher austerity measures. The time when the debtor nations of the oppressed world are driven to rebel against their creditor, oppressor nations draws nearer.

★

Mass strikes and explosive protests rocked the world in 2019 and 2020, before and during the pandemic, perhaps most notably in Haiti, Nigeria, Ethiopia, India, Chile, Bolivia, France and the US.

In India, where capital has started its bid to expropriate the last small farmers, 250 million people staged the largest ever general strike. The outcome of this struggle could determine how soon accumulation collapses for good, since 'modernising' these farms represents the final realm of monopolisation.

In the US, the racist police murder in May 2020 of George Floyd, a recently unemployed black man, sparked incendiary riots across the country, coming threateningly close to the White House itself.

A bonfire of civil rights has followed.[867] With the pandemic serving as a convenient pretext, the ruling classes have imposed yet more forms of social control, enclosure and surveillance across the whole world.[868]

The class struggle has already begun.

Notes

Introduction
1. Engels, "The part played by labour in the transition from man to ape", *The Dialectics of Nature*, Marx and Engels, *Collected Works*, Vol 25, Ch 9, pp460-1.
2. Willeit et al, "Mid-Pleistocene transition in glacial cycles explained by declining CO_2 and regolith removal", *Science Advances* vol 5, no 4, 3 April 2019.
3. "Climate deadline more like 18 months instead of 12 years, some experts say", GlobalNews.ca, 5 August 2019.
4. "IPCC reports 'diluted' under 'political pressure' to protect fossil fuel interests", TheGuardian.com, 15 May 2014.
5. "Big Oil's real agenda on climate change", InfluenceMap, March 2019.
6. To put that in context, the number of Syrian refugees reaching Europe during the war on Syria has been around one million.
7. Max Planck Institute for Chemistry and the Cyprus Institute, "Climate-exodus expected in the Middle East and North Africa", ScienceDaily.com, 2 May 2016.
8. Spratt and Dunlop, *Existential Climate-related Security Risk: A Scenario Approach*, Breakthrough – National Centre for Climate Restoration, May 2019.
9. "NASA: Earth is warming at a pace 'unprecedented in 1,000 years'", TheGuardian.com, 30 August 2016.
10. Zemp et al, "Global glacier mass changes and their contributions to sea-level rise from 1961 to 2016", *Nature.com*, 8 April 2019.
11. Farquharson et al, "Climate change drives widespread and rapid thermokarst development in very cold permafrost in the Canadian High Arctic", *Geophysical Research Letters*, 10 June 2019.
12. David Wallace-Wells, "The Uninhabitable Earth", *New York Magazine*, 17 July 2018. Also stored in the Arctic are ancient diseases, "in some cases, since before humans were around to encounter them" – meaning our immune systems "may not be equipped" to combat them – along with more recent bugs, such as the 1918 flu, smallpox and the bubonic plague. Many such organisms won't survive the thaw, but in 2017 a boy died and 20 others were infected by anthrax released when retreating permafrost exposed the frozen carcass of a reindeer killed by the bacteria at least 75 years earlier. 2,000 live reindeer were infected, too, carrying and spreading the disease beyond the tundra. Diseases like dengue fever and malaria could spread into the warming 'Global North'. Malaria, for instance, thrives in hotter regions not just because the mosquitoes that carry it do, too, but because for every degree increase in temperature, the parasite reproduces ten times faster.
13. Wallace-Wells, *The Uninhabitable Earth*, Penguin, New York, 2019, p12.
14. Ibid, p68.
15. Laybourn-Langton et al, *This is a Crisis: Facing Up to the Age of Environmental Breakdown*, Institute for Public Policy Research, 12 February 2019.
16. Wallace-Wells, 2018.
17. "Heatwaves sweeping oceans 'like wildfires', scientists reveal", TheGuardian.com, 4 March 2019.
18. Landrigan et al, "The Lancet Commission on pollution and health", *The Lancet*, vol 391, no 10119, 19 October 2017.
19. "Third of Earth's soil is acutely degraded due to agriculture", TheGuardian.com, 12 September 2017.
20. "Only 60 years of farming left if soil degradation continues", ScientificAmerican.com, 5 December 2014.
21. Baccini et al, "Tropical forests are a net carbon source based on aboveground measurements of gain and loss", *Science* Vol 358, Issue 6360, 13 October 2017.

22. "All but the one that killed the dinosaurs were caused by climate change produced by GHG. The most notorious was 252 million years ago; it began when carbon warmed the planet by five degrees, accelerated when that warming triggered the release of methane in the Arctic, and ended with 97% of all life on Earth dead. We are currently adding carbon to the atmosphere at a considerably faster rate; by most estimates, at least ten times faster. The rate is accelerating. This is what Stephen Hawking had in mind when he said... that the species needs to colonise other planets in the next century to survive." Wallace-Wells, 2018. During the Permian-Triassic extinction, atmospheric carbon levels had reached 1,000ppm.

23. According to some estimates, that would mean that whole regions of Africa and Australia and the US, parts of South America north of Patagonia and Asia south of Siberia would be rendered uninhabitable by direct heat, desertification and flooding. Wallace-Wells, 2019, p6.

24. University of Edinburgh, "Climate outlook may be worse than feared", *Earth and Environmental Transactions*, ScienceDaily.com, 9 December 2015.

25. Wallace-Wells, 2018, p14.

26. Schneider et al, "Possible climate transitions from breakup of stratocumulus decks under greenhouse warming", *Nature Geoscience* 12, pp163-7, 25 February 2019.

27. Will Denayer, "How climate change is rapidly taking the planet apart", Flashback-Economics.com, 20 July 2016.

28. Alberto Saldamando, a lawyer with the Indigenous Environmental Network, said: "The Paris accord is a trade agreement, nothing more. It promises to privatise, commodify and sell forested lands as carbon offsets in fraudulent schemes. These offset schemes provide a financial laundering mechanism for developed countries to launder their carbon pollution on the backs of the Global South. For example, the US's climate change plan includes 250 million megatonnes to be absorbed by oceans and forest offset markets. Essentially, those responsible for the climate crisis not only get to buy their way out of compliance but they also get to profit from it." Alston's report for the UN, published in June 2019, said that developing nations are expected to suffer at least 75% of the costs of climate change, despite the fact that the poorer half of the world's population generates just 10% of emissions. He said "those who have contributed the least to emissions... will be the most harmed" and warned that the effects could undo 50 years of progress on poverty reduction.

29. "Quarter of world's biggest firms 'fail to disclose emissions'", TheGuardian.com, 10 July 2019.

30. "North American drilling boom threatens major blow to climate efforts – report", TheGuardian.com, 25 April.

31. "Majority of European firms have no CO_2 reduction targets", TheGuardian.com, 19 February 2019.

32. George Monbiot, "Averting climate breakdown by restoring ecosystems: a call to action", NaturalClimate.Solutions.

33. Richard Seymour, "The climate strike is a source for hope – but new research shows it might be too late", Independent.co.uk, 16 March 2019.

34. Yanis Varoufakis, *The Global Minotaur: America, Europe and the Future of the Global Economy*, Verso, London, third edition, 2015, p161. A derivative is a contract, a bet, between two or more parties whose value is based on an agreed-upon underlying financial asset, index or security, such as bonds, commodities, currencies, interest rates, market indexes and stocks. Originally, derivatives were used as a means of hedging future price risk by individuals or companies that experience significant price volatility (oil, cattle, etc). For instance, if a cattle farmer was concerned about the future price he'd get for a herd of cattle when the time comes to slaughter them, he could hedge his risk by buying a derivative that gave him the right to sell his cattle at a particular price, no matter what the market turns out to be paying for

cattle at slaughter time. Regulated derivatives pass through transparent open exchanges. Unregulated, over-the-counter derivatives are privately traded between 'dealer' banks, priced on the dealers' valuation. The unregulated market overtook the unregulated market in the US in the 1990s, hitting $16.8 trillion in 1995 – twice the size of then US GDP. See Graham Summers, *The Everything Bubble*, 2017, loc 1283. The value of these bets is not the same as the value of the underlying asset, so the value of the bet fluctuates based on the value of the asset at any given time. If an asset depreciates, the value of the bet is worth less. This created a systemic issue for big banks trading in derivatives as 64% of unregulated derivatives ($11 trillion) were related to (falling) interest rates (Summers, *op cit*, loc 98-105).

35. Brazil's far right president Jair Bolsonaro, elected in 2018, promised to open the Amazon – which absorbs a quarter of all the carbon absorbed by the planet's forests – up to deforestation, threatening to release an estimated 13.12 gigatonnes of carbon between 2021 and 2030. For reference, in 2017 the US emitted 5 gigatonnes. By August 2019, fires in the Amazon had risen by more than 80% compared with 2018.

36. Asad Rehman, "The 'green new deal' supported by Ocasio-Cortez and Corbyn is just a new form of colonialism", Independent.co.uk, 4 May 2019.

37. Under capitalism, the worker is alienated from the products of their labour, which are appropriated and sold by the capitalist. Since those products are made from nature, the worker is also alienated from nature. The worker cannot rely on nature for his needs but must sell his labour to survive. Since man is a part of nature, he is therefore even alienated from himself. This estrangement is exacerbated by the centralising needs of capital accumulation, manifesting in the urban-rural divide.

38. Janet Burns, "How cannabis coevolved with humanity, and could save it now", Forbes.com, 21 March 2020.

1. The greatest overaccumulation of capital, the greatest ever capitalist crisis

39. Henryk Grossman, *The Law of Accumulation and Breakdown of the Capitalist System*, Pluto Press, London, 1992 (first published in 1929), p85.

40. Larry Fink, "BlackRock CEO Larry Fink tells the world's biggest business leaders to stop worrying about short-term results", BusinessInsider.com, 14 April 2015.

41. Democratic socialists in theory believe that socialism can be built by voting for 'socialist policies' through bourgeois democracy, the label at the same time implying that communists are 'authoritarian socialists' and anti-democratic. Yet while democratic socialists certainly aim to make capitalism more democratic, it is only communists who offer the full enfranchisement of the working class with the promise of participative and direct rather than merely representative democracy.

42. Yanis Varoufakis, "Capitalism will eat democracy – unless we speak up", December 2015, ted.com. In *The Global Minotaur* Varoufakis one-sidedly claims the "rhythm of the economy is set by large corporations"; that investment is determined by "optimism" (p46); and (entirely wrongly) that a reduction in wages and interest rates "deepens the recession" (p49). He recognises that value production tends towards zero, but says this only happens "the more successful corporations are" at replacing "human agency" with machinery, suggesting the process is not historical and can be reversed – that capitalism can be saved. He says capitalism is in crisis globally because of the US's "failure" to show "self-restraint" but insists it can be revived if the US leads on introducing a "global surplus recycling mechanism". This would do nothing to create new value and rely on surplus nations to voluntarily shrink their own economies. Moreover, the US is now a deficit nation.

43. Ron Surz, "Per capita world debt has surged to over $200,000", Nasdaq.com, 24 July 2019.

44. Michael Pento, *The Coming Bond Market Collapse*, Wiley, New Jersey, 2013, p53.

45. Typically a given bank's reserve funds (their deposits with the central bank) are meant to equate to about 10% of that bank's savings. Banks with excess capital lend it to each other. The interest rate on these loans is the base interest rate. In the case of the Federal Reserve in the US, this is called the Target Federal Funds Rate, considered the 'cost of money' in the financial system. If the rate is 0.5-1%, but the banks start lending money to each other at rates above this range, say 1.25%, then this money indicates that the cost of money in the system is getting 'expensive'. The Fed will start buying securities from the banks, taking them out of the system (putting them on its balance sheet) and putting money into it, increasing the base money supply in the financial system, forcing rates to go lower (money is more abundant so 'costs' less). The same process works in reverse: the Fed sells securities, puts assets into the financial system and takes money out, reducing the amount of base money circulating in the financial system, causing rates to rise and making money more expensive. So there is no exact rate central banks control.

46. John Burn-Murdoch and Magnus Bennetzen, "Where are the world's corporate cash reserves?", FT.com, 21 January 2014.

47. Robin Harding, "Corporate investment: a mysterious divergence", FT.com, 24 July 2013.

48. Cardiff Garcia, "The US Capital Stock: Old and busted, but why?", *FT Alphaville*, 1 November, 2013.

49. John Smith, *Imperialism in the Twenty First Century*, Monthly Review Press, New York, 2016, p292.

50. Households' surplus was 0.9% of GDP; the external balance made up the difference. Figures quoted from Martin Wolf, "Britain needs to whittle down corporate cash piles", FT.com, 16 February, 2012.

51. Martin Wolf, "Japan's unfinished policy revolution", FT.com, 9 April, 2013. Depreciation is a charge on income, so the sum of the two is less than gross retained earnings.

52. Quoted in Smith, ibid.

53. David Bowers, "Watch out as sovereigns eye company cash piles", FT.com, 8 February 2012.

54. David Yaffe, "Brexit intensifies Britain's crisis", *FRFI* 252 August/September 2016. All *FRFI* articles referenced can be found on the website revolutionarycommunist.org.

55. "Federal government: tax receipts on corporate Income", Federal Reserve Bank of St Louis.

56. "Corporation tax rates", FigureWizard.com.

57. When former Prime Minister David Cameron said, "I'm determined that the UK must not become a safe haven for corrupt money from around the world," it already was one. Of the 214,000 companies listed in the leaked Panama Papers, more than half were registered in UK overseas territories or crown dependencies, which have tax treaties with the City of London. Particularly popular is the British Virgin Islands (BVI). Some 950,000 businesses are incorporated there. Jersey held $1.7 trillion of deposits in 2013 and, together with Guernsey, generates around $100bn in revenue a year for British banks.

58. "Reality check: how much did the banking crisis cost taxpayers?", TheGuardian.com; "The real size of the bailout", MotherJones.com. According to Matt Taibi, "Companies like AIG, GM and Citigroup were given tens of billions of deferred tax assets – allowing them to carry losses from 2008 forward to offset future profits and keep future tax bills down. Official estimates of the bailout's costs do not include such ongoing giveaways. 'This is stuff that's never going to appear on any report,' says former bailout Inspector General Neil Barofsky. Citigroup, all by itself, boasts more than $50bn in deferred tax credits – which is how the firm managed to

pay less in taxes in 2011 (it actually received a $144m credit) than it paid in compensation that year to its since-ousted dingbat CEO, Vikram Pandit (who pocketed $14.9m)." "Secrets and lies of the bailout", *Rolling Stone*, 4 January 2013.

59. "US debt by president by dollar and percentage", TheBalance.com. The top three highest borrowing presidents: FD Roosevelt (1933-45; 1,048%; £240bn); Woodrow Wilson (1913-21; 727%; £20bn); and Ronald Reagan (1981-89; 186%; £1.86 trillion.)

60. "From taxes to transport: visualizing America's $27 trillion debt", World Economic Forum, 11 November.

61. Grennes et al, "Finding the tipping point – when sovereign debt turns bad", 2013.

62. "An honest debate about austerity and tax", FlipChartFairyTales.wordpress.com, 17 July 2017.

63. Ibid.

64. Ellie Mae MacDonald, "The gendered impact of austerity: Cuts are widening the poverty gap between women and men", LSE.ac.uk, 10 January 2010. In Britain, a woman earns 82p for every £1 a man earns.

65. Women's Budget Group, "Intersecting Inequalities", wbg.org.uk, 5 June 2018.

66. In the US, Josh Bivens writes for the Economic Policy Institute that, "Astoundingly, per capita government spending in the first quarter of 2016 – twenty-seven quarters into the recovery – was nearly 4.9% lower than at the trough of the Great Recession. By contrast, 27 quarters into the early 1990s recovery, per capita government spending was 3.6% higher than at the trough; 24 quarters after the early 2000s recession (a shorter recovery that did not last a full 27 quarters), it was almost 10% higher; and 27 quarters into the early 1980s recovery, it was more than 17% higher… If government spending following the Great Recession's end had tracked the spending that followed the early 1980s recession – the only other post-war recession of similar magnitude – governments in 2016 would have been spending almost a trillion dollars more in that year alone." "What should we know about the next recession?", EPI.org, 18 April 2019.

67. Watkins et al, "Effects of health and social care spending constraints on mortality in England: a time trend analysis", *British Medical Journal*, vol 7, issue 11, November 2017.

68. FlipChartFairyTales.wordpress.com, *op cit*.

2. Breakdown theory is crisis theory

69. Grossman, *op cit*, p85.

70. Karl Marx, *Capital* Vol 1, Penguin Classics, London, 1990, p125.

71. Grossman, *op cit*, p155.69.

72. Ibid, p31-2.

73. That higher labour-intensity produces higher profit rates has been confirmed by statistical mechanics. See Paul Cockshott, "How physics is validating the labour theory of value." For a more mathematical proof of the labour theory of value, see Andrew Kliman, "Debt, economic crisis, and the tendential fall in the profit rate: a temporal perspective", May, 1999.

74. Ibid, p133.

75. Marx, 1991, p358.

76. Grossman, *op cit*, p32.

77. Ibid. p59.

78. Ibid, p164.

79. Ibid, p33.

80. Before the Russian Revolution all of the major Marxist parties were "social democratic".

81. Quoted in ibid, p39.

82. Quoted in ibid, p43.

83. Ibid, p44.
84. Quoted in ibid, p45.
85. Quoted in ibid, p40.
86. Ibid, p45.
87. Ibid, p54.
88. Quoted in ibid, p55.
89. Quoted in ibid, p54.
90. Quoted in ibid, p56.
91. Ibid, p56.
92. Quoted in ibid, p51.
93. Ibid, p51.
94. Ibid, pp52, 55.
95. Opportunism didn't do the SPD much good. Having sided with the High Command of the Imperial Armed Forces and proto-fascist freikorps paramilitaries to slaughter communists and independent social democrats (and even some of their own militant supporters) – starting with the murder of leaders Rosa Luxemburg and Karl Liebknecht – when the 1929 crash made the SPD's social reforms completely unaffordable, the ruling class could no longer tolerate them and the same High Command turned to the Nazis to crush the SPD and its supporters in the labour movement. The SPD was outlawed and many SPD members, including Hilferding, were murdered.
96. Grossman, *op cit*, p199.
97. Ibid, p200.
98. Ibid.
99. Ibid, pp41-2.
100. Ibid, p48.
101. Ibid, pp50-51.
102. Grossman and Kuhn, *Capitalism's Contradictions: Studies of Economic Thought Before and After Marx*, Haymarket, Chicago, 2017, p127.
103. Grossman, *op cit*, p31.
104. Ibid, p30.
105. Ibid.
106. Ibid, p31.
107. Ibid, pp67-8.
108. Ibid, p71.
109. Ibid, p72.
110. Ibid.
111. Ibid.
112. Marx, *Capital* vol 3, Penguin Classics, London, 1991, p359.
113. Grossman, *op cit*, p75-6.
114. Ibid, p77.
115 Ibid, p76; Marx, 1991, p360.
116. Grossman, *op cit*, p77-8.
117. Ibid, p82.
118. Ibid.
119.Ibid, p96.
120. That we later show how capitalist corporations increasingly plan from within should not be confused with the idea of a planned capitalism as a whole, which competition for profits between individual capitals makes impossible; and as we see here could not prevent breakdown anyway.
121. Grossman, *op cit*, p156.
122. Ibid, p87.
123. Ibid, p108.

124. Marx, *Grundrisse*, Penguin Classics, London, 1993, p703.
125. Grossman, *op cit*, p135.
126. Ibid, p132.
127. Marx, 1991, p338.
128. Ibid, p361.
129. Tepper and Hearn, *The Myth of Capitalism: Monopolies and the Death of Competition*, John Wiley & Sons, 2018, xv.
130. Ibid, p200. Tepper and Hearn lament that business schools in US universities teach their students to eliminate rivals, and that if they find themselves in possession of a small competitor they should sell it to an interested monopoly rather than try and fail to compete (pp13-15). While complaining that "the government has been captured by the companies it is meant to regulate", they appeal to the very same rulers to change things with the utopian demand of breaking up the monopolies. "If we do not get reform, we will get a revolution that we have not chosen (p239)."
131. Bebchuck and Hirst, *The Spectre of the Giant Three*, Harvard Law School, May 2019.
132. Vitali et al, *The Network of Global Corporate Control*, PLOS ONE, 26 October 2011.
133. Brian Becker, *Imperialism in the 21st Century*, Liberation Media, 2015, p13.
134. Tepper and Hearn, *op cit*, p10.
135. Ibid, p9.
136. Marx, 1990, p748.
137. Grossman, *op cit*, p140.
138. Ibid, p142. Grossman here effectively anticipates the 'Just-In-Time' (JIT) production system perfected by Japanese carmaker Toyota and now the *de facto* standard for the modern car factory, whereby orders arrive more or less as they re required. Toyota describes JIT as: "A 'pull' system of providing the different processes in the assembly sequence with only the kinds and quantities of items that they need and only when it needs them. The primary objectives of JIT are to save warehouse space and unnecessary cost-carrying and to improve efficiency, which means organising the delivery of component parts to individual work stations just before they are physically required. To apply this flow efficiently means relying on ordering signals from *Kanban* [visual signal] boards or by forecasting parts usage ahead of time, though this latter method requires production numbers to remain stable. Use of JIT means that individual cars can be built to order and that every component has to fit perfectly first time because there are no alternatives available. It is therefore impossible to hide pre-existing manufacturing issues; they have to be addressed immediately." Toyota says that 30,000 or so components that go into a car can be assembled from raw material into the finished product in around 17-18 hours, whether that is at its mothership factories in Nagoya, or its many subsidiaries around the world.
139. Grossman: "... this cannot be emphasised enough – the reproduction process is not simply a valorisation process; it is also a labour process, producing not only values but also use-values. Considered from the side of use-value, increases in the productivity of labour represent not merely a devaluation of the existing capital, but also a quantitative expansion of useful things." *Op cit*, p144.
140. Marx, 1991, p355.
141. Quoted in Grossman, *op cit*, p147.
142. Quoted in ibid, p148.
143. Ibid, p148.
144. Ibid, pp148-9.
145. Marx, 1991, pp442-3.
146. Quoted in Grossman, *op cit*, p152.
147. Ibid, p153.

148. "Services close to 80% of UK economy", FT.com, 31 March.
149. Slavery became a fetter on capital because slaves are a form of constant capital and humans could not work as fast as improving machinery. Nor could it be enforced in urban settings. A contributing factor to the collapse of slavery in both the ancient Mediterranean and the US was its exhaustion of the agricultural land.
150. "Britain's biggest export: wealth", Economist.com, 9 January 2015.
151. France, for example, extracts 85% of 14 African countries' foreign reserves as colonial debt annually. Although the smaller European countries are part of this imperialist bloc and are therefore not oppressed nations in the traditional sense, they are dominated and plundered by Germany and France. If the so-called PIIGS nations – Portugal, Ireland, Italy, Greece and Spain – left the EU, they would take 58% of the value of Europe's banks with them. See James Bell, "Approaching the eurozone crisis", jrbml.wordpress.com, 27 September 2015. Europe initially gloated that the 2008 crisis was an Anglo-Celtic one. German banks ended up with an average ratio of €52 borrowed to every €1, a ratio worse than that racked up by Wall Street or the City of London (Varoufakis, *op cit*, p203). Whether Russia and China have become or are becoming imperialist is beyond the scope of this investigation.
152. Figures from "Financial flows and tax havens: combining to limit the lives of billions of people", Global Financial Integrity (GFI) and the Centre for Applied Research at the Norwegian School of Economics, December 2016. Quoted in Jason Hickel, "Aid in Reverse: how poor countries develop rich countries", TheGuardian.com, 14 January 2017.
153. Quoted in Smith, *op cit*, p49.
154. Mark Curtis, *The New Colonialism: Britain's Scramble for Africa's Energy and Mineral Resources*, War on Want, July 2016. "While the scale and scope of the UK's involvement in the exploitation of Africa's mineral resources is staggering, so too is the trail of social, environmental and human rights abuses left in its wake."
155. Smith, "The GDP Illusion", *Monthly Review*, 1 July 2012.
156. The term 'oppressed nation' used to refer to the colonies of the Empires. Since most of them have achieved at least nominal independence (and the empires have nominally ended), it is now not always a satisfactory definition. For example, while Ireland (occupied by Britain) and Palestine (occupied by Zionist Israel) remain oppressed nations in the old sense, Venezuela, for example, even though it is under attack from US imperialism, technically is not; it is a sovereign nation. General references to neocolonial, oppressed, exploited, underdeveloped or developing/emerging countries will have to suffice for this investigation. NB: According to Tony Norfield, author of *The City: London and the Global Power of Finance*, in 2010, Ireland's GDP amounted to €156bn. However, "from this sum a net income amounting to nearly €28bn was paid in wages, profits, interest and dividends to foreigners. Ireland did receive €1.5bn of EU subsidies, but against this it paid the EU €400m in taxes. Gross National Income accruing to Irish residents totalled €129.3bn, 17% less than the value of output in the domestic economy. So, nearly one-fifth ... from Ireland's annual output was paid to foreign investors. Owing to this factor, domestic incomes also tend to grow by an average of 0.5% less than that of output." See, "Ireland's imperial tithe", economicsofimperilaism.blogspot.com, 1 July 2011.
157. "High income" does not necessarily correlate to 'imperialist' nor "mid to low income" to 'oppressed/neocolonial/developing'. The high-income nations are: Australia, Austria, Canada, Denmark, Finland, Germany, Ireland, Italy, Japan, Netherlands, New Zealand, Norway, Portugal, Switzerland, United Kingdom, United States. Low- and middle-income nations: Algeria, Argentina, Bangladesh, Benin, Bolivia, Brazil, Cameroon, Central African Republic, Chile, Colombia, Costa Rica, Croatia, Ecuador, Egypt, El Salvador, Ghana, Guatemala, Honduras, Hong Kong, Hungary, India, Indonesia, Jamaica, Jordan, Kenya, South Korea, Madagascar,

Malawi, Malaysia, Mauritius, Mexico, Morocco, Nepal, Nicaragua, Nigeria, Oman, Pakistan, Panama, Papua New Guinea, Paraguay, Peru, Philippines, Romania, Saudi Arabia, Senegal, Slovenia, Sri Lanka, Thailand, Togo, Trinidad and Tobago, Tunisia, Turkey, Uruguay, Venezuela, Yemen, Zimbabwe.

158. The WDIs do not provide a value for Chinese MVA in 2002. Including China, total trade of low- and middle-income nations increased by 434.3%. In 2001, these 55 nations produced 61.2% of the combined GDP of all 156 low- and middle-income nations listed in the WDI tables; this rises to 79.4% if China is included.
159. Smith, *op cit*, pp96-7.
160. Grossman, *op cit*, p172.
161. Ibid.
162. Ibid, p122.
163. Ibid.
164. Ibid, p181.
165. Ibid.
166. Ibid, p197.
167. Ben Reynolds, *The Coming Revolution: Capitalism in the 21st Century*, Zero Books, 2018, loc 2774.
168. Ibid, p85.

3. Defining automation: the fourth industrial revolution?

169. *Aristotle's Politics*, translated by Carnes Lord, University of Chicago Press, book I, chapter 4, 2013.
170. Marx, 1993, p705.
171. Ibid, p702.
172. Marx would say the same of himself, for his work built on and corrected the idealist philosophy of Hegelian dialectics and the classical bourgeois political economy of the likes of David Ricardo and Adam Smith, who both posited a labour theory of value (one-sidedly focused on exchange-value), along with Simonde de Sismondi (and others who saw history as an evolutionary succession of systems), who, Grossman argues, was "the scientific discoverer of capitalistic dynamics". See Grossman, "Sismondi, Jean Charles Leonard Simonde de", Marxists.org, 1934.
173. Marx, *Capital*, 1990, pp496-7. The first generalised example of machine-aided mass production was the printing press, which revolutionised the production of text – the first globally mass-produced product – and images. The cost of books, which had been extremely labour intensive to make, fell to 2% in England of the price of an average manuscript prior to the advent of printing. "A man born in 1453, the year of the fall of Constantinople, could look back from his fiftieth year on a lifetime in which about eight million books had been printed, more than perhaps all the scribes of Europe had produced since Constantine founded his city in AD 330." Quoted in Reynolds, loc 122-31. "Ultimately, the explosion of production created by the printing press made it necessary to overcome the limitations of local markets," says Reynolds. "Thus, the printing press established the *industrial production paradigm*." (A production paradigm is the technical foundation of a mode of production.) While it took around 350 years for the industrial production paradigm to expand to other commodities, and 45 years for the steam-powered loom to overtake the handloom in textile production in Britain, it took only a decade for personal computers to make minicomputers obsolete (loc 569).
174. Genrikh Volkov, *Era of Man or Robot? The Sociological Problems of the Technical Revolution*, Progress Publishers, Moscow, 1967, p159.
175. Ibid, p40.
176. Marx, 1993, p705.
177. Volkov, *op cit*, p45.

178. Sam Lilley, *Automation and Social Progress*, Lawrence & Wishart, London, 1956, p13.
179. Volkov, *op cit*, p50.
180. Ibid, pp50-1.
181. The peasantry remains in some small vestiges of rural life in the oppressed world, particularly on the African continent. And a significant branch of artisanal labour has not yet been eliminated, namely, the traditional arts. The painter, for example, still produces commodities *before* securing a sale of their labour-power. In general, they do not own capital, locating this relationship as an artisanal one. While modern branches of the arts (beginning with film) work by the relations of capital and certain traditional artists operate as capitalists, the general organisation of the labour remains in this form.
182. For example, half the population in Nigeria now has access to the internet. But rather than going through the sequence of adopting landline access and then mobile access, as in Europe and North America, Nigeria leapfrogged the former and adopted mobile internet *en masse*. (Aaron Bastani, *Fully Automated Luxury Communism: A Manifesto*, Verso, London, 2019, p108.) This is not to claim that imperialism does not continue to under-develop the non-imperialist world. However, most countries have now industrialised to an extent that was obviously not true before the Second World War, even if this development has been severely limited due to imperialist parasitism. Grossman backs up the point: "It is not necessarily true that in countries recently opened up to capitalist production the organic composition is always lower. While West European capitalism may have needed 150 years to evolve from the organisational form of the manufacturing period into the sophisticated world trust, the colonial nations do not need to repeat this entire process. They take over European capital in the most mature forms it has already assumed in the advanced capitalist countries. In this way they skip over a whole series of historical stages, with their peoples dragged straight into gold and diamond mines dominated by trustified capital and its extremely sophisticated technological and financial organisation." Grossman, *op cit*, p183.
183. Volkov, *op cit*, pp162-4.
184. Ibid, p166.

4. 'Technological unemployment' and fearful rulers
185. Ibid, p18.
186. "Coming to an office near you", Economist.com, 18 January 2014.
187. Keynes, *Economic Possibilities for Our Grandchildren*, 1930, p3.
188. Acemoglu and Restrepo, *Robots and Jobs: Evidence from US Labor Markets*, National Bureau of Economic Research, March 2017. Another analysis, by the Institute for Public Policy Research, said that twice as many women as men work in occupations with a high potential for automation (9% compared to 4% of men), and that 64% of jobs in these occupations are held by women. Migrants and lone parents (typically women) are more likely to hold jobs with high automation potential.
187. "Rapid robot rollout risks UK workers being left behind, reports say", TheGuardian.com, 26 June 2019.
190. Frey, *Wealth Creation, Not Job Creation is Impact of Tech Industries*, Oxford Martin Programme on Technology and Employment, 2 May 2015.
191. "A Goldman trading desk that once had 500 people is down to three", Bloomberg.com, 30 April 2018.
192. Frey and Osborne, *The Future of Employment: How Susceptible are Jobs to Computerisation?*, Oxford Martin Programme on Technology and Employment, September 2013.

193. Frey and Chen, *Technology at Work v3.0: Automating e-Commerce from Click to Pick to Door*, Oxford Martin Programme on Technology and Employment, August 2017.
194. "America's first robot farm replaces humans with 'incredibly intelligent' machines", TheGuardian.com, 9 October 2018.
195. "Robocrop: world's first raspberry-picking robot set to work", TheGuardian.com, 27 May 2019. Just 1.5% (476,000) of the British workforce worked directly on farms in 2019, down from 22% in 1850 (already the lowest anywhere at that time). The figure is also 1.5% in the US, down from 21% in the 1920s. The urban population in the US rose from 39.6% of the population in 1900 to 79% in 2000; between 1900 and 2005 the number of US farms fell by 63% and the average farm size grew by 67%). Reynolds, *op cit*, loc 885. Mechanisation had already had a profound impact on US farming by 1900: the labour needed to produce one acre of wheat fell from 61 hours in 1830 to three hours 19 minutes in 1896. Loc 1757. Today, the agriculture problem is returning to the bleak days of the Great Depression, when the US government bought produce for a guaranteed profit or ordered its destruction to raise prices. From 1996 to 2006, the cost of producing corn was higher than its sale price. Rising demand as a result of droughts, crop failures and biofuel production boosted prices for a while, but by 2015 corn production became unprofitable again. "The amazing thing about this example is that it was not a digitised piece of information but a physical commodity that first demonstrated this possibility. US agriculture became so productive that it could no longer carry on the production of exchange value. An industry that could easily feed everyone in the country teetered on the verge of collapse while people were going hungry in the streets. [This] demonstrates that Marx's remarkable prediction was right. The collapse of production for exchange value is not just a theoretical possibility. We can already observe it happening. An agricultural system that sacrificed everything from environmental standards to food quality and safety in the search for profit can no longer sustain production for profit on an independent basis. US agriculture has to be subsidised permanently or it will be unable to operate in a capitalist market." Reynolds, *op cit*, loc 1789-1805.
196. "Every progress in industry reduces the price of production and hence increases the rate of ground rent. In agriculture, however ... ground rent declines. These capitalist determinants of profitability evidently form 'one of the greatest obstacles to a rational agriculture' – but this has nothing to do with diminishing returns of the soil. [William] Petty already told us (1699) 'that the landlords of his time feared improvements in agriculture because they would cause the price of agricultural products and hinc [hence] (the level of) rent to fall'." Grossman, *Henryk Grossman Works* vol I, edited by Rick Kuhn, Brill 2017, p126.
197. "'Dehumanising, impenetrable, frustrating': the grim reality of job hunting in the age of AI", TheGuardian.com, 4 March 2018.
198. Joseph Rowntree Foundation, "In-work poverty hits record high as the housing crisis fuels insecurity", jrf.org.uk, 7 December 2016.
199. For a Marxist analysis of the gig economy, see Luke Meehan, "The gig economy: new name for old exploitation", *FRFI* 254, December 2016/annuary 2017.
200. "Gig economy in Britain doubles, accounting for 4.7 million workers", TheGuardian.com, 28 June 2019.
201. "What jobs will still be around in 20 years? Read this to prepare your future", TheGuardian.com, 26 June 2017.
202. Deloitte predicts 114,000 legal jobs in Britain – 40% of the sector – are likely to be automated over the next 20 years, and says technology has already replaced 31,000.
203. *How ICT Technology Drives the UK Office Economy*, Centre for Economics and Business Research, October 2013, p2.

204. Despite high absolute growth in productivity, the rate of productivity growth has been slowing for a long time. In 1987 Nobel Peace prize-winning economist Robert Solow famously said, "You can see the computer age everywhere but in the productivity statistics."
205. Quoted in TheGuardian.com, *op cit*, 26 June 2017.
206. Quoted in TheGuardian.com, "Robot revolution: rise of 'thinking' machines could exacerbate inequality", 5 November 2015.
207. *Disruptive Technologies: Advances that will Transform Life, Business, and The Global Economy*, McKinsey Global Institute, p4.
208. The same law has seen internet bandwidth, where user capacity has grown by between 25 and 50% a year since 1983 and data storage, which has likewise enjoyed an exponential function in space-to-cost ratio, with a gigabyte of storage falling from around $200,000 in 1980 to just $0.03 in 2014. Storing data as DNA is likely to be the next big leap, although it is some way off. A single gram of human DNA is able to store 215 petabytes (215 million gigabytes) of information. Bastani, *op cit*, p46. The number of devices connected to the internet exploded from 313,000 in 1990 to 100 million in 2000 and 15 billion in 2015.
209. Adair Turner, *Capitalism in the Age of Robots: Work, Income and Wealth in the 21st Century*, Institute for New Economic Thinking, April 2018, p3.
210. Ibid, p3-4.
211. Ibid, p5.
212. Keynes, *op cit*, p3.
213. Grossman, 1992, p79.
214. Ibid, p80.
215. Quoted in ibid, p128-9.
216. Ibid, p129.

5. Workerless factories, globalisation in retreat and the crisis of imperialism

217. Ibid, p122.
218. Lilley, *op cit*, p15.
219. Efficiency is especially notable in terms of the hours, days and months saved by design work that can now be done on modern computers.
220. Quoted in TheGuardian.com, *op cit*, 5 November 2015.
221. Ibid.
222. Ibid.
223. *Executive summary: World Robotics 2017 Industrial Robots*, International Federation of Robotics.
224. Ibid
225. Ibid.
226. "Robot factories could threaten jobs of millions of garment workers", TheGuardian.com, 16 July 2016.
227. Turner, *op cit*, p34.
228. TheGuardian.com, 16 July 2016.
229. "Sewbots to replace humans at new US garment factory", TheManufacturer.com, 29 August 2017.
230. That China has 'liberalised' or 'opened up' its economy since the 1970s to one extent or another is not in dispute. A definitive position on China's social character, however, is beyond the scope of this investigation. Whether China remains socialist or has become capitalist is not determined by 'good' or 'bad' policy. A detailed examination of the relationship between China's working class and the means of production is required to assert a position on the matter. China itself has said that it is 'building socialism' via a 'capitalist road' and will achieve this goal around 2050.

This suggests that it is capitalist and makes it impossible to know how sincere the leadership is about building socialism. It comes across as more Bernsteinian than Leninist. Some have argued that China is also imperialist. Again we are not taking a definitive view here. China's role as a direct economic competitor to the US, its frequent export of capital through its loans and FDI, and the Belt and Road Initiative, may suggest that it has become imperialist. Chinese capital is certainly at a more virile stage of accumulation compared to US capital; but its debt quadrupled between 2007 and 2015; and its GDP growth rates have fallen consistently (along with consumption relative to GDP), indicating that China is also suffering from an ever-growing overaccumulation of capital. China has not shown anything like the aggression of the US in foreign policy, however, and has been an ally to countries like Cuba and Venezuela. It has, though, been involved in proxy wars (arguably usually in a defensive way in opposition to US imperialism) and has become the number one seller of armed drones to the United Arab Emirates and Saudi Arabia.

231. "China's robot revolution", FT.com, 6 June 2016.
232. "The company that builds iPhones is replacing workers with robots", BusinessInsider.com, 25 May.
233. "The world's first humanless warehouse is run only by robots and is a model for the future", CNBC.com, 30 October 2018.
234. Whereas NASA's first space shuttle had 2.5 million moving parts and SpaceX machines possess around 100,000, Relativity Space aims for its rockets to have a thousand moving parts or less, fewer than most cars.
235. Bastani, *op cit*, p123.
236. Reynolds, *op cit*, loc 589-673; 1813.
237. Bland, *op cit*, 6 June 2016.
238. Turner, *op cit*, p33.
239. Ibid.
240. Ibid, p35.
241. Ibid, p34.
242. Andrew Norton, "Automation will end the dream of rapid economic growth for poorer countries", TheGuardian.com, 20 September 2016.
243. "Premature deindustrialization in the developing world", Dan Rodrik's Weblog, 12 February 2015.
244. Varoufakis, *op cit*, p226.
245. The demonisation and intimidation of benefits claimants has undoubtedly played a major role in the scandal of 'unclaimed' ie unpaid benefits – over £10bn of benefits went unclaimed in the UK in 2016-17, while benefit fraud accounts for just 0.7% of the UK welfare budget.
246. China's industrial rise saw its tech companies Huawei, Oppo and Vivo account for 43% of global smartphone sales in 2017, eclipsing Apple in the US and Korea's Samsung. In response Trump accused China of stealing technology and trade secrets. China imports more than 95% of its high-end computer chips, used in mobile phones, telecommunications equipment and computers. In 2016 China spent $227bn importing chips, more than it spent on oil.
247. "WTO warns on rise of protectionist measures by G20 economies", FT.com, 21 June.
248. See, for example, "6 December 1993: Anti-Soviet warrior puts his army on the road to peace", independent.co.uk; "MI5 was complicit in the activities of Manchester bomber Salman Abedi", Alison Banville, MorningStar; "Now the truth emerges: how the US fuelled the rise of Isis in Syria and Iraq," Seamus Milne, TheGuardian.co.uk, 3 June 2015.
249. David Yaffe, "British economy: weak link in the imperialist chain", *FRFI* 248, December 2015/January 2016.

250. Ibid.

251. Ibid.

252. Ibid.

253. Ibid.

254. "Britain's missing billions: revised figures reveal UK is £490bn poorer than previously thought", Telegraph.co.uk, 15 October 2017.

255. Despite the fact that there has been little in the way of mass class struggle since the Miners' Strike in the 1980s, Britain is arguably closer to falling to socialism than anywhere else. Britain has a very low rate of profit, very high organic composition of capital and record low interest rates, plus a services-based working class. If trade were to end capitalism in Britain would become all but impossible, given that the country would not even be able to import the materials needed to 'reindustrialise' and recreate a valorisation base. The British ruling class would have to attack the middle classes, not just the working class. Given that imperialism has necessitated a huge dependence on imports, the British population may be particularly vulnerable.

256. A "worst case scenario" Whitehall document obtained by Sky News estimates that the value of the pound could fall by as much as 25%. The document also warned of "consumer panic", "law and order challenges" in the north of Ireland and "security gaps".

257. See David Yaffe, "Britain: Parasitic and decaying capitalism", *FRFI* 194 December 2006/January 2007.

258. See David Yaffe, "EU referendum: The position of communists", *FRFI* 251 June/July 2016.

259. It is clear that the EU cannot be reformed from within. Any treaty reform would require unanimity across member states, while any reform via secondary legislation would need the consent of the commission, the majority of governments and the majority of MEPs, and then the European court of justice. The EU helped to destroy Libya and Syria and then left refugees forced to flee these countries to drown in the Mediterranean Sea. The EU sees these people as no more than a surplus supply of labour. The 'liberal', 'progressive' EU has also paid private companies to militarise its borders and incarcerate the refugees who do survive the journey in inhumane detention camps. The EU is also paying African countries, such as Libya, to process migrants before they get a chance to reach Europe, effectively funding concentration camps on the African border. A senior African Union official said this "could create something like modern-day slave markets, with the 'best' Africans being allowed into Europe and the rest tossed back". Indeed, chattel slavery has returned to Libya in the wake of the overthrow of Muammar Gaddafi, under whom Libyans enjoyed the highest living standards on the continent. Médecins Sans Frontières (Doctors Without Borders), which has played a heroic role in rescuing many refugees, has cut ties with the EU in protest.

260. Lenin, *Collected Works*, Vol 21, pp339-343.

261. The Labour Party was just as split on the issue as the Tories. Corbyn came under mounting pressure from both the right of the party and its young left-leaning membership base to support a second referendum, whereas the more traditional Left of the party and the Labour MPs representing constituencies that voted to leave have broadly pushed for Brexit to go ahead.

262. The same can be said of Britain's falling self-sufficiency in food production, which in 2014 had decreased over the previous 30 years from 78% to 60%. See "Britain's food self-sufficiency is in long-term decline, warn farmers", TheGuardian.com, 7 August 2014.

263. Vauxhall's Ellesmere plant, which looked likely to close until France's PSA Group bought Vauxhall from General Motors in 2018, is the last light commercial

plant in the UK. Its Vivaro Life model is made by 300 robots and 13 humans. PSA said in July that the factory, which exports 80% of its production to mainland Europe, may have to be closed after Brexit.

264. Bastani, *op cit*, p37.
265. GMO data show that tangible investments in plant and machinery by US private industry steadily declined from 14% of output in 1980 to around 7% by 2011, whereas 'intangible' investments went in the opposite direction, making up two-thirds of total investments by US industrial firms.
266. Grossman, *op cit*, p121.
267. Ibid.
268. VI Lenin, *Imperialism: The Highest Stage Of Capitalism*, in Selected Works, London, 1969, p260.
269. See chapter 11. In summary, this social democratic arrangement involved a minimal nationalisation programme, including of large tracts of land, which enabled the building of mass social housing; a large expansion of state welfare (Britain has never been nor had a 'welfare state'); and the founding of the National Health Service (NHS).
270. Smith, *op cit*, p301.
271. "Pulled back in", Economist.com, 14 November, 2015.
272. Smith, *op cit*, p303.
273. Ibid, p308.
274. Ibid.
275. James Kynge and Jonathan Wheatley, "Emerging markets: The Great Unravelling", *FT*, 1 April, 2015.
276. "China tipped to continue stimulus as growth slows", FT.com, 21 January 2019.
277. "China GDP: annual growth rate", Trading Economics.
278. See James Kynge and Jonathan Wheatley, "Emerging Asia: the ill wind of deflation", FT.com, 4 October 2015.
279. *Global Financial Stability Report: Risks Rotating to Emerging Markets*, IMF, October 2015 update.
280. Kynge and Wheatley, *op cit*, 4 October 2015.
281. "China bets on expanding its way out of debt", FT.com, 22 May 2015.
282. Ibid.
283. Smith, *op cit*, p303.
284. Ibid.
285. Ibid, p304.

6. The final contradiction?
286. *Economic and Philosophic Manuscripts of 1844*, Wilder Publications, Blacksburg (US), 2011, p50.
287. *What Caught My Eye?* V61: "Lumpenproletariat and deglobalisation", Macquarie Research, 20 July 2016. The paper says that "while considerable attention is focused on cultural, religious or other causes [of political and social decay] we believe that at the end of the day economics is at the base of most human endeavours" and so the rise of populism is "not an aberration but a logical outcome". Governments will have "no choice" but to "provide minimum income guarantees and spending vouchers, and perhaps other rewards for higher spending, without any requirement to look for or hold a job. While some would call it socialism, we maintain that it is the inevitable and logical outcome of the Fourth Industrial Revolution." The bloodless final recommendation made to investors is to put their money into robotics and automation, genome augmentation, gaming and entertainment, skilling, "social and geopolitical dislocation", ie weapons, drones, security firms, and "facilitators and enablers".

288. 'Lumpenproletariat' refers to the declassed or destitute from all layers of society.
289. Bastani, *op cit*, pp43-4. The ASCI Red was a US military war games simulator the size of a tennis court.
290. Ibid, p47. Global solar capacity has doubled every two years – it increased by a factor of 100 between 2004 and 2014, finally making it competitive with fossil fuel.
291. Quoted in Rick Kuhn., "Economic Crisis and Socialist Revolution: Henryk Grossman's Law of Accumulation, Its First Critics and His Responses," p14.
292. 'Late capitalism' is a controversial term in Marxism and Mandel himself was dissatisfied with it. He did not claim to have identified a new epoch in capitalist development but "its specific traits in a new phase" (*op cit*, p8). "Traits" is a bit of a push; certainly he described new features arising from the intensifying continuation of the laws of capitalist development already identified by Marx.
293. Ernest Mandel, *Late Capitalism*, Verso, Second Edition, 1980, p209-11 (first published in 1972).

7. Factory fragmentation
294. Volkov, *op cit*, p44.
295. Quoted in Jeff Sparrow, "Sinister Automatons", *Counterpunch*, 1 November 2012.
296. Sparrow, ibid.
297. Translation: the workmanship was better than the subject matter.
298. Ibid.
299. *State of the Global Workplace: Employee Engagement Insights for Business Leaders Worldwide*, Gallup, 2013, p12.
300. Nick Dyer-Witherford, *Cyber Marx*, University of Illinois Press, 1999, pp49-50.
301. Quoted in Grossman, 1992, p100.
302. Grossman, 1992, p101.

8. Rescuing Marx's 'The Fragment on Machines'
303. Marx, 1993, pp701-2.
304. Ibid, p694.
305. Ibid, p692.
306. Ibid, p693.
307. Ibid, p694.
308. Ibid, p700.
309. Indirect labour being direct labour's conversion into machinery or 'objectified/ dead labour'.
310. Marx, 1993, pp705-6.
311. Quoted in Paul Mason, *Postcapitalism: A Guide to Our Future*, 2015, Penguin, p137.
312. "Once one copy of a piece of software has been written, the next million, or the next billion, or next 10 billion copies cost next to nothing." Turner, *op cit*, p3.
313. Mason, *op cit*, p137.
314. Ibid, p144.
315. Ibid.
316. Ibid, p144-5.
317. Marx, 1993, p706.
318. Mason, *op cit*, p137.
319. Ibid.
320. Ibid.
321. Ibid, p49.
322. Ibid, p70.
323. Ibid, p133.
324. Grossman, 1992, p118.

325. Mason, *op cit*, p55.
326. Marx, 1991, p319.
327. Engels, before editing it, described Marx's manuscript for vol III as an "incomplete first draft". Marx may well have added to vol III had he lived longer, or written a fourth volume. Moreover, Grossman points out that Marx's *Capital* anticipates that capitalism would eventually suffer from an absolute overaccumulation of capital. See chapter 10.
328. Marx, 1991, p372.
329. Marx, 1993, p708.
330. Bastani, *op cit*, p49.
331. Ibid, p59.
332. Ibid, p63.
333. 'Global South' has become something of a buzzword among left-wing academics who conveniently shy away from addressing the question of imperialism directly. It is a rather inadequate and euro-centric term – more than half of Africa is above the equator, for example, while Ireland, very much in the 'Global North' is an oppressed nation that remains colonised by Britain. Australia is below the equator but is an ally of the imperialist NATO. For those who wish to present imperialism as a static phenomenon – a specific grouping of certain nations – rather than a social system, the term is very useful. It essentially provides an *a priori* justification to support for the ambitions of the larger, semi-independent nations of the 'Global South', painting a world in which perhaps South African exploitation of the continent would not be as bad as European or US exploitation, or Indian expansion not as galling as British expansion. After all, they are in the 'Global South'!
334. Bastani acknowledges that the term "luxury" would be redundant by definition by the time everybody enjoyed a high standard of living.

9. The fantasy of fully automated capitalism
335. Mandel, *op cit*, p206-7.
336. When it turns out that as many or more jobs have been created as lost, the Left is often mocked for promoting the 'Luddite Fallacy'. However, as Turner notes (*op cit*, p25): "In their analysis of the potential distributional consequences of new machine deployment, the handloom weavers of the 1820s who joined Ned Ludd's campaign of machine destruction were entirely rational. For the first 30-40 years of the 19th century industrial revolution, labour's share of UK national income fell steeply, and real wages stagnated despite significant productivity improvements driven by automation. And if the steam driven factories had never been developed, many individual handloom weavers would have enjoyed higher real incomes throughout their lives. Smashing machines was rational, even if ineffective because technological progress could not in reality be halted."
337. In *Grundrisse* (p784) Marx quotes Elizabeth Tuckett's *A History of the Past and Present State of the Labouring Population*: "Owing to the introduction of machinery, in 1800 one person could do as much work as 45 in the year 1785. In the year 1800 the capital invested in mills, machinery etc appropriate for the wool trade was not less than six million pounds sterling and the total number of persons of all ages occupied in England in this branch was 1,500,000. Thus the productive power of labour grew 4,600%.... Hardly any manufacture had such an advantage from the improvements in science as the art of dyeing cloth through the application of the laws of chemistry."
338. Lilley, *op cit*, p142-3.
339. Elsby, *The Decline Of US Labor Share*, Brookings Institution, 2013, p31.
340. See Volkov, *op cit*, pp156-7.
341. Lilley, *op cit*, p214.

342. Volkov, *op cit*, pp119-20.
343. Ibid, p124.
344. Lilley, *op cit*, p143.
345. Ibid, p145.
346. Ibid, p146.
347. Volkov, *op cit*, pp104-5.
348. That and the fact that workers are being driven into low-paid, low-productivity services work. Turner makes the point that work as domestic servants boomed during the first industrial revolution, as wealthy capitalists had plenty of disposable income to spend on making their own lives easier, while attempting to quell social unrest by keeping as many people as possible out of unemployment. Now, in contrast to falling work in manufacturing, it is projected that job opportunities in social care, dietary and nutritional expertise etc, are going to rise the most.
349. Grossman, 1992, p120.
350. The nodes on a computer chip are measured by the nanometre (nm) – ie one billionth of a metre, or 100,000 times thinner than a sheet of paper. The smaller the node, the more can be fitted into the same small space. In 1965 when Moore published his theory, a single transistor spanned the width of a fibre of cotton and cost $8 in today's money. Now, billions of transistors can be squeezed onto a chip the size of a fingernail, with the cost per unit having fallen to a tiny fraction of a cent (Bastani, *op cit*, p43). Sales of the 10nm class began in 2016, following on from 14nm in 2014, 22nm in 2012, and 32nm in 2010. Production of the 7nm class began in June 2017 and the 5nm class is expected to go on sale in 2020.
351. "It doesn't matter if the newness of a commodity is real or artificially created through the propaganda of advertising. When Apple introduced its iPad, the newness was more than a perception but the same mechanism applied. As the exclusive seller of this product, Apple is able to command a price far above what it costs to make the product. Nobody else is permitted to make an iPad because its production is protected by patents. The growth of patents, after a slow but quite steady course since the late 19th century, exploded in the 1980s. Intellectual property rights became essential parts of international trade agreements, and both US and European authorities repeatedly lengthened the duration of patents and copyrights. There are patents on everything, and almost two million new ones are filed every year, including the right to use, develop and sell technologies, programmes, products, methods of research and production, procedures, even scents and colours, by anybody but the patent-owner and those licensed by them." – "Artificial scarcity in a world of overproduction: an escape that isn't", metamute.org, 19 May 2010.
352. Reynolds, *op cit*, 2352.
353. Mandel, *op cit*, p206-7.
354. "This is, of course, only true on an international scale. Theoretically, it is conceivable that a fully automated industry in the USA or West Germany could corner the surplus value necessary for the valorisation of its capital through exchange with non-automatically produced commodities from other countries. In practice, the social and political consequences of such a situation would be immeasurably explosive." – Footnote from *Late Capitalism*.
355. Ibid.

10. The final breakdown: destined to strike much earlier than a zero rate of profit
356. Esteban Ezequiel Maito, *The Historical Transience of Capital: The Downward Trend in The Rate of Profit Since XIX Century*, Universidad de Buenos Aires, 2014, p16.
357. Insurance companies also began to collapse because they could not afford to pay out on insurance policies called credit default swaps (CDSs), which effectively

allow one to bet that a person, company or country would default on their debts. When Lehman Brothers, the fourth largest investment bank in the US, failed in September 2008, American Insurance Group (AIG) had to be bailed out because most of Lehman's CDOs were insured by AIG, which had issued CDSs against Lehman's CDOs. AIG had placed $3bn in bets with no assets to cover potential losses. CDOs have not gone away – the Obama administration's plan for dealing with them was to allow banks to set up their own hedge funds that would purchase them *with public money*. This was the only option other than allowing most banks to go bankrupt. The equivalent to CDOs in Europe are eurobonds. In the eurozone, member states were responsible for bailing out the banks rather than the European Central Bank. But because of the currency union, member states could not devalue their currencies in order to make their own economies more competitive. That encouraged banks and hedge funds to take out CDSs on countries like Greece with capital that they could have otherwise lent them, pushing up interest rates on the loans Greece needed to finance its €300bn deficit (12% of national income in 2010, four times higher than the limit set by the EU). Germany refused to bail out Greece, refused interest rate relief, and refused to allow Greece to default. It was only when the Greek debt crisis panicked investors into refusing to buy anyone's bonds, fearing a global default, that the eurozone, the ECB and the IMF extended a €110bn loan to Greece – though at an interest rate high enough that the Greek public purse would never be able to repay this new loan on top of existing ones.

358. *Granma International*, 6 September 1998.
359. Martin Hart-Landsberg, "Portrait of the 2009-2019 US expansion", MRonline.org, 20 June 2019.
360. While austerity has pushed back the date of the next recession in Britain, the costs of preparing for Brexit – new Prime Minister Boris Johnson added another £2.1bn to no-deal preparations on top of the £6.3bn already made available by the Treasury – and the uncertainty Brexit has caused, with many banks and other companies moving operations elsewhere, would have brought the recession forwards. In the wake of the Brexit vote, investment in the UK by overseas companies and individuals fell from a £120bn surplus in the first half of 2016 to a £25bn deficit over the same period in 2017. This after BoE governor Mark Carney said that Britain's economy depended significantly on "the kindness of strangers". Japanese foreign minister Tarō Kōno has suggested that many Japanese companies operating in the UK – of which there are over 1,000 – would relocate to other countries in Europe in the event of a no-deal Brexit. If Britain left the EU without a transitional trade agreement in place, Britain would, overnight, cease to be part of the single market and customs unions. The legal basis for the free movement of goods between Britain and the EU would disappear, and instead the UK would have to abide by World Trade Organisation (WTO) rules, introducing tariffs of up to 40% on EU goods.
361. FDI is direct in the sense that it involves a company expanding its own operations in a country outside the one in which it is registered.
362. World Investment Report 2018, UNCTAD, 6 June 2018.
363. "The lasting effects of the financial crisis have yet to be felt", ChathamHouse.org, 12 January 2018.
364. The IMF cited the failure of regulators to impose tough restrictions on insurance companies and asset managers, which handle trillions of dollars of funds, along with the dramatic rise in lending by unregulated 'shadow' banks. Shadow banking – a reaction to tighter regulation of regular banks and low interest rates – includes lending by institutions such as hedge funds, property funds and private equity, as well as through derivatives. Britain's shadow banking sector is more than twice the size of any other economy's as a share of GDP. The US is the only country where

shadow banking assets are greater than those of the conventional banks. Again, the symptoms are worst in the most decayed countries.
365. Marx, 1993, p318.
366. Ibid, p748.
367. Marx, 1991, p350.
368. Ibid, p320.
369. Ibid, p317.
370. Ibid, p318.
371. Ibid.
372. Ibid, p319.
373. Michael Roberts, "The US rate of profit – the latest", TheNextRecession.wordpress.com, November, 2012.
374. Roberts, "The US rate of profit in 2017", TheNextRecession.wordpress.com, November 2018.
375. Roberts, *The Long Depression*, Haymarket Books, Chicago, 2016, p24.
376. Maito's calculation is simply the rate of return against fixed capital, due to the difficulty of tracking variable capital in real terms. He argues (*op cit*, p5): "The rate of return on fixed capital is sufficient to analyse the evolution of profitability.… The rate of profit on fixed capital tends to converge with the Marxian rate of profit in the long run [because] the growth in turnover speed of circulating capital steadily reduces the participation of that circulating capital in the total capital advanced, ie related to fixed capital." Arguably, including variable capital would make the rate even lower.
377. Roberts, "UK rate of profit and British economic history", TheNextDepression.files.wordpress.com, September 2015.
378. Maito, *op cit*, p19.
379. Quoted in Pento, *op cit*, p150.
380. Officialdata.org.
381. The 'core-periphery' dichotomy is another problematic starting point that sees the imperialist countries as the 'core' of a single Empire. This runs into the usual Kautskyist pitfalls as it obscures imperialist rivalry.
382. As part of the EU and NATO, Spain is an imperialist nation, even if it is not one of the major powers, and should therefore have been included as a 'core' country. While Australia is not in NATO it is a NATO ally and is therefore not oppressed by imperialism; it should have therefore been included with the 'core' nations. It also seems quite an oversight not to have included France. Neither can China, given its economic rise, be considered as part of the 'periphery'. However, for the purposes of showing that the rate of profit falls historically towards zero these problems do not affect our investigation.
383. Maito, *op cit*, p9.
384. Paul Schmelzing, "Eight centuries of global real interest rates, R-G, and the 'suprasecular' decline, 1311–2018", bankofengland.co.uk, 3 January 2020, p3, 39.
385. Ibid, p40.
386. Ibid, p74.
387. Ibid.
388. Ibid, p3.
389. Ibid, p56.
390. Ibid, p55.
391. Ibid, p74.
392. Mason, "What 700 years of falling interest rates tell us about our economic future," NewStatesman.com, 21 May 2020.
393. Grossman and Kuhn, *op cit*, pp131-2.
394. Maito, *op cit*, p17.

395. Marx and Engels, *The Communist Manifesto*, Penguin Classics, 2015, p20.
396. Rick Kuhn, "Capitalism's Collapse: Henryk Grossman's Marxism", *Science & Society* vol 59, 1995, p176.
397. Grossman, 1992, p187.
398. Ibid.
399. Ibid, p187.
400. Marx, 1991, p373.
401. Ibid, p330.
402. Marx, 1991, p360.
403. Grossman, 2017, pp384-5.
404. "Fed may not have enough firepower to prevent recession", CNBC.com, 16 August 2019.
405. One basis point is equivalent to 0.01% (1/100th of a per cent).
406. "Recession watch: Trump and markets could be set for a brutal reckoning", *TheAge.com.au*, 4 June 2019.
407. Marx and Engels, 2011, p90.
408. "Washington is flirting with a debt crisis. No one has a plan to stop it", CNN.com, 12 May 2019. The White House later struck a two-year deal with Democratic Party leaders in Congress to raise America's $22 trillion borrowing limit. The deal raised spending levels in both defence and non-defence areas by a total of $320bn, while cutting spending by much less than the $150bn in offsetting reductions sought by the Trump administration. Maya MacGuineas, president of the Committee for a Responsible Federal Budget, said the latest agreement was a "total abdication of fiscal responsibility by Congress and the president. There was a time when Republicans insisted on a dollar of spending cuts for every dollar increase in the debt limit. It's hard to believe they are now considering the opposite – attaching $2 trillion of spending increases to a similar-sized debt limit hike."
409. When Carillion, Britain's second largest construction company, went into liquidation in January 2018 it was the biggest collapse in the history of the British construction industry and one of the largest bankruptcies in recent British corporate history. Carrillion held 450 outsourced government contracts, worth 38% of its income in 2016. Carillion expanded with the growth of Private Finance Initiatives (PFIs). Outsourcing public services to private business started with Thatcher's Conservative government in 1979. PFIs were introduced in 1989 and expanded under the 1997-2010 Labour governments. With PFIs, the government contracts private firms to raise the money to build and operate public sector assets. The firms are then repaid, with interest, by taxpayers for periods up to 30 years. 90% of Carillion's work was itself outsourced to some 30,000 sub-contractors. See Trevor Rayne, "Carillion: What is hidden in the ruins", revolutionarycommunist.org, 1 February 2018.
410. Roberts, 18 November 2017.
411. See "244: Michael Pento: The Coming Bond Market Collapse: How to Survive the Demise of the US Debt", Cashflow Ninja, Youtube, 27 December 2017; and "The Coming Bond Market Collapse: Michael Pento, Pt-3", Youtube, The Lance Roberts Show, 30 April 2019. Pento says holders of gold could then spend it digitally using the crypto-currency platform Blockchain. Pento is an outright conservative libertarian who argues that the free market has been dead since Herbert Hoover became President and began pumping money into the economy (before The New Deal). He isn't particularly wrong (although the free market really ended around 1900). What he does get wrong is in thinking that this "indefinite Keynesianism" has been a strictly political choice. He claims crises would not occur if the US had not devalued the dollar against gold or ended the gold standard, but cannot see that that decision was prompted by the system's need to revive accumulation on a higher

level. He would "leave everything to the free market": no central control over the interest rate and no government stimuli – ie permanent deflation! Without government subsidies the private sector would die.

412. "Jim Rogers: The worst crash in our lifetime is coming", BusinessInsider.com, 9 June 2017.

413. Summers, *op cit*, 1768.

414. Before turning to the Nazis to crush the SPD and KPD, the owners of German heavy industry initially, in May 1932, regarded the economic policy articulated by Otto Strasser – whose 'left' faction of the party advocated support for strikes and nationalisations of banks and industry – as "simple-minded mercantilism" (which is highly protectionist). The industrialists, however, recognised that the traditional bourgeois parties did not have the mass base to enforce their desired anti-labour and anti-parliament policies. After this section of the ruling class, along with the agricultural elite, approached Hitler, the party's Economics Division was reorganised, with the industry-friendly Walther Funk taking over its leadership. Strasser began professing that "we recognise private property, we recognise private initiative… we are against the nationalisation of industry. We are against the nationalisation of commerce. We are against the planned economy in the Soviet sense." Quoted in David Abraham, *The Collapse of the Weimar Republic*, second edition, Holmes & Meier, New York, 1986, xxxv.

415. Summers, *op cit*, loc 2063.

416. Marvin Goodfriend, "Overcoming the zero bound on interest rate policy", richmond fed.org, August 2000.

417. Summers, *op cit*, loc 2764-2803.

418. Ibid, loc 2087-2115.

419. Ibid, 2199.

420. "The world's most valuable resource is no longer oil, but data", *The Economist*, 6 March 2017.

421. "What is Amazon, really?", QZ.com, 20 August 2017.

422. Work that is neither productive or unproductive is non-productive. It does not create surplus value but it does not require any outlay on wages, so nor is it a drain on surplus value in the way that work by 'third persons' is.

423. Amazon workers have been striking against poor pay, long hours (of up to 70 a week) and dangerous, inhumane working conditions. The company has responded by training management in union busting.

424. "The wave of unicorn IPOs reveals Silicon Valley's groupthink", Economist.com, 17 April 2019.

425. Spotify, the global leader in music streaming, founded in 2008, turned a profit for the first time in 2018 – and that is expected to be an anomaly. The music industry, which demands an ever greater slice of Spotify's revenues, has been hit hard by the emergence of this rental model. In 1999 the music industry generated revenues of $14.6bn in the US, a figure which had fallen to $7.65bn by 2016 (not accounting for inflation). This despite the fact that more people are listening to more music than ever before. Bastani, *op cit*, p234. Album sales in 2000-13, including digital and physical albums, declined by 74%. Reynolds, *op cit*, loc 2684.

426. Again, high official employment figures mask reality. A better measure is the labour force participation rate, which is the civilian labour force (ie, those employed and those unemployed and actively looking for work) divided by the civilian non-institutional population (ie, those not in the military or institutionalised). In May 2019, the labour force participation rate of 62.8% remained significantly below its 2008 peak (about 66%) and even further below the even higher peak reached at the turn of the century (about 67.5%). The decline in the labour force participation rate

means that, in reality, millions of workers have yet to return to the labour force, either to hold a job or to look for one. Hart-Landsberg, *op cit*.
427. "China stocks roar back after grim 2018", FT.com, 15 February 2019.
428. "Rising market is ignoring economic reality", FTAdviser.com, 22 February 2019.
429. Reynolds, loc 2170.
430. Varoufakis, *op cit*, p131.
431. Grossman, 1992, p192.
432. Ibid.
433. Ibid, p196.

11. Keynesian fantasies
434. Reynolds, *op cit*, loc 1969.
435. Paul Mattick, *Economics, Politics and the Age of Inflation*, "Chapter Six: The Great Depression and the New Deal", Marxists.org, 1977. All further Mattick quotes from the same source.
436. Kimberly Amadeo, "New Deal summary, programs, policies, and its success", TheBalance.com, 25 February 2015.
437. Varoufakis, *op cit*, p90.
438. Ibid, p88.
439. Ibid, p92.
440. Reynolds, *op cit*, loc 1517.
441. Varoufakis, *op cit*, p96.
442. Reynolds, op cit, loc 1969.
443. David Yaffe and Paul Bullock, "Inflation, the Crisis and the Post-war Boom", *Revolutionary Communist* No 3/4 November 1979, p12.
444. "Sterling devalued and the IMF loan", nationalarchives.gov.uk.
445. Although the Tories used plenty of stick in terms of police brutality against striking miners, they also used plenty of carrot in order to split the working class. Indeed, the workers who did remain in work saw their real wages rise. In addition, the government sold workers their council houses and offered them shares in newly privatised companies, such as British Telecom and British Gas, at far below the estimated market price. As Varoufakis writes (*op cit*, p138): "The much-vaunted shareowners' democracy lasted but a few days, as the co-opted workers immediately sold their shares to the conglomerates. They did the same thing with their council houses, in an attempt to move to better neighbourhoods and make some extra cash in the process, since much of the new house's price would be paid for with a mortgage. The newly privatised housing encouraged banks to extend mortgages and credit card facilities to families that had never had them. The concomitant increase in the demand for houses boosted their prices, and that gave the workers the illusion that they were getting richer."
446. William Blum, "Overthrowing other people's governments: The Master List," williamblum.org.
447. Summers, *op cit*, loc 946.
448. Ibid, loc 1043.
449. Ibid, 954.
450. Ibid, 1199.
451. Ibid, 1128-1135.
452. Ibid, 1219.
453. Ibid, 1344.
454. Ibid, 1474.
455. Ibid, 1540.
456. Ibid, 1596
457. Ibid, 1635.

458. Ibid, 1707.
459. Ibid, 1726-1733.
460. Germà Bell's essay "Against the mainstream: Nazi privatisation in 1930s Germany" shows that Nazi Germany "went against the mainstream trends in the Western capitalist countries, none of which systematically re-privatised firms during the 1930s". This debunked the commonly promoted view that privatisations in Chile and Britain in the 1970s and 80s had been the first privatisation policies in modern history. The last governments of the Weimar Republic took over firms in diverse sectors. Nazi manifestos and economic programmes promised nationalisations and made no mentions of privatisations (pp15-16), presumably in a bid to dupe workers. Initially the Nazis did make some nationalisations. Sectors that were re-privatised included steel, mining, banking, local public utilities, shipyards, ship-lines, and railways. Some public services, especially social services and services related to work, were also transferred to the private sector, mainly to organisations within the Nazi Party (p2).
461. In Nazi Germany, working hours were lengthened by 40%. Wages were forced down by 23% in 1929-32, only rising by 10% by 1939 despite full employment. Capital's share of national income in Germany had fallen from 29.4% in 1913 to 11.2% in 1930, but shot back up to 32.3% by 1938. Mandel, *op cit*, p173.
462. Keynes based this on the rate of rising living standards and accelerating capital accumulation, which he put down to "compound interest". "Mankind is solving its economic problem," he declared in his 1930 essay "Economic Possibilities for our Grandchildren" (*op cit*, p3-4). Keynes was not entirely wrong – automation means solving the economic question is indeed "in sight", as he put it, and he also recognised that the end of the "money-motive" would rid mankind of "pseudo-moralism".
463. "15 per cent increase in people working more than 48 hours a week risks a return to 'Burnout Britain', warns TUC", TUC.org.uk, 9 September 2015.
464. "Work Your Proper Hours Day – tackling the culture of unpaid overtime", TUC.co.uk, 22 February 2018.
465. Marx, 1990, p534.
466. As Mariana Mazzucato has shown in her book *The Entrepreneurial State* (Penguin, 2018), technological innovation under capitalism is almost always led not by the private sector, as has been mythologised by commercial propaganda, but by the state. From IT, biotech and nanotech to today's emerging green tech, Mazzucato shows that the private sector "only finds the courage to invest after the state has made the high-risk, long-term investments that the private sector cannot afford. The state socialises the risks, while rewards are privatised." Every technology that made the iPhone – the symbol of Silicon Valley superiority – was developed or funded by the state: the internet, GPS, touchscreen, battery, hard drive, voice recognition and AI. The state even takes a leading role in establishing commercial viability (p55). In fact the large private research and design centres in the US have "mostly disappeared" (p193). State funding for new technology firms is two to eight times the amount of investment from venture capital, whose risk of loss is 66.2% at seed stage and 53% at the start-up stage, but only around 20% at the third and pre-public stages (ibid). Small and medium enterprises also rely massively on state subsidies. In Britain they receive more collectively than the police force (p52).
The Soviet Union was, of course, far more innovative than it is given credit for. Inventions there included: the radio antenna; 2- and 3-D holography; artificial satellite; the programmable computer; the nuclear power plant and nuclear powered submarine; the AK assault rifle; the mobile phone; and Tetris. See "Russian inventions in the soviet era", inventions-handbook.com. NB: Central planning made it possible to speedily transport factories to the other side of the Urals after the

outbreak of WWII – within 12 months 2,500 major enterprises had been moved and brought into operation. Soviet armaments production was more efficiently organised than that of either the Allies or the fascists. For every million tonnes of steel the USSR produced 1.5 times more planes than the UK, 2.6 times more than Germany, and 3.2 times more than the US. The Soviet Union's industrial output quadrupled in 1928-38 while the advanced capitalist economies broke down into the Great Depression. See: "War and the Soviet Union: The Soviet victory over fascism", *FRFI* 49, May 1985. According to Lilley (*op cit*, p159), the volume of production in the USSR was four times greater than in the US in 1937, five times greater by 1949, nearly seven times greater in 1952 and nearly nine times greater in 1955.
467. Larry Elliott, "Governments have to invest in the fourth industrial revolution", TheGuardian.com, 16 July 2017.
468. "50 years of decline for UK steel industry", SkyNews.com, 20 January 2016.
469. Tuner, *op cit*, p29-30.
470. Bastani recognises that UBI is unaffordable and instead puts forward a demand for Universal Basic Services, including housing. This is a much better demand and is based on taking "much of the national economy under public ownership". Bastani argues this would be possible under social democracy thanks to falling prices. But while capitalism still exists such a wide-ranging outlay would depend on much higher taxes at a time when much of the private sector is suffering from ever-tighter profit margins. It would probably therefore have to happen, at best, during a *de facto* period of dual power, *a la* Venezuela, rather than mere social democracy.
471. Marx, 1993, p611.
472. The Resolution Foundation think tank calculated that £3.2m families would be an average of £2,400 a year worse off under UC compared to tax credits, with 600,000, mostly two-parent families, losing all benefit. Average rent arrears have gone up from £207 to £365. A two-child limit restricts the child element in UC and tax credits worth £2,780 per child per year to the first two children, saving the state £1bn a year by 2021 and pushing an additional 300,000 children into poverty by 2024, while 1 million children already below the breadline will be pushed into deeper hardship, according to Child Poverty Action Group. Nearly all families affected by the limit reported cutting back on essentials such as food, medication, heating and clothing as a result of the policy, which makes them miss out on at least £53 a week. Callous Tory ministers have defended the policy on the basis that it forces parents to take responsibility for their choices and teaches them that "children cost money". Yet the government has barely publicised the policy; only half those affected were aware of it before they became pregnant. Relatively few claimants have used a barbaric 'non-consensual sex exemption', dubbed the 'rape clause', which forces women to prove that their third or subsequent child was conceived as a result of rape to qualify for the exemption.
473. See James Bell, "We are not all Daniel Blake" for a communist review of *I, Daniel Blake*. *FRFI* 254 December 2016/January 2017.
474. Although the needs of capital determine legal immigration flows (see next footnote) the idea that Europe has been inundated with migrants is of course a racist myth. Only around 3% of the world's population live outside the country in which they were born, a figure which has remained relatively constant for decades. See Heaven Crawley et al "Unravelling Europe's "Migration Crisis"", Policy Press, 2017. In contrast, between 1850 and 1920, when there were no restrictions on the mobility of people across national boundaries – passports were seldom needed and immigrants were granted citizenship with ease – about 70 million people emigrated *from Europe*, 36 million of them to the US, 6.6 million to Canada, 5.7 million to Argentina, and 5.6 million to Brazil, settling on land cleared by the genocide of indigenous civilisations. The total migratory flow was equivalent to more than a

sixth – 17% – of the 408 million people living in Europe in 1900. This mass emigration to the Americas and Australasia mitigated the growth of pauperism and the reserve army of labour in Europe. As Smith (*op cit*, p108-113) points out, the unemployed in Africa and elsewhere today do not have the same option. If the same proportion had emigrated from the 'global south' since WWII as left Europe between 1850 and 1920, 800 million people would have moved north, expanding the total population of the more developed countries by 70%. Instead, a negligible 0.8% of the workforce of the developing world has migrated to work in the developed countries, 1/20th of the Europeans that emigrated in the earlier period.

475. The plunder and oppression of nations by imperialist powers is, clearly, inherently racist. Capitalism then is the material basis of racism and continually *reproduces* it. Immigration controls in the imperialist nations are an extension of this national oppression and therefore also inherently racist. The needs of capital tend to dictate the flow of immigration. When there is a boom and a labour shortage, immigration controls are relaxed in order to 'import' a new layer of cheap, super-exploited labour, which arrives with fewer rights and, usually, less economic support, than the rest of working class, meaning they have to accept the worst jobs and poorest living conditions. During times of crisis and a labour surplus, immigration controls tighten, and deportations increase. While Trump has stepped up the rhetoric and action against migrants, it should be remembered that this has been an intensification of what went before. A record three million deportations took place under Obama. NB: While the anarchist demand of 'no nations, no borders' is an agreeable long-term ideal, it is chauvinistic in the present conditions – socialist and oppressed nations require borders to repel imperialist aggression. Our slogan should be: controls on capital, not on labour.

476. Ground rent goes up according to land value, which rises as interest rates fall (which in turn fall depending on the size of overaccumulation) as land becomes a form of banking for surplus capital, necessitating the privatisation of social housing and the buying up of housing in general, even if it is left empty, to be sold on later at a higher price. In 1979, 42% of the population in Britain lived in publicly-funded housing; today the figure is less than 8%. After WWII large tracts of land were nationalised in order to build social housing, but half of the land in England is now owned by less than 1% of the population. Only 8.5% of the land in England falls under the custodianship of the public sector and in fact all the land ultimately belongs to the Crown. Across Europe 11 million homes lie empty while migrants and the homeless are told that there is no room at the inn. In Britain, the so-called "home-owning democracy", home ownership has fallen to its lowest level since 1985. Having risen from 22% in 1920 to 33% in 1940, 55% in 1980, and 74% in 2007, the proportion of adults who own their own home (or pay a mortgage) declined to 63.4% in 2016, the most dramatic fall in the EU. Average house prices rose from £25,000 in 1980 to £175,000 in 2008 and £228,000 in 2018. From 2010-17, the official number of evictions rose by 53% to 169 a day, but that only included the number that went through the courts. The private rented sector has shot up from 12% to 20% of all household tenures across Britain in little more than a decade. On average, rents claim 32% of income, or more than 40% in London. By contrast, rent in socialist countries has commonly been capped at 5% of income or less, and evictions have been outlawed.

477. "Labour's universal basic income would leave the poorest worst off", *The Spectator*, 3 August 2018. Compass modelled a UBI that paid £284 a month to every working-age adult and smaller payments for others. This would stand alongside, rather than replace, extant social programmes, adding £170bn a year to public spending – equivalent to 6.5% of GDP and more than is presently spent on the NHS. Bastani, *op cit*, p225.

478. "Scrap personal allowance and replace with a new weekly cash payment", NewEconomics.org, 11 March 2019.
479. Since those earning above £125,000 do not have a personal allowance in the current system, they would also not receive the new payment.
480. See Eddie Abrahams, "Zionist Israel: Its role in the Middle East" and Claudia Miller, "Unpicking the Zionist myth", revolutionarycommunist.org.
481. "Colombia: Unions demand government action following the murder of an in4igenous teacher", Education International, 26 October 2018.
482. Former army chief general Lord Dannatt said in 2019 that a 7% reduction of the defence budget in 2010 "resulted in a 20% cut in the size of the army, and I would actually suggest a 50% cut in what we can actually do". The Ministry of Defence needs to find a further £20bn of savings but in January 2019 May rejected a proposal to cut a further 11,000 soldiers from the army and 2,000 from the Royal Marines as "politically unacceptable". What is apparently acceptable is the recruitment of 16 and 17 year-olds, which made up 30% of those enlisted in 2019. Charlotte Cooper of the Child Rights International Network said: "The army is leaning on teenagers from the most deprived backgrounds to fix its recruitment crisis, using them to fill the riskiest roles because it can't persuade enough adults to enlist."
483. Paul Carter, "Could an army coup remove Jeremy Corbyn – just as it almost toppled Harold Wilson?", Telegraph.co.uk, 9 May 2018.
484. The idea promoted by some Corbyn supporters that he has returned the party to the days of 'real' or 'old' Labour is nothing to be proud of. The party was set up by middle class liberals and labour aristocrats to channel discontent into reformism and therefore win enough concessions to prevent a revolutionary force from emerging. As Grossman says, the Labour Party "immediately adopted the principles of the Fabians and trade unions" (2017, p99), ie reformism on mainly moralistic grounds. Labour has never been a socialist or democratic socialist party since its left wing has always been tied in a coalition to its liberal right. Furthermore, the impression given by much of the British left that Tony Blair was the first Labour prime minister to sanction genocide overseas is unconscionable. Clement Attlee, the darling of 'old' Labour and proud anti-communist, sanctioned imperialist terror in Korea, Malaya and elsewhere.
485. See Robert Clough, *Labour: A Party Fit for Imperialism*, Larkin Publications.

12. Proletarianisation and the historical demands of the productive forces
486. Lenin, *What Is To Be Done?*, Martino Publishing, 2013, p28.
487. "World Bank recommends fewer regulations protecting workers", TheGuardian.com, 20 April 2018.
488. "When the next recession comes, the robots will be ready", WashingtonPost.com, 24 January 2019.
489. "Job Polarization and Jobless Recoveries", nirjaimovich.com.
490. By 'Leninist' we refer to a vanguard party-led revolution, and proletarian dictatorship expressed through a nationwide network of workers' councils and an all-socialist state. We do so for clarity because 'Marxist' has been distorted by various trends, including by 'libertarian communists' who claim Marx did not stand for vanguardism or state power. In the *Communist Manifesto* Marx and Engels clearly state (p33): "The proletariat will use its political supremacy to wrest, by degrees, all capital from the bourgeoisie, to centralise all instruments of production *in the hands of the state*, [our emphasis] ie of the proletariat organised as the ruling class; and to increase the total of productive forces as rapidly as possible." In section IV of the *Critique of the Gotha Programme*, Marx says that the question of the transformation of the state "can only be answered scientifically… Between capitalist and communist society there lies the period of the revolutionary transformation of the one into the

other. Corresponding to this is also a political transition period in which the state can be nothing but *the revolutionary dictatorship of the proletariat.*" 'Leninism' then is really just Marxism (although Lenin is of course credited with updating the theory to include the development of imperialism, while also being the first communist leader to put successful revolutionary tactics into practice).

491. That the Soviet Union lasted 72 years in the face of unrelenting imperialist aggression – not to mention the backwards peasant economy it inherited – proved emphatically that socialism works. Any new system is bound to experience very challenging 'teething problems', especially in the face of counter-revolution.
The problems socialist societies have experienced have stemmed mainly from the leftovers of feudalism and capitalism, internal and external, especially the retarding influence, to whatever degree, of the law of value. The need to trade with capitalist countries undermined planning as fluctuating foreign prices could not be predicted. Money could therefore not be abolished (although it was used internally only as an index; see Grossman, 2017, p263) and meant allowing a black market to some degree made sense in order to build up foreign currency. In perhaps one of the most under-appreciated statements in Marxist literature, the *Manifesto* makes this clear (*op cit*, p33): "Of course, in the beginning, this cannot be effected except by means of despotic inroads on the rights of property, and on the conditions of bourgeois production; by means of measures, therefore, which appear economically insufficient and untenable, but which, in the course of the movement, outstrip themselves, necessitate further inroads upon the old social order, and are unavoidable as a means of entirely revolutionising the mode of production."
Ultimately this does have to be applied globally.

492. Smith, *op cit*, p101.
493. John Bellamy Foster, Robert W McChesney, and R Jamil Jonna, "The global reserve army of labor and the new imperialism", MonthlyReview.org, 1 November 2011.
494. Smith, *op cit*, p101.
495. EAP data from Laborsta, quoted in Smith, *op cit*, p115.
496. ILO, *Key Indicators of the Labour Market* 8th ed, quoted in Smith, *op cit*, p147.
497. Volkov, *op cit*, p102.
498. Alex Press, "White-collar unionization is good for all workers", TheNation.com, 29 January 2019.
499. "The American middle class is losing ground", PewSocialTrends.org, 9 December 2015.
500. Middle-income US Americans were defined as adults whose annual household income is two-thirds to double the national median, about $42,000 to $126,000 annually in 2014 dollars for a household of three.
501. Similarly in Britain, the Trussell Trust says that whereas it sent out 41,000 food packs in 2010, the number reached 1.2 million in 2017.
502. In Britain, the Money Advice Service says 17 million people of working age have less than £100 in personal savings.
503. Varoufakis, *op cit*, p128.
504. Amy Chozick, "Middle class is disappearing, at least from vocabulary of possible 2016 contenders", nytimes.com, 11 May.
505. Volkov, *op cit*, p164.
506. EAP data from Laborsta, quoted in Smith, *op cit*, p114.
507. The informal economy is the part of an economy that is neither taxed or regulated by any form of government.
508. Mike Davis, *Planet of Slums*, Verso, reprint edition, 2007, p14.
509. Smith, *op cit*, p102.
510. Quoted in ibid, p104.

511. Quoted in ibid, *op cit*, p104.
512. Reynolds, *op cit*, loc 2954-2990; "Africa's jobless youth cast a shadow over economic growth," UN.org, 2017.
513. John Lanchester, "The Robots are Coming", *London Review of Books*, 5 March 2015.
514. Bastani, *op cit*, p58.
515. Quoted in ibid, pp56-7.
516. Elsby, *op cit*, p15.
517. "Millennials are less entrepreneurial and fail more often", FT.com, 14 June 2018.
518. ILO, 2011, *op cit*, p58.
519. Ibid.
520. The United Socialist Party of Venezuela (PSUV) government continues to be threatened by a US-backed coup, not just because it has nationalised the world's largest oil reserves but because the higher wages and state-funded social programmes the Bolivarian Revolution has secured – lifting the vast majority of the Venezuelan working class out of extreme poverty – significantly curb the surplus value available to the valorisation of capital. The Bolivarian Revolution is yet to establish a proletarian dictatorship as capitalist parties have not been disempowered from participating in elections. Despite significant nationalisations, around 70% of the economy remains privately owned. This, along with US-imposed sanctions, is what creates economic problems for Venezuela, as the capitalists are able to hoard essential goods in blatant acts of sabotage. As Sam McGill has argued in *FRFI*, the PSUV badly needs to take foreign trade under a state monopoly in order to undermine this tactic. See McGill, "Venezuela: the visible hand of economic warfare", *FRFI* 260 October/November 2017. However, while a proletarian dictatorship has not been established, the fact that the PSUV has remained in power since 1999 shows that the working class has the upper hand in a situation of *de facto* dual power, rather than of mere social democracy. This is thanks to the working class's highly organised communal system and the fact that Hugo Chavez was able to replace many right-wingers in the army with loyal supporters. This has made the PSUV worthy of critical support from Venezuelan communists. The Venezuelan working class is fighting on the frontline in the global struggle for socialism.
521. Elsby, *op cit*, p15.
522. "A letter to Steven Pinker (and Bill Gates, for that matter) about global poverty," jasonhickel.org, 4 February 2019.
523. Indeed, repressive measures have always been required, including by anarchists. The only 'successful' anarchist 'revolutions' have employed prisons, although they have often done away with courts (presumably the absence of law and the right to a fair trial perversely make anarchists feel less 'authoritarian').
524. Total state ownership does not have to mean individual types of products are made in only one plant (although the practical, logistical problems of the transition have to be taken into account, as well as geographical ones – dams, for example, can only be located in certain places and can't be 'communally owned'), as was too often the case in the Soviet Union, which also had problems with rewarding 'optimisation' (maximum output), thereby incentivising exaggerated data feedback. We envisage moving towards a diffusion of all products being made as locally as possible, ie a transition from state ownership towards a mix of international and communal ownership, in a way that links sector enterprises together nationally and internationally – a kind of 'global commune'; with in-built incentives – improving working conditions, increased free time, etc – so that the focus is on human needs and wants.
525. A company can only centrally plan its own activity; the competition between companies knocks plans off course, while unanticipated changes in economic

growth and other factors mean an overall plan for an industry or an economy let alone the system as a whole is impossible. Whereas capitalist enterprises can plan based on attempted forecasts, socialist states can conduct plans based on goals. The capitalist state is always planning in terms of allocating funding etc but at certain stages of crisis it is forced to try to plan the economy as a whole, as is the case with Keynesianism, but to no avail. This only serves to show that a system which can plan the economy as a whole is required.

526. Kevin Farnsworth, a senior lecturer in social policy at the University of York, released a study in 2015, *The British Corporate Welfare State*. For the financial year 2011-12 he added up the subsidies and grants paid directly to businesses, which amounted to over £14bn – almost three times the £5bn paid out that year in income-based jobseeker's allowance. Add to that the corporate tax benefits, the value of cheap credit made available to banks and other businesses, the insurance schemes run by the government to protect exporters, the marketing for British business by the relevant state ministry, plus public procurement from the private sector, and Farnsworth calculated that direct corporate welfare cost British taxpayers nearly £85bn. This was a conservative estimate, and it did not include the public subsidy provided to bail out the banks.

527. In 2017 England's chief medical officer, Sally Davies, warned that "the world is facing an antibiotic apocalypse" because of the rapid growth of antimicrobial resistance (AMR) bacteria, threatening to throw civilisation backwards to a time before Alexander Fleming discovered penicillin in 1928. The pharmaceutical industry developed 13 classes of antibiotics between 1935 and 1968, but only two more between then and 1987. Since then no new classes have been developed, and none are in the pipeline, except for a small number of new individual antibiotics. This is perhaps the starkest example of capital becoming an ever-growing fetter on productivity. Even the Tory government effectively admitted that the profit motive deters Big Pharma from improving antibiotic drugs. In fact it even recognised that Big Pharma is responsible for *causing* AMR to develop in the first place. The Health Department said it would offer subsidies to incentivise the development of new antibiotics, adding: "Low returns on investment in development means industry does not innovate enough…. The way drugs companies are currently paid depends on the volumes they sell, meaning companies have an incentive to sell as many antibiotics as possible at the same time as government is trying to reduce antibiotic use." As antibiotics are used for relatively short periods and are often curative, they are not as profitable as drugs that treat chronic conditions – where investment is therefore directed – such as diabetes, psychiatric disorders or asthma. Antibiotics are becoming ineffective because they are over-used. But they are not just overprescribed (partly due to corruption); they are – to maximise profit, of course – pumped into animals as growth supplements and because animals are kept in overcrowded and therefore dirty conditions in captivity, breeding disease. The antibiotics crisis is particularly worrying in the context of global warming threatening to spread diseases around the world.

528. Mazzucato, *op cit*, p31.
529. "Do farmers make more from subsidies than agriculture?", FullFact.org, 11 August 2016.
530. Pento, *op cit*, p123.
531. Mazzucato, *op cit*, p31.
532. William Lazonick and Ken Jacobson, "End stock buybacks, save the economy", nytimes.com, 23 August 2018.
533. Mandel, *op cit*, pp228-9.
534. The 'Internet of Things' is expected to take up 20% of the world's energy needs.
535. Marx and Engels, *op cit*, p11.

13. Man vs machine: Postcapitalist techno-utopia or dictatorship of AI?
536. Volkov, *op cit*, pp16-17.
537. See Dyer-Witheford, *op cit*, pp28-30. Toffler was a former Marxist who argued that because "knowledge drives the economy" now, workers already "own a critical … share of the means of production" inside their heads and therefore no longer need to seize the means of production. This reconstitution of idealism, whereby the material world is determined by what exists inside man's head, makes for a lovely modern fairytale.
538. Roberts, "Robots and AI: utopia or dystopia? Part two", TheNextRecession.wordpress.com, 29 August 2015.
539. "In the development of productive forces there comes a stage at which productive forces and means of intercourse are called into existence, which, under the existing relationships, only cause mischief, and which are no longer productive but destructive forces (machinery and money)." Marx and Engels, *The German Ideology*, New York, 1960, p68.
540. The play introduced the word 'robot' to the English language.
541. Volkov, *op cit*, p14.
542. Ibid, p17.
543. Automation in the UK arms sector has coincided with jobs falling in that sector from 405,000 in 1980-81 to about 142,000 in 2016. Figures quoted in Rod Austin, "The arms trade needs moral balance – lives and livelihoods depend on it", TheGuardian.com, 27 June 2018.
544. "Instead of escaping the soul-killing mechanism of modern technological society," wrote the playwright Ernst Toller about his generation's exposure to the trenches, "they learned that the tyranny of technology ruled even more omnipotently in war than in peacetime. The men who through daring chivalry had hoped to rescue their spiritual selves from the domination of material and technical forces discovered that in the modern war of material the triumph of the machine over the individual is carried to its most extreme form."
545. Quoted in *Counterpunch, op cit*.
546. Peter Maurer, President of the International Committee of the Red Cross (ICRC), "Algorithmic warfare is coming. Humans must retain control", World Economic Forum, 26 Sep 2018.
547. Ibid.
548. Toby Walsh, "It's not too late to save the world from killer robots", TheGuardian.com, 6 April 2018.
549. Geist and John, *How Might Artificial Intelligence Affect the Risk of Nuclear War?*, RAND.org, 2018.

14. Capitalism wants the most destructive world war yet – but even that can't save it
550. Lee Adler, "Do we need another world war?", BusinessInsider.com, 9 November 2010.
551. Quoted in Grossman, 1992, p158.
552. Ibid, p158.
553. See John Pilger, "A world war has begun. Break the silence", JohnPilger.com, 20 June 2016.
554. Johan Galtung, "On the Coming Decline and Fall of the US Empire", transnational.org, 28 January 2004.
555. Medea Benjamin, "America dropped 26,171 bombs in 2016. What a bloody end to Obama's reign", TheGuardian.com, 9 January 2017.

556. "Trump is a hawk. 2017 proves it", Vox.com, 30 January 2018.

557. "France, Germany protect Iraq ties", WashingtonTimes.com, 20 February 2003.

558. As well as devaluing the dollar in order to attract foreign capital flows into the US to finance its deficits, the rise in interest rates that followed Nixon's decision to end the gold standard enabled the US to hammer enemy nations that had become reliant on low rate US loans during Bretton Woods. When interest rates soared, socialist states in Poland, Romania and Yugoslavia began to feel the pinch. Once they realised their grave dependency on US capital, they tried to repay their debts as quickly as possible, which meant imposing harsh austerity measures on their own workforces. The result was mass discontent and the first stirrings of organised opposition, such as the Polish trade union Solidarity, which, backed by US imperialism, spearheaded a chain of events leading to the first collapse of a socialist state. The interest rate rise also triggered the 'third world debt crisis', badly hurting a number of non-aligned countries led by national liberation parties. The IMF bailed them out but only on the conditions of exorbitant interest repayments, harsh austerity measures and the selling off of public assets to imperialist multinationals, rolling back many of the gains initially made by national liberations.

559. A country's current account is the broadest measure of its trade in goods, services, and income.

560. David Yaffe, "The world economy – facing war and recession", *FRFI* 171 February/March 2003.

561. "Has our government spent $21 trillion of our money without telling us?", Forbes.com, 8 December 2017.

562. Engels, *Anti-Dühring*, 1877, "Part II: Political Economy, III Theory of Force (Continuation)", Marxists.org.

563. See Trevor Rayne, "Blitzing Fallujah: Fitting up Iraq for democracy", *FRFI* 182 December 2004/January 2005.

564. "Secret memos expose link between oil firms and invasion of Iraq", Independent.co.uk, 19 April 2011.

565. "China's economy will overtake the US in 2018", Forbes.com, 29 April 2016.

566. Reynolds, *op cit*, 3104.

567. "Defense Disaster: Russia and China are crushing the US military in war games", *NationalInterest.org*, 11 March 2019.

568. Trevor Rayne, "China: On top of the world", 16 October 2018, *FRFI* 266, October/November 2018.

569. Grossman, *op cit*, p157-8. "When no such thing happened, [Kautsky went] on to deny the inevitability of the breakdown as such."

570. After 1935, the Comintern effectively ordered its national sections in Europe to take 'democratic socialist' routes to socialism. Whether you consider this a necessary tactical retreat or a capitulation to reformism, it failed in its aims – to 'not provoke' the spread of fascism and world war. The situation was, though, tremendously complex. Trotsky believed the Soviet Union could not survive without revolution in western Europe, while Stalin believed it could and in fact had no choice but to go it alone. Armed soviets had only ever formed under conditions of national military defeat, after all, when the workers had trained, conscripted soldiers on their side, and even then they mostly remained reformist (a fact we surely have to take into account when it comes to our attitude towards opportunism). The Soviet Union had hardly had a chance to progress from the carnage of WWI and the counter-revolutionary civil war that included invasions by 13 other nations. It can't be denied that following the defeat of the German Revolution in 1918-23, the prospects of a European let alone world revolution dissipated, meaning that – with minimal support from the western European working class – the Soviet Union was left isolated and probably had to prioritise its own survival, to keep its own population

on side. When armed soviets did then form at the end of WWII, communist parties directed by the Soviet Union settled for social democracy on the grounds that insurrections would be crushed by US troops (even though some US troops had started to mutiny). Starting another war, this time with the US, was a major concern, something the Soviet Union understandably did not want to risk after losing at least 20 million citizens during WWII. Moreover, the Soviet Union did not yet have the Atom bomb, the US having used it on Japan primarily as a warning to Moscow. WWII also decimated the communist and working class cadre, which allowed reformists to become more dominant within the Communist Party, strengthened by a general desire to end the bloc's isolation. While it would seem that Stalin proved to be correct at the time in terms of socialism's ability to survive in one country, it could be argued that the Soviet Union's rightward drift – from its reformist social democratic foreign policy that began under Stalin; to its domestic economic reforms after Stalin and the bloc's eventual collapse – proved Trotsky right in the long run. When it did collapse, this was partly because skilled workers and intellectuals wanted the higher wages their equivalents earned in imperialist countries (something that won't be a problem once full automation has made capitalism impossible). Social democrats and neoliberals took over the leadership of the party and slashed taxes supposedly in order to boost productivity (which had stagnated, at least in relative terms as the Soviet Union became more industrially mature) but this only collapsed the tax base and sparked hyperinflation. A ban on alcohol had also boosted the black market and a criminal class that did not pay any tax. In a 1991 referendum 77.85% of 146 million voters voted to reform but retain the Soviet Union; but they were ignored and too few mobilised militantly enough to prevent the counter-revolution. Six million excess deaths followed a huge contraction in industrial output, which never fully recovered after capitalist restoration.

571. Grossman, 1992, p49-50.
572. Ibid, p157.
573. Quoted in ibid, p157.
574. Ibid, p157.
575. Mattick, *op cit*.
576. Quoted in Grossman, 1992, p55.
577. While it does not take a Marxist analysis to predict that a world war today would be the most destructive ever, or that it would almost certainly result in nuclear conflagration, part of why it is important to show that capitalism is what makes war inevitable – rather than simply 'human stupidity' or 'lust for power' etc – is to prove that there is a solution that offers real lasting peace, ie socialism and communism, thereby combatting misanthropy and nihilism.
578. While communists at the time saw the world wars as the death pangs of capitalism, with hindsight they should arguably be viewed as the last birth pangs of monopoly capitalism.
579. Grossman, 2017, p138.
580. Michael Pettis, "Competitive devaluations threaten a trade war", FT.com, 1 December 2009.
581. Nafeez Ahmed, "The 'disintegration' of global capitalism could unleash World War 3, warns top EU economist", Medium.com, 21 February 2019.
582. Quoted in D Yaffe, "The Marxian Theory of Crisis, Capital and the State", 1972.
583. In February 2019 Trump announced that the US would be suspending its compliance with the 1987 Intermediate-range Nuclear Forces (INF) treaty, claiming that Russia had developed a new ground-launched cruise missile which violated the INF prohibition of missiles with ranges between 500km and 5,500km. Russia acknowledged its existence but claimed that its range does not violate INF limits. In July, Russian President Vladimir Putin signed a bill formalising Russia's withdrawal

from the same treaty. There is no evidence that Russia was already in violation of the treaty. While possible, it seems considerably unlikely given that Russia has been cutting its military budget. The second reason given by the US, that China is building a nuclear arsenal, unrestrained, is incredibly overstated and has nothing whatsoever to do with the INF, to which only Russia and the US were signatories. While the number of nuclear arms eliminated by the Treaty (around 2,000 Russian missiles and 800 US missiles) is not terribly significant relative to overall nuclear stockpiles, it carried significant weight as an agreement. The INF was the first arms treaty in history to eliminate an entire class of nuclear missile, ie ground-based mid-range nuclear weapons. This class of arms are particularly useful as offensive weapons, as they are easy to conceal and, thus, the risk of a retaliatory strike before a nuclear launch is lessened considerably. While mid-range nuclear arms were still deployed at sea or on aircraft prior to the US withdrawal, these deployments are not so easy to conceal. The significance of the US withdrawal from the INF is, therefore, a return of land-based, offensive nuclear arms. Perhaps more significantly from the perspective of international relations is that the US's decision firmly locates any conflict between it and Russia as occurring *within Europe – the only deployment location prohibited by the INF.*

584. Ukraine's so-called Maiden revolution of 2014 was a US-backed coup that put a far right coalition into power as part of the US's strategy to fragment Russia. The US aimed to remove Russia's naval base from Sevastopol in Crimea; break Russian military ties to industries in eastern Ukraine; bring Ukraine into the EU and NATO; and station NATO missiles on Ukrainian territory. Russia responded by incorporating Crimea and Sevastopol into the Russian Federation.

585. Kit Klarenberg, "Damaging ties: why Germany is the Integrity Initiative's 'most important target'", SputnikNews.com, 9 January 2019.

586. The US and Britain overthrew Iran's popularly elected Mosaddegh government – which nationalised British Petroleum – in 1953 and replaced it with an absolute monarchy which wiped out the country's left-wing forces. Poverty rose dramatically but has been cut by two-thirds since the bourgeois nationalist revolution of 1979. The US has been desperate to reinstall a proxy dictator ever since.

587. While there is no doubt that Israel lobbies the US very strongly for continued and absolute support, the idea that Israel controls the US government is absurd and anti-Semitic. As the Democratic Party's Joe Biden said more than 20 years before becoming US vice-president, "Israel is the best $3bn investment we make. Were there not an Israel the US would have to invent an Israel to protect our interests in the region." Luckily for the US, Britain had already invented Israel. Israel received $38bn in military aid from the US in 2018. Israel is a leader in the sector of arms miniaturisation, including "nanobots implanted into humans that can cause fundamental physical or psychic distortions", according to Jeff Halper's book *War Against The People* (Pluto Press, 2015), which details how Israel tests its weaponry on Palestinians in Gaza. Israel is also developing tiny surveillance and combat drones which draw inspiration from insect behaviour, and even conducting research into how to control insects for military purposes. See Toby Harbertson, "Israel's war against the people - review", revolutionarycommunist.org, 5 January 2016.

588. Sanctions are an act of aggression which deny countries the ability to import food, medicine and other essential goods. In 1996, Madeleine Albright, a Democrat, defended UN sanctions against Iraq which had resulted in the deaths of half a million children, saying: "We think the price is worth it."

589. For more detail on the emerging imperialist divisions, shifting alliances and the ideological, cyber and militaristic developments in "hybrid warfare", see James Bell,

"The Old World is Dying, Part one: the actuality of global war", Patreon.com/Prolekult, 14 July 2019.

590. In March 2019, the World Trade Organisation (WTO) ruled that Washington had failed to stop giving Boeing illegal subsidies which hurt Airbus – a year after it issued a ruling against EU subsidies to Airbus. Under WTO rules, the ruling paves the way for the EU to request the right to impose tariffs on US goods. The size of a potential retaliation would have to be based on the trade losses caused to Airbus.

591. "Chinese military deploys armored vehicles to Europe for the first time as Chinese medics train in Germany", *Military Times*, 10 July 2019.

592. Grossman, 1992, xi.

593. Ibid, p4.

594. Preamble to the Statutes, Third International, June-August 1920, international-communist-party.org.

15. Humanity's emancipation: higher communism and the single automated society

595. Volkov, *op cit*, p113.

596. Dyer-Witherford, *op cit*, pp40-2.

597. Marx and Engels, *op cit*, p15.

598. Marx, 1990, p617.

599. Ibid, p617-8.

600. Marx, "Speech at the Anniversary of the *People's Paper*", 14 April 1856, in Adoratsky and Dutt, *Karl Marx, Selected Works* vol 1 (London 1942), p428.

601. Marx, 1991, p368.

602. Lenin, "Imperialism, The Highest Stage Of Capitalism", *Collected Works*, Vol 22, Lawrence & Wishart, p266.

603. Helen Yaffe, *op cit*.

604. Volkov, *op cit*, p113.

605. See Helen Yaffe, "Ernesto 'Che' Guevara: a rebel against Soviet Political Economy", Marxists.org, 2006. Guevara concluded in 1966 that the Soviet Union "is returning to capitalism". "He challenged the reliance on capitalist categories to organise the socialist economy, particularly the operation of the law of value... the profit motive, interest, credit, individual material incentives and elements of competition," writes Yaffe. While Guevara accepted that the law of value could not be abolished in one or several countries while so much of the world remained capitalist, he believed it could have been suppressed to a much more radical extent. Guevara's analysis contrasts with the assertion made by many Trotskyists that socialism cannot exist in one country, that it has to become global to succeed. While this is of course preferable and the end goal (perhaps even true in the long run), to believe that the whole world can become socialist at more or less the same time is idealistic (especially before a final breakdown) – one country has to become socialist first by default – and is therefore a *de facto* counter-revolutionary position. Cuba today demonstrates, despite the island's isolation, that socialism can survive and, to an extent, thrive in one country. Cuba could not have free, world class health care and education and a trailblazing science sector if it was not socialist (some Trotskyists, and Maoists, claim that Cuba is not socialist, despite the likelihood that Trotsky himself would disagree with them). "In Cuba, Guevara's analysis was revisited in the mid-1980s in the period known as Rectification, which pulled the island away from the Soviet model before it collapsed, arguably contributing to the survival of Cuban socialism," writes Yaffe. Guevara also lamented the policy of peaceful co-existence with imperialism that the Soviet Union adopted. Peaceful co-existence could never be sustained because the Soviet Union was a barrier to

necessary capitalist expansion; but the conditions for socialist revolution rarely existed anywhere after WWII.

606. Already before mergers and acquisitions take place, we see corporations forced to turn to cooperation with their rivals because they cannot afford the cost of production alone. The car manufacturing industry is a vivid example, with Toyota, for instance, teaming up with fellow Japanese brand Subaru and German marque BMW respectively to build its last two sports cars, the GT86 and the Supra.

607. Volkov, *op cit*, p169.

608. Similarly, that monopoly capitalism is followed by socialism, a united public monopoly, negates the claim by some communists that a socialist US (or 'USSA', as if the 'R' in USSR denoted Russia instead of Republic) would be 'illegitimate' and remain settler-colonial (the same accusation is usually levelled at the Soviet Union and Cuba), meaning the indigenous and black ('New Afrikan') populations represent *de facto* nations within the US. Therefore, because communists support the right of oppressed nations to self-determination, even when they are capitalist, the US should be abolished, with new treaties bringing back new and old national borders, such as an independent Black Nation state in the south. Certainly indigenous reservations should have sovereignty within a socialist union (as with oblasts in the Soviet Union), but abolishing the US nation-state and returning to former borders is simply not an option given that indigenous people are now massively outnumbered. It is subjectively argued that the US could not be decolonised unless indigenous people became the ruling classs of each new state. This forgets that socialism raises the working class to the position of ruling class, and would therefore make the black and indigenous people a part of a socialist US ruling class by definition. Deprivatising the land in the US as a whole and institutionalising equal rights, underpinned by economic rights that cannot exist in capitalism, in a new constitution, would move the US beyond settler-colonialism, for settler-colonialism depends on the preservation of private property and economic-based discrimination. Most importantly, socialism would end unemployment and the artificial scarcity that inflicts poverty on black and indigenous people. Here then is a theoretical and concrete solution to the question of decolonisation and which *meets the material needs of the black and indigenous people*. Another demand, for reparations to be paid both to the new indigenous nations and the countries around the world that have been plundered by US imperialism is not possible under capitalism as it would make everyone in the country much poorer – if a government were to instal it now it would provoke way too much opposition and push many people into the arms of the far right. It is more likely that the remaining capitalists will be the ones to receive reparations (through long-term payments, as was the case with slave-owners) in order to save lives through disincentivising counter-revolutionary violence. Whether the tax base could also bare long-term payments for victims of colonialism would have to be assessed, but it seems unnecessary given that workers will receive all the value they create minus direct taxes under socialism. Instead we should probably follow the example of Cuba, which shares its world class leadership in health care by sending doctors (human resources being material wealth under socialism) around the world to treat patients and educate new doctors. (While internationalist pride and honour is part of the incentive, other incentives are of course involved.) If socialism is rejected as the road to decolonisation, then the demand for decolonisation and reparations become academic, akin to demanding the abolition of slavery by reintroducing universal war. The US is monopoly capitalist – the next stage in its development is the lower stage of communism. Marx wrote extensively on the US and supported Lincoln once Lincoln committed to abolishing slavery, but never argued for any separatist Black Nation. The black US proletariat is not descended from one African nation and is entitled to all of the US, not a part of it. At

a time when the rest of the world sits in the crosshairs of US nuclear terror, attempts by some communists to isolate anyone who questions this utopianism seems extraordinarily US-centric. Although the desire behind these demands is understandable and the commitment to them admirable, they are only isolating themselves from the masses.

609. Marx, 1993, p708.

610. Ibid.

611. Obviously isolated socialist states of the past and present have had to invest in militarism, weakening their civilian economies significantly, to defend themselves from imperialist aggression. The reality is that state militarism could not be dismantled until the whole world is socialist, after which nation-states would wither away to the tune of an everlasting world peace.

612. In order to measure free time in real terms, socialist states of the future will have to take all factors into account. In Volkov's book, he writes (*op cit*, p129): "To get an idea of the leisure hours proper, we have to deduct the time taken up by sleep, eating, personal hygiene, preparation of meals, cleaning, washing and travel to and from work. This time varies. A survey of the Economic Institute of the Siberian Department of the Academy of Sciences of the USSR shows that it is far greater in the case of women (25-50% greater than with men) and also greater in the case of residents of Novosibirsk and Krasnoyarsk than those of Moscow (the difference being about one hour)." A survey in the mid-1960s by the Laboratory of Sociological Research at Leningrad University, covering 100 workers of the Kirov plant, showed that 30% of time was taken up by sleep and meals, 6% by odd jobs at home and personal hygiene, and about 7% by travelling to and from work. Leisure therefore represented 26%, ie six hours daily. Assuming that the average across the Soviet Union was three to four hours daily, when holiday was added the amount of free time amounted to about 1,500 hours, approaching the 1,814 hours of average working time. Volkov commented: "For the first time in history, the working man has gained the opportunity to devote almost as much time to free creative activity and his spiritual development as to work."

613. See Volkov *op cit* pp132-47 for a detailed assessment of how this began to develop in the USSR."To be deprived of creative activity will be the most severe form of punishment. Not without reason did the utopian socialist [Étienne-Gabriel] Morelly suggest that the way to deal with loafers in the society of the future is to deprive them of work and thus 'punish idleness with idleness'." Marx described this new period in the history of mankind as the "kingdom of freedom", because work driven by necessity and outside expediency comes to an end.

614. Marx, 1993, p711.

615. Ibid, pp711-2.

616. "In place of the old bourgeois society, with its classes and class antagonisms, we shall have an association, in which the free development of each is the condition for the free development of all." Marx and Engels, 2015, p35.

617. Spokesman, 1993. The authors also advocate a party-less state system of lot-drawing instead of elections in order to make the people genuinely sovereign and politicised. Although we sympathise we tend to think this would not be possible, given the importance of expertise, until world socialism is fully secure and the transition towards higher communism has begun in earnest.

618. The more moribund capitalism becomes the more we can already see historical trends (back) towards a genderless and raceless society emerging, with the increasing struggle for and recognition of transgender and non-binary civil rights, and the still relatively new emergence of multiculturalism, interracial families etc. Like all forms of healthcare, gender transitioning in Cuba is free. In its efforts to combat bigoted and chauvinistic attitudes, the National Center for Sex Education

raises consciousness about what it terms 'sexual diversity'. See Lucy Roberts, "Cuba: A radically different approach to LGBT rights", RATB.org.uk, 9 May 2019.

619. Capitalism may not have originated gender and therefore sexism but it does continually *reproduce* it. Women's oppression under capitalism takes a particular form in relation to how social production is organised – in sum, a dual oppression that compels women to reproduce (ie bear, raise and maintain) the working class (children and men) *gratis* at home – making housework privatised – while also comprising part of a cheap reserve army of labour. This is why women's struggles have made more progress in the workplace, because capital has anyway needed a growing valorisation base, than with demands for paid housework, which would change housework from non-productive to unproductive labour. The division created by the breadwinner-homemaker dynamic makes women dependent on men for security, privileging men, and also reproduces the conventional gender and heteronormative binaries. Homophobia and transphobia can therefore be considered extensions of sexism. That the relationship between men and women, to a limited extent, started to level out under monopoly capitalism manifested from technological and productivity advances, including labour-saving domestic devices, the need to expand the valorisation base, the growing expense of home-owning, and the reduced need for manufacturing workers, ie the typical working class man (the latter factor contributing simultaneously to a societal 'crisis of masculinity' and the increasing manifestation of gender fluidity). However, the deeper capitalist crisis becomes the more women's gains are reversed and the more women are pushed back into the confines of the home. Universal Credit, for example, creates incentives for single-earner households, due to the withdrawal of benefits from two-earner households. Furthermore, UC is paid in one lump-sum into one bank account (usually the primary earner's). These measures are likely to increase the number of households with one primary earner and a partner that is either a second earner or not earning. Women are much more likely than men to be the latter, increasing their dependence upon their male partners for security. The capitalist mode of production is *the fundamental material basis* for the oppression of women and therefore their emancipation can only be achieved by overthrowing it and introducing socialist relations of production, which will increasingly socialise the responsibility of house and care work, *liberate* the family from its status as an economic unit and therefore women from their status as mere instruments of production. Gradually, the family as we know it may be 'abolished' as humans return to raising children communally, but it may take a number of generations for this to become the norm. In hunter-gatherer societies, the male and female sex practiced a form of group marriage, and as paternity could not be established descent was traced through the mother. The emergence of agriculture, private property and surplus production relegated women from a position of equality to the position of producing workers to work the land. As the obvious inheritors of private property had to be legitimate heirs, this precipitated the invention of monogamous marriage and the enforced fidelity of the wife, replacing the matrilineal system with a patrilineal one so that paternity could be determined. Communism then will also complete the 'sexual revolution' as women will no longer have to 'sell sex' to men in return for security; contraception will be abundant and free for all; and the material basis for exploitative sex work will of course also disappear. People will finally be able to enjoy relationships free of economic considerations. A number of studies showed that both women and men had much more satisfactory sex lives in East Germany than in West Germany because sex was seen as a natural need and something to share rather than trade. (Ghodsee, *op cit*, pp132-9.) Indeed, recent questions about falling birth rates have been coupled with bemusement from liberals as to why millennials are having less sex.

620. Ableism refers to the structural oppression faced by disabled people under class society. As with racism and sexism, it did not originate under capitalism, as evidenced by the trade in 'dwarves' for 'freak shows' under the Roman empire or certain feudal societies. Rather, it has adopted a particular form under capitalism. As capital creates working environments based upon bolstering productivity, those workers who are not suited to such environments are viewed as underproductive and, therefore, undesirable. *It is then capital rather than individuals' impairments that disables workers.* This is compounded when job losses and benefit cuts lead to poor mental health etc. To bring up their productivity, capitalists would be required to adapt the workplace to their needs. While this is now a formal right in many imperialist nations, reality tells a different story. For example, in May 2019, 48.7% of the 7.6 million economically active disabled people in Britain were unemployed, with a further 3.3 million people considered as economically inactive. While the capitalist attitude to disability is inaccurate – disabled workers are not axiomatically unproductive; they may be when their needs are not met with adaptations – it serves to create conditions of super-exploitation for those disabled people in employment. As the view is such that disabled people are unproductive, those workers with disabilities in employment are viewed as deserving less. This is expressed in the generally lower rate of pay awarded to disabled workers and even explicitly with arguments that disabled workers should not be allowed as much income put forward in the bourgeois media.

621. This is not to claim that sexism, disableism, racism, homo/queerphobia and transphobia would disappear overnight, but that the material basis for their reproduction will progressively disappear during the course of building socialism, especially as abundance erases class antagonisms and demographics continue to integrate and evolve. In the meantime, better and more accessible education will help to tackle cultural chauvinistic attitudes that have permeated all classes, while equal rights will be underpinned by economic rights. The very ability to provide full employment and higher living standards for all will limit friction and competition between people.

622. Marx, 1993, p712.
623. Volkov, *op cit*, p46-7.
624. Ibid, p91.
625. Ibid.
626. Dyer-Witherford, "Red Plenty Platforms", *Culture Machine* 14, 2013, p8.

627. Most working class people recognise the shallowness of bourgeois democracy because even discounting vote-rigging efforts via discriminatory restrictions and gerrymandering, it inherently disenfranchises them. They cannot afford to run, their class is not represented, term limits preclude the recall of politicians and, other than the odd referendum, they do not get any direct say in any decision-making. In 2016, almost 50% of the eligible US electorate did not vote in the presidential election. In contrast, Cuba's proletarian democracy – where 16 year-olds are eligible to vote – sees regular turnouts of over 80%. Candidates to the Municipal Assembly are nominated in public by neighbourhood committees, student unions, farmers' organisations and trade unions. Over 15,000 candidates are elected every two and a half years to make up 169 Municipal Assemblies of People's Power. At the local level, voters can nominate two to eight candidates at public meetings. They are elected if they receive 50% of the votes of all the people registered to vote in their district. Delegates are elected directly by the voters, who have the power to recall them. Candidates receive no financial benefit from their positions and spend no money to promote their campaigns. The Municipal Assembly votes on which candidates become deputies to the National Assembly of People's Power and which will become delegates to the Provincial Assembly. Women make up 43% of the

National Assembly, ranking Cuba third in the world in female participation in government. On 24 February 2019, the people of Cuba approved a new Constitution. 8,945,521 Cubans – the vast majority of the population – participated in the process of debating the draft constitution. 133,680 meetings took place, with Cubans abroad also contributing; 1,706,872 spoken interventions were made at the meetings and as a result 783,174 modifications, additions or eliminations to the draft constitution were made. A referendum on the final version was approved by 84.4% of the turnout. For a comparison between British democracy and Soviet democracy, see *The Soviets and Ourselves* by KE Holme, edited by Colette Boulanger. As for party democracy, the system of democratic centralism allows for open debate but all members are expected to uphold decisions once members have voted on them.
628. Lilley, *op cit*, p167.
629. Ibid, p159.
630. Ibid, p162.
631. Ibid, p165-7.
632. Denayer, *op cit*.

16. Against extinction: For a green (hemp-based) industrial revolution that is actually green
633. Ibid
634. John Beddington, "Food, energy, water and the climate: a perfect storm of global events?", UK Government Office of Science, 2009.
635. "NASA-funded study: industrial civilisation headed for 'irreversible collapse'?", TheGuardian.com, 14 March 2014.
636. Reynolds, *op cit*, loc 3349.
637. Bastani, *op cit*, p99.
638. Most of this demand is going to come from the developing nations, enabled, as we shall see, by falling commodity prices. Due to production relocation and increased energy efficiency, demand for energy in the world's richest countries has started to decline, but only slightly. The British state claims that the country's energy consumption peaked at the turn of the millennium and has fallen by 2% every year since, meaning Britain's energy use in 2018 was actually lower than in 1970. (Ibid, p99-100.) In June 2019 Britain was able to declare that fossil fuels produced less than half of UK electricity for first time. However, the government does not count emissions from consumption of goods and services from other parts of the world. Factoring in the emissions embedded in imports, UK emissions have fallen by as little as 7% since 1990. ("Are the UK's emissions really falling or has it outsourced them to China?", CarbonBrief.org, 19 March 2015.) While claiming victory at home, the British state's UK Export Finance body, which provides lines of credit and insurance to help British companies win business overseas, spent £2.6bn in recent years to support the UK's global energy exports, £2.5bn of which was handed to fossil fuel projects. Only 4% of the funding, or £104m, was used to support renewable energy projects, according to the environmental audit committee. Whatever progress Britain has made, the Committee on Climate Change has said that only one of 25 vital emissions-cutting policies in 2018 had been delivered in full, and warned that Britain was on course to miss emissions-cutting targets for 2025 and 2030. It added that Britain's preparations for extreme weather events had seen severe funding cuts that left the population vulnerable. The then Chancellor Philip Hammond said in June 2019 that transitioning to a zero-carbon economy would cost the British state £1 trillion and necessitate further cuts to public services.
639. Bastani, *op cit*, p38.

640. "None of the world's top industries would be profitable if they paid for the natural capital they use", Grist.org, 17 April 2013. 'Natural capital' refers to ecological materials like clean water or a stable atmosphere.

641. In perhaps the best example of the overproduction crisis, between 1969 and 1997 the vehicle population in the US grew six times faster than the human population. The number of cars increased two and a half times as fast as the number of households, and twice as fast as the number of drivers. See "Number of cars is growing faster than human population", nytimes.com, 21 September 1997. Although cars will become less prevalent, the ones we do make will be much better, since the fetter on production has stymied innovation and made sports cars unprofitable.

642. The amount of plastic produced each year is roughly the same as the entire weight of humanity – and 91% of it doesn't get recycled. 8.3bn tonnes have been produced since the 1950s. An estimated 12.7 million tonnes end up in the oceans every year, a truckload every minute. The UN Environment Programme says that, at current rates, there will likely be more plastic in the sea than fish by 2050. One study warns of the "near-permanent contamination of the planet". Imperialist nations have long exported recyclable waste to poorer countries but the latter have started to reject it, saying much of it arrives illegally and contaminated. Britain is rapidly running out of landfill capacity. It was declared 'the dustbin of Europe' in 2010 for burying more than 18.8 million tonnes of household waste, two million tonnes more than any other EU nation. Much recyclable and biodegradable material ends up lingering in landfill, starved of oxygen and light, because brands mix them in hard-to-separate ways with non-recyclables for aesthetic purposes. Austerity has seen massive cuts to recycling collections.

643. The world produces enough food to feed 10 billion people, but roughly one third (1.3 billion tonnes) of the food produced for human consumption is wasted or lost every year and around 2.1 billion suffer from malnutrition. This is the anarchy of capitalist production and distribution. It must be acknowledged, however, that technological advances have achieved relative progress, with the number of people living in hunger having halved to 10% of the world's population in just the past 10 years (Bastani, *op cit*, p164) (although food prices and hunger have started to rise again since 2016.) This continues to disprove the Malthusian theory, still promoted by the likes of *The Population Bomb* author Paul Ehrlich, that increases in food production led to overpopulation and therefore falling average living standards.

644. The ever-increasing overproduction of commodities is an expression of the deepening crisis of capitalism. Commodities are commodities in their simple form, but they are also commodity capital. "Overproduction of capital, not of the individual commodities – although overproduction of capital always includes overproduction of commodities – is thus simply overaccumulation of capital." Marx, 1991, p359.

645. Global Footprint Network.

646. Michael Parenti, *Against Empire*, City Lights Books, San Francisco, 1995, p209.

647. Franck et al, "Harvesting the sun: New estimations of the maximum population of planet Earth", *Ecological Modelling*, June 2011.

648. Indeed, while most fringe right-wingers and fascists until now have denied the existence of climate change and framed it as a conspiracy theory (Trump has claimed, for example, that it was dreamed up by China to undermine the US economy) a presently small 'eco-fascist' trend accepts the existence of climate change and cites overpopulation as the cause, and therefore advocates depopulation as the solution.

649. This is the real basis of the misogynist anti-abortion lobby; if the basis for their 'pro-life' stance was a moral one, they would not be *de facto* pro-child poverty, pro-war and pro-ecocide, etc.

650. This tends to coincide with birth rates declining relative to child mortality. Poor or expensive medical care keeps birth rates high.
651. Marx, 1990, pp783-4.
652. Global Resources Outlook 2019.
653. At current rates, 2020 will be the first time in human history that there will be more people over the age of 65 than under the age of five. By 2050 there will be more people over 65 than under 14. "This is perhaps the crowning achievement of our species," says Bastani. "Nowhere else in nature do the old outnumber the young." *Op cit*, p138.
654. Meanwhile, some women have started a 'birth strike' to protest the lack of action on climate change and because they feel it would be morally wrong to bring children into a world that is on the brink of ecological and civilisational collapse.
655. Kristen Ghodsee, *Why Women Have Better Sex Under Socialism And Other Arguments For Economic Independence*, Vintage, London, p60.
656. Aamna Mohdin, "The fastest shrinking countries on Earth are in Eastern Europe", QZ.com, 24 January 2018. Ghodsee, *op cit*, p60.
657. Ghodsee, *op cit*, p61.
658. Ibid, p66.
659. Women now comprise almost 60% of all professionals in Cuba and more than half of scientists (compared to 25% in Europe).
660. "Americans are dying younger, saving corporations billions", Bloomberg.com, 8 August 2017.
661. Bastani, *op cit*, 143.
662. "Humans causing climate to change 170 times faster than natural forces", TheGuardian.com, 12 February 2017.613.
663. Andreas Malm, "The Anthropocene Myth", JacobinMag.com, 3 March 2015.
664. "The energy complex: meeting the world's energy needs", FidelityInternational.com.
665. "Consumption by the United States", public.wsu.edu.
666. "US military is the world's number one consumer of fuel", QSEnergy.com, 11 February 2010.
667. Wallace-Wells, 2019, p33.
668. Jason W Moore, *Anthropocene or Capitalocene? Nature, history, and the crisis of capitalism*, PM Press, 2016.
669. Granados et al, "Climate Change and the world economy: short-run determinants of atmospheric CO_2", *Environmental Science & Policy*, Vol 21, August 2012, pp50-62.
670. Quoted in Jason Hickel, "Why Branko Milanovic is wrong about de-growth", JasonHickel.org, 19 November 2017.
671. Mazzucato, *op cit*, p155. This progress has largely been driven by Chinese state investment. See further on.
672. 80% of the world's population inhabits areas with sufficient sunlight to rely exclusively on solar.
673. Bastani, *op cit*, p103-5.
674. Ibid, pp11-14.
675. "BP and Shell planning for catastrophic 5°C global warming despite publicly backing Paris climate agreement", Independent.co.uk, 27 October 2017.
676. Demand is also growing because of rising temperatures. For instance, demand for air conditioners and fans – which already account for 10% of global electricity consumption – is expected to triple or quadruple between now and 2050. Wallace-Wells, *op cit*, p42. Designing buildings with bigger windows to allow more natural daylight in would also reduce energy used for lighting.

677. "How Google, Microsoft, and Big Tech are automating the climate crisis", Gizmodo.com, 21 February, 2019.

678. "We could be witnessing the death of the fossil fuel industry – will it take the rest of the economy down with it?", AlterNet, 22 April 2016. The report adds: "At a speech at the London School of Economics in February, Jaime Caruana of the Bank for International Settlements said that outstanding loans and bonds for the oil and gas industry had almost tripled between 2006 and 2014 to a total of $3 trillion. This massive debt burden, he explained, has put the industry in a double-bind: in order to service the debt, they are continuing to produce more oil for sale, but that only contributes to lower market prices. Decreased oil revenues mean less capacity to repay the debt, thus increasing the likelihood of default."

679. Nafeez Ahmed, "Welcome to the Age of Crappy Oil", Vice.com, 18 August 2016.

680. Underlining the intensifying geo-strategic rivalries, in 2004 the International Energy Agency said the world's dependence on Middle Eastern oil would only deepen. It said global demand for oil would rise from 82.4 million barrels per day in 2004 to 121 million in 2030, a 50% increase, with the global oil supply share of Oil Producing and Exporting Countries (OPEC) rising from 35% to over 50%. Oil trade between producer and consumer countries would double. "Most of that additional trade will have to pass through vital choke-points, sharply increasing the possibilities of supply disruption," it said.

681. "Fossil fuel subsidies are a staggering $5 trillion per year", TheGuardian.com, 7 August 2017.

682. "42% of global coal power plants run at a loss, finds world-first study", CarbonTracker.org, 30 November 2018.

683. "G20 nations triple coal power subsidies despite climate crisis", TheGuardian.com, 25 June 2019.

684. Democratic socialists in the imperialist nations can be pretty shameless about their pro-imperialist chauvinism. The reference to the "free world" in particular exposes Johnson's anti-communism.

685. Brad Johnson, "The Green New Deal Needs WWII-Scale Ambition", JacobinMag.com, 3 March 2019.

686. Ibid.

687. Indeed, it is largely for this reason that the US has fallen behind in developing clean energy; having played a leading role in solar and wind in the 1980s (the first silicon solar cells were invented in the US in the 1950s) its leading manufacturers were lost through acquisition and bankruptcy, partly because falling fossil fuel prices made them uncompetitive. The US now lags behind a number of European countries as well as Japan and China. Even with large state support, venture capitalists have been reluctant to invest. Solyndra, the one-time darling of clean tech, received a $527m loan from the government but, after investing in an automated factory, the price of raw silicon collapsed and the costs of competing technology plummeted as a result of Chinese state investment. Venture capitalists pulled $1.1bn out of the company, it went bust and the government loan was wasted. Solyndra tried to sue the Chinese companies it blamed for its collapse and Republicans responded not by blaming venture capital's risk aversion but by repeating their standard slogan that the state cannot be trusted to "pick winners" and attacked the loan programme – even though it was designed to attract venture capital. The irony is that Chinese companies succeeded where US companies failed because state clean energy investment in China has been much higher. See Mazzucato, *op cit*, p135-142.

688. Leonid Bershidsky, "In Germany, The Green New Deal Actually Works", Bloomberg.com, 13 February 2019.

689. See "Germany's green energy shift is more fizzle than sizzle", *Politico*, 23 March 2018.

690. Dénes Csala, "Germany's plan for 100% electric cars may actually increase carbon emissions", The Conversation, 26 February 2017.

691. "Fabricating [solar] panels requires caustic chemicals such as sodium hydroxide and hydrofluoric acid, and the process uses water as well as electricity, the production of which emits greenhouse gases." NationalGeographic.com, "How Green Are Those Solar Panels, Really?", 11 November 2014.

692. Rehman, *op cit*.

693. See *The Rivers are Bleeding: British Mining in Latin America – Updated*, WarOnWant.org, April 2019.

694. "Leading scientists set out resource challenge of meeting net zero emissions in the UK by 2050", nhm.ac.uk, 5 June 2019.

695. Clough et al, "Imperialism relentlessly driving climate change", revolutionarycommunist.org, 28 May 2019.

696. Backed by the US and British governments, the World Bank is exploiting the indebtedness of neo-colonies to extend its Enabling Business Agriculture indicator to 80 developing countries, requiring them to establish land titles on all common land to enable its sale to agribusiness multinationals. Between 2001 and 2014, agribusiness land grabs in Africa totalled 56 million hectares.

697. See the Prolekult documentary *Selling Extinction* and Cory Morningstar, Wrong Kind of Green.

698. In the geopolitical context, the fact China has the most mineral reserves on the planet, and given a transition to renewable energy infrastructure would make oil redundant, the transition has huge relevance to oil and the dollar. Presently, OPEC prices oil exclusively in dollars, necessitating the currency's presence in oil consuming nations (including Europe). Should a transition occur, then China would necessarily benefit and the dollar lose much of its gravity as the world's reserve currency. It would not install China's reminibi as the reserve currency for more than a relatively short period as, unlike oil, when the minerals are purchased and the infrastructure installed, minerals are not burned into thin air.

699. "History of hemp", Hemp.com.

700. Jeremy Briggs, "Hemp fuel guide", CBDoiled.com.

701. Grace Kaucic, "A sustainable alternative to fossil fuels: hemp & biofuel", HempHistoryWeek.com, 18 April 2019.

702. "Hemp seed nutrition", HempTank.co.uk.

703. "Hemp, and lots of it, could be one climate solution", *Huffington Post*, 6 December 2017. The extra 40 billion tonnes of carbon dioxide that is being pumped into the atmosphere each year could be offset in theory by planting three crop cycles per year of hemp on 6.5 billion acres of land. While that is an impossible figure to reach (and undesirable given the need for variation in vegetation and biodiversity) – only four billion acres of land, 37% of the Earth's land surface, is currently used for farmland – we shall see further on how much larger parts of the world could be freed up for hemp and other forms of green farming (and all the ways hemp can make emissions negative).

704. Gabriel Propkin, "How much can forests fight climate change?", *Nature.com*, 15 January 2019.

705. Briggs, *op cit*.

706. Kaucic, *op cit*.

707. A report by British MPs on the Environmental Audit Committee, Fixing Fashion, said that textile production contributes more emissions than international aviation and shipping combined, consumes lake-sized volumes of freshwater and

creates chemical and microplastic pollution. 300,000 tonnes of clothing is burned or buried in the UK every year. The government rejected the committee's recommendation to charge 1p for every garment to raise £35m a year for better clothing collection and sorting, saying it could only be considered by 2025. It also rejected the proposal to ban the incineration and landfilling of unsold clothes. Wrap, a clothing recycling charity, has lost 80% of its government funding since 2010.

708. Napper and Thompson, "Release of synthetic microplastic fibres from domestic washing machines: Effects of fabric type and washing conditions", *Marine Pollution Bulletin*, Vol 112, Issues 1-2, sciencedirect.com, 15 November 2016.

709. Jambeck et al. "Plastic waste inputs from land into the ocean", *Science*, 13 February 2015.

710. Sebille et al, "A global inventory of small floating plastic debris", *Environmental Research Letters* vol 10, no 12, IOPscience.iop.org, 8 December 2015.

711. Bangor University, "Microplastic pollution widespread in British lakes and rivers, study shows", phys.org, 7 March 2019.

712. "Microplastics discovered in human stools across the globe in 'first study of its kind'", EurekAlert.org, 22 October 2018.

713. "The Next Big Thing in 'Green' Packaging Is Hemp Bioplastic", GreenEntrepreneur.com, 29 November 2018.

714. "10 x Stronger Than Steel In The 1940s: Henry Ford's Hemp Car", Collective-Evolution.com, 25 February 2015.

715. Ben Dronkers, *Hanf Magazine*, Issue 4, November 2018, p55.

716. Alex Corren, "8 ways hemp can save the world", Medium.com, 17 May 2018.

717. The same is true of hemp bricks, which are made in combination with mycelium from fungus.

718. Quoted in Graham Durrant, "Why we should build with hempcrete", HempTank.co.uk, 30 May 2019.

719. "Better-than-zero-carbon buildings", UKhempcrete.com.

720. Dr Mike Lawrence, "Growing our way out of climate change by building with hemp and wood fibre", TheGuardian.com, 25 September 2014.

721. "Hemp walls saved India's ancient ellora caves", Seeker.com, 3 November 2016.

722. See Matt Weeks, "Hemp fabric to hemp plastic, is hemp really able to do all of this?", RxLeaf.com, 22 October 2018. Analysis by *Ethical Consumer* magazine in 2019 showed that producing toilet paper is becoming increasingly unsustainable. The growing demand for 'luxury' four-ply and quilted toilet roll is fuelling the use of virgin pulp in a bid to create the softest product. Kimberly-Clark, one of the biggest suppliers of toilet tissue worldwide, reduced the proportion of recycled wood pulp used in its total fibre from just under 30% in 2011 to 23.5% in 2017. The magazine said this was driving unnecessary deforestation, but for the sake of capital accumulation it is necessary. If people don't want to run out of toilet paper, they're going to have to fight for hemp-based socialism!

723. "Hemp fibres 'better than graphene'", BBC News, 13 August 2014.

724. "Alternet Systems Inc engages professor David Mitlin to launch hemp supercapacitor initiative", *Business Insider*, 18 October 2018.

725. "The hemp battery performs better than the lithium battery", CannabisTech.com, 16 August 2017.

726. "How to turn leaves into solar panels", actu.epfl.ch 3 February 2012.

727. Eben Bayer, "The Mycelium Revolution is upon us". *Scientific American*, 1 July 2019.

728. Bastani, *op cit*, 118.

729. Ibid, pp38-9.

730. Ibid, p119.

731. Leigh Phillips, *Austerity Ecology & the Collapse-porn Addicts: A defence of growth, progress, industry and stuff*, Zero Books, pp175-204.
732. See Joe Martino, "How hemp became illegal: the marijuana link", Collective-Evolution.com, 5 December 2012.
733. See Bewley-Taylor et al, *The Rise And Decline Of Cannabis Prohibition*, Transnational Institute, 2014, p3.
734. The ban was lifted during WWII because hemp imported from the Philippines was cut off after Pearl Harbour. The US government launched a film to encourage hemp farming called Hemp For Victory.
735. In July 2019, Canadian cannabis firm Sundial Growers bought Spalding-based Bridge Farm Group in Lincolnshire, England. The farm will be used to grow hemp and expanded to an estimated 3.8 million square feet, making it "one of the biggest fully automated growing structures in Europe". The expropriation of such a facility will be symbolic of the British Revolution.
736. Nutt et al, "Drug Harms In The UK: A Multicriteria Decision Analysis", *The Lancet* 376 (9752): 1558-1565, 2010.
737. Matt Weeks, "Cannabis kills all types of cancer cells that science has tested so far", RxLeaf.com, 27 November 2018.
738. *The Cannamanual*, Global Cannabinoids Solutions, p98.
739. Morgan and Zimmer, *The Myth Of Marijuana's Gateway Effect*, druglibrary.org, 1995.
740. *The Exit Drug*, Weedmaps, YouTube, 23 March 2018. Between 2000-15, the opioid crisis in the US saw more than 500,000 mostly white working class people in small towns and rural communities die prematurely from both illegal and legal opioid drug use. Legal prescription opioids – overprescribed by bribed doctors – now kill more people than both heroin and cocaine combined. (In 1949, 50 million of China's 400 million population were drug addicts, a legacy of Britain's Opium Wars on the Chinese people. By 1974, drug addiction was a memory. "Mao reconsidered", MRonline.org, 18 October 2017.)
741. CBD and THC have such an effective medical function because humans have an endocannabinoid system (ECS) – a network of cannabinoid receptors all over our bodies that provide chemical feedback for cellular communication. Talk about reuniting humanity with nature – there is an evolutionary link between cannabis and the human body! These receptors are located on inflammatory cells, white blood cells, lymphocytes and throughout the nervous system. They have anti-inflammatory effects and various properties that have health benefits. When you stimulate the cannabinoid type 1 receptor you reduce pain transmission into the nervous system, for example. CBD and THC therefore provide the same pain relief as opioids but without the potential addictiveness. For example, THC mimics and therefore complements or makes up for an underproduction of anandamide – an endocannabinoid – producing a calming effect on irritated neurons. (Those who do not have an underproduction of anandamide should not use cannabis too frequently. Like other drugs, nor is it always safe to mix with other drugs/medicines.) This area of medicine and anatomy is hugely under-researched due to prohibition. It was not until the 1990s that the ECS in humans was even discovered. We now know that the ECS is involved in fighting almost all diseases, opening the way for researchers to re-analyse how they should be treated. It may be that the ECS can be manipulated not just therapeutically but through vibrations and bioelectricity.
742. University of Mexico, "THC found more important for therapeutic effects in cannabis than originally thought", ScienceDaily.com, 26 February 2019.
743. University of York, "Risk of psychosis from cannabis use lower than originally thought, say scientists", ScienceDaily.com, 20 April 2017.

744. Anderson et al, "Association of marijuana laws with teen marijuana use", JAMA Pediatrics, 8 July, 2019.

745. "Associations between adolescent cannabis use frequency and adult brain structure: A prospective study of boys followed to adulthood", *Drug and Alcohol Dependence* volume 202, 1 September 2019, pp191-199.

746. Rarely taken into account is the fact that black market cannabis is usually mixed with tobacco – itself linked to psychosis – and contaminated with heavy metals, pesticides and potency-strengthening synthetics that are much stronger than natural THC and can damage the ECS and even cause death. The right kind of synthetic cannabinoids can be better than crude cannabis as they can target disease in a much more focused way, while digesting extract oil is more medicinally beneficial than inhaling through the lungs. The effects of cannabis, which is a family of medicines rather than one, are highly personal and cannot be assessed with double-blind trials or treated like a pharmaceutical. It is not a single substance; it contains more than 500 identified chemical constituents. What is not widely understood about THC is that it heightens lucidity, something which can be 'a shock to the system' but also a state of being that you can learn to operate on if you do not take too much. So while it can amplify already-existing paranoia or anything else in your subconscious (if you do take too much), it can also amplify happiness and creativity. In a society that did not give people so much to worry about the experience would be mostly blissful and intellectually empowering. In a communist world it would not be surprising if it eventually became much more common for people to learn how to operate on a higher plane of consciousness by using THC or other lucidity-heightening drugs (Silicon Valley workers are already renowned for 'microdosing' psychedelics for inspiration and focus). Recent potentially groundbreaking findings for psilocybin, the active compound in 'magic mushrooms', found that just a single high dose of the drug is effective at treating symptoms of both depression and anxiety in late-stage cancer patients. It is thought that psychedelics (banned during the Vietnam War in order to target anti-war protestors) hold the key to not only treating but healing the brain, opening up the possibility for effective treatments for post-traumatic stress disorder and degenerative diseases like dementia.

747. "Cannabis-derived compound may help treat schizophrenia", MedicalNewsToday.com, 5 June 2017.

748. In October 2018, Victoria Atkins MP – the British *drugs minister* – recused herself from responding to points relating to cannabis and synthetic cannabinoids in a debate about drug consumption rooms "due to the potential for a conflict of interest with my husband's business interests". Atkins, who opposes legalisation and decriminalisation, is married to Paul Kenward, managing director of British Sugar. Atkins therefore directly benefits financially from prohibition. Furthermore, former British Prime Minister Theresa May's husband Philip's £1.4 trillion investment firm Capital Group is GW's biggest shareholder. (Among Capital Group's other investments are General Dynamics, the company which runs migrant concentration camps in the US; it also manufactures weapons.) This flagrant corruption: keeps mafias (which enslave trafficked children, who are treated by the justice system as criminals instead of victims) in business; scores of (disproportionately young and black) people criminalised and incarcerated for non-violent drug offences; and forces old, disabled and ill people to obtain their medicine outside of the law, meaning they are often persecuted for growing their own. Parents of epileptic children in Britain have been forced to obtain private prescriptions overseas and then smuggle the medicine back into the country. (Illicit cannabis in Britain is worth £3bn a year, according to University College London, making it more profitable than alternatives. Cannabis profits are therefore often used by mafias to subsidise other areas of illegality, meaning legalisation would reduce crime in other areas, too. In England

and Wales, there were 2,917 deaths related to illicit drugs in 2018 – a year-on-year increase of 16%. At 51 deaths per million of the population, England and Wales' drug death rate is now more than double the European average (22 per million) and over 12 times that of Portugal, which decriminalised drugs in 2001.) However, May's monopoly cannot resist forever. As prices fall, more investors are becoming interested in the industry and demanding reform. In July 2019, the Adam Smith Institute recommended legalising recreational cannabis. While it obviously promoted private ownership, it did call for the expungement of cannabis-related convictions, and backed the regulation of cannabis social clubs and the right to grow your own, a demand made by working class patients who are concerned that legal recreational cannabis will remain prohibitively priced. In Canada, supply is yet to meet demand and so patients have continued to access their medicine from illegal community dispensaries, which the state has now started to crack down on, presumably on behalf of 'Big Pot'.

749. Other studies have linked pollution to heart disease, Alzheimers, cancer, diabetes, miscarriages and more. A recent comprehensive review concluded that air pollution may be damaging every organ and virtually every cell in the human body. Schraufnagel et al, "Air Pollution and Noncommunicable Diseases", *Chest Journal*, vol 155, issue 2, pp409-416.

750. "Vigorous US endeavour, including the use of unreliable scientific data and considerable influence over the recently established World Health Organisation (WHO), did much to ensure that cannabis was condemned within the 1961 Single Convention as a drug with particularly dangerous properties.... Cannabis never passed the test of a scientific review by WHO experts against the criteria required for inclusion of any psychoactive substance in the UN schedules of controlled drugs." Bewley-Taylor et al, *op cit*, p3.

751. Three billion people still cook or access heat and light from biomass, primarily the burning of wood, dung and crop residue. According to the WHO this accounted for 36% of global respiratory infections in 2002, 22% of chronic obstructive pulmonary disease and almost 2% of all cancers. The falling prices of renewable and clean energy are bringing electricity to parts of the world that have until now gone without it. For example, in Kenya in 2009, a radio, solar-powered mobile phone charger and enough electricity for four hours of light and television cost $1,000, but that has fallen to $350. Bastani, *op cit*, p109-111.

752. According to a report by consultancy firm Prohibition Partners, a legal cannabis industry in Africa could be worth more than $7.1bn a year by 2023 if legislation is introduced in a few of the continent's major markets. The report notes that the plant's medicinal properties have given it "an exalted status in local folklore" in Africa for thousands of years. Africa has one of the highest user rates of cannabis in the world, at 13.2% – 76 million from a population of 1.2 billion. Many farmers in Africa have turned to illegal cannabis cultivation anyway as the only means of subsistence following a decline in demand for other crops, such as tobacco. The UN estimates that 38,000 tonnes of illegal cannabis is produced across Africa each year, with a market value of billions of dollars. "This agricultural expertise in cannabis farming could position Africa as a leading producer of cannabis," says the report.

753. Briggs, *op cit*.

754. Herer, *The Emperor Wears No Clothes*, Access Unlimited, California, 1985, p11.

755. "How CO_2 could be the future of fuel", VICE on HBO, 13 September 2018.

756. *Nature* magazine has dismissed all scenarios built on carbon capture and storage as "magical thinking" because it would require so many large-scale plantations. One estimate suggests the number of large-scale plants that would have to open per day to stop the 2°C rise would be one and a half for the next 70 years. In 2018, there were 18 in total. Wallace-Wells, 2019, p45-6.

757. "Carbon emissions had levelled off. Now they're rising again", NationalGeographic.co.uk, 13 November 2017.
758. "This gasoline is made of carbon sucked from the air", NationalGeograhic.com.au, 8 June 2018.
759. "Climate change: 'magic bullet' carbon solution takes big step", BBC News, 3 April 2019.
760. See "5. Quote of the Day", Axios.com, 3 April 2019.
761. Tim Smedley, "The technology that turns CO_2 into rock", Medium.com, 18 January.
762. "UK 'sky mining' facility creates carbon-negative diamonds", *Engineering and Technology*, 30 October 2020. Producing a one carat diamond requires the shifting of around 1,000 tonnes of rock and earth, consumes almost 4,000 litres of water, and generates more than 100kg of carbon emissions. A 'sky mining' facility extracts carbon dioxide from the atmosphere, which is then liquified, purified and mixed with hydrogen split from molecules of rainwater to make methane. This is inserted into a diamond mill, where the diamonds are grown in balls of plasma at around 8,000°C via chemical vapour deposition. The entire process is powered with wind and solar energy. Gold that is 'golden than gold' can also be produced in labs. See "New form of lab-made gold is better and golder than nature's pathetic version", iflscqence.com, 5 July 2018. Competition (especially from China) has already compelled the De Beers diamond mining multinational to invest in synthetic diamond production, with the per carat price plummeting from $4,200 in May 2018 to $800 just three months later (compared to $6,000 for a mined diamond).
763. F Kestner (1912), quoted in Grossman, *op cit*, pp175-6.
764. Marx, 1991, p203-4.
765. "$180bn investment in plastic factories feeds global packaging binge", TheGuardian.com, 26 December 2017.
766. Wallace-Wells, 2019, p178.
767. Jason Hickel, "Clean energy won't save us – only a new economic system can", TheGuardian.com, 15 July.
768. Quoted in Mazzucato, *op cit*, p130.
769. "Global air transport continues to expand", WorldwatchInstitute.org, 17 December 2013. Only 1% of exports by volume go in aircraft but because they tend to be the most expensive goods, they account for 35% of global trade by value. The number of passengers travelling by plane increased 95-fold from 31 million in 1950 to 2,957 million in 2012. The cumulative climate impact of aviation to date in 2012 was equivalent to about 40% of all surface transport modes, even though motor vehicles are far more numerous than planes. "Relative to all sources of GHG emissions, the sector is responsible for about 4% of climate change, and its role is rising rapidly," says the report.
770. "Climate change – the facts", BBC, 18 April 2019.
771. Wallace-Wells, 2017.
772. It has been estimated that every degree Celsius of warming costs, on average, 1.2% of GDP. 50% of GDP could be destroyed by climate change by 2100, although this is likely a conservative estimate. For every half-degree of warming, it is estimated that societies will see a 10-20% increase in the likelihood of armed conflict. See Hsiang et al, "Estimating economic damage from climate change in the United States", *Science*, vol 356, issue 6345, ScienceMag.com, 30 June 2017, pp1362-1369.
773. Quoted in Wallace-Wells, *op cit*, 2019, p122.
774. Wallace-Wells, 2019, p13.
775. Mazzucato, *op cit*, p130.
776. Ibid, p132.

777. "The power of China's energy efficiency policies", The French Institute of International Relations, 5 September 2018.
778. Echo Huang, "For every $1 the US put into adding renewable energy last year, China put in $3", QZ.com, 9 April 2018.
779. Mazzucato, *op cit*, p130.
780. "China is crushing the US in renewable energy", CNN.com, 18 July 2017.
781. Ibid.
782. A feed-in tariff is a payment made to households or businesses generating their own electricity through the use of methods that do not contribute to the depletion of natural resources, proportional to the amount of power generated.
783. Ibid.
784. Huang, *op cit*.
785. Volkov, *op cit*, p54.
786. Ibid.
787. Volkov, *op cit*, pp56-7.
788. Ibid, p63.
789. Ibid, p55.
790. David Hetfield, "Socialism is good for the environment", *FRFI* 214, April/May 2010.
791. At least 30% of crops and 90% of wild plants need natural pollinators like bees to survive. In the six years to 2013, more than 10 million bee colonies were lost, nearly twice the normal rate of loss. Shortages of bees in the US have increased the cost to farmers renting bees for pollination services by up to 20%. One of the factors behind the die-off is thought to be the introduction of a new breed of insecticide called neonicotinoids, which, as the name suggests, says Wallace-Wells "effectively turned all the bees into cigarette fiends" (2019, p152).
792. "Why does Cuba have the healthiest bees?", People's World, 9 October 2018.
793. Going back to the importance of hemp, a study in North Carolina during July to September 2018 found that hemp "exhibits mass pollen shedding" when "many crops have completed bloom leading to a dearth of nutritional resources for pollinators", which sees bees becoming stressed as they search for pollen sources to feed their young. "Thus, hemp becomes a valuable pollen source for foraging bees." See Colton O'Brien, "What is with all the buzzing? Exploring bee diversity in industrial hemp", esa.confex.com, 11 November 2018. It has also been found that honey, wax, and brood production thrive after feeding bee hives with a special formulated syrup containing high levels of THC. See "Naturally infused honey & the effects of cannabis on bees", Vimeo.com.
794. "Cuba's urban farming revolution: how to create self-sufficient cities", Architectural-Review.com, 17 March 2014.
795. Hetfield, *op cit*.
796. Volkov, *op cit*, p58-9.
797. Ibid, p60.
798. Ibid, p60-1.
799. Ibid, p62.
800. At present the average ingredient in a person's meal in the US travels 1,150 miles before consumption, while 70% of a food's final retail price comes from transportation, storage and handling. Bastani, *op cit*, p181. At present, 36 % of all mammals are human; almost all the rest, 60%, are captive, awaiting slaughter.
801. George Monbiot, "Lab-grown food will soon destroy farming – and save the planet," TheGuardian.co.uk, 8 January 2020.
802. Bastani, *op cit*, p168-175. While advocating cellular agriculture may seem at odds with our argument for reuniting man and nature, it is hard to see how any state could swiftly force so many people to give up meat without causing serious

social conflict, while it will also help to safeguard against shortages in general. Furthermore, technology is made from nature and is therefore *a part of nature*. Cellular agriculture may potentially smooth the way in both the process of weaning people off of conventional meat and reclaiming land from agribusiness for state-run collective farming. In the long run, perhaps humans will give up meat altogether. Many of the world's best athletes, including weightlifters, are now switching to plant-based diets and seeing huge improvements in their performance. Scientists have conducted experiments showing that switching to plant-based diets (even over organic meat) significantly reduces the chances of getting heart disease and cancer, and improves physical and sexual health. In the last decade archeologists have started to believe that early humans ate mostly plants; that human teeth are designed to eat plants, not meat, and the same is true of the digestive system in general. (See the documentary *The Game Changers*.) While a more in-depth investigation is required, it is probable that the introduction of private property and the labour-intensity of agriculture is what brought about the dominance of meat-eating. The damage capitalism has done to the soil has also diminished the nutritional density of our fruit and vegetables. Methods which are showing success in reversing this that socialism should look at upscaling on state-run collective farms are hydroponics and permaculture (see the documentary *The Need To Grow*.)

803. Marx, 1991, p911.
804. Bellamy Foster, "Late Soviet ecology and the planetary crisis", MonthlyReview.org, 1 June 2015.
805. Quoted in ibid.
806. Quoted in ibid.
807. Quoted in ibid.
808. Quoted in ibid.
809. It was not until the post-Soviet era that Vladimir Putin was finally to sign altogether out of existence Stalin's Group I of protected forests – those under the highest level of protection and preservation. Ibid.
810. Quoted in ibid.
811. Quoted in ibid.
812. Quoted in ibid.
813. Quoted in ibid.
814. "Hurricane tips from Cuba", nytimes.com, 29 July 2013.
815. NASA's Saturn V, first launched in 1967 remains the tallest, heaviest and most powerful vehicle ever built. Only now that manufacturing prices are nosediving is a more powerful launch vehicle being built, by SpaceX.

Conclusion: socialism or extinction
816. Marx and Engels, 2011, p89.
817. Quoted in Smith, *op cit*, p315.
818. Although the absolute number of slaves in the US continued to grow, the number relative to the whole population tended to fall before slavery was abolished in the US (approx. 25% in 1790 versus 16% in 1860). ("Population of the United States, 1790-1860," ncpedia.org). Similarly, the proportion of manufacturing workers in the total workforce under capitalism in the US has tended to fall (26.4% in 1970 versus 8.51% in 2018). Marx wrote in support of the 'bourgeois republic' in the North against the slave oligarchy of the South, convinced that the complete abolition of slavery was a precondition for the emancipation of the US working class and that "labour in white skin cannot achieve dignity as long as it is despised in a black skin". Furthermore, writes Grossman, slavery's "inherent expansionist tendencies limited the possibilities for northern industrial capital and hence the development of the industrial proletariat". Slavery was inherently dependent on expansion since

land was cultivated by means of extensive farming – the intensive nature of slave labour exhausted the land. To preserve themselves, slavers had to export slavery by seizing new territory. For Marx, the US form of slavery differed to the purely consumptionist system of antiquity (the ancient past) because it was part of the present profit-making system that served the world market. Abraham Lincoln's election in 1860 came with the demand from Republicans to limit slavery to the South, to push it back out of the 'free states'. The union therefore became worthless to the South. Its war against the North was not a defensive one for the status quo but a war of aggression and conquest. "It was not difficult to predict that, in this case, the living standards of the white working class of the North would gradually be forced down to the level of the slaves," says Grossman. Lincoln eventually realised that, to save the Union – and its most agriculturally fertile regions – slavery would have to be abolished. "It was an unavoidable struggle between two social systems that could no longer peacefully coexist, because the continued existence of the one was only possible by virtue of its victory over the other!" Grossman, 2017, pp455-8. Soviet leaders that promoted peaceful co-existence with imperialism apparently did not adopt the same sort of logic, although the position was more likely driven by the impossibility of defeating US imperialism at that time.

819. Armed soviets usually only formed under conditions of national military defeat. There must be some hope now, because *everybody would lose in a world war*, and because the economy is going to sink into an unprecedented crisis, that revolutions will be possible without losing a world war first.

820. Quoted in Grossman, 2017, p433.

821. Marx and Engels, *op cit*, p2.

822. Volkov (*op cit*, p111): "Whereas the worker is the object from which moneyed wealth is derived, the capitalist is the subject of this wealth. He is wealth personified. Material wealth is incarnated in the individual instead of the individual being the incarnation of wealth. The petty world of the bourgeois, in which man devotes himself to accumulating things (in their concrete or moneyed form) instead of things being devoted to man, is just as dehumanised, if not more so, as the world of the hired worker whom society robs both physically and spiritually. The principle of private property permeates and subjugates the individual. Things possess man rather than the reverse. His strength (and his weakness) does not lie in his own physical and spiritual potentialities, but in his moneyed wealth. Wealth rises above the individual instead of being the individual's wealth and his inner and most essential quality. This is why Marx condemned bourgeois political economy based on moneyed wealth as a systematic 'negation of man' and laid bare the inhuman nature of capitalist relations."

823. "Nuclear weapons: experts alarmed by new Pentagon 'war-fighting' doctrine", TheGuardian.com, 19 June 2019.

824. Indeed, religion is dying alongside the law of value in the most economically advanced countries – 70% of 16 to 29 year-olds in Britain identify with no religion, for example, according to a study by St Mary's University. ("… the miracles of gods [are] rendered superfluous by the miracles of industry…". Marx, 1844, p56.) Rising scarcity, however, as capitalism collapses, is likely to see religion rise again somewhat. The abolition of the law of value will underpin the 'completion' of the Enlightenment and eventually abolish superstition for good.

825. This is not to claim that revolutions will necessarily succeed first in the imperialist countries. While revolution in the imperialist countries is now very important and more likely than ever given their high development, low rates of profit and downwardly mobile middle classes, the proletariat remains proportionally bigger – and poorer – in the non-imperialist countries. Ordinarily it would therefore probably take revolutions in the latter to spur revolutions in the

former, having cut off the imperialist parasite's source of wealth. However, we have also seen that this process has started 'organically', with automation spurring the insourcing of production, while capitalism threatens to collapse everywhere simultaneously. Marx and Engels originally thought that revolution would begin in England but later changed their position, having come to the conclusion that the Irish would free the English and not vice-versa. (See David Yaffe, *Ireland: Key to the British Revolution*, Larkin Publications.) The socialist revolution instead began in Russia, the most underdeveloped imperialist nation, and only spread to other underdeveloped countries. Despite that, it is not unreasonable to argue, given what our investigation has revealed, that Marx and Engels' original prediction, that the most developed countries would become socialist first, is now possible again. It would certainly help the proletariat in the neo-colonies – arguably, the sadistic viciousness of imperialist reaction, especially in Korea and Vietnam, had the desired effect of deterring much of the oppressed world from the call to fight for socialism.

826. Pilger, *op cit*, 20 June 2016. Bell, *op cit*, 14 July 2019. See also Bell's excellent Prolekult documentary *History is Marching*.

827. "All you wanted to know about nuclear war but were too afraid to ask", TheGuardian.com, 16 July 2018.

828. "Threat of nuclear weapons use has risen, says Lords Committee", parliament.uk, 24 April 2019.

829. "'We used to talk during the Cold War': top US general urges communication with Moscow", RT, 15 April 2019.

830. Andrei Platonov, "On the First Socialist Tragedy", 1934.

831. The best chance for the neo-colonies to become independent from imperialism has always been to become socialist. You can become independent from one imperialist state only to become dependent on another. Because capitalism is now so close to expiring, any national liberation struggle today is only going to succeed in the long run if it becomes socialist. The most successful national liberation struggles have been led by communists. This is what Fidel and Raúl Castro and Che Guevara came to understand so well – that the only way to expel US colonialism was to nationalise industry in order to reduce dependence on foreign investment. It was through this line of argument that they won enough support to make the revolution in Cuba a socialist one – it was not until two years after the revolution that Fidel Castro declared its character to be socialist. In fact, the Cuban communists gave the national bourgeoisie ample opportunity to cut their ties with the US, but this proved to be impossible. As Guevara said: "The national bourgeoisie were basically importers. Their interests were entangled with imperialism and they were against us. We destroyed them, both economically and politically." "Memorandum of conversation between Mao Zedong and Ernesto 'Che' Guevara", p3.

832. Enforcing slavery (up to about 20% of the Nazi Empire's population) and the Holocaust was unsustainable due not only to the resistance of slaves (productivity was extremely low) but also because of the mounting fuel costs involved.

833. "In proportion as the exploitation of one individual by another is put an end to, the exploitation of one nation by another will also be put an end to. In proportion as the antagonism between classes within the nation vanishes, the hostility of one nation to another will come to an end." Marx and Engels, 2015, p30.

Afterword

834. Rosa Luxemburg, *The Essential Rosa Luxemburg*, edited by Helen Scott, Haymarket, Chicago, 2008, p43.

835. Mandel certainly made an important contribution but, like so many, he could be guilty of over-complicating the theory. His criticism of Grossman was pedantic to

the point of being obtuse, claiming that Grossman "failed" because of a focus on one contradiction – overaccumulation – instead of the myriad contradictions. But Grossman did no such thing, for he showed why the myriad of contradictions always *resulted* in overaccumulation. Mandel even claimed that Grossman misunderstood the role of competition and "forgot" to deal with the "historical and social element" of the value of labour power (see Kuhn *op cit*, footnote 8, p187), presumably because he did not deal explicitly with automation. Even so, Grossman had shown that capitalism would collapse from an absolute overaccumulation of capital, before a zero rate of profit and therefore before full automation could be achieved. Mandel's book in 1968 was timely amid the emerging crisis of Keynesianism and in refuting the prevalent theories of post-industrialism, which asserted that technology was eradicating the contradictions that produced capitalist crisis. *Late Capitalism* is particularly good on automation and effectively upholds "The Fragment on Machines" without distorting it. However, Mandel's work has plenty of shortcomings. He implies, for instance, like some other Trotskyists, that workers in underdeveloped countries are no more exploited than their counterparts in imperialist nations. See Smith, *op cit*, pp203-22 for a critique of this and other incorrect theories of imperialism among contemporary academics, including from David Harvey, perhaps the most well-known current Marxist academic.

836. Mattick was a 'council communist' who was against a large, centralised state, not just because he feared it would become oppressive but also unresponsive. He advocated the commune as the basic unit of governance, with each commune electing members to military and economic planning committees, and so on. This was not too dissimilar from Lenin's backing of a "commune state" in the April. That the central organs of the state came to be so large was surely a manifestation of the Soviet Union's isolation in the face of imperialist aggression. That Grossman supported the Soviet Union despite the hostility of its leadership towards his theoretical work gives us an idea of his principled anti-sectarianism.

837. Grossman, 2017, p280.

838. Ibid, pp596-7.

839. Quoted in Kuhn, *op cit*, p189.

840. Grossman, 2019, p143.

841. Lenin, "The Collapse of the Second International", *Collected Works* vol. 21, Lawrence & Wishart, London, 1974 (1915), pp214-5.

842. In 2011, Treasury Secretary Timothy Geithner told Congress that a US government default would cause interest rates to spike the world over because US treasury bonds represent the benchmark borrowing rate. If the government defaulted and either refused to pay interest or said it would pay bonds back at a fraction of the face value, trillions of dollars in what were previously safe assets would be wiped out. Geither said the US government may as a result have to stop paying the salaries of soldiers and other government officials. "Secretary Geithner sends debt limit letter to Congress," treasury.gov, 1 June 2011.

843. While the chances of relatively swift and peaceful revolutions on the basis of mass defections are far from guaranteed – some revolutions will obviously take longer, perhaps much longer, than others – we *do not dogmatically rule the possibility out*, as, for example, Maoists have done. Maoists believe that because Lenin's relatively sudden and peaceful revolution proved to be a one-off (it was the counter-revolution and the scarcity produced by capitalist breakdown that was extremely violent), the science of revolution has moved on – universally – to that of the protracted people's war. While this may turn out to be correct, it must at least be questioned since *no revolution has been tested in the circumstances of capitalism's final breakdown*. Not to mention the fact that many protracted people's wars – some lasting decades – have not succeeded, either (because they have operated in

circumstances where the masses have been passive, or remained reformist). In the context of a final breakdown it does not seem outlandish to suggest that capitalism *could* fall as swiftly as the Soviet Union fell. (This is not to suggest that the fall of the Soviet Union was not very violent; but, because of mass defections, it did not involve years of war.) Whether the 'Maoist' approach becomes necessary can only really be judged as developments materialise, based on all sorts of variables, from country to country – as was the case during the Chinese Revolution itself, when Mao abandoned the Communist International's disastrous popular front tactic and took an independent path. Maoism, however, seems to tend towards adventurism/ accelerationism (premature action, ie without enough support/demanding more than the productive forces are capable of at a given time). Mao's Cultural Revolution and Great Leap Forward are examples of leaping over necessary stages of steady development and progress. This was partly fuelled by the *danwei* system of welfare benefits that overincentivised production, resulting in an unsustainable increase in the extraction of grain. Mao himself admitted to not fully understanding Marxist economics. With regards to the Sino-Soviet split, although both sides were guilty of sectarianism, it should probably be considered largely symptomatic of their relative isolation in a capitalist world, their underdevelopment and the remaining strength of the law of value globally at that point in history – although again it must be stressed that socialism is not going to be a totally harmonious political utopia!

844. Quoted in Grossman, 2017, p136.

845. The Red Army included many senior army personnel who had served the Tsar. *The Manifesto* (p17) anticipates a "portion of the bourgeoisie" taking the side of the proletariat, just as a portion of the feudal nobility sided with the bourgeoisie; while Lenin stressed that socialism needed bourgeois experts to train workers in highly skilled technical work, to farm, and so on. Guevara worked tirelessly to convince middle class technicians and the like to work for the revolution. That military personnel in the US donated more to Bernie Sanders than to fellow Democrat Joe Biden and Trump combined suggests that there is some potential to win them over as the crisis deepens. See *"Which Democratic candidates are national security employees opening their wallets for"*, ForeignPolicy.com, 8 November 2019.

846. Grossman, 2017, p254.

847. See *The Lost Revolution* by Chris Harman for an assessment of the complications and mistakes that arose during the German Revolution. For example, a premature attempt by the KPD to launch a general strike in 1921 when striking workers had only just gone back to work (everyone who did not support it were called 'scabs') was denounced by Lenin as an act of "ultraleft lunacy" and a failure to win over the "majority" of workers through "systematic class struggle". Harman, *The Lost Revolution*, Bookmarks, London, p215. Part of the problem is that new converts tend to be too gung-ho. The Bolsheviks dealt with this not by condemning them but by lauding their courage while trying to 'hold them back' with 'your time is coming' type speeches and stressing the importance of winning the majority in the soviets before power could be both seized and then held on to in the face of counter-revolution. The opposite problem also existed: in 1923, during hyperinflation, a fully prepared insurrection was called off at the last moment, essentially bottled by the leadership because it was suddenly felt that independent social democrats would not support the action, when hundreds of thousands of communists and workers were ready to fight. The KPD's membership declined again and it sunk into relative irrelevance as new leaders adopted a 'united front from below' stance that refused to talk to reformist leaders and labelled social democrats 'social fascists'. Membership picked up again as the SPD started to accept austerity measures after 1929 and the fight against the Nazis intensified, but by nowhere near enough to prevent catastrophe, with the SPD instead continuing to seek compromise.

848. Communists have to take into account the fact that 'bourgeois conservatism' (sometimes overstated) has penetrated all classes – most of us are born into bourgeois 'nuclear' families, after all – and is not something that can be 'drilled out' of the masses via a swift 'cultural revolution'. Socialist Cuba, for example, has to contend with the historical influence of catholicism, meaning socially progressive policies are sometimes opposed by the majority of the population. Culture continually evolves over protracted periods of time. It is not uncommon for the poorest workers and countries (where social conservatism is a legacy of European colonialism) to be the most socially conservative. The transition towards communal living and the realisation of post-scarcity will see social conservatism wither away, but over many decades. Part of this social conservatism is 'identity politics' (the primacy of nationality, gender etc over class) which (if it is not blatantly weaponised for the purposes of divide and rule or imperialist plunder) should usually be treated as we treat religion, as a private matter and 'sigh of the oppressed' (Marx).

849. Communists can fail to merge scientific socialism with the mass movement: through left deviationism (usually referred to as infantile ultraleftism or adventurism) or right deviationism (usually referred to as opportunism or tailism). The former involves revolutionaries isolating themselves from the mass movement by running too far ahead of it, either in rhetoric or action; or demanding more from the productive forces than is possible at the time; the latter involves 'dissolving' into the movement by supporting reforms but failing to press for the final goal of actual socialism in word and/or practice. Although we do not claim that Lenin never made any mistakes – he changed his mind on a number of occasions and admitted to making insincere criticisms of some opportunists – his work surely got the closest to maintaining the right political line. For an important discussion on Lenin and the merger theory, see *Lenin Rediscovered: What Is To Be Done? in Context* by Lars T Lih.

850. "The Cooperative Instinct," *Greater Good Magazine*, 21 September 2012.

851. Quoted in "Birds do it. Bats do it," *Greater Good Magazine*, 1 November 2009.

852. Marx, *Critique of the Gotha Programme*, Dodo Press, 2009 [1875], p8.

853. "Get drunk without a hangover on synthetic booze", Telegraph.co.uk, 22 January 2015.

854. Both a popular front (championed by Stalin) and a united front (championed by Trotsky) necessitate that working class forces enter into an alliance with reformist forces. Under a popular front, the right to criticise other organisations within this alliance is set aside for the sake of unity, whereas under a united front it is maintained. The right to criticism is a necessity if one is to retain an independence of organisation and of politics. To eschew it means that one must fall in line on *all* positions once the front has adopted them, likely rendering communist forces (who start out in the minority) as little more than mouthpieces for reformism. This renders the objective of forming such a front – that 'to fight for the hegemony [leadership] of proletarian politics over this alliance' – all but impossible. Communists should give some level of critical support to a popular front so as not to isolate themselves from the mass movement, but only by taking up the position of a united front. Stalin's flip-flop between the hard left sectarian line that social democrats were 'social fascists' – effectively alienating a large proportion of the masses during a period in which the *majority* of workers supported social democracy – and the soft opportunism of giving uncritical support to these very same 'social fascists', is a useful example of how both left and right deviationism can scupper the merger of scientific socialism and the mass movement. The bitterness felt towards the German SPD was justified but emotions cannot be allowed to cloud judgement. Trotsky was right when he wrote in his 1933 article "The German Catastrophe" that: "Instead of helping to aggravate the discord between Communism's principal political

adversary and its mortal foe – for which it would have been sufficient to proclaim the truth aloud instead of violating it – the Communist International convinced the reformists and the fascists that they were twins; it predicted their conciliation, embittered and repulsed the Social Democratic workers, and consolidated their reformist leaders. It was necessary to exploit to the limit the contradiction between reformism and fascism – in order to weaken fascism, at the same time weakening reformism by exposing to the workers the incapacity of the Social Democratic leadership. These two tasks fused naturally into one." By Stalin's logic, in Russia all of the Menshevik rank and file and the soviets themselves were social fascists until they swung behind the Bolsheviks. It was not a line Lenin used to win them over – "Bread, peace, and land" and "All power to the soviets", once they had finally lost their illusions in social democracy, is what did that. The Stalin-Trotsky dichotomy that still sows so much sectarianism on both sides distracts from Lenin's tactical superiority. While Trotsky rejected an alliance between the proletariat and the poor peasants (a counter-revolutionary position when the proletariat was in the minority) and Stalin offered critical (if temporary) support for the provisional bourgeois government to put pressure on it to end the war, Lenin called for an alliance between the proletariat and the poor peasants and "no faith in the provisional government". To their credit, Trotsky and Stalin both moved to Lenin's position. Note that Lenin did not raise the slogan of "down with the provisional government" before the majority had lost faith in the provisional government. He and the Bolsheviks also supported a 'workers' government', ie an all-social democratic government, while refusing to enter it, in order to show the masses that even this could not resolve the crisis.
855. Harman, *op cit*, p216.
856. Lenin, "The Discussion on Self-Determination Summed Up", "10. The Irish Rebellion of 1916", *Collected Works*, Marxists.org.

Update: The covid-19 crash
857. The World Wildlife Fund puts the spread of zoonotic diseases down to "the trade and consumption of high-risk wildlife; deforestation and conversion; expansion of agriculture and unsustainable intensification and animal production". The pandemic appears then to be yet another symptom of the demands of capital accumulation. (Any conspiracy – many theories abound – would be motivated by the same thing.) Monoculture contributes by denying animals the normality of co-evolving with nature, causing harmless microbes to transform into diseases. The outbreak is said to have come from bats in a wildlife market in Wuhan, China, but it is possible that China was just the first to report it – the virus is also said to have been present in the US a month beforehand (WSJ.com, 1 December). There are some genuine reasons to suspect that the severity of covid-19 has been seriously overstated by a sleight of hand to justify lockdowns, mass lay offs, civil rights rollbacks, privatisations and the ramping up of public debt to subsidise Big Pharma and Big Tech. According to Dr John Lee, a recently retired professor of pathology: "Every positive test for covid-19 must be [registered] in a way that it just would not be for flu or most other infections... The vast majority of respiratory deaths in the UK are recorded as bronchopneumonia, pneumonia, old age or a similar designation... If the patient has, say, cancer, motor neurone disease or another serious disease, this will be recorded as the cause of death, even if the final illness was a respiratory infection." Because the infection rate at the outset of the pandemic was ten to 20 times higher than testing could keep up with, "the headline death rate due to this virus is likely to be ten to 20 times lower [than the initially feared 5%; the rate was, as of 29 October, 1.15% in high income countries and 0.23% in low-income countries with younger populations (imperial.ac.uk)], say 0.25-0.5%. That puts the covid-19 mortality rate in the range associated with infections like

flu." (*Spectator.co.uk*, 28 March). (The H1N1 mortality rate was originally feared to be 1-5% but turned out to be 0.02%. BBC, 2 April.) He elaborates (30 May): "Very early on in the epidemic, rules surrounding death certification were changed – in ways that make the statistics unreliable. Guidance was issued which tends to reduce, rather than increase, referrals for autopsy ["usually requested by a coroner to ascertain the cause of death... Autopsy studies typically show major discrepancies between actual findings and clinical diagnosis in a quarter to a third of cases... [But] at a time when autopsies could have played a major role in helping us understanding this disease, the Chief Coroner issued guidance [on 26 March] which seemed designed to keep covid-19 cases out of the coronial system: 'The aim of the system should be that every death from covid-19 which does not in law require referral to the coroner should be dealt with via the [death certification] process.' And even guidance produced by the Royal College of Pathologists in February stated: 'In general, if a death is believed to be due to confirmed covid-19 infection, there is unlikely to be any need for a post-mortem examination to be conducted.'"]. Normally, two doctors are needed to certify a death, one of whom has been treating the patient or who knows them and has seen them recently. That has changed. For covid-19 only, the certification can be made by a single doctor, and there is no requirement for them to have examined, or even met, the patient. A video-link consultation in the four weeks prior to death is now felt to be sufficient for death to be attributed to covid-19. For deaths in care homes the situation is even more extraordinary. Care home providers, most of whom are not medically trained, may make a statement to the effect that a patient has died of covid-19. In the words of the Office for National Statistics, this 'may or may not correspond to a medical diagnosis or test result, or be reflected in the death certification'. From 29 March the numbers of 'covid deaths' have included all cases where covid-19 was simply mentioned on the death certificate – irrespective of positive testing and whether or not it may have been incidental to, or directly responsible for, death. From 29 April the numbers include the care home cases simply considered likely to be covid-19." (The US, Italy, Germany and Hong Kong also count any death of a patient who has covid-19 as a death caused by covid-19 (BBC, 2 April)). In January, peak flu season in Britain, the number of flu cases plummeted to a 130-year low, by 95% compared to the five-year average (Royal College of General Practices), when covid-19 cases were at their highest point. Britain downgraded its death toll by 5,377 the previous August as it included people with positive tests from months earlier. This was changed to 28 days. In Public Health England's (PHE) analysis for 21 March 2020-1 January 2021, 7,511 excess deaths in which other illnesses were listed as the underlying cause of death were registered as covid-19 deaths. Deaths from heart disease, stroke, circulatory disease, dementia and Alzheimer's, urinary and liver diseases, and from causes other than covid-19, were 11,013 over the five-year average, with 5,057 of these listed as covid-19 deaths. When deaths from the underlying cause were below the five-year average, as they were for cancer, Parkinson's disease, acute respiratory infections, chronic lower respiratory diseases, and other respiratory diseases (particularly the last three), 2,454 deaths were registered as covid-19 deaths. From 21 March-8 January, there had been 76,220 excess deaths in England overall – up 19.74% on the expected number (462,241 vs 386,021) based on the five-year average – with 82,160 deaths with covid-19 mentioned on the death certificate overall. But among excess deaths in England and Wales (which has 5% of England's covid deaths), 140 a day have been at home "very few of which are from covid-19" (*BMJ*, 18 November). Extrapolating that figure over a year would equate to 51,100. *The Lancet* reported "substantial increases" in "avoidable" cancer deaths (20 July). The waiting list for operations rose to 4.5 million, with people waiting for more than a year rising 137-fold from 1,398 in November 2019 to 192,169 a year later. Hospital admissions for routine treatment fell by 27% (NHS England, 14 January). While some precautions may be necessary to protect the most vulnerable people and slow down the spread of a new disease while its lethality is being assessed so that hospitals (already decimated by capital) are not overburdened, the effectiveness of lockdown (closing pubs and restaurants encourages 'underground' gatherings where 'social distancing' is less likely to be regulated; the virus is bound to spread via food distribution; and so on) and its wider impact, such as on mental health and domestic abuse, must also be taken under consideration. Numerous studies since March 2020 have argued that lockdowns had little effectiveness in suppressing transmission but seriously harmed public health. (See: Bendavid et al, *European Journal of Clinical Investigation* ("there is no evidence that more restrictive non-pharmaceutical interventions ('lockdowns') contributed substantially to bending the curve of new cases in England, France, Germany, Iran, Italy, the Netherlands, Spain, or the United States in early 2020"; Chaudry et al, *The Lancet* ("government actions such as border closures, full lockdowns, and a high rate of covid-19 testing were not associated with statistically significant reductions in the number of critical cases or overall mortality"); Kuhbandner et al, University of Regensburg ("official data from Germany's RKI agency suggest strongly that the spread of the coronavirus receded autonomously, before any interventions become effective"); Wood, University of Edinburgh ("the decline in infections in England… began before full lockdown… [S]uch a scenario would be consistent with… Sweden, which began its decline in fatal infections shortly after the UK, but did so on the basis of measures well short of full lockdown"); Homburg and Kuhbandner, datascienceassn.org ("Flaxman et al allege that non-pharmaceutical interventions imposed by 11 European countries saved millions of lives. We show that their methods involve circular reasoning."); Rice, *British Medical Journal (BMJ)* ("the addition of interventions restricting younger people might actually increase the total number of deaths from covid-19"); Cohen and Lipsitch, HHS Public Access ("interventions that reduce but do not eliminate exposure can paradoxically increase the number of cases of severe disease by shifting the burden of infection toward older individuals"); Woolf et al, JAMA ("restrictions imposed by the pandemic (eg stay-at-home orders) could claim lives indirectly through delayed care for acute emergencies, exacerbations of chronic diseases, and psychological distress (eg drug overdoses). In 14 states, more than 50% of excess deaths were attributed to underlying causes other than covid-19"); Karáth, *BMJ*; ("Belarus's President… [who has recently fended off a US-backed coup] refused to impose a lockdown, close schools, or cancel mass events…Yet the country's death rate is among the lowest in Europe"); Thomas et al, *Biosecurity and Bioterrorism* ("the negative consequences… are so extreme… they should be eliminated from serious consideration"); Letizia et al, *New England Journal of Medicine*; De Larochelambert, *Frontiers in Public Health*; Gibson, *New Zealand Economic Papers*.) Arguably lockdowns could be shorter and more decisive under socialism because of secure and consistent economic interests (while vaccines and contact tracing systems would be more trustworthy). Under capitalism, lockdowns will only get worse as the system continues to collapse. A regional tier system has already been put in place in Britain, possibly the first stage of plans to effectively balkanise the population indefinitely. Liberals and social democrats in Britain, though, keep calling for harder lockdowns, only to then act surprised when extraordinary powers are abused by an authoritarian Tory government, which claims to be acting to protect public health when it has done the opposite. The government forced care homes, while starving them of resources, including staff, to accept untested and positive patients (BBC, 29 July) – something Labour left-wingers never seem to mention in their calls for harder lockdowns – making lockdown all but pointless. One way or another, this smacks of eugenics. The details were covered up "to protect commercial interests" (The Guardian, 27 August). With enough state support, people with symptoms would be incentivised to self-isolate. Low sick pay has forced many people to continue working after being told to stay home ("£13 a day isn't enough – isolating workers need proper sick pay", TUC.co.uk, 27 August). As a result, black and minority ethnic people, overrepresented in the NHS and low-paid work, have been disproportionately affected both by the virus (Manchester.ac.uk, 12 January) and the punitive measures enforcing lockdown, with a sharp rise in 'stop and search', which went up by 40% ("Coronavirus: Disproportionate number of BAME people fined", BBC, 3 June). (They have also disproportionately lost more jobs, according to the TUC (*FT*, 20 January). In the US, mortgage failures are highest in predominantly black counties (Black Knight Inc); and black-owned small businesses have seen their business activity fall three times more than white counterparts (-41% vs -17%; -32% for Hispanic; -26% Asian) (National Bureau of Economic Research)). Health Secretary Matt Hancock said one in three people with covid-19 are asymptomatic (the *British Medical Journal* (*BMJ*) says it's 80%, 2 April) and labelled them a "silent danger". A *BMJ* editorial (21 December) reported that a city-wide prevalence study of almost 10 million people in Wuhan found "no evidence" of asymptomatic transmission and said rapid testing of asymptomatic people was a waste of scarce resources. The Tory government, which blames the public for not following lockdown rules when the infection rate goes up, can now justify a harsher lockdown any time it feels any kind of political threat (in a country where, compared to France, for example, resistance to austerity has been almost non-existent). As Linda Bauld, a professor at the University of Edinburgh, has said, Downing Street's "blame game" consists of reproaching young people and threatening to impose larger fines. Prime Minister Boris Johnson complained about people "brazenly defying" restrictions when a very high 90% of the public have followed them (BMJ.com, 7 January). Yet he defended his unelected chief aide Dominic Cummings, who drove to a beauty spot on his wife's birthday to "test his eyes" (ChronicleLive.co.uk, 25 May) and then 260 miles to his parents, supposedly to seek childcare when his wife had covid-19, on a day that happened to coincide with the death of his uncle, Lord Justice Laws. People reportedly started to follow guidelines less strictly as a result (Independent.co.uk, 3 June), which was perhaps the intended outcome. The Tory Party is badly divided on the issue of lockdown, since some sections of capital are doing well out of it at the expense of others, resulting in inconsistent rules ("Independent shops hit out at high street chains trading during lockdown", TheGuardian.com, 7 November). Despite having a pandemic down as one of the biggest threats to national security, in the past few years the government slashed spending on stockpiles of protective equipment for NHS staff (BBC, 28 April 2020). Funding vaccines, of course, means heaping more debt on to the public. Some of the concerns about their effectiveness and safety cannot be smugly dismissed as conspiracy theory. (See, for example: "Will covid-19 vaccines save lives? Current trials aren't designed to tell us", *British Medical Journal* (*BMJ*), 22 October; "Informed consent disclosure to vaccine trial subjects of risk of covid-19 vaccines worsening clinical disease", *International Journal of Clinical Practice*, 28 October; "Unlicensed vaccine manufacturers are immune from some, but not all, civil liability", Full Fact, 4 September; "Victims of swine flu jab to get £60m payout", TheTimes.co.uk, 2 March 2014.) An alleged cache of email exchanges between EU officials and the European Medicines Agency showed the drug regulator was uncomfortable about fast-tracking approval for the Pfizer and Moderna jabs (*Le Monde*, 18 January). The British government postponed the second dose from three to 12 weeks after the first – which many people had already received – to 'get more people protected sooner' when Pfizer said there was no data to suggest the first shot continued to be effective after 21 days. Conflicts of interest among the government's covid-19 advisors were covered up (*BMJ*, 9 December), although it later emerged the UK's chief scientific adviser Sir Patrick Vallance has a £600,000 shareholding in GlaxoSmithKline, which has been contracted for a vaccine.

Under threat of legal action, the UK government released details about NHS covid data deals with Google, Microsoft, Amazon and the Cummings-linked Faculty (Open Democracy, 5 June). The *BMJ* has accused the government of "state corruption" and "suppressing science". The privatisation of the NHS has been accelerated and contracts awarded with no competition, oversight or due diligence (British Medical Association, 23 July). Vallance later claimed a variant of the virus in Britain – the country most in need of a deep depression (and therefore a longer lockdown) – had mutated into the most lethal one in the world. There have been up to 20,000 mutations identified but "in reality, mutations rarely impact outbreaks dramatically" (Grubaugh et al, nature.com). Covid-19 is expected to become as mild as the common cold (NewScientist, 21 January). 40-60% of unexposed people are thought to have immunity due to covid-19's similarity to already circulating coronaviruses (Grifoni et al) and PHE found that people who recover from covid-19 have a similar level of protection against future infection as those who receive a vaccine (at least for the first five months, the time it had to conduct the research). Yet former Labour Prime Minister Tony Blair – notorious for selling the lie of 'weapons of mass destruction' to justify invading Iraq – is calling for the introduction of 'health passports', meaning only those who have a vaccine would be allowed to travel. Such fascistic plans and the corporate 'we're all in this together' facade were particularly exposed when, to keep prices high, the Gates Foundation and imperialist states reneged on promises to waiver patents, meaning nine in 10 poorer nations are expected to be denied the vaccine in 2021 (Kaiser Health News, 25 August; TheNational.scot, 9 December). By the British government's logic, this would allow the virus to mutate, potentially rendering the first vaccines outdated – creating the need for new ones and another big pay day for Big Pharma. Scepticism of vaccines is high in African nations due to centuries of ongoing medical abuse at the hands of colonialism. (In Britain, up to 72% of black people said they were unlikely to have the jab (UK Household Longitudinal Study).) A UK parliamentary committee found that "routine healthcare in some countries has ground to a halt, and people fear starvation and unemployment more than they do the pandemic. Covid-19, and its countermeasures, have increased rates of gender-based violence and child marriage". (Labour adopted a policy of cancelling 'third world' debt 'owed' to Britain, later rejected by new leader, Keir Starmer.) These counter-measures have been largely influenced by Microsoft tycoon Bill Gates, the second richest man on Earth (now the US's number one owner of farms). The Gates Foundation (worth $51bn) has shareholdings in several pharmaceutical giants. "The foundation appears to see the Global South as both a dumping ground for drugs deemed too unsafe for the developed world and a testing ground for drugs not yet determined to be safe enough for the developed world," according to *The Grayzone* (8 July, 2020). Oxford's Clinical Infectious Diseases Periodical has contended that "the only cause of polio is likely to be the vaccine". Many others have come to similar conclusions about the vaccines Gates promotes. As the second largest contributor to the World Health Organisation (WHO), after the US, the WHO (which gets 80% of its funding privately) "doesn't decide how these funds are spent – the foundation does". The Gates Foundation has also donated millions of dollars to mainstream media outlets and Gates even starred in a docu-series on Netflix about how to stop a pandemic a few weeks before covid-19 hit the US. In 2017 Gates started buying up oxygen tank supplies – and now there is a global shortage (*Borgen*, 9 November). In January, Microsoft filed a patent to allow the company to 'digitally revive' deceased loved ones as online chatbots, using the individual's "images, voice data, social media posts, and electronic messages" in a sick bid to profit off and prolong people's grief and loneliness. As Alex Gutentag writes, the ruling class has ramped up its class war: "Indefinite closures have never before been used as a disease control method on a global scale... In March, unprecedented policies were rationalised through shocking stories and videos from northern Italy... Unknown to many was [the impact of] privatisation and a shrinking hospital system regularly overwhelmed by influenza... Chronic understaffing and lockdown-induced layoffs in nursing homes severely exacerbated covid's death toll.... In New York hospitals sent over 6,300 elderly covid patients back into nursing homes... Isolation is as deadly as obesity or smoking 15 cigarettes a day... Economic shutdown has weakened global pension funds and they may not recover... Because literacy and education levels are a main predictor of longevity, learning losses represent years of life stolen from students. Moreover, cases of severe abuse and mental-health related ER visits are surging for children... Many hospitals had to close due to lack of revenue from routine surgeries and procedures. 1.4 million hospital staff were laid off in April while private health insurance companies doubled their earnings... A static social order is being solidified... the wealthy have political and social privileges..., while the more low-income someone is, the more they are treated as contaminated... Only 40% of the workforce can afford to stay home... income is the main determinant of covid mortality.... Internationally, ... devastation will be compounded by famine and the increased spread of diseases like tuberculosis. In July, closed food markets were linked to 10,000 child deaths a month. Crops are rotting while the number of people facing acute hunger this year has doubled to 265 million... At the start of the crisis, vocal segments of the American Left argued that economic shutdown was a way to resist capitalism. This demonstrated a deep misunderstanding of the way financiers can profit from economic contraction." "The Great Covid Class War", thebellows.org, 16 December 2020.

858. "This was the fastest 30% sell-off ever, exceeding the pace of declines during the Great Depression", CNBC.com, 23 March 2020.
859. Smith, "Why coronavirus could spark a capitalist supernova", MR Online, 4 April 2020.
860. Gaby Hinsliff, TheGuardian.com, "The next wave of coronavirus disruption? Automation", 30 April 2020.
861. Pam Martens and Russ Martens, "The Federal Reserve now owns 15 percent of the US Treasury Market; at its current rate, it could own the whole market in less than two years", Wall Street on Parade, 28 March 2020.
862. Grossman, 2017, p314.
863. "UK Interest Rate History – dramatic 300 year Base Rate graph," BLA.co.uk.
864. Nic Fleming, TheGuardian.co.uk, 23 January 2021.
865. "8 predictions for the world in 2030", WEForum.org, 12 December 2016.
866. Quoted in Smith, 4 April 2020.
867. British parliament passed a bill authorising informants to break the law, without explicitly ruling out crimes such as murder, torture or serious sexual offences. Labour abstained. (TheCanary.co.uk, 17 October.) In November, parliament banned protests. Civics Monitor said that 87% of the global population now lives in countries that are 'closed', 'repressed' or 'obstructed', up 4% on a year earlier. "The use of detention as the main tactic to restrict protests only shows the hypocrisy of governments using covid-19 as a pretence to crack down on protests, [as] the virus is more likely to spread in confined spaces like prisons."
868. One example: "Exclusive: GCHQ giving Boris Johnson 'real-time' intelligence to tackle covid", Telegraph.co.uk, 18 November 2020. Violent rioting by armed Trump supporters marching on Congress after his election defeat to Democrat Joe Biden – five people died – will inspire further crackdowns. The EU, meanwhile, poured cold water on talk of 'returning to normal' relations by continuing de-dollarisation (Reuters, 19 January). German chancellor Angela Merkel rejected Biden's call for the US and EU to form a bloc to 'contain' China (Politico, 27 January).)

Printed in Great Britain
by Amazon